The Future of Mental Health, Disability and Criminal Law

This book brings together contributions from 23 world-leading scholars and commentators that address a range of contemporary and pressing international themes in mental health, disability and criminal law. The authors use the work of internationally renowned academic, Emeritus Professor Bernadette McSherry, as a springboard to reflect on recent developments in these areas of law and to anticipate the future directions they may take. In doing so, they aim to inform and inspire a new generation of mental health, disability and criminal law scholars, advocates and reformers.

The book is divided into four substantive sections: reforming mental health and disability law; regulating coercion and restrictive practices; improving access to justice and the criminal law; and transforming mental health law. It also includes an introduction from the editors and an afterword from Emeritus Professor McSherry.

The book is aimed at regulators, policymakers, lawyers, clinicians, consumer advocates and academics who are interested in the urgent and contentious issues surrounding the reform and development of mental health, disability and criminal law. It will help them understand the key issues and problems and presents suggestions for reform. The book is interdisciplinary and international in its focus.

Kay Wilson is a Melbourne Post-Doctoral Research Fellow at Melbourne Law School.

Yvette Maker is a senior lecturer at the University of Tasmania, Australia and an Honorary Senior Fellow at Melbourne Law School.

Piers Gooding is a Research Fellow at Melbourne Law School and an associate of the Melbourne Social Equity Institute.

Jamie Walvisch is a senior lecturer at Melbourne Law School and the University of Western Australia.

The Future of Mental Health, Disability and Criminal Law

Essays in Honour of Emeritus Professor Bernadette McSherry

Edited by
Kay Wilson, Yvette Maker, Piers Gooding and Jamie Walvisch

Routledge
Taylor & Francis Group
LONDON AND NEW YORK

First published 2024
by Routledge
4 Park Square, Milton Park, Abingdon, Oxon OX14 4RN

and by Routledge
605 Third Avenue, New York, NY 10158

Routledge is an imprint of the Taylor & Francis Group, an informa business

British Library Cataloguing-in-Publication Data
A catalogue record for this book is available from the British Library

Library of Congress Cataloging-in-Publication Data
Names: Wilson, Kay (Legal researcher), editor. | Maker, Yvette, editor. | Gooding, Piers, editor. | Walvisch, Jamie, editor. | McSherry, Bernadette. hounoree.
Title: The future of mental health, disability and criminal law : essays in honour of Emeritus Professor Bernadette McSherry / edited by Kay Wilson, Yvette Maker, Piers Gooding and Jamie Walvisch.
Description: Abingdon, Oxon ; New York, NY : Routledge, 2024. | Includes bibliographical references and index.
Identifiers: LCCN 2023015087 | ISBN 9781032396071 (hardback) | ISBN 9781032396323 (paperback) | ISBN 9781003350644 (ebook)
Subjects: LCSH: Mental health laws—English-speaking countries. | Mental health laws—Australia. | LCGFT: Festschriften.
Classification: LCC K3608 .F88 2024 | DDC 344.04/4—dc23/eng/20230720
LC record available at https://lccn.loc.gov/2023015087

ISBN: 978-1-032-39607-1 (hbk)
ISBN: 978-1-032-39632-3 (pbk)
ISBN: 978-1-003-35064-4 (ebk)

DOI: 10.4324/9781003350644

The Open Access version of chapter 9 was funded by University of Melbourne Early Career Researcher Grant 503454.
The Open Access version of chapter 13 was funded by Australian Research Council.

Contents

Table of Cases *viii*
Table of Statutes *xi*
List of Contributors *xix*
Foreword *xxv*
Preface *xxviii*
Acknowledgments *xxx*
List of Acronyms and Abbreviations *xxxii*

PART I
Reforming Mental Health and Disability Law 1

1 What Is the Future of Mental Health, Disability and Criminal Law? 3
KAY WILSON, YVETTE MAKER, PIERS GOODING AND JAMIE WALVISCH

2 Making the Future Happen: Law Reform Lessons From the Victorian Royal Commission 11
MARY DONNELLY

3 The Human Right to Health and the *Mental Health and Wellbeing Act 2022* (Vic) 34
PENELOPE WELLER

4 Benefitting From Hindsight: What the *Mental Capacity Act* and Its Implementation Can Teach Us About CRPD Implementation 54
PETER BARTLETT

PART II
Regulating Coercion and Restrictive Practices 71

5 Who Approves the Use of Restrictive Practices in Australia? The Case for a Uniform Authorisation Process 73
JOHN CHESTERMAN

6 Chemical Restraint Use and Reform in Health Care and Disability Settings 88
IAN FRECKELTON

7 Who Do We Turn To? Safeguarding Residents in Aged Care Settings From Abuse and Neglect in New Zealand 114
KATE DIESFELD

8 Some Concerns About Arbitrary Detention of Elderly People in Secure Rest Home Care 137
JOHN DAWSON AND FRANCES MATTHEWS

PART III
Improving Access to Justice and the Criminal Law 159

9 Whydunnit?: Causal Explanations in Sentencing Offenders With Mental Health Problems 161
JAMIE WALVISCH, ANDREW CARROLL, TIM MARSH AND JAYDIP SARKAR

10 Finetuning a Jurisprudence of Risk 186
CHRISTOPHER SLOBOGIN

11 The Rights of Persons With Sensory Disabilities to Participate in Juries 203
LISA WADDINGTON AND PAUL HARPUR

PART IV
Transforming Mental Health Law 227

12 Challenging the Foundations of Mental Health Law: Using Articles 12 and 14 of the CRPD as a Framework to Deconstruct and Reimagine Mental Health Law 229
ANNA ARSTEIN-KERSLAKE

13 The Digital Turn in Mental Health and Disability Law: Actuarial Traditions and AI Futures of Risk Assessment From a Human Rights Perspective 244
PIERS GOODING AND YVETTE MAKER

14 Regulating Rights: Developing a Human Rights and Mental Health Regulatory Framework 267
SIMON KATTERL AND SHARON FRIEL

15 Standing Up Against the Weight of History: The Importance of Lived Experience in the Mental Health Context 298
ERANDATHIE JAYAKODY AND MALITHA PERERA

Afterword 318
BERNADETTE MCSHERRY

Index *321*

Table of Cases

A, B and C v Y and Z [2012] EWHC 2400 (COP) 56
A Clinical Commissioning Group v N [2017] UKSC 22 64
AH [2021] EWCA Civ 1768 57
Alexopoulos v R [2022] VSCA 145 180
An NHS Trust v ST (Refusal of Deprivation of Liberty Order) [2022] EWHC (Fam) 91–2
Arthars v R (2013) 39 VR 613 165
B v Forsey 1988 SLT 143
Barefoot v Estelle, 463 US 880 (1983) 192
Beasley v Australia, Communication No 11/2013, UN Doc CRPD/C/15/D/11/2013 ..... 203, 215–6
Bonnington Castings v Wardlaw [1956] 1 All ER 615 177
Bowen v R [2011] VSCA 67 171
Carroll v R [2011] VSCA 150 168
CC v KK and STCC [2012] EWCOP 2136 57
College of Nurses of Ontario v Theodossiou, 2020 CanLII 456 (ON CNO) ... 92
Conway v Jaques (2005) 250 DLR (4th) 178 92
Croke v Ireland [2000] ECHR 680 14
Daubert v Dow Chemical Co, 509 US 579 (1993) 192
Department of Health v D (1999) 18 FRNZ 233 149
Devers v Kindilan Society (2010) 116 ALD 23 214
Director of Proceedings v Oceania Care Co Ltd [2022] NZHRRT 8 118
Director of Proceedings v The Ultimate Care Group Ltd [2022] NZHRRT 17 ..... 118, 119
Director of Public Prosecutions v Brown [2020] VCC 196 177
Director of Public Prosecutions v Missen [2019] VSC 32 177
Director of Public Prosecutions v O'Neill (2015) 47 VR 395 180
Director of Public Prosecutions v Patterson [2009] VSCA 222 171
Director of Public Prosecutions v UA [2018] VSC 423 178
Director of Public Prosecutions v Weidlich [2008] VSCA 203 167
Entick v Carrington (1765) 19 Howell's State Trials 1029; 95 ER 807 (KB) 148
Estelle v Smith, 451 US 454 (1981) 192

Fox v Percy (2003) 214 CLR 118 206
Gagnon v Scarpelli, 411 US 778 (1973) 199
Gardner v Florida, 430 US 360 (1977) 198
HL v United Kingdom [2004] 40 ECHR 761 .... 14, 15, 59, 143, 151, 154
HYY (Guardianship) [2022] VCAT 97 82–3
Jackson v Indiana, 406 US 715 (1972) 191
Johnson v Cockrell, 306 F 3d 249 (5th Cir, 2002) 193
Johnson v United Kingdom, 2250/93, judgment of 24 October 1997 (ECHR) 64
Johnson v United States, 576 US 591 (2015) 190
Johnston v R [2013] VSCA 362 171
Jurek v Texas, 428 US 262 (1976) 189, 190
Kansas v Hendricks, 521 US 346 (1997) 191
Kioa v West (1985) 159 CLR 550 36
Kolanis v United Kingdom, 517/02, judgment of 21 June 2005 (ECHR) ... 64
LB (Re), 2010 CanLII 21401 (ON CCB) 92
LB v AJ, 2021 CanLII 5858 (ON HPARB) 92
Lockrey v Australia, Communication No 13/2013, UN Doc CRPD/C/15/D/13/2013 .... 203, 215–6
Loli v MWY, FAM 2009–004–1877, Auckland Family Court, 14 January 2011 148
London Borough of Brent v SL [2017] EWCOP 5 60
Long v State, 2009 WL 960598 (Tex Crim Ct App, 2009) 190
MM v Secretary of State for Justice [2018] UKSC 60 149–50
Nenno v State, 970 SW 2d 549 (Tex Crim Ct App, 2009) 193
O'Connor v R [2014] VSCA 108 165
Opinion 17HDC00352 (2020), Case 17HDC0035, 30 June 2020 ... 118–119
Opinion 18HDC01049 (2021), Case 18HDC01049, 19 February 2021 118
P v Cheshire West and Chester Council [2014] UKSC 19 14
Paparone v R [2000] WASCA 127 168
PBU and NJE v Mental Health Tribunal (2018) 56 VR 141 .... 36, 41
R v Bournewood and Community Mental Health NHS Trust; Ex parte L [1999] 1 AC 458 .... 141, 142
R v Dolheguy [2020] VSC 704 170
R v Hayes [2010] QCA 96 176–7
R v M'Naghten (1843) 8 ER 718 182
R v Peta (2007) 2 NZLR 627 194
R v Pritchard (1836) 7 C&P 303 183
R v Secretary of State for the Home Department; Ex parte Simms [2000] 2 AC 115 .... 146, 150
R v Special Commissioner; Ex parte Morgan Grenfell and Co Ltd [2002] UKHL 21 146
R v Surtees [2022] VSC 124 171
R v Verdins (2007) 16 VR 269 163

R v Vuadreu [2009] VSCA 262 171
R (Barry) v Gloucestershire (1997) 2 All ER 1 64
R (Davey) v Oxfordshire County Council [2017] EWCA Civ 1308 64
R (Rose) v Thanet Commissioning Group [2014] EWHC 1182 64
R (Ross) v West Sussex PCT [2008] EWHC 2252 (Admin) 64
Re ADP [2003] WASAT 131 93
Re Application for Guardianship Order (BCB) (2002) 28 SR (WA) 338 92
Re BTO, Guardianship and Administration Board (WA), 14 October 2004 93
Re LB, 2010 CanLII 21401 (ON CCB) 92
Re JP [2004] WASAT 3 93
Re SB (A Patient: Capacity to Consent to Termination) [2013] EWHC 1417 (COP) 57
Ross v R [2015] VSCA 302 165
Seling v Young, 531 US 250 (2001) 191
Shtukaturov v Russia, 44009/05, judgment of 27 March 2008 (ECHR)... 57
State v Guise, 921 NW 2d 26 (Iowa, 2018) 198
Taylor v Louisiana, 419 US 522 (1975) 208
TC and UB v Komisia za zashtita of diskriminatsia and VA (2021) (C-824/19 ECLI:EU:C:2021:862 .... 203, 217–18
United States v Dempsey, 830 F 2d 1084 (10th Cir, 1987) 207
United States v Field, 483 F 3d 313 (5th Cir, 2007) 192
United States of America v Archie W Brawner, 471 F 2d 969 (DC Cir, 1972) 183
Varga v State, 2003 WL 21466926 (Tex Crim Ct App, 2003) 190
Welsh Ministers v PJ [2018] UKSC 149–50
Winterwerp v Netherlands 6301/73 [1979] ECHR 4 151
Woods v New Zealand Police [2020] NZSC 141 150
Wright v R [2015] VSCA 88 166
Youngberg v Romeo, 457 US 307 (1982) 191

Table of Statutes

Australia

Aged Care Act 1997 (Cth) 79, 80, 83, 100
s 54.10(1)(f) 80
Aged Care and Other Legislation Amendment (Royal Commission Response) Act 2022 (Cth)
sch 9 83
Aged Care and Other Legislation Amendment (Royal Commission Response No 1) Act 2021 (Cth)
s 3 80
Aged Care and Other Legislation Amendment (Royal Commission Response No 2) Bill 2021 (Cth)
s 1 83
Charter of Human Rights and Responsibilities Act 2006 (Vic) 22, 36, 83, 220, 270
s 10(c) 40
Crimes (Mental Impairment and Unfitness to be Tried) Act 1997 (Vic) 182, 289
s 6(1) 183
Criminal Code 1995 (Qld)
s 52 182
Disability Act 2006 (Vic)
pt 6A 74, 75, 84
pt 6B 74, 75, 84
pt 7 .... 74, 75, 84
s 3 100
Disability Services Act 2006 (Qld)
pt 6 75
s 145(1) 98
s 145(2) 98
Equal Opportunity Act 2010 (Vic)
pt 8 272
pt 10 272

Forensic Disability Act 2011 (Qld)
s 50 ... 77
s 56 ... 77
s 61 ... 77
Guardianship and Administration Act 2000 (Qld)
ch 5B ... 75, 81
pt 3 ... 81
s 12 ... 81
s 80R ... 81
s 11B ... 79
sch 2 ... 81
Guardianship and Administration Act 2019 (Vic) ... 28, 82
s 3 ... 82
s 30 ... 82
Human Rights Act 2019 (Qld) ... 83
Medical Treatment Planning and Decisions Act 2016 (Vic) ... 28
s 3 ... 74
Mental Health Act 2007 (NSW)
s 12 ... 274
s 14 ... 274
s 68 ... 274
Mental Health Act 2009 (SA) ... 98, 100, 126
s 21 ... 274
Mental Health Act 2013 (Tas) ... 100
s 3 ... 98
s 6 ... 274
s 40 ... 274
Mental Health Act 2014 (Vic) ... 7, 22, 34–5, 44, 268, 269, 270, 280, 282, 284, 285, 286
s 3 ... 76
s 5 ... 274
s 11(1) ... 268
ss 19–22 ... 268
ss 68–71 ... 268
s 70 ... 48
s 71 ... 48
s 105 ... 76
s 110 ... 76
s 113 ... 76
s 228 ... 273, 282
Mental Health Act 2014 (WA)
s 25 ... 274
Mental Health Act 2015 (ACT)
s 58 ... 274

s 66 274
s 101 274
Mental Health Act 2016 (Qld) 100
ch 8 77
s 3 274
s 12 274
s 246 77
s 247 89
s 249 89
s 250 89
s 256 77
s 270
Mental Health and Wellbeing Act 2022 (Vic) 7, 22, 27, 28–9, 34, 36, 42–50, 88, 312
pt 3 46
s 2 76
s 3 77
s 3(1) 98
s 12 43–4
s 12(c)(ix)(B) 76
s 16 45
ss 16–28
s 18 45
s 19 45
ss 78–84 46
s 79 46
s 80 46
s 81 .... 46, 76
s 82 46
s 83 47
s 84 47
s 85 47
s 85(3) 47
s 86 47
s 87 47–8
s 87(3)(c) 48
s 89(1)(a)(ii) 48, 49
s 89(3)(a)–(b) 48
s 89(4) 48
s 89(4)(b) 48
s 127 .... 89, 101
s 128 101
s 139 77
s 143 312
s 161(1(g)–(h) 89

National Disability Insurance Scheme Act 2013 (Cth)
s 181E(1)(a) 273, 282
National Disability Insurance Scheme (Restrictive Practices and Behaviour Support) Rules 2018 (Cth) 100, 104
r 6 99
r 6(b) 99
r 8 100
r 9 100
r 10 100
r 11 100
r 12 100
r 13 100
r 22 100
r 24 100
Powers of Attorney Act 1998 (Qld)
s 32 82
sch 2 82
Powers of Attorney Act 2014 (Vic) 82
s 3 82
s 22 82
Quality of Care Amendment (Reviewing Restraints Principles) Principles 2019 (Cth) 96
Quality of Care Principles 2014 (Cth) 96, 100
Senior Practitioner Act 2018 (ACT) 75, 84
Sentencing Act 1991 (Vic) 180
Victorian Collaborative Centre for Mental Health and Wellbeing Act 2021 (Vic) 27

Canada

Canadian Charter of Rights and Freedoms 1982
s 7 138

International Instruments

Additional Protocol to the American Convention on Human Rights in the Area of Economic, Social and Cultural Rights
art 6 214
African Charter on Human and Peoples' Rights
art 15 214
Charter of Fundamental Rights of the European Union 216
art 26 218
Convention on the Elimination of All Forms of Discrimination Against Women
art 7 213
art 11(1)(a) 214

Convention on the Rights of Persons with Disabilities ... 3, 6, 11, 13, 15, 22, 36, 38–42, 45, 47, 59–62, 65–7, 105, 125–6, 132, 191, 203, 210, 211–12, 216, 218, 231, 239, 258, 260, 319
art 2 ... 56, 214
art 3 ... 39
art 4(2) ... 64
art 4(3) ... 17
art 5 ... 211
art 5(1) ... 211–12
art 5(3) ... 218
art 9 ... 210, 211
art 9(1) ... 210
art 9(2)(h) ... 214
art 10 ... 39
art 12 ... 11, 39, 40, 48, 54, 57, 231, 232–4, 236–40
art 12(5) ... 63
art 13 ... 216, 219
art 14 ... 11, 39, 42, 63, 138, 231, 234–5, 236–40, 258
art 14(1)(b) ... 235
art 15 ... 39, 232
art 16 ... 39, 56
art 17 ... 232
art 19 ... 63, 232
art 21 ... 210, 211
art 21(a) ... 210
art 21(b) ... 211
art 22 ... 258
art 23 ... 232
art 25 ... 39, 259
art 25(a) ... 39
art 25(b) ... 39
art 25(c) ... 39
art 25(d) ... 39
art 25(e) ... 39
art 25(f) ... 39
art 27 ... 218
art 27(1)(g)–(h) ... 215
art 27(1)(i) ... 214
art 29(b) ... 213–14
Convention on the Rights of the Child
art 32 ... 214
European Convention on Human Rights ... 14
art 5 ... 14, 138, 143
art 5(1) ... 138
art 5(2)–(4) ... 140

art 5(4) 138, 152
art 6 208
European Social Charter (Revised) 1996
art 1 214
Employment Equality Directive 2000/78/EC 210, 217, 219
art 2(2)(a) 218
art 4(1) 218
art 5 218
International Convention on the Elimination of All Forms of Racial Discrimination
art 5(e)(i) 214
art 5(f) 210
International Covenant on Civil and Political Rights 139, 140, 258
art 4 .... 210, 211
art 6 232
art 8(3)(a) 214
art 9 .... 139, 151, 258
art 9(1) 138
art 9(4) 138, 152
art 14 .... 208, 258
art 17 258
art 19 210
art 25 213
art 25(c) 210
art 26 .... 210, 211
International Covenant on Economic, Social and Cultural Rights 37
Preamble 211
art 2 211
art 6 214
art 13 211
Optional Protocol to the Convention against Torture and other Cruel, Inhuman or Degrading Treatment or Punishment 123, 125, 132
Treaty on the European Union 216
Treaty on the Functioning of the European Union 216
art 19 217
United Nations Charter
Preamble [2] 211
arts 55–56 211
Universal Declaration of Human Rights
Preamble [1] 211
art 2(1) 37
art 9 138
art 10 208

art 12 ... 37
art 21 ... 213
art 23(1) ... 214
art 25 ... 37
Vocational Rehabilitation and Employment (Disabled Persons) Convention ... 214

India

Mental Healthcare Act 2017 ... 24

Ireland

Mental Health Act 2001 ... 14, 23
s 75 ... 17
Mental Treatment Act 1945 ... 14

New Zealand

Accident Compensation Act 2001 ... 116
Crimes of Torture Act 1989
s 26 ... 123
Health and Disability Commissioner Act 1994 ... 115, 116
s 52(2) ... 116
Health and Disability Commissioner (Code of Health and Disability Services Consumers' Rights) Regulations 1996 (NZ) ... 116
r 4(1) ... 118, 119
Health Practitioners Competence Assurance Act 2003 ... 116
Mental Health (Compulsory Assessment and Treatment Act 1992
s 29 ... 149
s 40 ... 149
s 41 ... 149
s 59 ... 149
New Zealand Bill of Rights Act 1990
s 22 ... 139
Protection of Personal and Property Rights Act 1988 ... 144
s 10 ... 148
s 10(1) ... 146, 147
s 10(4) ... 147
s 18(3) ... 153
s 19(1) ... 153
s 98(5) ... 153
s 98A ... 153

Scotland

Mental Health (Care and Treatment) (Scotland) Act 2003 23

Turkey

Turkish Disability Act 2014 15

United Kingdom

Belfast (Good Friday) Agreement Act 1998 12
Care Act 2014 152
Court of Protection Rules 2017 57
r 1.2(1)(d) 57
r 14.2(e) 57
Criminal Procedure (Insanity) Act 1964
ch 84 s 4 183
Government of Wales Act 1998 12
Human Rights Act 1998 138
Mental Capacity Act 2005 .... 6, 54–5, 58–9, 61–2, 65–6, 151
s 4 153
s 4A 14
s 4B 14
s 16A 14
s 17B 150
s 73 150
Mental Capacity (Amendment) Act 2019 .... 60, 154
Mental Health Act 1959 .... 15–16, 18
Mental Health Act 1983 .... 16, 17, 18–19, 149
Mental Health Act 2007 .... 16, 19, 59
Mental Health Bill 2002 20
Scotland Act 1998 12

United States of America

Americans with Disabilities Act 1990 205
Armed Career Criminal Act of 1984
§ 924(e) 190
Constitution
amend V 138
Federal Rules of Evidence
r 702 192
Model Penal Code 2017
§ 6.06(2)(a) 189
Texas Code of Criminal Procedure
art 37.071(b) 190

Contributors

Anna Arstein-Kerslake is a Professor in Human Rights at the Irish Centre for Human Rights at the University of Galway, Ireland. She is also an Associate Professor at Melbourne Law School where she founded the Disability Human Rights Clinic and has led multiple large scale research projects on legal personhood. She is an internationally recognised socio-legal academic in the fields of human rights, disability rights and gender justice. She has published widely in these areas.

Peter Bartlett is Nottinghamshire Healthcare NHS Trust Professor of Mental Health Law in the School of Law and Institute of Mental Health at the University of Nottingham.

Andrew Carroll has worked as a forensic psychiatrist in both treatment and assessment roles in Australia for over two decades. He currently carries out treatment work in a prison clinic and medicolegal assessment work in both criminal and civil fields. He also is an adjunct associate professor at the Centre for Forensic Behavioural Science (Swinburne University of Technology). He is also Co-Director at 'Our Curious Minds', a mental health training enterprise. He has published on a range of topics including the interface between mental disorder and sentencing in the criminal courts. He has published papers in conjunction with Bernadette McSherry on topics including drug-associated psychoses and recovery-oriented risk management.

John Chesterman is the Queensland Public Advocate. A lawyer and historian by training, John has expertise in the fields of human rights, guardianship, supported decision making, powers of attorney and elder abuse. Prior to taking up his current position, John was Victoria's Deputy Public Advocate. He has previously undertaken a Churchill Fellowship on the topic of adult safeguarding.

John Dawson is Professor of Law at the University of Otago, in New Zealand. Since the 1980s, he has published extensively on mental health law, especially law governing community treatment orders. He has an LLD for publications in this field. He was a member of the OCTET team that conducted a randomised controlled trial of the English community treatment order scheme. With George Szmukler he has proposed the 'fusion' of mental health and adult guardianship legislation into a single legal scheme. He conducts evaluation research, consults to law reform bodies, is a qualified barrister and solicitor, and has published previously in the field.

Kate Diesfeld is Professor of Law at Auckland University of Technology in New Zealand. Professor Diesfeld was a court investigator for the State of Alaska and then graduated from University of San Diego School of Law. In Los Angeles, she advocated for people with developmental disabilities as a staff attorney with Protection and Advocacy, Inc. She held academic roles at Kent Law School (England), the University of Waikato (NZ) and Auckland University of Technology (NZ). She was AUT's Director of the National Centre for Health Law and Ethics and Chair of AUT's Ethics Committee. In England, she represented clients before the Mental Health Review Tribunal.

Mary Donnelly is Professor of Law at University College Cork, Ireland. She publishes widely in mental health and capacity law and is co-editor of the *Routledge Handbook of Mental Health Law* (forthcoming, 2023). She is Associate Editor of the *International Journal of Law and Psychiatry* and is a member of the Editorial Board of the *Medical Law Review* and *Medical Law International*. She is Joint-Chair of the HSE National Consent Policy Advisory Group. She was Chair of the Expert Group to develop Codes of Practice for the Assisted Decision-Making (Capacity) Act 2015 (Ireland) and was a member of the Expert Group to Review the Mental Health Act 2001 (Ireland). She is a member of the Mental Health Commission Legislation; the HSE Assisted Decision-Making Implementation Group and is Vice Chair of the National Research Ethics Committee (CT-A).

Ian Freckelton AO KC is a King's Counsel in full-time practice as a barrister throughout Australia. He is Professor of Law and a Professorial Fellow in Psychiatry at the University of Melbourne; Adjunct Professor of Forensic Medicine at Monash University; a judge of the Supreme Court of Nauru; and a member of Victoria's Coronial Council. He is Past President of the Australian and New Zealand Association of Psychiatry, Psychology and Law; a 25-year member of the Mental Health Tribunal of Victoria; and an elected Fellow of the Australian Academy of Health and Medical Sciences, the Australian Academy of Social Sciences and the Australian Academy of Law. Ian is the Editor of the *Journal of Law and Medicine* and the Founding Editor of *Psychiatry, Psychology and Law*. In 2021, he was made an Officer of the Order of Australia (AO) for distinguished service to law and the legal profession across fields including health, medicine and technology.

Sharon Friel is an ARC Laureate Fellow, Professor of Health Equity and Director of the Planetary Health Equity Hothouse and Menzies Centre for Health Governance at the School of Regulation and Global Governance

(RegNet), Australian National University. Her research focuses on the political economy of health; governance and the planetary, social and commercial determinants of health inequities. She has previously published in these areas highlighting the importance of addressing the global consumptogenic system.

Piers Gooding is a Research Fellow at Melbourne Law School and Associate of the Melbourne Social Equity Institute. He is a socio-legal researcher whose work concerns the law and politics of disability and mental health. He is the author of *A New Era for Mental Health Law and Policy* (CUP, 2017) and serves on the editorial board of the *International Journal for Mental Health and Capacity Law*. Dr Piers Gooding has received several awards for his research, including an Australian Research Council Discovery Early Career Research Award (2020) and a Menzies Australian Bicentennial Fellowship (2011).

Paul Harpur is an Associate Professor at the TC Beirne School of Law, the University of Queensland, Australia. Associate Professor Harpur's principal area of interest lies in international and comparative disability law, the UN *Convention on the Rights of Persons with Disabilities*, and comparative anti-discrimination and disability laws. He is funded on an Australian Research Council Future Fellowship (FT210100335). Additionally, he is an International Distinguished Fellow at the Burton Blatt Institute, Syracuse University, an Academic Fellow at the Harvard Law School Project on Disability and chairs the University of Queensland Disability Inclusion Group. Associate Professor Harpur has visited at the Burton Blatt Institute, Harvard Law School, the National University Ireland, Galway, and is a former Fulbright Future Scholar and dual Paralympian.

Erandathie Jayakody draws on her personal experience of living with a mental health condition and peer support to promote the consumer perspective. Coming across a peer support network and finding her 'people' was a life changing experience and one that changed the narrative of her recovery. Erandathie is a member of the Independent Panel to review Victoria's Compulsory Treatment Criteria and Decision-making Laws and a tribunal member at the Mental Health Tribunal, Victoria. She developed the 'Consumers Leading in Governance' pilot programme – the first specialist governance programme developed by and for mental health consumers in Australia. She was a member of the Expert Advisory Committee to the Royal Commission into Victoria's Mental Health System.

Simon Katterl is a consultant on mental health, human rights and regulation. Simon's work is grounded in his lived experience of mental health issues, as well as his studies in law, politics, psychology and regulation. Simon previously worked for the Victorian Equal Opportunity and Human Rights Commission, the Mental Health Complaints Commissioner, Victoria Legal Aid and provides consultancy to several agencies, including the Royal Commission into Victoria's Mental Health System. Simon's research has focused on mental health-related vilification, human rights breaches within mental health systems and the shortcomings of regulatory oversight processes and was co-author on *Not Before Time: Lived Experience-Led Justice and Repair*.

Yvette Maker is a senior lecturer at the University of Tasmania, Australia and an Honorary Senior Fellow at Melbourne Law School. She has a background in law and social policy and her current work focuses on the disability- and gender-related dimensions of law, policy and practice. She edited *Restrictive Practices in Health Care and Disability Settings* with Bernadette McSherry (Routledge, 2021) and is the author of *Care and Support Rights After Neoliberalism* (CUP, 2022).

Tim Marsh completed a law and a science degree at Melbourne University. After working as a solicitor at the Office of Public Prosecutions, Tim went to the Bar in 2003, reading with Mark Rochford QC. In 2011 Tim joined Victoria Legal Aid as a senior public defender. In 2013 he was appointed as Chief Counsel, and for the next seven years led VLA Chambers, before deciding to return to the Bar in November 2020. Tim was counsel in the landmark case of *DPP v Walters*, which saw the controversial 'baseline sentencing' reforms declared 'incapable of practical application' by the Court of Appeal. While Tim practices in all areas of crime, he has a strong practice in mental impairment and disability law. His work at first instance and on appeal in this area has helped clarify and reshape how the Victorian Courts treat offenders with mental illnesses.

Frances Matthews qualified in medicine in 1982 in England and has worked in hospitals and community settings in the UK, Ireland, Canada and New Zealand. She was called to the Bar in Ireland in 2012, and has worked as a legal researcher and human rights advocate for older people's charities. Dr Matthews holds a Master of Laws and a Master of Bioethics and Health Law degree from the University of Otago. Her special interest is the human rights of older people and those with disabilities. She currently works as a GP and medicolegal advisor in New Zealand. Her PhD in law concerns detention in dementia care in New Zealand.

Bernadette McSherry is Emeritus Professor of Law at Melbourne Law School and was the Foundation Director of the Melbourne Social Equity Institute from 2013 to July 2020. She is an elected Fellow of the Academy of the Social Sciences Australia and the Australian Academy of Law. She is a Commissioner with the Victorian Law Reform Commission and previously served as a Commissioner on the Royal Commission into Victoria's Mental Health System.

Malitha Perera is an occupational therapist and a financial counsellor who has worked in various operational, clinical and strategic leadership roles in mental health. He is passionate about addressing inequities that impact on our collective health and wellbeing. He holds a Diploma of Financial Counselling, Bachelor of Occupational Therapy, Bachelor of Psychological Science and Master of Public Health.

Jaydip Sarkar is a consultant forensic psychiatrist and personality disorder specialist at Forensicare, Melbourne. He was previously Adjunct Assistant Professor and a clinical lecturer in Singapore. Dr Sarkar trained in the UK and provides expert testimony in multiple jurisdictions. His active interest and testimony in capital punishment cases led to a precedential judgment in Singapore. He has particular clinical and therapeutic skills with victims of trauma, family violence and offenders with personality disorder who commit serious offences. He has received awards for 'outstanding service contribution', major 'clinical process improvements' and 'public healthcare clinician', in the UK and in Singapore. He has published widely, contributed to and co-edited an award-winning British Medical Association book.

Christopher Slobogin occupies the Milton Underwood Chair at Vanderbilt University Law School. He has published several books, and over 200 articles and chapters, primarily on criminal justice topics. He is one of the five most cited criminal law and procedure scholars in the United States over the past five years, according to the Leiter Report. He has received both the American Board of Forensic Psychology's Distinguished Contribution Award and the American Psychology-Law Society's Distinguished Contribution of Psychology and Law Award, the only law professor to receive both awards. He has appeared on *Good Morning America*, *Nightline*, the *Today Show*, *National Public Radio*, and many other media outlets, and has been cited in over 5,000 law review articles and treatises and more than 200 judicial opinions, including five US Supreme Court decisions. Slobogin holds a secondary appointment as a professor in the Vanderbilt School of Medicine's Department of Psychiatry.

Lisa Waddington is the European Disability Forum Professor of European Disability Law at the Faculty of Law, Maastricht University, the Netherlands. Professor Waddington's principal area of interest lies in European and comparative disability law, the UN *Convention on the Rights of Persons with Disabilities*, and European and comparative equality law in general. She is a senior expert for a number of networks and organisations, including the European Network of Legal Experts in the Non-discrimination Field and the European Disability Expertise network. She is a member of the Maastricht Centre for European Law, the Netherlands Network for Human Rights Research, the Maastricht Centre for European Law and the Berkeley Center on Comparative Equality and Anti-Discrimination Law. Professor Waddington has been a visiting professor at the University of British Columbia, Vancouver, the University of Melbourne and Leeds University.

Jamie Walvisch is a senior lecturer at Melbourne Law School and the University of Western Australia. He is a criminal law scholar with a strong law reform background. He has previously worked as a research and policy officer at the Victorian Law Reform Commission, where he co-authored reports on defences to homicide, disputes between co-owners and workplace privacy; a research analyst for the Australian Institute of Criminology, where he co-authored reports on road rage and fraud; and Senior Research Officer at the Judicial College of Victoria, where he developed the *Victorian Criminal Charge Book* (the main judicial reference book used by judges and legal practitioners in Victorian criminal jury trials). His current research focuses on the intersection between law, psychiatry and psychology, especially in the sentencing context. His work and advocacy in this area have resulted in significant changes to Victorian law.

Penelope Weller is a professor of law in the Graduate School of Business and Law at RMIT University in Melbourne. She has published over 50 articles and chapters concerned with human rights and mental health law. From 2008–2013 Penelope Weller worked closely with Professor McSherry at Monash University as a Postdoctoral Research Fellow and later Deputy Director of the Centre for the Advancement of Law and Mental Health (CALMH). She has previously co-authored a volume with Professor McSherry.

Kay Wilson is a Melbourne Post-Doctoral Research Fellow at Melbourne Law School, a lawyer, scholar and writer with an interest in mental health, disability and human rights law. She has a Bachelor of Arts and Laws and an Honours degree in psychology from Monash University and a PhD in law from the University of Melbourne. She is the author of *Mental Health Law: Abolish or Reform* (Oxford University Press, 2021) and is published in Australian and international peer-reviewed journals. She was also a researcher on Professor McSherry's *Rethinking Mental Health Laws* and *Seclusion and Restraint Projects* and has published papers in Australian and international journals. In 2015, she won the Dontas Travelling Fellowship to Greece to give a paper on seclusion and restraint.

Foreword

For over a century and a half, in Victoria, Australia, there have been two kinds of 'mentally ill' people: those who are free citizens and those who are subject to state-sanctioned psychiatric treatment. This is the case, in Victoria and elsewhere, courtesy of mental health laws which create haves and have-nots of persons with freedom of choice in psychiatric treatment.

Free citizens I'll call 'Class 1' and the others 'Class 2'.

Class 2 exists because it is widely accepted that some people are unaware they have this thing called mental illness. And for that reason, they don't seek treatment. Or perhaps they had treatment and didn't like it. Or perhaps they prefer alternatives to the conventional psychiatric treatment served up by the state.

The cohort of people in Class 2 make up the supply side that creates the demand for stand-alone mental health laws with provision for compulsory treatment. The compulsory component is deemed a clinical and legal necessity. Most people are unaware these laws even exist until they are touched by it personally.

Under these laws a segment of those considered mentally ill are siphoned off into Class 2 by the state's psychiatric assessment and treatment apparatus. Those in Class 2 are then given psychiatric treatment whether they want it or not. The streaming of mentally ill persons with its Class 2 limitations on rights and freedoms is justified by a line of thought which says that in a civilised state, we strive to protect our most marginalised and would like everyone with mental illness to get the treatment they need.

In 2008, I became an agent of the state, working as a member of what is now called the Mental Health Tribunal for the state of Victoria. I was tasked with deciding whether a person provisionally in Class 2 would remain there or be cut loose to Class 1 and beyond. A state hospital psychiatrist had already made a preliminary decision about who went where. Those who ended up in Class 2 presented before members of the tribunal a short time later for independent scrutiny and we had the right of veto.

I made these decisions as a layperson ('community member') on a panel of three, sitting alongside a lawyer and a medico. I took this work very seriously for a number of reasons: (1) because it's serious; (2) I'd experienced a short stint in Class 2 myself; (3) I often wondered how an instrumental music teacher like me ended up a as member of the tribunal; and (4) I was getting paid an obscene amount of money for this work.

This is where I met Bernadette McSherry, a lawyer. My colleagues and I saw Bernadette only rarely due to her limited availability, but we always looked forward to working with her. Bernadette was a good operator who also took this work seriously – mental health law is her thing and she's good at it. I also thought it was cool when people who'd helped design the content of the law stuck around to apply it.

Bernadette had a natural affinity for engaging with Class 2 people even when they were unhinged. And she was equally adept at talking to the clinicians who provided their treatment. Speaking to all present in exactly the same manner, language and tone of voice, Bernadette was able to create what I call an 'atmosphere of equal engagement'. In tribunal hearings, for that hour at least, a person in Class 2 could instinctively feel that they were being listened to and accorded equal consideration to others in the room. This may not seem like such a big deal, but for many people it's not an easy thing to do without sounding forced.

In these hearings Bernadette as the Chair initiated a discussion which, in addition to being legally on point, also revealed the full impact of Class 2 treatment arrangements beyond just the clinical benefits they were intended to deliver. This was important for me because I was becoming aware of cases, both at work and on the consumer beat, where the single-minded pursuit of optimum clinical outcomes had had a broad detrimental effect. In some Class 2 cases, the protracted and unrelenting feeling of loss of autonomy had inadvertently extinguished all hope. (This is not intended as a criticism of the clinicians working in the system. These individuals are doing their very best in a crisis-driven environment with the tools they have available.) The hopelessness phenomenon is best understood as an occasional by-product of prolonged compulsory treatment.

Following widespread consternation about the high per capita rate of people on Community Treatment Orders in Victoria, a new law was constructed and became operational in 2015. The mental health infrastructure got a cash injection to cope with the increased demands of the new law. And then a funny thing happened.

Nothing.

The rate of compulsory treatment (the outpatient variety in particular) dipped and then climbed again. We found ourselves with non-binding Advance Statements, a Second Psychiatric Opinion Scheme which doesn't challenge diagnoses and a Mental Health Complaints Commissioner who won't issue compliance notices. We wanted to believe in things like supported decision-making and the dignity of risk but, for Class 2 citizens, the song remained the same. *What they say, you do.*

Not that long afterwards, in 2019, Bernadette was appointed a commissioner of the Royal Commission into Victoria's Mental Health System. She and her fellow commissioners confirmed an open secret – the mental health system was 'broken' (for people in both the 1st and 2nd classes) and the mental health law, not long in operation, was no longer fit for purpose.

So a new law is again on the horizon and what shall we put in it this time?

To be honest, I don't think it really matters. Having lived through the most recent change I've come to the conclusion that it's not what's *in* the law that counts. It's more about people and the attitudes of those who administer the law. If various provisions of *the Act* are routinely ignored with no consequences, then those provisions may as well not be there. If we are to say 'but those provisions are aspirational' then around we go again – the same parts of the mental health infrastructure comply while the rogue element goes up the river.

In the modern era, any efforts to redesign the law should include what is currently known as the 'lived experience' perspective. It makes sense that end users of public mental health services, Class 1 and 2 citizens, should get a seat at the table during the law's consultation and design phase and also in the various points of its administration thereafter. Likewise, people with lived experience should be involved in reform of other parts of the mental health infrastructure.

Lived experience input is not just a shopfront to make us feel good about ourselves. Nor will lived experience input achieve much if others around the table are fearful of people with mental illness. Class 2 citizens make up a sizeable chunk of the group of end users, and so they should be made to feel welcome at the table too.

Class 1 end users are sometimes chosen exclusively for lived experience input for ease of operation and the comfort and satisfaction of others. But when end users are from Class 1 alone, lived experience is of mental health treatment devoid of limitations on rights and freedoms. For as long as the state avails itself of a Class 2 compulsory treatment mechanism, it has a moral obligation to seek out and engage with Class 2 lived experience.

The Royal Commission into Victoria's Mental Health System exposed way too many shocking instances of dysfunction throughout the mental health infrastructure and not all of them can be attributed to a lack of resources. This book, put together as a tribute to Bernadette's work, with its many and varied contributors, I hope will help turbocharge the implementation of the Royal Commission's recommendations and assist in reform of the law, of the system, of its people and their attitudes.

Bernadette and I don't work together on the Mental Health Tribunal anymore. After many years she decided it was time to finish up. It feels like some legal rigour and an element of compassion departed with her that day.

Duncan Cameron
Community Member – Mental Health Tribunal

Preface

This collection is a Festschrift in honour of Emeritus Professor Bernadette McSherry on the occasion of her retirement, following an esteemed academic career spanning over 30 years. The author and editor of ten books and more than 160 book chapters and peer reviewed journal articles, she has published key texts in the mental health, disability and criminal law fields, including the highly regarded *Managing Risk: The Law and Ethics of Risk Assessment and Preventive Detention* (Routledge, 2014); *Rethinking Rights-Based Mental Health Laws* (co-edited with Penelope Weller, Hart, 2010) and *Principles of Criminal Law* (co-authored with Simon Bronitt, Thomson Reuters, 2017, 4th ed). She has obtained numerous awards and grants, including a prestigious Australian Research Council Federation Fellowship for the project *Rethinking Mental Health Laws: An Integrated Approach*. She has also led large research projects on the impact of the United Nations *Convention on the Rights of Persons with Disabilities* on mental health law, and on the minimisation, with a view to elimination, of the use of seclusion and restraint in mental health, disability and aged care settings.

Prior to entering academia, Bernadette McSherry was a practising lawyer and Associate to Mr Justice Gobbo of the Supreme Court of Victoria, Australia (1987–1990). After completing a PhD at Osgoode Hall Law School, York University in Canada in 1996, she held positions including Louis Waller Chair of Law and Professor of Law at Monash University, Adjunct Professor of Law at Melbourne Law School and Foundation Director of the University of Melbourne's Melbourne Social Equity Institute. She was appointed a Fellow of the Academy of Social Sciences in Australia and a Fellow of the Australian Academy of Law in 2011.

Bernadette McSherry's contribution has extended well beyond the Academy. She served as a member of the Victorian Mental Health Tribunal from 2001 to 2018, as a Victorian Law Reform Commissioner from 2018 and most recently as a commissioner on the Royal Commission into Victoria's Mental Health System. She was President of the Australian and New Zealand Association of Psychiatry, Psychology and Law from 2016 to 2018. She has also conducted consultancies to Australian government agencies, United Nations bodies and civil society organisations.

We first came to work with Bernadette early in our academic careers, as doctoral students or post-doctoral researchers at the University of Melbourne and Monash University. Our motivation for compiling the collection was to acknowledge the substantial contribution she has made to the fields of mental health, disability and criminal law in scholarship and practice, and especially to promoting an interdisciplinary approach to these fields that included both legal and non-legal perspectives.

A second motivation was to recognise the many other influences that Bernadette McSherry has had on the Academy and wider community. These include her strong, ongoing support for junior scholars through mentoring and advocacy and, perhaps most significantly, her role in challenging the 'Ivory Tower' of academia to foster a community of researchers whose work is led by, or conducted in collaboration with, affected communities and contributes to the pursuit of social equity. Her work in this area has manifested most strongly in a determination to ensure that mental health consumers and people with disability have 'a seat at the table' and a voice in developing the laws, policies and practices that affect them. In recognition of this work, she was awarded the 2017 Mental Health Services (TheMHS) Award for Exceptional Contribution to Australian and New Zealand mental health services.

The willingness of colleagues across disciplines and around the globe to contribute chapters to this collection, and to offer generous comments on one another's papers at a workshop in her honour in April 2022, demonstrates the breadth of Bernadette McSherry's influence and the high regard in which she is held by her peers.

While she has formally retired, we are in no doubt that Emeritus Professor McSherry's influence will long continue, through her ongoing scholarship and other professional activities in the fields of policy and law reform, through the continued influence of her work in the fields of mental health, disability and criminal law, and via the formative influence she has had on so many scholars (among whom we count ourselves) as well as policymakers, advocates and activists.

Kay Wilson
Yvette Maker
Piers Gooding
Jamie Walvisch

Acknowledgments

The editors thank Andrew Simon-Butler for his invaluable research and editing assistance and Sandra Pyke for compiling the Index and Tables of Cases and Legislation. They also express their deepest gratitude to the chapter authors for their generous contributions and patience with our editorial suggestions and queries.

John Chesterman thanks the editors for their tireless good work.

Kate Diesfeld deeply appreciates the information provided by Hanny Naus, Professional Educator, Elder Abuse and Neglect Prevention, Age Concern New Zealand. The editors' and peers' recommendations were very constructive. The analysis is her own.

Mary Donnelly is grateful for the invaluable feedback on Chapter 2 from Dr Anna Arstein-Kerslake, Professor Peter Bartlett, Dr Paul Harpur, Dr Yvette Maker and Dr Kay Wilson (any errors in spite of their efforts are the author's alone).

Piers Gooding would like to acknowledge the research funding of the Australian Research Council (ARC No. DE200100483), which partially funded his work on this book.

Yvette Maker and Piers Gooding thank Bernadette McSherry, Jeannie Paterson and the 2022 workshop participants for their generous comments on Chapter 13.

Erandathie Jayakody would like to acknowledge the extraordinary and tireless work of Anthony Stratford (1953–2023) in promoting the voice of lived experience in Australia and internationally. Meeting him changed her recovery trajectory and the course of her life. This is the transformational power of peer support. She wants to express her gratitude for his counsel and guidance over the years. She acknowledges that her work, including this chapter, is inspired by his many years of work. Erandathie Jayakody and Malitha Perera would like to thank Piers Gooding and Rebecca Duke for their critique in the drafting of this chapter.

Lisa Waddington and Paul Harpur gratefully acknowledge the support of Caitlyn Donohoe (4th year Arts/Laws student, The University of Queensland), who assisted with researching and editing their chapter.

Jamie Walvisch would like to acknowledge the research funding of the University of Melbourne (Early Career Researcher Grant 503454), which supported his work on Chapter 9 and paid for it to be made Open Access.

Kay Wilson thanks her co-authors and co-editors for their incisive comments; it has been wonderful working with you on this project. Dr Kay Wilson also thanks all the contributors for their chapters, participating in the workshop, producing multiple drafts and very patiently responding to emails. She would also like to thank Emeritus Professor McSherry for her inspiration, guidance, support and friendship.

Acronyms and Abbreviations

ACNZ	Age Concern New Zealand
ACRC	Abuse in Care Royal Commission (New Zealand)
ACT	Australian Capital Territory
AHRC	Australian Human Rights Commission
AI	Artificial intelligence
ALRC	Australian Law Reform Commission
AMA	Australian Medical Association
CAT	*Convention Against Torture and Other Cruel, Inhuman or Degrading Treatment or Punishment*
CEDAW	*Convention on the Elimination of All Forms of Discrimination Against Women*
CESCR	Committee on Economic, Social and Cultural Rights
CJEU	Court of Justice of the European Union
COMPAS	Correctional Offender Management Profiling for Alternative Sanctions
CQC	Care Quality Commission (England)
CRC	*Convention on the Rights of the Child*
CRPD	*Convention on the Rights of Persons with Disabilities*
CRPD Committee	Committee on the Rights of Persons with Disabilities
CTO	Community treatment order
Disability Royal Commission	Royal Commission into Violence, Abuse, Neglect and Exploitation of People with Disability (Australia)
DoLS	Deprivation of Liberty Safeguards
EARS	Aged Care New Zealand Elder Abuse Response Service
ECHR	*European Convention on Human Rights*
ECtHR	European Court of Human Rights
EPOA	Enduring power of attorney
EU Charter	*Charter of Fundamental Rights of the European Union*
HDC	Health and Disability Commissioner (New Zealand)
HDCA	*Health and Disability Commissioner Act 1994* (NZ)
HEPF	Health Equity Power Framework
HRMHRF	Human Rights and Mental Health Regulatory Framework

HRRT	Human Rights Review Tribunal (New Zealand)
ICCPR	*International Covenant on Civil and Political Rights*
ICERD	*International Convention on the Elimination of All Forms of Racial Discrimination*
ICESCR	*International Covenant on Economic, Social and Cultural Rights*
ICRMW	*International Convention on the Protection of the Rights of all Migrant Workers*
IMM	Independent Monitoring Mechanism (New Zealand)
LE Strategy	Driven by Lived Experience Framework and Strategy
LPS	Liberty Protection Safeguards
MCA	*Mental Capacity Act 2005* (England and Wales)
MHA 1959	*Mental Health Act 1959* (UK)
MHA 1983	*Mental Health Act 1983* (England and Wales)
MHA 2001	*Irish Mental Health Act 2001*
MHA 2007	*Mental Health Act 2007* (England and Wales)
MHA 2014	*Mental Health Act 2014* (Vic) (Australia)
MHCC	Mental Health Complaints Commission (Victoria, Australia)
MHWB Act 2022	*Mental Health and Wellbeing Act 2022* (Vic)
MHWC	Mental Health and Wellbeing Commission (Victoria, Australia)
MIND	National Association for Mental Health (UK)
MSD	Ministry of Social Development (New Zealand)
NDIS	National Disability Insurance Scheme (Australia)
OPCAT	*Optional Protocol to the Convention against Torture and other Cruel, Inhuman or Degrading Treatment or Punishment*
PBSP	Positive Behaviour Support Plan
Percy Report	Report of the Royal Commission on the Law Relating to Mental Illness and Mental Deficiency (1957) (UK)
PPPR Act	*Protection of Personal and Property Rights Act 1988* (NZ)
PWD	Person with disability
RAI	Research assessment instruments
RC	Royal Commission
RCACQS	Royal Commission into Aged Care Quality and Safety (Australia)
SAFEHOME	Stopping Aberrant Fatal Events by Helping Overcome Mental Extremes
TEU	*Treaty of the European Union*
TFEU	*Treaty on the Functioning of the European Union*
UDHR	*Universal Declaration of Human Rights*
UNHRC	United Nations Human Rights Committee

VCAT	Victorian Civil and Administrative Tribunal
Victorian Royal Commission	Royal Commission into Victoria's Mental Health System (Australia)
VLRC	Victorian Law Reform Commission (Australia)
WHO	World Health Organization

Part I

Reforming Mental Health and Disability Law

1 What Is the Future of Mental Health, Disability and Criminal Law?

Kay Wilson, Yvette Maker, Piers Gooding and Jamie Walvisch

Introduction

Mental health, disability and criminal law are under pressure. As Mary Donnelly points out in Chapter 2 of this volume, the source of this pressure on states is both external and domestic. At the international level, calls for a 'paradigm shift' have been driven by the entry into force of the *Convention on the Rights of Persons with Disabilities* (CRPD) in 2008, while reforms in various jurisdictions, including – for the purposes of this book – in high-income common law countries, have been influential in setting standards and guiding innovation. At the domestic level, a spate of scandals, adverse judicial findings and inquiries, along with greater input from persons with lived experience are, in the words of Erandathie Jayakody and Malitha Perera in Chapter 15 of this volume, challenging the 'deficit' narrative of mental illness and disability and collectively creating change. Still further, pressures are exerted by the broad demographic changes of an ageing global population, and the professionalisation of care previously provided informally by (mostly) women, which create challenges of how to best support older persons, especially those who may be frail or have dementia and other complex needs. In addition, mental health, disability and criminal law are not exempt from the influences of emerging technologies, especially artificial intelligence, that are sweeping the world and infiltrating almost every aspect of life in the 21st century. In this maelstrom, some of the hallmarks of mental health, disability and criminal law – including their role in social exclusion, institutionalisation and damaging restrictive practices and incarceration – are becoming increasingly untenable. As Peter Bartlett writes in Chapter 4 of this volume, 'the status quo ante manifestly must change'. But, *how*? As mental health, disability and criminal law twist and warp under the tension of heated debate and widespread discontent, where exactly are they going? Will they buckle under the strain? And just what might emerge in the aftermath?

The chapters in this edited volume explore these and other difficult questions about the future of mental health, disability and criminal law. At the same time, they honour the career of Emeritus Professor Bernadette McSherry, an internationally recognised scholar who has dedicated her career to advancing

DOI: 10.4324/9781003350644-2

scholarship and addressing the complex questions in these fields. McSherry is an Emeritus Professor of Law at Melbourne Law School, the University of Melbourne and was Foundation Director of the Melbourne Social Equity Institute. She recently retired following an academic career spanning 30 years. To mark this occasion, this volume brings together 23 world-leading scholars and commentators from Australia, Ireland, the Netherlands, New Zealand, the United Kingdom and the United States, most of whom have collaborated or worked with McSherry in the preceding decades. The contributors were invited to develop and extend McSherry's work by reflecting on and anticipating the future directions of mental health, disability and criminal law. The chapters in this collection use McSherry's work as a springboard to reflect on her vast contribution to scholarship and practice in the fields of mental health, disability and criminal law, while making their own contribution to developing and shaping these areas of law. In doing so, they aim to inform and inspire a new generation of mental health, disability and criminal law scholars, advocates and reformers.

Building on the Contributions of Emeritus Professor Bernadette McSherry

The scope of this volume demonstrates the deep well of inspiration that Bernadette McSherry's career (described in the Preface) has provided for the contributors. Few legal scholars have contributed as much to the development of mental health, disability and criminal law in Australia and New Zealand and beyond. Drawing on her background in law, psychology and political sociology, McSherry's scholarship and law reform practice has influenced government policies and legislative frameworks around the common law world. Her work on coercive treatment and preventive detention regimes has helped shape debates about the power of the state to regulate those considered at risk of harmful behaviour and has sparked the creation of a body of interdisciplinary work that challenges coercive mental health and criminal laws (e.g. McSherry and Keyzer 2011; McSherry and Freckelton 2013; Gooding and McSherry 2018). She has also conducted major projects on the impact of the CRPD on mental health law, and on the minimisation and elimination of seclusion and restraint in mental health, disability and aged care settings (see e.g. McSherry 2014, 2017; Brophy et al. 2016; Maker and McSherry 2019; McSherry and Maker 2021). Her seminal paper 'Legal Capacity Under the Convention on the Rights of Persons with Disabilities' (McSherry 2012), in which she sets out the various approaches to 'legal capacity' including the 'status approach', 'cognitive approach' and 'functional approach' under the CRPD, has been widely cited and its lasting impact exemplifies the clarity and acuity of her scholarship.

The Importance of Lived Experience Perspectives

A key feature of Bernadette McSherry's scholarly work and academic practice has been its concern with the perspectives, experiences and human rights of persons with lived experience of disability and mental health service use or diagnosis. This volume has similarly sought to foreground the voices of people with lived experience, consistent with the motto of the disability rights movement, 'nothing about us, without us'. Many of the academic authors in the collection have lived experience of disability, mental health conditions or mental health service use themselves, and the volume also contains contributions from three lived experience authors: Simon Katterl, Erandathie Jayakody and Duncan Cameron, who have written about the importance of lived experience and how *they* would like to see mental health law, policy and practice reformed. Further, all chapters that were not written by persons with lived experience have been reviewed by Duncan Cameron or Erandathie Jayakody to provide the editors and contributors with feedback on each chapter from a lived experience perspective.

Terminology

The language used to describe persons with disabilities and especially mental health service users and those with mental health conditions in scholarly literature and common parlance is context-dependent and potentially fraught (Walvisch 2017). As has been observed by the Australian Law Reform Commission (2014), language in this field has long been problematic, because terms which were once deemed socially acceptable are now considered to be derogatory, creating the ongoing need for a new lexicon. Further, language often reflects underlying theoretical issues; for instance, the separation between 'impairment' and 'disability' in the social model of disability, or the reclaiming of certain terms like 'mad' as self-identifiers (Wilson 2021). For this reason, rather than impose uniform terminology in this collection, the editors have invited contributors to use the terminology they consider most appropriate. This means inconsistencies between chapters are a deliberate editorial and authorial choice to reflect the pluralism and evolution of terminology in these three intersecting fields.

The Structure of This Volume

The contributions to this volume are arranged under four themes that encompass the different strands of McSherry's work: Reforming Mental Health and Disability Law (Part I; Chapters 1–4); Regulating Coercion and Restrictive Practices (Part II; Chapters 5–8); Improving Access to Justice and the Criminal Law (Part III; Chapters 9–11); and Transforming Mental Health Law (Part IV; Chapters 12–15).

The contributions in Part I consider the potential for future reform to mental health and disability law in line with human rights requirements and some of the challenges facing legislators, policymakers, practitioners and consumers in pursuing reform. Part II focuses on the regulation of one aspect of mental health, disability and aged care services – coercion and restrictive practices. It identifies some areas which are ripe for reform and others that have been stubbornly resistant to change. Part III turns to matters relating to criminal law and access to justice, focusing particularly on the role of mental health experts and risk assessment procedures in forensic processes, as well as recent developments in the inclusion of people with disability as jurors in several jurisdictions. Finally, the contributions in Part IV explore some of the emerging frontiers of mental health and disability law, including chapters that address the potential of human rights and lived experience perspectives to drive significant transformations of existing regulatory schemes in the mental health and disability sectors, and which consider the implications of rapidly developing technologies for forensic mental health risk assessment.

A Vision for the Future

So what, then, do the contributors to this volume think the future of mental health, disability and criminal law might be? Rather than offering a single specific snapshot, the chapters in this collection provide a kaleidoscope of glimpses of the future from multiple angles and perspectives.

After reviewing the sources of mental health law reform and the history of law reform processes in the United Kingdom, Mary Donnelly (Chapter 2, 'Making the Future Happen: Law Reform Lessons From the Victorian Royal Commission') envisages the Royal Commission into Victoria's Mental Health System (2021) (Victorian Royal Commission) in Australia as offering a significant blueprint for moving forward internationally, not only with respect to its substantive findings, but also in its modelling of a process of continual and widely consultative mental health law reform and dedicated funding. Anna Arstein-Kerslake (Chapter 12, 'Challenging the Foundations of Mental Health Law: Using Articles 12 and 14 of the CRPD as a Framework to Deconstruct and Reimagine Mental Health Law'), in accordance with the views of the CRPD Committee, the international body for monitoring and implementing the CRPD, goes even further by reimagining mental health law as protecting persons with mental health disability from a loss of rights, rather than authorising coercion and involuntary detention and psychiatric treatment.

However, despite the high hopes created by the CRPD and the Victorian Royal Commission, other chapters in the collection emphasise that the implementation of reform and the realisation of rights presents considerable challenges. Peter Bartlett (Chapter 4, 'Benefitting From Hindsight: What the *Mental Capacity Act* and Its Implementation Can Teach Us About CRPD Implementation') observes that much can be learnt from the pitfalls revealed during the implementation of previous 'breakthroughs' such as the *Mental Capacity Act 2005* (UK) in England and Wales. As Bartlett warns, efforts to realise the human rights of persons with disabilities can be thwarted by shortcomings of the legal system ('courts act like courts'), the entrenched power structures of the medical and legal establishments ('professionals act like professionals'), governments with little interest in providing real remedies and the sad reality that changing the law does not necessarily change practice or social attitudes. In a similar vein, Penelope Weller (Chapter 3, 'The Human Right to Health and the *Mental Health and Wellbeing Act 2022* (Vic)') is concerned that the aspirations of the Victorian Royal Commission to realise the highest attainable standard of mental health and wellbeing, including the importance of informed consent, may have been provisionally lost in translation within the text of the new *Mental Health and Wellbeing Act 2022* (Vic). John Dawson and Frances Matthews (Chapter 8, 'Some Concerns About Arbitrary Detention of Elderly People in Secure Rest Home Care') also point out that shaky legal foundations and questionable practices mean that many older persons are subject to arbitrary detention in aged care facilities in violation of their right to liberty, and ponder how that liberty might be protected.

Many of our authors emphasise that the future of mental health, disability and criminal law may not need more legislation, but rather better regulation, oversight and accountability. For instance, Simon Katterl and Sharon Friel (Chapter 14, 'Regulating Rights: Developing a Human Rights and Mental Health Regulatory Framework') critique the Mental Health Complaints Commission (MHCC) of Victoria, which was introduced by the *Mental Health Act 2014* (Vic). They propose using a new 'Human Rights and Mental Health Regulatory Framework' to ensure that the mistakes of the MHCC are not repeated and that proper regulatory oversight of the mental health system is introduced. Similarly, Kate Diesfeld (Chapter 7, 'Who Do We Turn To? Safeguarding Residents in Aged Care Settings From Abuse and Neglect in New Zealand') expresses concern that many older persons in aged care are subject to elder abuse. She reviews the gaps in the complaints, regulatory and oversight systems in New Zealand, drawing out lessons from comparable jurisdictions with ageing populations.

Of particular concern to our contributors is the use, regulation and oversight of restrictive practices like seclusion and restraint in a variety of health and care settings, which have severe human rights implications. In this regard, John Chesterman (Chapter 5, 'Who Approves the Use of Restrictive Practices in Australia? The Case for a Uniform Authorisation Process') points out the weaknesses, power imbalances and complications caused by Australian federalism in regulatory regimes which rely on the actual or substituted consent of persons to restrictive practices, particularly in aged care. Chesterman makes the case for a stricter and more accountable regulatory approach using behaviour support plans, which aim to drive down rather than merely authorise the use of restrictive interventions. Ian Freckelton (Chapter 6, 'Chemical Restraint Use and Reform in Health Care and Disability Settings') aims his cross hairs at the controversial use, definition and regulation of chemical restraint across health and aged care settings in light of the revelations and recommendations of Royal Commissions in Australia into mental health and disability in recent years.

While most persons with mental health conditions and disabilities never commit crimes (and are more likely to be victims of crime), how the criminal justice system responds to those who are found guilty of an offence raises many questions about the future application of the criminal law and the use of technology and medical expertise in psychological assessments. Jamie Walvisch, Andrew Carroll, Tim Marsh and Jaydip Sarkar (Chapter 9, 'Why-Dunnit?: Causal Explanations in Sentencing Offenders With Mental Health Problems') consider how judges should take into account the complex and often uncertain relationship between an offender's mental health condition and their history of offending in making sentencing determinations. Drawing on Nigel Walker's notion of 'possibility' explanations, they present a framework for how medical experts and legal counsel can best guide courts by providing robust retrospective explanations of the role of mental health conditions in an individual's past offending. Christopher Slobogin (Chapter 10, 'Finetuning a Jurisprudence of Risk') is concerned about how the future risks of reoffending are assessed in the sentencing, post-sentencing and preventive detention contexts. He points out the potential of algorithms, and the development of a 'jurisprudence of risk', to provide a more accurate, transparent and less biased way of identifying low risk offenders compared with the often prejudiced and inaccurate ways in which humans currently make decisions. By contrast, Piers Gooding and Yvette Maker (Chapter 13, 'The Digital Turn in Mental Health and Disability Law: Actuarial Traditions and AI Futures of Risk Assessment From a Human Rights Perspective') examine the drawbacks of automation and algorithmic technologies in risk assessment and raise human rights concerns with the use of predictive technology in forensic mental health care. Without ruling out the rights-enhancing possibility of some technological developments, they argue that considerable caution is required in the use of algorithmic approaches, acknowledging the 'structured clinical judgment' advocated by McSherry as likely presenting the 'least worst option'.

Finally, it is certain that the future of mental health, disability and criminal law involves greater inclusion of persons with lived experience at all levels of law, policy-making, service provision, the court system and individual health care decision-making. In this regard, Lisa Waddington and Paul Harpur (Chapter 11, 'The Rights of Persons With Sensory Disabilities to Participate in Juries'), both academics with lived experience of disability, envisage a future court system in which jurors with sensory disabilities are able to discharge their civic duties on an equal basis with others and ensure that the jury system is truly representative of the diversity of the community. Erandathie Jayakody and Malitha Perera (Chapter 15, 'Standing Up Against the Weight of History: The Importance of Lived Experience in the Mental Health Context') argue that persons with lived experience have a unique expertise, and that the historical exclusion of persons with lived experience from mental health law, policy and systems has resulted in dysfunctional and inherent structural biases, requiring urgent correction. Simon Katterl and Sharon Friel (noted earlier) argue that the contributions of persons with lived experience can be used as an important regulatory tool to address power imbalances, keep regulation focussed on human rights, ensure accountability of regulators from third parties and reduce the risk of regulatory capture. Duncan Cameron ('Foreword') draws on his lived experience to point out that in practice the letter of the law may be less important than the attitudes and compassion of the people who participate in and administer it. And it is perhaps by the exchange of ideas and sharing of experiences, through incisive and persuasive research and scholarship in edited volumes such as this, that hearts and minds are opened and ultimately won.

While there is certainly much scope for reform, on balance the contributors to this volume have painted a picture of the future development of mental health, disability and criminal law which is more positive than negative – less coercive, more responsive and more inclusive – as well as making a plea for immediate action to realise that vision. They are ambitious for legal, systemic and social change, while being realistic about the many obstacles in making real, substantive and enduring improvements rather than just mechanically ticking boxes or tinkering around the edges. Of course, a book such as this which speculates about the future always risks becoming outdated by the effluxion of time, as what was the future becomes the past. Yet, obsolescence would be a very welcome sign of success – if it means that mental health, disability and criminal law are improved and transformed as our contributors argue they must. But whatever the future of mental health, disability and criminal law may be, there is no doubt – as attested by the production of this volume – that it would not be the same without the influence of Emeritus Professor Bernadette McSherry. Thus, while looking back on McSherry's career, *The Future of Mental Health, Disability and Criminal Law* seeks to leave a contemporary and forward-looking legacy.

References

Australian Law Reform Commission (2014) *Equality, Capacity and Disability in Commonwealth Laws.* Available www.alrc.gov.au/publication/equality-capacity-and-disability-in-commonwealth-laws-alrc-report-124/ (accessed 23 December 2022).

Brophy, L.M., Roper, C.E., Hamilton, B.E., Tellez, J.J. and McSherry, B.M. (2016) 'Consumers and Their Supporters' Perspectives on Poor Practice and the Use of Seclusion and Restraint in Mental Health Settings: Results from Australian Focus Groups', *International Journal of Mental Health Systems*, 10(6): 1–10.

Gooding, P. and McSherry, B. (2018) 'Alternatives to Compulsory Detention and Treatment and Coercive Practices in Mental Health Settings', *Journal of Law and Medicine*, 26(2): 300–5.

Maker, Y. and McSherry, B. (2019) 'Regulating Restraint Use in Mental Health and Aged Care Settings: Lessons from the Oakden Scandal', *Alternative Law Journal*, 44(1): 29–36.

McSherry, B. (2012) 'Legal Capacity Under the Convention on the Rights of Persons with Disabilities', *Journal of Law and Medicine*, 20(1): 22–27.

McSherry, B. (2014) 'Mental Health Laws: Where to From Here?' *Monash University Law Review*, 40(1): 175–97.

McSherry, B. (2017) 'Regulating Seclusion and Restraint in Health Care Settings: The Promise of the Convention on the Rights of Persons with Disabilities', *International Journal of Law and Psychiatry*, 53: 39–44.

McSherry, B. and Freckelton, I. (eds) (2013) *Coercive Care: Rights, Law and Policy*, Abingdon: Routledge.

McSherry, B. and Keyzer, P. (eds) (2011) *Dangerous People: Policy, Prediction, and Practice*, London: Routledge.

McSherry, B. and Maker, Y. (eds) (2021) *Restrictive Practices in Health Care and Disability Settings: Legal, Policy and Practical Responses*, Abingdon: Routledge.

Royal Commission into Victoria's Mental Health System (2021) *Final Report*. Available https://finalreport.rcvmhs.vic.gov.au/ (accessed 23 December 2022).

Walvisch, J. (2017) 'Defining "Mental Disorder" in Legal Contexts', *International Journal of Law and Psychiatry*, 52: 7–18.

Wilson, K. (2021) *Mental Health Law: Abolish or Reform?* Oxford: Oxford University Press.

2 Making the Future Happen

Law Reform Lessons From the Victorian Royal Commission

Mary Donnelly

Introduction

Professor Bernadette McSherry's scholarship on mental health law is marked by a focus on human rights as an instrument of change (McSherry and Weller 2010; McSherry and Freckelton 2013; McSherry and Maker 2021). From this perspective, she asks important questions about how human rights norms can be woven into the fabric of mental health service delivery. Her work eschews the simple dichotomies which have tended to dominate in debates around Articles 12 and 14 of the United Nations *Convention on the Rights of Persons with Disabilities* (CRPD) and instead identifies a more expansive and interconnected framework for human rights engagement (McSherry and Wilson 2015; McSherry 2017). This approach to human rights is reflected in the work of the Royal Commission into Victoria's Mental Health System (Victorian Royal Commission), of which Bernadette McSherry was one of the four commissioners. This mammoth piece of work, comprising an Interim Report published in 2019 and a five-volume final report published in 2021 (Victorian Royal Commission Report), sets out an ambitious plan to 'redesign Victoria's mental health and wellbeing system' (Royal Commission into Victoria's Mental Health System Summary and Recommendations (Executive Summary) 2021: 4). The rich and multi-faceted Victorian Royal Commission Report provides ample material for analysis from a wide range of perspectives, both within Victoria and internationally. Writing from an Irish perspective, I am especially interested in the Victorian Royal Commission Report's contribution to policy discourse beyond Victoria and in particular in how it can contribute to a better understanding of the processes of mental health law reform.

Although much more than a law reform project, law reform plays a central role in the Victorian Royal Commission Report. In this respect, the Victorian Royal Commission Report is one of many mental health law reform projects, conducted across different times and different jurisdictions. The pace and range of reform internationally has increased in the wake of the CRPD as States Parties have worked to prepare for their initial reports to the Committee on the Rights of Persons with Disabilities (CRPD Committee). Although law reform projects of one kind or another have been part of mental health law from its earliest iteration as a distinct discipline (Unsworth 1991), there

DOI: 10.4324/9781003350644-3

has (to my knowledge at least) been limited comparative analysis of law reform in this sphere. There is clearly a great deal to be learnt from how different jurisdictions approach the matter of reform. However, there are challenges in developing a basis for comparative analysis which is simultaneously sufficiently rigorous and sufficiently granular. The Concluding Observations of the CRPD Committee, issued at the conclusion of its reviews of States' implementation of the CRPD, and the World Health Organization (WHO) Mental Health Atlas (2020) provide helpful data. However, these are limited in what they cover. The CRPD Committee's Concluding Observations are restricted because the Committee's view that abolition of mental health law is the only CRPD-compliant approach limits its engagement with the range of law reform possibilities, while the WHO Mental Health Atlas provides only a high-level picture of legislative developments. Thus, these sources present only a partial picture of the impact of reforms of mental health law in the jurisdictions covered.

While recognising the value of broad – and deep – comparative work on mental health law reform, this chapter is more circumspect in its ambition. Using the Victorian Royal Commission Report as an entry point, it focuses less on the outcomes of law reform and more on the process which led to those outcomes. This is on the basis that law reform processes are important in their own right and that the way we approach law reform has consequences both for the law reform project's legitimacy and its potential to effect successful change. While recognising that the context for the Victorian Royal Commission's work will not necessarily be replicated in other jurisdictions, this chapter nonetheless argues that the Victorian Royal Commission's approach to law reform provides a template for other jurisdictions, both in its proposals and in the process it employed. Before turning to the specifics of the Victorian Royal Commission at work, this chapter begins by contextualising mental health law reform. It identifies differing impetuses for law reform and then, focussing primarily on the experience of the United Kingdom, it looks more closely at the diverse law reform processes which can be employed. It should be noted that, following the devolution of law-making authority in certain areas from the United Kingdom (UK) Parliament to the devolved legislatures in Wales, Scotland and Northern Ireland in the late 1990s (*Government of Wales Act 1998*; *Scotland Act 1998*; *Belfast (Good Friday) Agreement Act 1998*), mental health law reform has proceeded along different trajectories in the different UK jurisdictions. Accordingly, there are now quite distinct mental health laws in England and Wales, Northern Ireland and Scotland. Any discussion of post-devolution reforms in this chapter is concerned with England and Wales.

The second part of the chapter outlines the key law reform proposals in the Victorian Royal Commission Report, before identifying two central elements of the Victorian Royal Commission's process: its approach to the collection and presentation of evidence and its adoption of a system-wide analysis. This chapter concludes by identifying some lessons to be taken from the Victorian Royal Commission's approach.

Reforming Mental Health Law: Turns, Twists and Detours

Lady Hale (2007: 19), writing extra-judicially, described mental health law as an attempt 'to reconcile three overlapping but often competing goals: protecting the public, obtaining access to the services people need and safeguarding users' civil rights'. The attempt to reconcile these goals has been at the heart of all of the mental health reform projects (both in the UK and more broadly) discussed later. This section presents an overview of how these have worked, first identifying the different kinds of impetus for law reform and then exploring the processes employed.

Mental Health: The Impetus for Reform

Law reform projects do not simply happen but rather emerge in response to a wide range of political and/or legal imperatives. We need to understand these imperatives if we are to evaluate the processes employed and the reform choices made. One possible categorisation distinguishes between those imperatives which are external to the jurisdiction, typically arising from requirements of international or regional human rights instruments, and those which emerge from within the jurisdiction, usually emerging when difficulties in the existing system reach a tipping point. These categories are by no means watertight. As recounted by Gráinne de Búrca (2021: 17), international human rights standards can provide an important basis for domestic grassroots engagement, which in turn can help create a domestic impetus for reform. Moreover, jurisdictions influence each other; for example, as discussed later, the growing recognition of patient autonomy in the United States, beginning in the 1970s and the consequent civil rights-based judicial interventions in mental health law, were highly influential on domestic law reform processes in other jurisdictions.

External Impetus

Externally imposed requirements for mental health law reform are relatively new. Legislative reform is a key element of the CRPD, and the CRPD Committee has consistently reinforced the significance of law reform in its General Comments and Concluding Observations. From a mental health perspective, two strands of law reform can be identified in the CRPD Committee's communications. The first concerns positive requirements on States Parties to enhance the rights of persons with disabilities (Gooding 2017; Wilson 2021). These include the identification of a requirement on States Parties to 'holistically examine' their laws to ensure the equal right to legal capacity (General Comment (GC) No. 1, 2014: para 7) and to 'take action to develop laws and policies to replace regimes of substitute decision-making by supported decision-making, which respects the person's autonomy, will and preferences' (GC No. 1 2014: para 26). The second strand is focused on the repeal of existing laws, including those which allow for substitute decision-making (GC No. 1 2014: para 28) and mental health laws which allow for compulsory admission (Guidelines on Art. 14 2015: para 10) or treatment (GC No. 1 2014: para 42).

The first of these strands has been normatively uncontentious. States Parties (and their law reform processes) have of course diverged as to how the obligation to support should be given effect (Donnelly 2022), but the appropriateness of an obligation to develop decision-making supports has not been seriously questioned. The repeal (or abolitionist) element of the CRPD Committee's law reform agenda has attracted more controversy. Several States Parties, including Australia, Canada, Egypt, Estonia, Georgia, Ireland, the Netherlands, Norway, Poland, Singapore, Syria and Venezuela, have issued reservations or declarations in respect of the CRPD Committee's identification of a requirement to repeal all substitute decision-making regimes. Of more direct relevance to this chapter are the critiques of an abolitionist approach to mental health law, especially in the absence of alternative safeguarding structures (Freeman et al. 2015; Wilson 2021, 2022). Consequently, while many States Parties have taken steps to reduce the use of compulsion, no State Party has (yet) entirely repealed all aspects of compulsion under mental health law, although Peru is sometimes cited as having come closest (Encalada 2021).

Moving to regional human rights instruments, the *European Convention on Human Rights* (ECHR) provides one example of such instruments as external drivers of reform. The different legal character of the ECHR means that it is less overtly directional than the CRPD. Nonetheless, the ECHR was a key driver behind reform of Irish mental health law; the *Irish Mental Health Act 2001* (MHA 2001) was introduced following the settlement reached in *Croke v Ireland* [2000], where it was agreed that the complainant would withdraw his case before the European Court of Human Rights (ECtHR) provided that the Irish State would reform the (highly problematic) *Mental Treatment Act 1945*. ECHR-compliance was also the force behind the introduction of the Deprivation of Liberty Safeguards (DoLS) in England and Wales (*Mental Capacity Act 2005*: sections 4A, 4B and 16A). The DoLS were introduced following the decision of the ECtHR in *HL v United Kingdom* [2004] that the absence of any formal legal procedures meant that HL's admission (as an adult lacking capacity) to a psychiatric facility was in breach of the liberty protections set out in Article 5 of the ECHR. The DoLS are formal procedures which were originally intended to apply in situations where a person was admitted to a hospital or care home and lacked the capacity to consent to the admission. However, following the decision of the UK Supreme Court in *P v Cheshire West & Chester Council* [2014], the scope of the DoLS was expanded to apply in any situation where a person who lacks capacity is subject to continuous supervision and control and is not free to leave their place of residence (the 'acid' test for deprivation of liberty) (Series 2022: 173–78).

While an external impetus can lead to law reform, it is less clear that it will lead to successful law reform (Hathaway 2002). There is a risk of formulaic reform, introduced to comply with external requirements without the depth of engagement required to make the reforms meaningful. Ezgi Taşcıoğlu's (2022) critique of the engagement of the Turkish government with the CRPD provides a useful example. Taşcıoğlu (2022: 199–201) shows that while the government amended the *Turkish Disability Act No. 2378* in 2014, following Turkish ratification of the CRPD, practices on the ground remained largely unchanged. She points out the limitations of the state reporting process under the CRPD in achieving real change in the absence of domestic commitment to change (2022: 207–10). The DoLS saga in England and Wales (Law Commission 2017; Harding 2021; Series 2022) offers another angle on the limitations of compliance-driven law reform. The DoLS introduced in the wake of *HL v United Kingdom* [2004] were highly technical, legalistic, expensive and largely ineffective in delivering real protection. Peter Bartlett (2014: 4) sums up the impact of the DoLS on practice as follows:

> No doubt buttressed by the technical legal wording of the resulting legislation, the result is that care providers, insofar as they think about the DoLS at all, seem to perceive it as a technical legal problem, with a technical legal solution – not something that can actually benefit [the service user/consumer] in any tangible way.

These examples show that, while external reform requirements can be effective in instigating law reform, if these are to change domestic practices, deeper engagement with underlying social, political and cultural contexts is needed (see Bartlett in Chapter 4 of this volume). As de Búrca (2021: 30) has argued, 'the longer success of human rights campaigns often depends on the level of underlying social support and wider mobilization'. In light of this, we can turn to domestic impetus for reform.

Domestic Impetus

Domestic impetus for law reform emerges when it becomes sufficiently apparent to the political system that existing legal frameworks are no longer workable. The reasons for this may include broader social change, effective lobby groups, increased costs, public fears, public scandals and/or damning evidence from various forms of oversight bodies (Unsworth 1987). While these factors will play out differently in each jurisdiction, the repeated mental health law reform activities in the UK (and post-devolution, England and Wales) over the last half century or so make this an informative choice for a (truncated) tour of the many and varied domestic impetuses for reform.

Kathleen Jones (1972) famously described UK mental health law as a pendulum swinging between two extremes of legalism and medicalism. While this dichotomous characterisation may lack nuance (Wilson 2021: 36), its basic taxonomy remains useful. The return to 'medicalism' in the *Mental Health Act 1959* (UK) (MHA 1959) is therefore a useful starting point for consideration. The MHA 1959 came about following the Report of the Royal Commission on the Law Relating to Mental Illness and Mental Deficiency (1957) (the Percy Report), which had been convened in 1954 as the move from institutional to community-based care was starting to take hold. In this new climate, cumbersome 'quasi-criminal' (Percy Report: para 348) legal processes to prevent inappropriate admission no longer made sense and a looser, lighter touch legal approach was seen as being more in line with the changing times (Fennell 1996: 328–29; Rapaport and Manthorpe 2009: 255–58). Reflecting this, the Percy Report (and the MHA 1959 which followed) reduced the role of 'hard' law in the admission process, opting instead for greater medical autonomy coupled with various non-judicial oversight mechanisms, including second opinion safeguards and mental health reviews. John Hamilton (1983: 1721), the Medical Director of Broadmoor Hospital, described the resulting Act as being, in its day, 'regarded at home and abroad as a most enlightened piece of progressive legislation, heralding a new era in the care of the mentally disordered'.

Two decades on, the MHA 1959 had begun to look quite different in a changed landscape. Psychiatric practices were changing as the 'pharmacological revolution' took hold and multi-disciplinary teams were becoming established. Trust in the medical profession had reduced and the values of patient autonomy and patient rights were gaining traction, initially in the United States (Rothman 1991) and then in the United Kingdom (Wilson 2014). Meanwhile high-profile scandals were drawing public attention to the levels of neglect and abuse that were occurring in British psychiatric hospitals (Hamilton 1983: 1722). From this impetus, there emerged the 'new legalism' of the *Mental Health Act 1983* (MHA 1983), which included a statutory standard for admission and a right to a tribunal review (Shapland and Williams 1983; Szmukler and Gostin 2021).

The impetus for the next phase of legislative reform came from a very different place. This time, 'the risk posed to the public by those with mental illness, and the failings of the mental healthcare system to adequately manage those risks, was the major driver of the perceived need for reform' (Wessely 2018: 7T). The *Mental Health Act 2007* (MHA 2007) in England and Wales presaged a move to a more risk-focused approach to mental health law, characterised by John Fanning (2020) as the 'new medicalism'. This included broadening the definition of mental disorder as well as introducing provision for compulsory community treatment. Perhaps unsurprisingly, given its focus on risk, the period following the MHA 2007 coming into force saw a significant increase in the use of compulsory powers with the rate of involuntary hospitalisations shooting up from 51.7 per 100,000 in 1988-89 to 114.1 per 100,000 in 2015/16 (Wessely 2018: 49). A further law reform project, chaired by psychiatrist Sir Simon Wessely, was announced in October 2017. The impetus for reform this time is summarised by the Chair as follows:

> There is a clear case for change: the rate of detention is rising; the patient's voice is lost within processes that are out of date and can be uncaring;

> there is unacceptable overrepresentation of people from black and minority ethnic groups amongst people detained; and people with learning disabilities and or [sic] autism are at a particular disadvantage. We are also concerned that we are out-of-step with our human rights obligations.
> (Wessely 2018: 45)

One further domestic impetus which does not emerge from the preceding discussion is that which underpinned the review of the MHA 2001 in Ireland. The MHA 2001 (section 75) includes a requirement that, no later than five years after the establishment day of the legislation, the Minister for Health must carry out a review of the legislation and make a report in this regard to the Oireachtas (the Irish Parliament). This kind of automatic review clause has the advantage of keeping mental health law on the political agenda; however, it also runs the risk that a review, and any reform proposals it devises, will be formulaic rather than substantive.

Even from this brief account, it emerges that the decision to reform is highly responsive to broader social and political pressures. It also emerges that law reform is generally treated as something separate from – and largely subsequent to – underlying changes in policy and practice. Practices and policies evolve, and law reform is then introduced to address these. Thus, although there have been some moves to broaden the vision – see for example, the identification of 'system-wide enablers' in the most recent review of the MHA 1983 (Wessely 2018: 209–19) – the interactions between law and the broader mental health system, including factors such as economics/funding, staffing and broader culture, receives limited attention in law reform processes. As discussed later, the systems approach adopted by the Victorian Royal Commission provides an important counterpoint to this. Before this, a closer look at processes in operation shows both the significance of process and, drawing again on the UK example, the variety of processes employed.

Law Reform Processes in Operation

Mental health law reform processes are significant for both normative and instrumental reasons. From a normative perspective, the legitimacy of reform proposals is dependent on the rigour, care and inclusiveness of the process employed to develop these. An overtly political or an evidentially or analytically sloppy process will not (and should not) withstand normative scrutiny. Viewed instrumentally, a law reform process which has not gained at least some degree of stakeholder confidence will struggle to deliver meaningful change. The significance of process and in particular the importance of comprehensive integration of the service user/consumer contribution at all tiers of the law reform process is reinforced by Article 4(3) of the CRPD. This requires all States Parties to 'closely consult with and actively involve persons with disabilities . . . through their representative organisations' in developing and implementing legislation and policies to give effect to the CRPD. As Paul

Harpur and Michael Stein (2022) argue, this requirement may constitute a 'tipping point' in ensuring participation by persons with disabilities in relevant processes.

A focus on process pays attention to a variety of factors. These include the role and independence of the review body; the terms of reference for the review, including how expansive or tightly constrained these are; the membership and expertise of the review body and the locus of decision-making authority. Also relevant is the quality of the evidence relied upon to ground findings and to support recommendations made, including the range and reliability of evidence used; the scope and scale of consultation; and the integration of the outcome of consultation into the review. Bearing this in mind, it is informative to take a closer look at the variety of law reform processes which have been employed in just one (admittedly active) jurisdiction: the UK and (post-devolution) England and Wales.

Process in Practice

The Percy Report shows a Royal Commission in action. As described by Mintrom, O'Neill and O'Connor (2021: 80), Royal Commissions are 'governmental entities established by the head of state to investigate and report on specific matters of public concern'. Although Royal Commissions have fallen out of favour in the UK in recent times (Barlow 2013), traditionally, they had a level of standing compared with other processes arising from 'their perceived independence, neutrality, and transparency' (Mintrom, O'Neill and O'Connor 2021: 81). The Percy Commission sat for three years and consulted extensively, including at least some consultation with people with first-hand experience of mental illness and their family members or carers (Rapaport and Manthorpe 2009: 254). The members of the Commission had wide experience in mental health-related issues and a commitment to what we would now call social justice (Rapaport and Manthorpe 2009: 253). The Percy Commission produced a 324-page, evidence-based report and almost all of its recommendations were given effect in the MHA 1959 (Rapaport and Manthorpe 2009: 262). While some elements of the process, especially the level of involvement of service users/consumers, would not stand up to modern scrutiny, for its time, this might reasonably be described as a successful law reform project.

The legislation which followed the MHA 1959, the MHA 1983, emerged from quite a different process. In light of societal changes, in 1972 the Royal College of Psychiatrists established a Working Party to review the MHA 1959. However, unlike previous reform processes, this time there was a strong and organised alternative voice to that of the establishment. The National Association for Mental Health (MIND) and its legal officer, Larry Gostin, provided a powerful policy analysis, drawing heavily on principles, including the adoption of the least restrictive alternative and the application of due process values, which had been emerging in the United States (Gostin 1975). MIND proved itself to be an effective lobbying force (Hilton 2007: 220–22) and following the enactment of the MHA 1983, MIND estimated that two-thirds of the Act's new provisions had been advocated for by MIND (Hilton 2007: 225–26).

The next phase in the reform cycle offers a further insight into the politics of law reform. Following the emergence of public concerns about a perceived threat posed by people with mental illnesses, an expert review group comprising of 12 members and chaired by the legal academic Professor Genevra Richardson was convened in July 1998. The group was tasked with undertaking a 'root and branch review' of the MHA 1983, and specifically with providing recommendations regarding the introduction of measures for compulsory community treatment (Report of the Expert Committee 1999: 140). However, as Jill Peay (2000: 6), a member of the expert group, explains, '[t]he Richardson Committee was set up with a fairly clear brief. It was not our task to formulate policy, rather to enable the legislative framework to reflect government policy'. The Richardson Committee grounded its legal analysis in a set of underlying principles which it used to direct its approach to law reform. The principles identified were: patient autonomy, consensual care, non-discrimination, reciprocity, respect for diversity, equality, respect for carers, effective communication and provision of information, and evidence-based practice (Peay 2000: 9). These principles, and in particular, the identification of reciprocity (the State's obligation to provide quality care if requiring individuals to be subject to compulsion) were remarkably prescient (and indeed we will see many of them reflected in the Victorian Royal Commission Report). These principles were carefully integrated into a workable set of recommendations which were unanimously agreed by all members of the expert group. The Richardson Report was presented to the UK government in July 1999. However, it was not published until November 1999 when it appeared alongside a Green Paper setting out the government's view on mental health reform (Department of Health 1999). The Green Paper was a very different kind of document, described by one member of the Richardson Committee (Dr Nigel Eastman) as having taken 'part of the skeleton of Richardson, but abandoning its ethical heart' and by another of having abandoned its 'principled musculature' (Peay 2000: 8). The MHA 2007 reflected the Green Paper rather than the Richardson Report and, as described earlier, the period since its enactment has seen a substantial increase in the use of compulsory powers.

The most recent law reform project in England and Wales, the Wessely Review, was formally commissioned by the Prime Minister of the UK and afforded a much broader remit than that of the Richardson Review. The Wessely Review's Terms of Reference (Department of Health and Social Care 2017) identified specific concerns (including rising rates of detention, disproportionate levels of detention of black and minority ethnic groups and a range of stakeholder concerns) and required the Review to work with stakeholders to make recommendations to government. The Terms of Reference (Department of Health and Social Care 2017) explicitly recognised that some of the solutions were likely to lie in practice rather than in legislation and stated that the Review 'should consider practice-based solutions where possible'. The Review was chaired by a psychiatrist and the three Vice Chairs were a retired High Court judge (Sir Mark Hedley), a Rabbi and member of the House of Lords (Baroness Julia Neuberger) and a service user and Serious Mental Illness Living Consultant (Steven Gilbert) (Wessely 2018: 34). Gilbert chaired a 13-member Service User and Carer Group which comprised people who had either been detained under the MHA 1983 or had cared for someone detained and this Group provided a separate evaluation of the Report (Wessely 2018: 35–38). This deeper engagement of service users/consumers and the more extensive terms of reference are positive features and an indication that service user/consumer involvement is becoming an established and essential part of law reform processes. The Wessely Review reported in December 2018, setting out 150 recommendations (Wessely 2018: 297–314) aimed at enhancing human rights protections and affording a central role to the service user/consumer voice in all aspects of mental health decision-making (Laing 2022: 163–65). A Government White Paper which accepted the vast majority of the Wessely Review's recommendations was published in January 2021 (Laing 2022: 165), and a draft Mental Health Bill was published in June 2022. Compared with the Richardson Review, this might therefore be described as a politically successful review. However, as Judy Laing (2022: 175) argues, ultimately the success or failure of the measures introduced will depend on resources and the provision of 'system-wide supports and enablers'. Yet, this is something which, because of the way in which this law reform project (and indeed all the other projects discussed earlier) was established, the Review was unable to address in other than a minimal way. As will be seen later, the Victorian Royal Commission approach offers a fresh perspective on this key aspect of law reform.

The Victorian Royal Commission at Work

As with the UK, mental health law reform has a long history in Australian jurisdictions (see Jayakody and Perera in Chapter 15 of this volume). One of the most recent major reform processes was the Royal Commission established by the Victorian Government in February 2019. Its aim (in the words of the Victorian Premier, who is the head of the state government) was to fix a 'broken system' (Royal Commission into Victoria's Mental Health System Interim Report 2019 (Interim Report)). The extensive review of the Victorian mental health system presented in the Victorian Royal Commission's Interim Report suggests that this was not an overstatement. The Victorian Royal Commission estimated that over 1.1 million Victorians experienced a mental illness each year and that a further 1.5 million were at risk of experiencing such an illness (Interim Report: 27–28). For a range of reasons, the Victorian mental health system was unable to cope with this. Problems identified by the Victorian Royal Commission included an inability for individuals to access mental health services, difficulties in navigating the system, barriers to services and services which were uninclusive and exclusionary.

The political choice of a Royal Commission is indicative of the scale of the problem. Royal Commissions are expensive and time-consuming, although they do have a degree of prestige in Australia and an 'air of independence and impartiality which translate well to the general public' (Mintrom, O'Neill and O'Connor 2021: 82). One criticism of Royal Commissions has been their vulnerability to the political process. As Mintrom, O'Neill and O'Connor (2021: 81) describe, '[o]nce the final report has been submitted, governments can choose to simply ignore recommendations or respond only to those that suit their political goals'. Notably, however, the Victorian Government of the day committed in advance to implementing all of the Victorian Royal Commission's recommendations (Executive Summary 2021: 31). (However, for a critique of the Victorian Government's early attempts to implement the Victorian Royal Commission through its new *Mental Health and Wellbeing Act 2022* (Vic) see Weller in Chapter 3 of this volume.)

Royal commissioners are independent of government and are typically 'drawn from the ranks of highly respected members of society' (Mintrom, O'Neill and O'Connor 2021: 82). Like all policy influencers, the work of commissioners 'call[s] for skills in strategic thinking, gathering evidence, making arguments, working in teams, conflict management, negotiating, networking, and engaging multiple audiences' (Mintrom, O'Neill and O'Connor 2021: 83). This Royal Commission comprised four members from different professional backgrounds: the Chair, Penny Armytage, is a former senior public servant with extensive review/public inquiry experience; Dr Alex Cockram is a psychiatrist and leader in mental health care; Professor Allan Fels AO is an economist and former chair of the Australian Competition and Consumer Commission and a carer for a family member with schizophrenia; and Professor Bernadette McSherry, who, as this book sets out, is an esteemed legal academic with extensive engagement in public service. While representatives from law and psychiatry are almost always part of mental health law reform projects, the inclusion of public sector and economics expertise at this high level brought a broader set of skills and experience and indicated from the outset that this project was aimed at a much higher level of integration than the norm. In addition to the four commissioners, there was an eight-member Expert Advisory Committee which comprised members with lived, professional and sector experience of the Victorian mental health system (Interim Report: 11).

The Victorian Royal Commission delivered an Interim Report in November 2019 with nine recommendations for immediate action. A central recommendation of this Interim Report (2019: 560) was the introduction of a new ring-fenced levy or tax to fund the ongoing operation of the mental health system. The Royal Commission's final five-volume report was published in February 2021. This set out 65 recommendations across the mental health system which were intended to deliver 'transformational reform' (Executive Summary 2021: 18 et seq). As described by the Royal Commission itself, the aim was that reforms would 'rebalance the system so that more services will be delivered in community settings, and extend beyond a health response to a more holistic approach to good mental health and wellbeing' (Executive Summary 2021: 20). All aspects of the rich analysis in the Victorian Royal Commission's Report merit close engagement. However, given the focus of this chapter, the primary concern is with the law reform elements and in particular with the processes employed by the Royal Commission in developing these.

Legislative Reform Proposals

A core element of the Victorian Royal Commission's recommendations is that a new *Mental Health and Wellbeing Act* should be introduced to replace the *Mental Health Act 2014* (Vic) (MHA 2014). The MHA 2014 had been introduced in the wake of Australia's ratification of the CRPD and following a five-year consultation process. It introduced a range of measures which aimed to minimise the use and duration of compulsion and to introduce greater respect for human rights, supported decision-making and recovery-oriented practice (Royal Commission into Victoria's Mental Health System Final Report 2021 (RC Report) Vol. 4: 17). The Victorian Royal Commission concluded that, despite its recency, the MHA 2014 needed to be replaced. It set out several reasons for this view. First, it identified the narrow scope of the MHA 2014 which, like mental health legislation in most other jurisdictions, was narrowly focussed on compulsory admission and treatment and had 'little relevance for people who are not subject to, nor at risk of being subject to, compulsory treatment orders' (RC Report Vol. 4: 22). Secondly, 'despite the extensive consultation processes, the best efforts of many, and the careful and considered drafting of the legislation', the aspirations behind the MHA 2014 to embed supported decision-making and recovery-oriented practice had not been realised (RC Report Vol. 4: 23). This was primarily because supported decision-making and recovery-oriented practice had not been embedded into treatment, support and care (RC Report Vol. 4: 26). Thirdly, there were contradictions between the MHA 2014 and the applicable human rights frameworks, as set out in the Victorian *Charter of Human Rights and Responsibilities Act* and in the CRPD (RC Report Vol. 4: 29–30). Finally, the Commission identified the lack of clear accountability structures under the MHA 2014 (RC Report Vol. 4: 32) (see also discussion of the inadequacies of the MHA 2014 and need for greater accountability by Cameron in the Foreword and Katterl and Friel in Chapter 14 in this volume).

The *Mental Health and Wellbeing Act* as proposed by the Victorian Royal Commission, and passed by the Victorian Parliament in August 2022, aims to shift the legislative focus away from compulsion towards the delivery of treatment and the enhancement of wellbeing, with the underpinning goal being delivery on the right to the highest attainable standard of mental health and wellbeing (RC Report Vol. 4: 35–36). The Act presents a new vision of mental health law as an enabler of mental health and wellbeing, rather than as a mechanism for compulsion. This is not to say that the Act absolutely prohibits the use of compulsory admission or treatment. It retains the possibility of compulsory treatment as a last resort, however, as outlined in detail in an 89-page chapter, the Commission proposed a range of measures to ensure that compulsory treatment is only used as a last resort (RC Report Vol. 4: 359–447). While a statement of this kind of goal has now become a feature of most mental health law reform processes, the systems approach adopted by the Commission (and discussed further later) exhibits a level of practical grounding which substantially exceeds such proposals elsewhere. Moreover, the Commission concluded that a necessary goal of the redesigned system was working towards the elimination of restrictive practices. As described by the Commission, '[a]ny lesser aspiration will impair the efforts to achieve a system that is safe for both consumers and staff, and that provides the highest standard of treatment, care and support for people experiencing severe distress or who are in crisis' (RC Report Vol. 4: 300).

The *Mental Health and Wellbeing Act 2022* (Vic) engages a variety of legal tools to give effect to the vision of mental health law as an enabler of mental health and wellbeing in practice (RC Report Vol. 4: 39–40). First, it uses objectives and principles to guide interpretation of the Act. These are aimed not just at guiding courts but also providing a basis for engagement for people living with mental illness and their families, carers and supporters; as well as for service delivery and the resolution of complaints (RC Report Vol. 4: 40–41). The primary objective of the Act is the delivery of the highest attainable standard of mental health (see also discussion of the Victorian Royal Commission and the right to health by Weller in Chapter 3 of this volume). This has three clearly stated elements: promoting conditions in which people can enjoy good mental health and wellbeing; reducing inequities in access to and delivery of mental health and wellbeing services; and providing a diverse range of comprehensive, safe, high quality mental health services. The guiding principles are the full and effective participation in society by people with mental illness; the protection and promotion of human rights; supporting people with mental illness to make decisions for themselves; recognition and promotion of the value of families, carers and supporters; the promotion of recovery-based practices; and the provision of appropriate compulsory assessment and treatment only as a last resort (RC Report Vol. 4: 37).

The use of interpretative objectives and guiding principles is a relatively common feature of mental health laws in many jurisdictions (see *Mental Health Act 2001* (Ireland); *Mental Health (Care and Treatment) (Scotland) Act 2003* (Scotland)). However, the Victorian Royal Commission's Act as proposed and passed by the Victorian Parliament can be distinguished from these in two respects. The first is its robust focus on delivering the highest attainable standard of mental health and the inclusion of an explicit requirement that the Department of Health and mental health and wellbeing services make decisions in line with the Act's objectives (RC Report Vol. 4: 37). Secondly, the Act emphasises structures and systems. It provides the legislative basis for a set of new bodies and roles (a Mental Health and Wellbeing Commission; a Chief Officer for Mental Health and Wellbeing; and Regional Mental Health and

Wellbeing Boards) and an expanded role for complaint processes (RC Report Vol. 4: 39). As part of this, the Act provides for greater accountability and reporting arrangements for service providers, which in turn is linked back to the objectives and principles of the Act. The Act also provides for the establishment of multiagency panels to co-ordinate the range of services which people with mental illness may require (RC Report Vol. 4: 39). Finally, it introduces an array of concrete measures to ensure that compulsion actually is a measure of last resort. These include provision of (opt-out) non-legal advocacy for consumers placed, or at risk of being placed, on compulsory treatment orders; greater adoption of supported decision-making practices; simplified provisions on compulsion; and strong monitoring arrangements for restrictive practices.

Some elements of the Act reflect reforms or reform proposals in other jurisdictions. Efforts to reduce the use of compulsion are now relatively commonplace, as are attempts to introduce forms of supported decision-making into mental health law. The question of access also now features on many law reform agendas, whether through references to the highest attainable standard of health as an underlying principle for mental health legislation (Richardson Report 1999) or, as in the Indian *Mental Healthcare Act 2017*, by the introduction of a right to access mental health care (Duffy and Kelly 2019; Pathare and Kapoor 2022). However, the Victorian Royal Commission's proposals extend beyond this and seek to set out a new and more expansive telos for mental health law. In this, the Commission looks beyond the three goals Lady Hale identified (set out earlier) to incorporate the enhancement of mental health in all its forms into mental health law and to put in place the elements required to deliver on this.

Underpinning Evidence

As identified earlier, both the legitimacy and the success of law reform proposals depend on the quality of the evidence that informs them. The Victorian Royal Commission's proposals are underpinned by a substantial body of evidence and by an explicit intention to place the service user/consumer at the heart of the reform process (see also Wilson, Maker, Gooding and Walvisch in Chapter 1 of this volume). The Royal Commission links this to its systems approach (discussed later), drawing on expertise which indicates that this has been the key to the most successful health care reforms in recent times (RC Report Vol 1: 66). As described in the Interim Report, the Royal Commission conducted its inquiry through consultations, submissions, hearings, its own research and analysis and contributions by leading experts (Interim Report: 14).

The consultative process was extensive; there were 61 sessions in 21 locations attended by more than 1,650 people, with consultees invited to reflect on what was working well, not well, and how things might be improved (Interim Report: 14). There were 3,267 submissions, including 52 submissions in which the person making the submission was supported by the Commission (Interim Report: 18). There were also public hearings which were focussed on issues of particular concern (including stigma, prevention and early intervention; access to and navigation of the mental health system; families and carers; rural and regional; Aboriginal and Torres Strait Islander people; LGBTQI+ and culturally and linguistically diverse communities; community resilience; suicide prevention; prioritisation and governance of mental health services) and a series of targeted engagements (Interim Report: 18). The Victorian Royal Commission also engaged with a wide range of research, including research which it had specifically commissioned and specialist advisory panels (Interim Report: 22) as well as with the Expert Advisory Committee.

The range and quality of evidence employed by the Victorian Royal Commission is undoubtedly impressive, reflecting a deep and multi-faceted inquiry as well as indicating broad and inclusive consultation. Beyond this, a distinguishing feature of the Victorian Royal Commission Report, when compared with equivalent reports, is the space and weight which it accords to personal stories and case studies. Each chapter of the Report features multiple of these stories or case studies, some of them accompanied by photographs and many of them containing considerable detail. As the Report describes, 'these stories provide the individual's personal recollection of their interactions and experiences with Victoria's mental health system' (RC Report Vol. 1: xvii). Thus, while the Royal Commission chose the stories it included, the stories themselves are unmediated. It is clear from the Royal Commission's own observations that these stories had a powerful impact on its deliberations (RC Report Vol. 1: 3–4).

The inclusion of stories like these is a powerful device (Massaro 1989) which links the Victorian Royal Commission's work back to the real-world experiences of people impacted by mental health law. This adds a legitimacy and depth to the Royal Commission's proposals, engendering empathy in the reader and humanising the people for whom negotiation of the mental health system has been an unavoidable part of their lives. There are also instrumental benefits to the inclusion of unmediated personal narratives of this kind. The analysis by Mintrom, O'Neill and O'Connor (2021: 92) of some of the most successful Australian Royal Commissions identifies the role of narrative framing in making recommendations hard for politicians to ignore (2021: 92). Thus, across the most successful Royal Commissions, 'a lesson we draw is the importance of taking time to listen to people and empathise with the stories they tell and the views they express' (Mintrom, O'Neill and O'Connor 2021: 92). The effect is to bind people together in their commitment to change in ways that go beyond material interest and engage also with emotion (Mintrom, O'Neill and O'Connor 2021: 92).

A Systems Approach

Probably the most distinctive element of the Victorian Royal Commission's work is its adoption of a systems approach. This reflects the broader inquiry with which it was tasked, specifically to report on 'how Victoria's mental health system can most effectively prevent mental illness, and deliver treatment, care and support so that all those in the Victorian community can experience their best mental health, now and into the future' (Interim Report: 11). A systems approach to reform is grounded in the well-established view that society should be regarded as a social system, comprising a range of sub-systems. Derived initially from the biological sciences, this view was adopted in a social context by the American sociologist Talcott Parsons (1951) and developed by, amongst others, the German sociologist Niklas Luhmann (2012). While systems theory (and especially Luhmannian systems theory) can be highly abstract (King and Thornhill 2003), the Royal Commission's systems approach draws substantially on the more practically grounded work of the Australian health systems expert, Professor Jeffrey Braithwaite (for further discussion of Braithwaite's theories see Katterl and Friel in Chapter 14 of this volume). Quoting from Braithwaite and colleagues (2013: 57–58), the Commission outlines the core elements of how systems operate as follows:

> Complex systems are a group of visible and invisible interconnected parts that function together to achieve a goal. They are often characterised by:
>
> - interdependent relationships with other systems
> - deep, interdependent relationships between system parts, including parts that operate as a 'system within a system'
> - dynamic behaviour, including an ability to self-organise, adapt, learn and develop new features over time in response to change, the outcomes of which are often unpredictable.
>
> (RC Report Vol. 1: 55)

As the Victorian Royal Commission recognised, complex systems are unpredictable. Thus, '[c]hanges in one part of a complex system have the potential to create large changes in other parts of the system that can be seemingly unrelated in time, proximity or proportion to the initial change' (RC Report Vol. 1: 56). This means that some system changes can have unintended consequences (RC Report Vol. 1: 58). It also means that system change cannot simply be achieved by directing the system to produce an outcome; instead, change is achieved by 'shifting the underlying conditions that hold the most influence over how the system, and those people within the system, operate' (RC Report Vol. 1: 58). This then means that reform can require changes to parts of the system that 'appear distant, unrelated or even counterintuitive to achieving the desired outcome' (RC Report Vol. 1: 58). In light of this, the Royal Commission employed a four-stage systems change framework (Davidson and Morgan 2018) in developing its proposals. The first stage defines the purpose of the system and of the planned change; the second seeks to gain clarity and a better understanding of the problems and conditions that affect the system; the third stage finds leverage through identifying the parts within the system where interventions will have the greatest impact; the final stage involves acting strategically through taking steps to create and sustain positive change (RC Report Vol. 1: 62).

Although the Victorian Royal Commission's systems approach extended well beyond law reform, the systems change framework can be seen throughout the law reform proposals made. The need for a clear vision and purpose is expressed through the objectives and principles of the *Mental Health and Wellbeing Act 2022* which was proposed by the Royal Commission and subsequently enacted, and the various ways these are reinforced (RC Report Vol. 1: 75). In seeking to understand the system, the Royal Commission identified the complexity of mental health and its causes; the scale and diversity of system parts and how they interrelate; and the divergent perspectives on mental health among key stakeholders ('those who regulate, fund, govern, use, need, work in or benefit from') in the system (RC Report Vol. 1: 61). It also identified the different kinds of conditions of the system. These incorporate readily visible parts, such as government policies, organisational practices and the allocation of resources; observable parts, such as relationships and connections or power dynamics; and, hidden parts, such as underlying beliefs and values (RC Report Vol. 1: 77). Through this analysis, the Royal Commission identified 'systems levers' through which change could be effected. It describes a systems lever as a place 'where a seemingly small or discreet shift in one part of the system produces big changes across the system' (RC Report Vol. 1: 77).

A key systems lever identified by the Victorian Royal Commission was the statutory establishment of the Victorian Collaborative Centre for Mental Health and Wellbeing. This had been identified as a key action in the Interim Report (RC Report Vol. 1: 77), which noted that the model is already well established in respect of cancer and cardiac diseases (Interim Report: 394). The aim of the Collaborative Centre is 'to provide adult clinical and non-clinical services, emphasise the participation and inclusion of people with lived experience, and conduct interdisciplinary research' (Interim Report: 392). The idea of bringing together service delivery (within the local community) and interdisciplinary research is that this 'enables people with lived experience to participate in the design, development and production of research programmes and reinforces the translation of research and evidence into high quality care' (Interim Report: 392).

The establishment of the Collaborative Centre is also intended to play a strategic role in sustaining the law (and broader system) reform project into the future. Thus, as the Victorian Royal Commission describes, while the Collaborative Centre is just one institution, it 'holds a mandate to influence mental health treatment, care and support across Victoria, with a view to changing some of the "deeper" characteristics of the system' (RC Report Vol. 1: 77). In the first phase of implementation of the Royal Commission Report, the *Victorian Collaborative Centre for Mental Health and Wellbeing Act 2021* (Vic) received Royal Assent in November 2021 and the steps to establish the Collaborative Centre are underway at the time of writing. Crucially, the legislation requires that at least two members of the Board of the Centre are persons who have had experience of mental illness or psychological distress, at least two members are persons who have supported such persons and that one of the two directors of the Centre must be a person with experience of mental illness or psychological distress. McSherry (2023) argues that this statutory specification creates the potential 'for not only effective service delivery but also ground-breaking interdisciplinary research'.

Conclusion

It is difficult to envisage a time when law reform ceases to be part of the mental health landscape. For this reason, there is a need for a systemic understanding of law reform processes. This chapter has looked more closely at law reform and has argued that the quality of the processes employed is inherently linked both to the legitimacy of the law reforms proposed and to their chances of success. The innovative law reforms proposed by the Victorian Royal Commission reflect the process used in their development, and the emphasis placed on the involvement at every level of the service users/consumers that the system is established to serve. It will be instructive (and important) to see how effectively the Royal Commission's proposals work in practice. At the time of writing, implementation of some of the Royal Commission's proposals is underway in Victoria. In addition to the establishment of the Collaborative Centre (discussed earlier), a crucial element of implementation has been the introduction of the ring-fenced mental health levy recommended by the Royal Commission. The Mental Health and Wellbeing levy came into effect on 1 January 2022 and is paid as a payroll tax surcharge by employers with national payrolls of more than $10 million per annum. All revenues raised by the levy must be spent on the Victorian mental health system where they are to supplement the funding commitments of the Victorian Government. The availability of a steady and reliable income stream should allow for future planning and for the delivery of other Royal Commission recommendations. The *Mental Health and Wellbeing Act 2022*, which was described by the Deputy Premier at its second reading as 'unapologetically aspirational' (Victoria 2022: 2661), was passed by the Victorian Parliament in August 2022 and received royal assent on 5 September 2022, with the intention that it will come into force on 1 September 2023.

However, there is still a good deal of political work to be done. A significant pillar of the Victorian Royal Commission's recommendations is a structured move towards the abolition of restrictive practices. This is not delivered in the *Mental Health and Wellbeing Act 2022*. Instead, an Independent Review is to be carried out to provide formal advice to the Victorian Government on the law regarding compulsory treatment and restrictive interventions and on the relationship between the *Mental Health and Wellbeing Act 2022* and other Victorian health care legislation, including the *Guardianship and Administration Act 2019* and the *Medical Treatment Planning and Decisions Act 2016*. It is anticipated that the outcome of this review will require legislative reform of the *Mental Health and Wellbeing Act 2022* (Parliamentary Debates 2022: 2665), although how (and whether) this is approached will depend on the work of the Committee overseeing the review and the political climate at that time.

The work of the Victorian Royal Commission offers lessons for law reform processes in other jurisdictions. If we compare the Victorian Royal Commission with the more traditional processes reviewed in the first part of the chapter, the most far-reaching lesson is the enormous potential of a system-wide review in which law reform is only one component, informed by the methodologies of the system change framework used by the Victorian Royal Commission. Clearly, this kind of review requires extensive and highly sophisticated engagement as well as considerable resources and realistically is likely to be a once-in-a-generation endeavour. Nonetheless, if the Victorian experiment can be shown to work, it will provide a valuable template for law- and policy-makers in other jurisdictions. There are also other, possibly more easily realisable, lessons from the Victorian Royal Commission's work which can be integrated into more traditional law reform processes, including those discussed above. First, the Victorian Royal Commission shows that deep involvement of service users/consumers at every stage of the process is essential and that this needs to become established practice in all reform processes. While more recent law reform processes, such as the Wessely Review in England and Wales, have been far better at drawing on the expertise of service users/consumers, the Victorian Royal Commission Report shows both normative and instrumental benefits in integrating unmediated service user/consumer voices into the final report. Secondly, there are lessons to be learnt from the strategic elements of the Victorian Royal Commission's approach. The accurate identification of system levers will undoubtedly be more challenging where the reform analysis is primarily focussed on the legal system. Nonetheless, a law reform methodology which recognises the importance of finding levers and thinking strategically is still likely to have more chance of effecting meaningful change than one which does not take account of strategic elements. Finally, and possibly most significantly, the Victorian Royal Commission shows ways to think about law reform which expand and reinterpret the telos of mental health law and the kind of legal interventions which might be considered in the mental health sphere. For these reasons, the Victorian Royal Commission (and Professor Bernadette McSherry) have done the broader world of mental health law reform some considerable service.

References

Cases

Croke v Ireland [2000] ECHR 680.
HL v United Kingdom [2004] ECHR 471.
P v Cheshire West & Chester Council and Anor [2014] UKSC 19.

Legislation

Mental Health and Wellbeing Act 2022 (Vic).
Mental Health Bill 2022 (EW). Available www.gov.uk/government/publications/draft-mental-health-bill-2022 (accessed 11 November 2022).

Books, Journal Articles and Other Texts

Barlow, P. (2013) *The Lost World of Royal Commissions*, London: Institute for Government. Available www.instituteforgovernment.org.uk/blog/lost-world-royal-commissions (accessed 11 November 2022).

Bartlett, P. (2014) 'Reforming the Deprivation of Liberty Safeguards (DoLS): What is it Exactly That we Want?' *European Journal of Current Legal Issues*, 20(3). Available http://eprints.nottingham.ac.uk/27970/1/465 (accessed 11 November 2022).

Braithwaite, J., Clay-Williams, R., Negus, P. and Plumb, J. (2013) 'Health Care as a Complex Adaptive System', in E. Hollnagel, J. Braithwaite and R. Wears (eds) *Resilient Health Care, Ashgate Studies in Resilience Engineering*, Surrey: Taylor and Francis, 57–73.

Committee on the Rights of Persons with Disabilities (2014) *General Comment No. 1 Article 12 – Equal Recognition Before the Law*, 11th sess, UN Doc CRPD/C/GC/1. Available www.ohchr.org/en/documents/general-comments-and-recommendations/general-comment-no-1-article-12-equal-recognition-1 (accessed 11 November 2022).

Committee on the Rights of Persons with Disabilities (2015) *Guidelines on Article 14 of the Convention on the Rights of Persons with Disabilities*, 14th sess. Available www.ohchr.org/Documents/HRBodies/CRPD/14thsession/GuidelinesOnArticle14.doc (accessed 11 November 2022).

Committee on the Rights of Persons with Disabilities (2022) *Concluding Observations*. Available https://tbinternet.ohchr.org/_layouts/15/treatybodyexternal/TBSearch.aspx?Lang=en&TreatyID=4&DocTypeID=5 (accessed 11 November 2022).

Davidson, S. and Morgan, M. (2018) *Systems Change Framework*, Hobart: Tasmanian Department of Health.

de Búrca, G. (2021) *Reframing Human Rights in a Turbulent* Era, Oxford: Oxford University Press.

Department of Health (1999) *Reform of the Mental Health Act 1983: Proposals for Consultation*, London: HMSO. Available https://assets.publishing.service.gov.uk/government/uploads/system/uploads/attachment_data/file/265574/4480.pdf (accessed 11 November 2022).

Department of Health and Social Care (2017) *Terms of Reference: Independent Review of the Mental Health Act 1983*. Available www.gov.uk/government/publications/mental-health-act-independent-review/terms-of-reference-independent-review-of-the-mental-health-act-1983 (accessed 11 November 2022).

Donnelly, M. (2022) 'Support Relationships in Law: Framing, Fictions and the Responsive State', in M. Donnelly, R. Harding and E. Taşcıoğlu (eds) *Supporting Legal Capacity in Socio-Legal Context*, Oxford: Hart Publishing, 19–38.

Duffy, R. and Kelly, B. (2019) 'The Right to Mental Healthcare: India Moves Forward', *British Journal of Psychiatry*, 214(2): 59–60.

Encalada, A.V. (2021) 'The Potential of the Legal Capacity Law Reform in Peru to Transform Mental Health Provision', in M.A. Stein, F. Mahomed, V. Patel

and C. Sunkel (eds) *Mental Health, Legal Capacity, and Human Rights*, Cambridge: Cambridge University Press, 124–39.
Fanning, J. (2020) *New Medicalism and the Mental Health* Act, Oxford: Hart Publishing.
Fennell, P. (1996) *Treatment Without Consent: Law, Psychiatry and the Treatment of Mentally Disordered People Since 1845*, London: Routledge.
Freeman, M.C., Kolappa, K., de Almeida, J.M., Kleinman, A., Makhashvili, N., Phakathi, S., Saraceno, B. and Thornicroft, G. (2015) 'Reversing Hard Won Victories in the Name of Human Rights: A Critique of the General Comment on Article 12 of the UN Convention on the Rights of Persons with Disabilities', *Lancet Psychiatry*, 2(9): 844–50.
Gooding, P. (2017) *A New Era for Mental Health Law and Policy: Supported Decision-Making and the UN Convention on the Rights of Persons with Disabilities*, Cambridge: Cambridge University Press.
Gostin, L. (1975) *A Human Condition: The Mental Health Act from 1959 to 1975: Observations, Analysis and Proposal for Reform*, London: MIND.
Hale, B. (2007) 'Justice and Equality in Mental Health Law: The European Experience', *International Journal of Law and Psychiatry*, 30(1): 18–28.
Hamilton, J. (1983) 'Mental Health Act 1983', *British Medical Journal*, 286(6379): 1720–25.
Harding, R. (2021) 'Safeguarding Freedom? Liberty Protection Safeguards, Liberty and the Rule of Law', *Current Legal Problems*, 74(1): 329–59.
Harpur, P. and Stein, M. (2022) 'The CRPD as a Global Tipping Point for the Participation of Persons with Disabilities', in W.R. Thompson (ed) *Oxford Research Encyclopedia of Politics*, Oxford: Oxford University Press. Available https://oxfordre.com/politics (accessed 11 November 2022).
Hathaway, O.A. (2002) 'Do Human Rights Treaties Make a Difference?' *Yale Law Journal*, 11(8): 1935–2042.
Hilton, C. (2007) 'Changes Between the 1959 and 1983 Mental Health Acts (England and Wales), with Particular Reference to Consent to Treatment for Electroconvulsive Therapy', *History of Psychiatry*, 18(2): 217–29.
Jones, K. (1972) *A History of the Mental Health Services*, London: Routledge and Keegan Paul.
King, M. and Thornhill, C. (2003) *Niklas Luhmann's Theory of Politics and Law*, London: Palgrave Macmillan.
Laing, J. (2022) 'Reforming the Mental Health Act 1983: Will More Rights Lead to Fewer Wrongs?' *Medical Law Review*, 30(1): 158–76.
Law Commission (UK) (2017) *Mental Capacity and Deprivation of Liberty – Report.* Available www.lawcom.gov.uk/project/mental-capacity-and-deprivation-of-liberty/ (accessed 11 November 2022).
Luhmann, L. (2012) *Introduction to Systems Theory* (P. Gilben, trans.), Cambridge: Polity Press.
Massaro, T.M. (1989) 'Empathy, Legal Story-Telling and the Rule of Law: New Words, Old Wounds', *Michigan Law Review*, 87(8): 2099–127.
McSherry, B. (2017) 'Regulating Seclusion and Restraint in Health Care Settings: The Promise of the Convention on the Rights of Persons with Disabilities', *International Journal of Law and Psychiatry*, 53: 39–44.
McSherry, B. (2023) 'Interdisciplinary Collaboration in the Mental Health Sector: The Role of Law', in B. Kelly and M. Donnelly (eds) *Routledge Handbook on Mental Health Law*, London: Routledge.

McSherry, B. and Freckelton, I. (eds) (2013) *Coercive Care: Rights, Law and Policy*, New York: Routledge.

McSherry, B. and Maker, Y. (eds) (2021) *Restrictive Practices in Health Care and Disability Settings: Legal, Policy and Practical Responses*, Abingdon: Routledge.

McSherry, B. and Weller, P. (eds) (2010) *Rethinking Rights-Based Mental Health Laws*, Oxford: Hart.

McSherry, B. and Wilson, K. (2015) 'The Concept of Capacity in Australian Mental Health Law: Going in the Wrong Direction?' *International Journal of Law and Psychiatry*, 40: 60–69.

Mintrom, M., O'Neill, D. and O'Connor, R. (2021) 'Royal Commissions and Policy Influence', *Australian Journal of Public Administration*, 80(1): 80–96.

Parsons, T. (1951) *The Social System*, London: Routledge and Keegan Paul.

Pathare, S. and Kapoor, A. (2022) 'Enabling Supported Decision-Making in India's Mental Healthcare Act, 2017: Learnings from a Low Resource Country Setting', in M. Donnelly, R. Harding and E. Taşcıoğlu (eds) *Supporting Legal Capacity in Socio-Legal Context*, Oxford: Hart Publishing, 135–56.

Peay, J. (2000) 'Reform of the Mental Health Act 1983: Squandering an Opportunity?' *Journal of Mental Health Law*, 3: 5–15.

Rapaport, J. and Manthorpe, J. (2009) 'Fifty Years On: The Legacy of the Percy Report', *Journal of Social Work*, 9(3): 251–67.

Report of the Expert Committee: Review of the Mental Health Act 1983 (1999) London: HMSO.

Report of the Expert Group on the Review of the Mental Health Act 2001 (2015) Dublin: Department of Health. Available https://assets.gov.ie/15986/af32aee7c6ce4747aef4962b11d716d8.pdf (accessed 11 November 2022).

Report of the Royal Commission on the Law Relating to Mental Illness and Mental Deficiency (1957) London: HMSO.

Rothman, D. (1991) *Strangers at the Bedside: A History of How Law and Bioethics Transformed Medical Decision Making*, New York: Basic Books.

Royal Commission into Victoria's Mental Health System Interim Report (2019) Available http://rcvmhs.archive.royalcommission.vic.gov.au/interim-report.html (accessed 11 November 2022).

Royal Commission into Victoria's Mental Health System Final Report (2021) Available https://finalreport.rcvmhs.vic.gov.au/ (accessed 11 November 2022).

Royal Commission into Victoria's Mental Health System Summary and Recommendations (Executive Summary) (2021) Available https://finalreport.rcvmhs.vic.gov.au/wp-content/uploads/2021/02/RCVMHS_FinalReport_ExecSummary_Accessible.pdf (accessed 11 November 2022).

Series, L. (2022) *Deprivation of Liberty in the Shadows of the Institution*, Bristol: Bristol University Press.

Shapland, J. and Williams, T. (1983) 'Legalism Revived: New Mental Health Legislation in England', *International Journal of Law and Psychiatry*, 6(3): 351–69.

Szmukler, G. and Gostin, L. (2021) 'Mental Health Law: "Legalism" and "Medicalism" – "Old" and "New"', in G. Ikkos and N. Bouras (eds) *Mind, State and Society: Social History of Psychiatry and Mental Health in Britain 1960–2010*, Cambridge: Cambridge University Press, 69–83.

Taşcıoğlu, E. (2022) 'Performing Disability Rights: State Reporting and Turkey's (Non) Engagement with the CRPD', in M. Donnelly, R. Harding and E. Taşcıoğlu (eds) *Supporting Legal Capacity in Socio-Legal Context*, Oxford: Hart Publishing, 195–212.

Unsworth, C. (1987) *The Politics of Mental Health Legislation*, Oxford: Clarendon.

Unsworth, C. (1991) 'Mental Disorder and the Tutelary Relationship: From Pre- to Post-Carceral Legal Order', *Journal of Law and Society*, 18(2): 254–78.

Victoria (2022) *Victorian Parliamentary Debates*, Legislative Assembly, 23 June (James Merlino, Deputy Premier, Second Reading Speech of Mental Health and Wellbeing Bill), 2660–66.

Wessely, S. (2018) *Modernising the Mental Health Act: Increasing Choice, Reducing Compulsion: Final Report of the Independent Review of the Mental Health Act 1983*, London: Crown Copyright.

Wilson, D. (2014) *The Making of British Bioethics*, Manchester: Manchester University Press.

Wilson, K. (2021) *Mental Health Law: Abolish or Reform?* Oxford: Oxford University Press.

Wilson, K. (2022) 'The CRPD and Mental Health Law: The Conflict about Abolition, the Practical Dilemmas of Implementation and the Untapped Potential', in F. Felder, L. Davy and R. Kayess (eds) *Disability Law and Human Rights*, Cham: Palgrave Macmillan, 171–98.

World Health Organization (2021) *Mental Health Atlas 2020*. Available www.who.int/publications/i/item/9789240036703 (accessed 11 November 2022).

3 The Human Right to Health and the *Mental Health and Wellbeing Act 2022* (Vic)

Penelope Weller

Introduction

The Royal Commission into Victoria's Mental Health System (Victorian Royal Commission) laid out an ambitious plan for the transformation of Victoria's mental health system. The Victorian Royal Commission's interim and final reports underpin the urgency of this task by describing a dysfunctional and broken system. The Victorian Royal Commission's (2021) five-volume Final Report outlines 65 very detailed and wide-ranging recommendations. As one of the four commissioners, Bernadette McSherry's appointment reflects the esteem in which her research into mental health law and practice is held, and reflects the considerable impact of her academic work. While it is difficult to summarise the breadth of the recommendations in a few lines, it is sufficient to say the Victorian Royal Commission envisaged fundamental systemic and cultural reform. Accepting the recommendations, the Victorian Government allocated AUD$3.8 billion dollars to mental health system reform in the 2021–22 State Budget. The Victorian Collaborative Centre for Mental Health and Wellbeing (Royal Commission into Victoria's Mental Health System 2021: recommendation 63) is being established at the time of writing, and the *Mental Health and Wellbeing Act 2022* (Vic) (Royal Commission into Victoria's Mental Health System 2021: recommendation 42) was recently passed by the Parliament of Victoria. The legislation will establish key elements of new system architecture, including new regional Mental Health and Wellbeing Boards (Royal Commission into Victoria's Mental Health System 2021: recommendation 4(2)), the Mental Health and Wellbeing Commission (Royal Commission into Victoria's Mental Health System 2021: recommendation 44), the Chief Officer for Mental Health and Wellbeing (Royal Commission into Victoria's Mental Health System 2021: recommendation 45(1)) and an 'opt out' model for independent mental health advocacy (Royal Commission into Victoria's Mental Health System 2021: recommendation 56).

With respect to the need for new legislation, the Victorian Royal Commission detailed the failure of the previous Act, the *Mental Health Act 2014* (Vic), to protect the rights of people with mental illness and psychological distress

DOI: 10.4324/9781003350644-4

in Victoria despite its rights-based stance and innovative features. Calling for a fresh approach, the Victorian Royal Commission outlined the need for new principles-driven legislation that would establish the necessary infrastructure, including new statutory bodies noted previously (see also the discussion by Donnelly in Chapter 2 of this volume). The new structures are to be animated by a commitment to meaningful leadership by those with lived experience of mental illness and psychological distress, including in the design, implementation and evaluation of mental health services (Royal Commission into Victoria's Mental Health System 2021: recommendation 28). On the question of compulsory treatment, the Victorian Royal Commission recommended that the statutory provisions permitting compulsion be retained, but simplified and clarified such that they are no longer the defining feature of Victoria's mental health laws (Royal Commission into Victoria's Mental Health System 2021: recommendation 42(2)(f)). It was recommended the legislation would also contain 'measures to reduce rates and negative impacts of compulsory assessment and treatment, [and] seclusion and restraint' (Royal Commission into Victoria's Mental Health System 2021: recommendation 42(2)(e)). The Victorian Royal Commission set a clear goal for the elimination of seclusion and restraint practices in Victoria within ten years (Royal Commission into Victoria's Mental Health System 2021: recommendation 54(1)).

The overarching recommendation to repeal the *Mental Health Act 2014* (Vic) and enact a new Mental Health and Wellbeing Act included the recommendation that the replacement Act contain 'new objectives and mental health principles, with its primary objective to achieve the ***highest attainable standard of mental health and wellbeing for the people of Victoria***' (Royal Commission into Victoria's Mental Health System 2021: recommendation 42(2)(a) [emphasis added]). It would do this by:

- promoting conditions in which people can experience good mental health and wellbeing;
- reducing inequities in access to, and the delivery of, mental health and wellbeing services; and
- providing a diverse range of comprehensive, safe and high-quality mental health services.

(Royal Commission into Victoria's Mental Health System 2021: recommendation 42(2)(a))

With these words, the Victorian Royal Commission stated its commitment to improving the health and wellbeing of people with mental illness and psychosocial distress.

The first point to make about this stance is that it adopts an outcomes approach (see Royal Commission into Victoria's Mental Health System 2021: recommendations 1 and 2). The second is to observe that the Victorian Royal Commission recommends that the legislation is framed with a fundamental human right in mind: the right to the highest attainable standard of health and mental health (hereafter, the right to health). Australia is a party to all the relevant conventions supporting the right to health. While such conventions are not binding in domestic Australian law without specific legislative incorporation (*Kioa v West* 1985), there is a general expectation that Australia will comply with its international human rights obligations. In Victoria, human rights are explicitly incorporated into state law through the operation of the *Charter of Human Rights and Responsibilities Act 2006* (Vic) (Charter). The Charter requires the state's public authorities to act in accordance with human rights by making it 'unlawful for a public authority to act in a way that is incompatible with a human right or, in making a decision, to fail to give proper consideration to a relevant human right' (Charter: section 38(1)). While there are recognised limitations to the scope of Charter, the Victorian Supreme Court in *PBU & NJE v Mental Health Tribunal* 2018 has emphasised the utility of the Charter and international human rights conventions, notably the United Nations *Convention on the Rights of Persons with Disabilities* (CRPD), in the interpretation of state law, including Victoria's mental health law.

The aim of this chapter is to consider whether the new *Mental Health and Wellbeing Act 2022* (Vic) (MHWB Act 2022) fully enacts the Victorian Royal Commission's recommendation to make the right to health its primary objective. The first part of this chapter examines the content of the right to health in international human rights law. This part demonstrates the centrality of the right to informed consent with respect to health and mental health care in international human rights law, as a mechanism that gives substance to the principles of dignity, autonomy and respect for self-determination. The second part of the chapter examines the contribution of the CRPD to the development of the right to health. This part illustrates the significance of both understanding human rights as universal, interdependent and interrelated, as well as giving credence to the lived experience of those who receive mental health care and treatment. The analysis in parts one and two shows that the right to informed consent is central to realising the right to health. The third part examines the provisions of the MHWB Act 2022 and considers whether its text supports the right to informed consent. The chapter argues that despite the inclusion of statutory principles attending to the circumstances of vulnerable people in the mental health system, the new MHWB Act 2022 fails to provide effective protection for the right to informed consent to mental health treatment and care – and on that basis fails to uphold the right to health. Notably, the MHWB Act 2022 will not come into effect until September 2023. At the time of writing the Victorian Government has convened an 'independent review panel', led by Justice Shane Marshall AM, which is going to examine provisions in the Act on compulsory treatment, restrictive practices, advance directives and personal medical decision-making as the legislative drafters wanted more time to consider these complex provisions (Victoria 2022). Noting that further legislative amendments are likely to result from this review, this chapter considers the MHWB Act 2022 as at 30 September 2022.

The Evolution of the Right to Health

The right to health is an embedded human right in international human rights law. Health is a variable human attribute dependent upon individual, social, political and material conditions (Toebes 1999; Eyles and Woodsm 2014; Prah-Ruger 2010). The right to health is therefore not a right to 'be healthy', but a right to access the social, economic, legal, environmental and personal conditions that enable human health without discrimination (see General Comment No. 14 of the Committee on Economic, Social and Cultural Rights (CESCR) 2000).

The original articulation of the right to health in the *Universal Declaration of Human Rights* (UDHR) contained a firm emphasis on equity and the broader social determinants of mental health and wellbeing (Meier 2010). The translation of Article 25 UDHR into the binding provisions of the *International Covenant on Economic, Social and Cultural Rights* (ICESCR) saw the distribution of elements of Article 25 across several of ICESCR's articles. Article 12 of the ICESCR contains obligations that relate directly to health care and the prevention of ill-health. Specifically, these obligations concern infant mortality, industrial hygiene, disease prevention and health service provision. With these foci, Article 12 has provided a robust framework for international development with respect to the right to health, albeit in light of the limitations afforded by the principle of progressive realisation. The principle of progressive realisation enables States Parties to the ICESCR to take steps toward fulfilment of the rights 'to the maximum of its available resources' (Article 2(1)). Realisation of the right to health, however, is subject to the overarching principles of equality and non-discrimination, meaning that a State Party to the ICESCR must ensure that the provision of health care and related services does not discriminate against marginalised groups, such as women, those of racial or other minority groups, or those with disabilities (CESCR 2000: para 30; MacNaughton 2009).

A major step in the articulation of the right to health was the CESCR (2000) General Comment No. 14 on the right to the highest attainable standard of health and mental health. General Comment No. 14 remains the foundational statement of the contemporary content of the right to health in international human rights law (Gable and Gostin 2009). It reinforces States Parties' obligations to provide the material conditions necessary to support human health and wellbeing by setting out the minimum economic and social standards required by the right, broadly understood. General Comment No. 14 recognises the full range of socio-economic factors influencing health and mental health, including new threats such as emerging diseases, inequality in resource distribution and gender difference. The core content of the right encompasses freedom to control one's own health and body and the parallel obligation of States to provide health care and public health facilities and services that are available, accessible, acceptable and of good quality. 'Availability' refers to facilities, goods and services, including health systems, hospitals, clinics, trained medical professionals and medicines, and to the underlying determinants of health such as safe and potable drinking water and adequate sanitation (CSECR 2000: para.12(a)). 'Accessibility' includes the overlapping dimensions of access without discrimination and physical and economic access, including affordable and accessible health-related information (CSECR 2000: para.12(b)). 'Acceptability' refers to respect for medical ethics and cultural sensitivities (CSECR 2000: para.12(c)). 'Quality' refers to the availability of scientifically and medically appropriate treatment, skilled medical personnel, scientifically approved and unexpired drugs, appropriate hospital equipment, safe and potable water and adequate sanitation (CSECR 2000: para.12(d)). The right to health also imposes obligations on States Parties to provide health care services that are physically, geographically and economically accessible; ethical; personally acceptable; scientifically, medically and culturally appropriate; and that attend to the needs of the most vulnerable (Toebes 1999).

General Comment No. 14 also recognises that the right to health is closely related to the realisation of other human rights such as the right to dignity, life, non-discrimination, equality, the prohibition against torture, privacy, access to information and the freedoms of association, assembly and movement. Although the elements of the right to physical heath are widely recognised, the right to mental health is less well developed (Stavert and McGregor 2018). How respect for human rights is to be given substance in the context of mental health care and treatment and in mental health law has generated heated debate about the human rights obligations arising from the CRPD. Much of that debate centres on the question of informed consent and the legitimacy of compulsory mental health treatment and remains unresolved (Wilson 2020). Indeed, the CRPD continues to pose significant challenges to the traditional assumptions that have shaped the development of rights-based mental health laws in developed western nations (see McSherry and Weller 2010).

Mental Health, Human Rights and the CRPD

While it has long been recognised that the right to health and mental health applies to those with disabilities, the substance of the right has not been understood or observed in practice. The CRPD is the first binding international agreement addressing the human rights of those with disabilities (Quinn and Degener 2002). The CRPD has generated a profound shift in human rights thinking by challenging some key assumptions that have hitherto shaped the law. That task was made possible by the participation of people with disabilities and their representative organisations in the treaty drafting process. Key features of the CRPD are its insistence on the equal enjoyment of human rights for those with disabilities and the adoption of a social model of disability that recognises disability as arising from the intersection of impairment and barriers to social participation (Weller 2018). Thus, the CRPD has an explicit social development dimension. The broad categorisation of persons with disabilities reaffirms that all people with disabilities must enjoy all human rights and fundamental freedoms on an equal basis with others, while the details in the CRPD's articles provide guidance about the necessary adaptations that will enable people with disabilities to effectively exercise those rights.

As noted earlier, the right to health encompasses the full suite of social, political and legal determinants of health. In this sense, all provisions of the CRPD have relevance for the right to health. The specific affirmation of the right to enjoy the highest attainable standard of health and mental health, however, appears in Article 25 of the CRPD. Article 25(a) requires States Parties to ensure that people with disabilities have access to health services that are gender sensitive and are of the same range and quality as are available to others, including sexual and reproductive health and public health programmes. People with disabilities are also entitled to services that are needed because of their disabilities (Article 25(b)). These must be provided close to their communities (Article 25(c)), be of good quality and include early intervention and prevention services appropriate for different populations such as the young and the aged. Health and mental health services must be provided in ways that are consistent with human rights, including based on free and informed consent (Article 25(d)). (I will return to informed consent shortly.) Services, including health insurance, must be provided without discrimination on the basis of disability (Article 25(e)). People with disabilities must not be denied health care, health services or food and fluids based on disability (Article 25(f)).

Article 25 must be read in the context of other articles in the CRPD. These include Article 10 on the right to life, Article 12 on equality before the law, Article 14 on the right to liberty, Article 15 on the right to be free from degrading treatment and punishment and Article 16 on the right to be protected from all forms of violence, exploitation and abuse. As obligations derived from these articles may arise in the course of even routine provision of health and mental health care, they must be kept in mind in any analysis of whether health and mental health care and treatment accords with human rights. The starting point of the CRPD, however, is the proposition that people with disabilities, including those with mental health and psychosocial disabilities, are entitled to engage with health and mental health care on an equal basis with others, including based on free and informed consent (Article 25(d)).

The principle of informed consent is central to the right to health and mental health because it reflects the principles of autonomy, dignity and self-determination. Article 3 of the CRPD enshrines the principles of inherent dignity, individual autonomy and the right to make one's own choice. Free and informed consent, which is a voluntary decision to accept health care treatment or some other intervention following the provision of appropriate information, is widely accepted as a guiding principle in health care (Beauchamp and Childress 2001). More recently it has been explicitly recognised as a central concept in human rights law and jurisprudence (Pritchard-Jones 2019). It is lauded as the principal mechanism for ensuring respect and protection of a patient's autonomy, self-determination and physical and mental integrity in the context of health and mental health care (Faden and Beauchamp 1986:

7). Respecting informed consent in its fullest sense is therefore a critical component of a human rights response. In Victoria, the obligation to respect the right to free and informed consent to medical treatment is protected under section 10(c) of the Charter, for a 'person must not be . . . (c) subjected to medical or scientific experimentation or treatment without his or her full, free and informed consent,' although there are many exceptions to the principle in law and practice.

In established law, the principle of informed consent rests on the question of mental capacity. Mental capacity is the requirement that the person is able to understand, retain, use and weigh information relevant to a particular question to arrive at and communicate a decision (Donnelly 2010: 139). Mental capacity assessments are supposed to provide a 'bright line' that determines who can or cannot give informed consent (Gooding 2015). Article 12 of the CRPD challenges the operation of mental capacity determinations by requiring that people with disabilities are provided with the support they need to make decisions, that decision-making support is underpinned with appropriate safeguards and that the outcome of the decision-making process accords with the rights, will and preferences of the person (Flynn and Arstein-Kerslake 2014). As noted earlier, there remains an unresolved debate about how legal capacity principles in Article 12 of the CRPD should be operationalised in practice. Nevertheless, Bernadette McSherry's (2012) seminal piece on the distinction between legal and mental capacity has fundamentally shaped the understanding of Article 12 of the CRPD. Her subsequent work on support for decision-making in mental health contexts (McSherry and Butler 2015) and for those who are deemed 'unfit to plead' in the criminal justice system (Arstein-Kerslake et al. 2017; see McSherry et al. 2017) provides compelling examples of how support for decision-making supports human rights outcomes (see also Preface and Wilson, Maker, Gooding and Walvisch in Chapter 1 of this volume).

The debate about mental capacity, informed consent and support for decision-making is especially challenging in the context of mental health care and treatment. In most jurisdictions, while mental health treatment and care is provided on a voluntary basis, it can also be provided compulsorily under mental health legislation. Mental health laws typically set out the circumstances in which a person may be detained and treated without their consent. The usual grounds are that the person is at risk of harming themselves or others and there is deemed to be 'no less restrictive alternative'. While such laws often work well in acute circumstances, mental health laws raise at least five human rights considerations whenever mental health treatment is contemplated. First, when considering if a person will be able to provide consent to proposed treatment it is important that the legal standard of mental capacity and consent is not pitched too high. If that is the case, the danger is that a person may be denied the right to make their own decision with respect to voluntary mental health treatment. As Justice Bell confirmed in the Victorian Supreme Court decision of *PBU & NJE v Mental Health Tribunal*, the mental capacity standard is necessarily a low one lest it be used as a discriminatory standard:

> It is not required that [persons] make, or are able to make, a rational and balanced decision in relation to the decision. It is enough that the person, like most people, is able to make and communicate a decision in broad terms as to the general nature, purpose and effect of the treatment. Personal autonomy and the dignity of the individual are at stake. A person does not lack the capacity to give informed consent simply by making a decision that others consider to be unwise according to their individual values and situation. To impose upon persons having mental illness a higher threshold of capacity, and to afford them less respect for personal autonomy and individual dignity, than people not having that illness, would be discriminatory.
>
> (*PBU & NJE v Mental Health Tribunal*: para 280)

Moreover, depending on the scope of the law, a legal lacuna may arise if it is determined that the person lacks mental capacity and needs mental health treatment but does not meet requisite risk criteria. The human rights risk is that the person does not receive care.

A second human rights problem arises if the fact that compulsory mental health treatment powers can be invoked is used to 'encourage' a reluctant person to accept voluntary treatment. Research into the experience of compulsion suggests that coercion of this kind is a very common experience in mental health settings (Newton and Mullen 2011). In law, coercion of this kind vitiates consent, thus rendering the provision of mental health treatment unlawful.

A third problem arises if compulsory mental health treatment powers are invoked or applied incorrectly. This can occur if the scope of the risk criteria is misunderstood. Wrongful or unlawful detention and/or treatment may offend the right to respect for liberty and security of the person (CRPD: Article 14).

A fourth human rights danger lies in the possibility that the provision of treatment under mental health legislation is enforced by the use of restrictive practices. While the use of seclusion and restraint is often regulated under mental health laws, there is widespread concern that seclusion, physical restraint and chemical restraint are used inappropriately and too frequently and are often harmful (see Chesterman in Chapter 5 and Freckelton in Chapter 6 of this volume). Improper use of such powers is likely to contravene the United Nations *Convention against Torture and Other Cruel, Inhuman or Degrading Treatment or Punishment* (CAT) (Weller 2019; cf Wilson 2020). The use of routine or inappropriate seclusion and restraint in mental health and other settings has significant consequences for the health and wellbeing of those who are restrained, including the possibility of injury and in extreme cases death (see Chieze et al. 2019). Inappropriate use of seclusion and restraint is incompatible with the right to health and mental health, and in some cases with the right to life. McSherry's scholarship on the use of seclusion and restraint has succeeded in bringing significant attention to the problems associated with such practices in both mental health and aged care (Kumble and McSherry 2010; McSherry 2013, 2017; Brophy et al. 2016; see also Melbourne Social Equity Institute 2014; McSherry and Maker 2021). Significantly, the Victorian Royal Commission recommended the elimination of seclusion and restraint within ten years.

A fifth risk arises if the compulsory treatment criteria are not constantly reassessed or are interpreted differently at different stages of care, resulting in the possibility that the person's ongoing detention and treatment is unlawful and contrary to the right to respect for liberty and security of the person (CRPD: Article 14) (see Dawson and Matthews in Chapter 8 of this volume).

In summary, the human rights approach expressed in the CRPD provides a set of principles that ensure that those with disabilities enjoy human rights on an equal basis with others. Applied to the provision of mental health care, those principles provide a framework to ensure that people with disabilities are provided with appropriate, acceptable and high-quality care.

The *Mental Health and Wellbeing Act 2022*

How mental health legislation articulates compulsory treatment powers is therefore central to the realisation of human rights. As noted, the Victorian Royal Commission recommended new legal architecture for Victoria which included four key recommendations with respect to mental health law. These were: (1) the adoption of a principles-based approach to new mental health legislation; (2) the simplification, but not removal, of compulsory detention and treatment criteria; (3) the adoption of an 'opt out' model for independent mental health advocacy; and (4) measures to reduce the use of seclusion and restraint. The MHWB Act 2022, due to commence in September 2023, is intended to embody the Commission's recommendations. As noted previously, while the Victorian Royal Commission urged that the right to health and mental health be positioned as the primary objective of the legislation and sought to elevate the quality of mental health care, it did not make specific recommendations with respect to informed consent. Further, as noted earlier, provisions in relation to compulsory treatment, seclusion, restraint and advance directives are currently subject to an Independent Review which will recommend further reforms.

Objectives in the MHWB Act

The Victorian Royal Commission recommended that the primary objective of a new MHWB Act should be 'to achieve the highest attainable standard of mental health and wellbeing for the people of Victoria' (Royal Commission 2021: recommendation 42(2)(a)). That is to be achieved by promoting the conditions in which people can experience good mental health and wellbeing, reducing inequities in access to services and ensuring safe and high-quality services. The objectives of the MHWB Act 2022 are listed in its section 12:

Objectives

In pursuit of the highest attainable standard of mental health and wellbeing for the people of Victoria, this Act has the following objectives:

(a) to promote conditions in which people can –

 (i) experience good mental health and wellbeing; and
 (ii) recover from mental illness or psychological distress;

(b) to reduce inequities in access to, and the delivery of, mental health and wellbeing services;
(c) to provide for comprehensive, compassionate, safe and high-quality mental health and wellbeing services that promote the health and wellbeing of people living with mental illness or psychological distress and that –

 (i) are accessible; and
 (ii) respond in a timely way to people's needs and recognise that these needs may vary over time; and
 (iii) are consistent with a person's treatment, care, support and recovery preferences wherever possible; and
 (iv) are available early in life, early in onset and early in episode; and
 (v) recognise and respond to the diverse backgrounds and needs of the people who use them; and
 (vi) provide culturally safe and responsive services to Aboriginal and Torres Strait Islander people in order to support and strengthen connection to culture, family, community and Country; and
 (vii) connect and coordinate with other support services to respond to the broad range of circumstances that influence mental health and wellbeing; and
 (viii) include a broad range of treatment options with the aim of providing access to the same treatment and support irrespective of whether a person is receiving voluntary or compulsory treatment; and
 (ix) include a broad and accessible range of voluntary treatment and support options –

  (A) to enable a reduction in the use of compulsory assessment and treatment; and
  (B) to enable a reduction in the use of seclusion and restraint with the aim of eliminating its use within 10 years;

(d) to promote continuous improvement in the quality and safety of mental health and wellbeing services including by ensuring that the experiences of people living with mental illness or psychological distress, and the people receiving treatment, their carers, families and supporters, are at the centre of changes in practices and service delivery and the design and evaluation of systems;

(e) to protect and promote the human rights and dignity of people living with mental illness by providing them with assessment and treatment in the least restrictive way possible in the circumstances;

(f) to recognise and respect the right of people with mental illness or psychological distress to speak and be heard in their own voices, from their own experiences and from within their own communities and cultures;

(g) to recognise, promote and actively support the role of families, carers and supporters in the care, support and recovery of people living with mental illness or psychological distress;

(h) to promote and support the health and wellbeing of families, carers and supporters of people living with mental illness or psychological distress;

(i) to recognise and value the critical role of the clinical and non-clinical mental health and wellbeing workforce and to support and promote the health and wellbeing of members of that workforce;

(j) to promote the mental health and wellbeing principles.

This list appears to follow the Victorian Royal Commission's approach but does not place the statutory emphasis on respect for the right to mental health and wellbeing. Rather, the statutory emphasis is on the experience of good mental health, wellbeing and recovery.

Importantly, 'recovery' is not defined in the MHWB Act 2022, despite the term being used multiple times throughout. Unfortunately, the failure to provide a definition of recovery replicates one of the limitations of the *Mental Health Act 2014* (Vic). Recovery has at least two meanings. On the one hand, clinical recovery refers to the medical model concept of 'recovery' or cure from a disease and illness, indicated by the absence of signs and symptoms. On the other, the consumer movement tends to refer to recovery as a holistic concept embracing one's personal journey and the idea of living well (Anthony 1993). The consumer notions of recovery tend to challenge pharmacological approaches that emphasise the elimination of symptoms and subordinate or ignore the wellbeing of the person. 'Recovery oriented practice' adopts the broader sense of recovery to refer to an approach to care that recognises the importance of lived experience, hope and empathy. Research into recovery-oriented practice provides an evidence base for the utility of this approach (Meadows et al. 2019). The failure to define recovery in the new legislation underscores the narrow focus of its objectives. Avoiding a definition of recovery misses the opportunity to redirect the objectives of medical intervention and pharmacological treatment.

Health and Wellbeing Principles of the MHWB Act 2022

The objectives are followed by the 'mental health and wellbeing principles' (MHWB Act 2022: sections 16–28). These principles appear to offer a holistic approach to decision-making under the MHWB Act 2022 but again do not mention the principle of informed consent. The most relevant principles for decision-making are the dignity and autonomy principle (MHWB Act 2022: section 16), the least restrictive principle (section 18) and the supported decision-making principle (section 19). The supported decision-making principle states that:

> Supported decision making practices are to be promoted. Persons receiving mental health and wellbeing services are to be supported to make decisions and to be involved in decisions about their assessment, treatment and recovery including when they are receiving compulsory treatment. The views and preferences of the person receiving mental health and wellbeing services are to be given priority.
>
> (MHWB Act 2022: section 19)

As noted, the provision of support for decision-making is a central principle in the CRPD. In the MHWB Act 2022, the supported decision-making principle refers to making decisions and being involved in decisions if the patient is a compulsory patient. As is explained more fully later, the standard of involving people in decisions, even when priority is given to their views and preferences, is a more limited standard than would be afforded by principles of informed consent.

The least restrictive principle is similarly opaque. According to the MHWB Act 2022, the least restrictive principle requires that:

> Mental health and wellbeing services are to be provided to a person living with mental illness or psychological distress with the least possible restriction of their rights, dignity and autonomy with the aim of promoting their recovery and full participation in community life. The views and preferences of the person should be key determinants of the nature of this recovery and participation.
>
> (MHWB Act 2022: section 18)

A careful reading of this passage shows that unlike the supported decision-making principle, the person's views and preferences are 'key determinants', but only with respect to the nature of the person's recovery and participation. From a human rights perspective, the concept of least restriction should be understood in terms of the subjective experience of the person (Weller 2019). The MHWB Act 2022 offers a narrower approach.

Perhaps the most relevant principle is the 'dignity and autonomy principle'. This principle is defined by the Act as:

> The rights, dignity and autonomy of a person living with mental illness or psychological distress is [sic] to be promoted and protected and the person is to be supported to exercise those rights.
>
> (MHWB Act 2022: section 16)

The reference to rights in this principle could be construed as a suggestion that those with mental capacity are entitled to make their own decisions. In the absence of clear language in the legislation, however, as is discussed later, the 'dignity and autonomy principle' may have little impact on the way the substantive provisions of the new legislation are construed, particularly as the substantive provisions in Part 3 the Act appear to contradict the mental health and wellbeing principles. To add to the confusion, Part 3, which I discuss in the next section, is governed by its own set of 'decision-making principles for treatment and interventions'.

Decision-Making Principles and Substantive Provisions

Part 3 of the MHWB Act 2022 includes the substantive provisions with respect to treatment, beginning with five '[d]ecision making principles for treatment and interventions' (section 78–84). Section 79 emphasises safe, high-quality care:

> Compulsory assessment and treatment is to be provided with the aim of promoting the person's recovery and transitioning them to less restrictive treatment, care and support. To this end, a person who is subject to compulsory assessment or treatment is to receive comprehensive, compassionate, safe and high-quality mental health and wellbeing services.

Section 80 recognises the detriment of compulsory treatment and restrictive interventions:

> The use of compulsory assessment and treatment or restrictive interventions significantly limits a person's human rights and may cause possible harm including – (a) serious distress experienced by the person; and (b) the disruption of the relationships, living arrangements, education or employment of the person.

Section 81 asserts the absence of a therapeutic benefit to the use of 'restrictive interventions':

> The use of restrictive interventions on a person offers no inherent therapeutic benefit to the person.

Section 82 recognises the balancing of harm principle:

> Compulsory assessment and treatment or restrictive interventions are not to be used unless the serious harm or deterioration to be prevented is likely to be more significant than the harm to the person that may result from their use.

Section 83 recognises the will and preferences of the person:

> The will and preferences of the person are to be given effect to the greatest extent possible in all decisions about assessment, treatment, recovery and support, including when those decisions relate to compulsory assessment and treatment.

Section 84 gives power to the Chief Psychiatrist to prepare guidelines with respect to the principles.

It remains to be seen whether such guidelines will address how a person's 'rights, will and preferences', as required by the CRPD, will be ascertained or how the 'decision-making principles' will encompass the use of advance statements and nominated persons (see Stavert 2021). These mechanisms of support for legal capacity are provided for in the legislation but not addressed in the decision-making principles. The substantive legislative position is that they *may* be taken into account by the treating psychiatrist.

The key question is whether and how the decision-making principles will operate. The principles are seemingly intended to discourage the use of compulsory treatment and clarify that the person's will and preference should remain an important consideration, even when the person is subject to compulsory treatment. As with the health and wellbeing principles, however, the defining feature of both the decision-making principles and the substantive provisions of the MHWB Act 2022 is the persistent avoidance of the question of mental capacity and the right to informed consent. The following paragraphs examine the relevant provisions.

Section 85 of the MHWB Act 2022 imposes a general obligation on treating psychiatrists to presume the mental capacity of those seeking treatment and to seek informed consent. The obligation to seek informed consent coupled with a presumption that the person has capacity to give it, is an important step forward. In theory, such provisions should encourage the use of voluntary treatment and discourage compulsory treatment. Section 85(3), however, excuses clinicians from seeking informed consent if he or she 'reasonably considers' that the person does not have mental capacity to give informed consent. Anecdotally, consumers of mental health services report that the presumption of mental capacity operates as a mechanism that permits those who agree with clinical assessments to be admitted as voluntary patients, while those who question or reject assessment and treatment are admitted under compulsory treatment powers (see also Bartlett 2011). If this is true, it denotes a significant departure from standard legal principles. In summary, there is no firm mechanism supporting the right to informed consent for compulsory patients despite the elements of informed consent being set out in section 86 of the Act.

Section 87 of the MHWB Act 2022 sets out the requirements of a functional mental capacity test, including the important – and less common – requirement that 'the person being assessed [for mental capacity] is provided with appropriate supports to enable the person to give informed consent' (section 87(3)(c)). While the recognition of support is welcome, the requirement of 'appropriate supports' appears to fall far below the CRPD requirements of support for legal capacity and decision-making safeguards as set out in Article 12. The central question from a human rights perspective is whether sufficient support for legal capacity will be provided to enable a person to provide informed consent, or to ensure that a decision is guided by the person's 'rights, will and preference'. On both these counts, the narrow scope of the statutory obligations in the MHWB Act 2022 appears to fall short of international human rights standards.

The most obvious contravention of human rights in the MHWB Act 2022 is the apparent conflation of treatment refusal with a lack of mental capacity. As is noted earlier, it is well established in health law (and recognised in international human rights law) that those who are able to give informed consent are entitled to accept or refuse treatment. However, the MHWB Act 2022 overrides a person's right to refuse treatment. It states that if a patient does not have capacity to give informed consent, or 'has capacity to give informed consent but does not give informed consent to the treatment proposed by an authorised psychiatrist' (section 89(1)(a) (ii)) then the psychiatrist may make the treatment decision if the clinician is satisfied that it is 'clinically appropriate' and there is 'no less restrictive way for the patient to be treated' (section 89(3)(a-b)). Section 89(4) sets out a list of considerations that the psychiatrist, 'to the extent that is reasonable in the circumstances, must have regard to', in deciding the less restrictive way for the patient to be treated, including – notably – considering 'any beneficial alternative treatment that is reasonably available' (section 89(4)(b)).

These new sections replicate almost exactly section 70 and section 71 of the legislation currently in force (the *Mental Health Act 2014* (Vic)). These provisions are highly significant because they give authorised psychiatrists the power to impose psychiatric treatment if they think it is appropriate – whether or not the person has mental capacity. In theory the guiding principles and decision-making principles should influence the way treatment decisions are made under these provisions. However, the same framework was included as a key innovation in the *Mental Health Act 2014* (Vic). In that instance, the provisions did not result in a change to the way treatment decisions were made with section 71 of the 2014 Act operating as a key source of power. As was noted by the Victorian Royal Commission, many of the aspirations of the *Mental Health Act 2014* (Vic) were not realised.

Discussion

In theory, the inclusion of objectives and principles in mental health legislation, framed by the overarching principle of the realisation of the right to the highest attainable standard of health and mental health and underpinned by an obligation to presume capacity and seek informed consent, should shift thinking about compulsory treatment decisions, rights, risk and the importance of respect for the autonomy and self-determination of the people who use mental health services (see also discussion of the importance of legislative principles by Donnelly in Chapter 2 of this volume). In practice, legislative regimes that replicate the substantive provisions of previous acts are unlikely to change the existing way clinicians and others utilise those powers. Arguably, this may depend on whether they have the opportunity to understand the intent of the legislation. The importance of principles as a statutory interpretation tool and their potential impact in the context of practical decision-making under the Act should form part of a concerted education campaign and implementation plan. Such training should be framed by an effort to impart an understanding of human rights, including the importance of mental capacity, legal capacity and informed consent in the disability and mental health context, and should be undertaken by and with all stakeholders. The impact of human rights training will be enhanced if it is possible to generate a shared understanding amongst consumers, carers, service providers and clinicians of the intent of the provisions and their relationship to human rights standards. If this were done, the MHWB Act 2022 could make a powerful contribution to cultural change in the mental health system as was envisaged by the Victorian Royal Commission.

Without a clear recognition of the human rights prohibition against coercion and clear statutory direction with respect to informed consent, however, the impact of the legislation may remain muted. The principles approach in the MHWB Act 2022 raises significant questions about the meaning of the new legislation. Because the MHWB Act 2022 retains the power to override treatment decisions 'if the person has capacity to give informed consent but does not give consent' (section 89(1)(a)(ii)), while providing only vague references to the entitlement of mental health consumers to participate in decisions, there is a risk that this legislation will continue to override the decisions of people with mental illness and psychological distress, and *even those with mental capacity* to provide informed consent. Indeed, there is now a fundamental disjuncture between the substantive provisions and the principles precisely because the question of mental capacity, legal capacity and informed consent has not been addressed in the principles. As is noted earlier, the Victorian Royal Commission recommended that compulsory treatment powers be retained but simplified so that compulsory treatment was no longer the focus of the legislation. Compulsory treatment provisions have been retained, but they are far from simple. The legislation is unwieldy and unclear. Rather than ensuring that compulsory treatment ceases to be the focus of the legislation, it seems that compulsion remains front and centre in the decision-making logic.

A human rights approach in mental health care recognises that informed consent is a fundamental starting point for any discussion of mental health care and treatment if it is to be guided by care and compassion. It is not an approach that aims to abandon people as is argued by some, but rather an approach that privileges person-centred care by giving timely advice and active ongoing support to make decisions in a way that respects the person and acknowledges their personal and social needs. As the Victorian Royal Commission recommended, significant cultural change is needed to create a system of humane and responsive care and treatment where compulsion is truly an option of last resort. The provisions of the MHWB Act 2022 are currently ill-suited to supporting those objectives. It is hoped that the pending Independent Review of the legislation, noted earlier, provides an opportunity to set a new course.

Conclusion

This chapter has argued that the right to health and mental health should be at the core of State responses to mental health care and treatment and should include a concerted effort to understand and implement the right to informed consent. Informed consent encapsulates the core content of the right to health and mental health, including the freedom to control one's own body and to access timely and appropriate health care. In failing to respect the right to informed consent, Victoria's new MHWB Act 2022 (as passed) has missed an opportunity to provide a robust framework for mental health care and treatment that is consistent with human rights.

References

International Instruments

Committee on Economic, Social and Cultural Rights (2000) *General Comment No. 14 – The Right to the Highest Attainable Standard of Health (Article 12 of the International Covenant on Economic, Cultural and Social Rights)*, 23rd sess, UN Doc E/C.12/2000/4.

Committee on the Rights of Persons with Disabilities (2014) *General Comment No. 1 – Article 12: Equal Recognition before the Law*, 11th sess, UN Doc CRPD/C/GC/1.

Convention Against Torture and Other Cruel, Inhuman or Degrading Treatment or Punishment (1985) Opened for signature 4 February 1465 UNTS 85 (entered into force 26 June 1987).

Convention on the Rights of Persons with Disabilities (2007) Opened for signature 30 March, 2515 UNTS 3 (entered into force 3 May 2008).

International Covenant on Economic, Social and Cultural Rights (1966) Opened for signature 19 December 1966, 993 UNTS 3 (entered into force 3 January 1976).

Universal Declaration of Human Rights (1948) *GA Res 217A(III)*, 3rd sess, 183rd plen mtg, UN Doc A/810.

Cases

Kioa v West (1985) 159 CLR 550.

PBU & NJE v Mental Health Tribunal (2018) 56 VR 141.

Legislation

Charter of Human Rights and Responsibilities Act 2006 (Vic)
Mental Health Act 2014 (Vic)
Mental Health and Wellbeing Act 2022 (Vic)

Books, Journal Articles and Other Texts

Anthony, W.A. (1993) 'Recovery from Mental Illness: The Guiding Vision of the Mental Health Service System in the 1990s', *Psychosocial Rehabilitation Journal*, 16(4): 11–23.

Arstein-Kerslake, A., Gooding, P., Andrews, L. and McSherry, B. (2017) 'Human Rights and Unfitness to Plead: The Demands of the Convention on the Rights of Persons with Disabilities', *Human Rights Law Review*, 17(3): 399–419.

Bartlett, P. (2011) 'The Necessity Must be Convincingly Shown to Exist: Standards for Compulsory Treatment for Mental Disorder under the Mental Health Act 1983', *Medical Law Review*, 19(4): 514–47.

Beauchamp, T. and Childress, J. (2001) *Principles of Biomedical Ethics*, 5th edn, Oxford: Oxford University Press.

Brophy, L.M., Roper, C.E., Hamilton, B.E., Tellez, J.J. and McSherry, B.M. (2016) 'Consumers' and Their Supporters' Perspectives on Barriers and Strategies to Reducing Seclusion and Restraint in Mental Health Settings', *Australian Health Review*, 40(6): 599–604.

Chieze, M., Hurst, S., Kaiser, S. and Sentissi, O. (2019) 'Effects of Seclusion and Restraint in Adult Psychiatry: A Systematic Review', *Frontiers in Psychiatry*, 10: 491.

Donnelly, M. (2010) *Healthcare Decision-making and the Law: Autonomy, Capacity and Limits of Liberalism*, Cambridge: Cambridge University Press.

Eyles, J. and Wood, K. (2014) *The Social Geography of Medicine and Health*, Abingdon: Routledge.

Faden, R.R. and Beauchamp, T.L. (1986) *A History and Theory of Informed Consent*, New York: Oxford University Press.

Flynn, E. and Arstein-Kerslake, A. (2014) 'Legislating Personhood: Realising the Right to Support in Exercising Legal Capacity', *International Journal of Law in Context*, 10(1): 81–104.

Gable, L. and Gostin, L. (2009) 'Mental Health as a Human Right', in A. Clapsham and M. Robinson (eds) *Realizing the Right to Health*, Zurich: Rüffer & Rub, 249–61.

Gooding, P. (2015) 'Navigating the "Flashing Amber Lights" of the Right to Legal Capacity in the United Nations Convention on the Rights of Persons with Disabilities: Responding to Major Concerns', *Human Rights Law Review*, 15(1): 45–71.

Kumble, S. and McSherry, B. (2010) 'Seclusion and Restraint: Rethinking Regulation from a Human Rights Perspective', *Psychiatry, Psychology and Law*, 17(4): 551–61.

MacNaughton, G. (2009) 'Untangling Equality and Non-discrimination to Promote the Right to Health Care for All', *Health and Human Rights*, 11(2): 47–63.

McSherry, B. (2012) 'Legal Capacity Under the Convention on the Rights of Persons with Disabilities', *Journal of Law and Medicine*, 20(1): 22–27.

McSherry, B. (2013) 'The Legal Regulation of Seclusion and Restraint in Mental Health Facilities', *Journal of Law and Medicine*, 21(2): 251–54.

McSherry, B. (2017) 'Regulating Seclusion and Restraint in Health Care Settings: The Promise of the Convention on the Rights of Persons with Disabilities', *International Journal of Law and Psychiatry*, 53: 39–44.

McSherry, B., Baldry, E., Arstein-Kerslake, A., Gooding, P., McCausland, R. and Arabena, K. (2017) *Unfitness to Plead and Indefinite Detention of Persons with Cognitive Disabilities: Addressing the Legal Barriers and Creating Appropriate Alternative Supports in the Community*, Melbourne Social Equity Institute. Available https://socialequity.unimelb.edu.au/__data/assets/pdf_file/0009/2598507/Unfitness-to-Plead.pdf (accessed 29 December 2022).

McSherry, B. and Butler, A. (2015) 'Support for the Exercise of Legal Capacity: The Role of the Law', *Journal of Law and Medicine*, 22(4): 739–44.

McSherry, B. and Maker, Y. (eds) (2021) *Restrictive Practices in Health Care and Disability Settings: Legal, Policy and Practical Responses*, Abingdon: Routledge.

McSherry, B. and Weller, P. (eds) (2010) *Rethinking Rights-Based Mental Health Laws*, Oxford: Hart Publishing.

Meadows, G., Brophy, L., Shawyer, F., Enticott, J.C., Fossey, E., Thornton, C.D., Weller, P.J., Wilson-Evered, E., Edan, V. and Slade, M. (2019) 'REFOCUS-PULSAR Recovery-oriented Practice Training in Specialist Mental Health Care: A Stepped-wedge Cluster Randomised Controlled Trial', *Lancet Psychiatry*, 6(2): 103–14.

Meier, B. (2010) 'Global Health Governance and the Contentious Politics of Human Rights: Mainstreaming the Right to Health for Public Health Advancement', *Stanford Journal of International Law*, 46(1): 1–50.

Melbourne Social Equity Institute (2014) *Seclusion and Restraint Project: Report.* Available https://socialequity.unimelb.edu.au/__data/assets/pdf_file/0017/2004722/Seclusion-and-Restraint-report.PDF (accessed 29 December 2022).

Newton, G. and Mullen, R. (2011) 'Coercion in Psychiatric Care: Systematic Review of Correlates and Themes', *Psychiatric* Services, 62(5): 465–70.

Prah-Ruger, J. (2010) 'Health Capability: Conceptualization and Operationalization', *American Journal of Public Health*, 100(1): 41–49.

Pritchard-Jones, L. (2019) 'Exploring the Potential and the Pitfalls of the United Nations Convention on the Rights of Persons with Disabilities and General Comment No. 1 for People with Dementia', *International Journal of Law and Psychiatry*, 66: 101467.

Quinn, G. and Degener, T. (2002) *Human Rights and Disability: The Current Use and Future Potential of United Nations Human Rights Instruments in the Context of Disability*, United Nations. Available www.ohchr.org/en/publications/special-issue-publications/human-rights-and-disability-current-use-and-future (accessed 29 December 2022).

Royal Commission into Victoria's Mental Health System (2021) *Final Report.* Available https://finalreport.rcvmhs.vic.gov.au/ (accessed 29 December 2022).

Stavert, J. (2021) 'Supported Decision-making and Paradigm Shifts: Word Play or Real Change?', *Frontiers in Psychiatry*, 11: 571005.

Stavert, J. and McGregor, R. (2018) 'Domestic Legislation and International Human Rights Standards: The Case of Mental Health and Incapacity', *The International Journal of Human Rights*, 22(1): 70–89.

Toebes, B. (1999) *The Right to Health as a Human Right in International Law*, Antwerp: Hart Publishing.

Victoria (2022) *Parliamentary Debates*, Legislative Assembly, 23 June (James Merlino, Deputy Premier, Second Reading Speech of Mental Health and Wellbeing Bill).

Weller, P. (2018) 'Article 25: Health', in I. Bantekas, M.A. Stein and D. Anastasiou (eds) *The United Nations Convention on the Rights of Person with Disabilities: A Commentary*, Oxford: Oxford University Press, 705–33.

Weller, P. (2019) 'OPCAT Monitoring and the Convention on the Rights of Persons with Disabilities', *Australian Journal of Human Rights*, 25(1): 130–49.

Wilson, K. (2020) 'The Abolition or Reform of Mental Health Law: How Should the Law Recognise and Respond to the Vulnerability of Persons with Mental Impairment?' *Medical Law Review*, 28(1): 30–64.

4 Benefitting From Hindsight

What the *Mental Capacity Act* and Its Implementation Can Teach Us About CRPD Implementation

Peter Bartlett

Introduction

The *Mental Capacity Act 2005* (MCA) in England and Wales introduced significant changes to English capacity law. While it did not purport to introduce the 'paradigm shift' of the United Nations *Convention on the Rights of Persons with Disabilities* (CRPD), it was a big deal, and the resulting experience provides a range of practical lessons for CRPD implementation, in particular of Article 12 (equal recognition before the law) and its effects on laws relating to mental capacity. This chapter explores those lessons.

The purpose of the chapter is not to define or defend a particular interpretation of the CRPD. It takes as a given that Article 12 requires a significant refocusing onto the will and preferences of the person with disability (PWD), and that support for that person is to be provided to realise that; and it accepts the overall direction of the CRPD towards equality, non-discrimination, social integration and the direct involvement of PWDs in the establishment of policy and its implementation. The status quo ante manifestly must change. That was, after all, why the CRPD was viewed by States Parties as needed, and those values infuse the text: this cannot be about cosmetic alterations around the edges of law as it applies to the PWD. Beyond those general directions, it is not concerned with the specifics of divergent interpretations. The issues in this chapter will apply to whatever interpretation is eventually adopted.

Consistent with that, it is perhaps appropriate to start with a positive point: the experience of the MCA demonstrates that fundamental legal change is possible. At the core of the MCA is the abolition of mental incapacity as a legal status. There is no longer any mechanism in English law to declare prospectively that an individual lacks capacity either generally or relating to classes of decisions or individual decisions, and the rights of a person to make decisions cannot in law be prospectively restricted. Admittedly, that change can be overstated: both the MCA and common law may disallow decisions taken by the PWD if he or she is found to lack the capacity to make a decision at the time the decision was or is being taken (see further discussion of mental capacity and informed consent by Weller in Chapter 3 of this volume). This chapter does not claim that the MCA is CRPD-compliant – there is a separate

DOI: 10.4324/9781003350644-5

literature on that question (see, e.g., Bartlett 2020; Clough 2018, 2022; Donnelly 2017; Martin et al. 2016). Nonetheless, the abolition of incapacity as a legal status is a significant shift, and a salient reminder: things can be different.

At the same time, the experience of MCA implementation points up a variety of technical difficulties (Bartlett 2022). For purposes of understanding CRPD interpretation, this chapter will discuss four of these:

- Implementation of the CRPD involves the fundamental rights of PWDs, and for that reason judicial oversight cannot (and must not) be avoided. That is pivotal in a democracy, but courts behave like courts. That raises an array of classic socio-legal issues about access to justice, process, delay, alienation and costs. That in turn affects the substance of the law: the situations over which courts adjudicate have to be reasonably static.
- Implementation of the CRPD will rely to a considerable degree on professionals. As courts behave like courts, so professionals behave like professionals. All the issues in the classic literature on how professionalism works and how professionals behave will be as relevant here as anywhere else in the social system.
- Legal structures do have their effects and limitations, and they are problematic: rights do not necessarily have meaning unless appropriate remedies are provided, and those remedies may go well beyond a judicial declaration. Governments are often hesitant to provide meaningful remedies and, particularly in the arena of social and cultural rights, courts are often hesitant to make the orders that would make rights real for the affected persons.
- Changing the law does not change practice. That is implied in the three previous points, of course, but the CRPD raises the problem to new levels. As we move towards integration of PWDs into the community, the issue is not just about changing professional practice, or practices in particular locations; it is about changing a great deal of society.

None of these problems are new; all have been the stuff of the law and society movement and its successors since the 1970s at least. They do however pose significant challenges to the introduction of the sort of meaningful change that the CRPD calls for. This chapter now explores each of these in turn.

Courts Behave Like Courts

A role for the courts (or, sometimes, perhaps tribunals) is inescapable in the implementation of human rights legislation, and that will be the case for domestic legislation implementing the CRPD. In jurisdictions that believe in the rule of law, disputes relating to an individual's human rights must be able to be decided by independent judicial bodies. That is significant not merely as a point of principle, but a point of practice, since legitimate questions can arise on how rights are to be interpreted, and rights under the CRPD are no exception. Ambiguities can arise even within the terms of a single article: at what point, for example, do measures taken to protect the PWD from violence, exploitation and abuse (CRPD: Article 16) themselves become exploitative or abusive? At what point does 'reasonable accommodation' impose 'a disproportionate or undue burden' (CRPD: Article 2)? These obligations will be implemented by individual States Parties by domestic legislation,[1] of course, and it is generally that legislation which the courts will have to interpret, rather than the CRPD itself; but the tensions remain, and courts will be needed to resolve them.

Good practices no doubt exist in many parts of the world, often the result of the dedication of devoted people working in sometimes difficult economic and social circumstances. Courts are, in that sense, not the only route to human rights compliance. Courts are vital bodies that can challenge bad practice, however: they can give the CRPD rights teeth. If we want the rights to be meaningful, courts have to be part of the picture.

Courts behave like courts, though. That means the procedures and legal trappings well known to socio-legal scholars for generations. Procedures take time and require evidence. Some cases in the Court of Protection, the court charged with the administration of the MCA, run on for a number of years. In Series and colleagues' (2017: 3) study of the Court of Protection, the median times were actually much shorter – roughly four months for decisions regarding personal care, and nine months for property and affairs. For these procedures to work effectively, the facts need to be reasonably static for the period of the court process. That includes facts relating to the manifestations of the disability itself and the decisions to be taken, and relating to the will and preferences of the PWD. Consistent with that, the Court of Protection jurisprudence tends to concern (and be at its strongest concerning) people with relatively static conditions, such as dementia and learning disabilities. The claim that capacity under the MCA is 'decision and time specific' must therefore be viewed with some scepticism: it will depend on how time-specific the evidence and the situation are.

Occasionally, the court does make a finding that is time specific, as in the following finding by Hedley J, as to capacity to make a will:

> In the event, I have concluded that I cannot make a general declaration that X lacks testamentary capacity, but that needs to be strongly qualified. There will undoubtedly be times when he does lack testamentary capacity. There will be many times when he does not do so. The times when he does lack such capacity are likely to become more frequent. It follows that, in my judgment, any will now made by X, if unaccompanied by contemporary medical evidence asserting capacity, may be seriously open to challenge.
>
> (*A, B, and C v X and Y* [2012]: para 37)

That may well be an entirely accurate assessment and consistent with the ethos of the MCA, but it may be of limited assistance if the facts may be materially different within hours or days: the parties could find themselves back in court almost immediately, with the burdens (including the financial burdens) that this implies. Admittedly, under the main interpretations of the CRPD and Article 12, capacity may not be the issue of concern to the court, but other key facts may be equally volatile. For people with some forms of mental disability, this creates real difficulties in designing a system.

Court systems are complex, and the PWD is likely to need a lawyer. That in turn has effects that are problematic in CRPD terms. At the very least, it places an intermediary between the PWD and the judge: the voice of the PWD is filtered. It is also likely to remove the hearing into a professionalised legal sphere: a universe of experts 'in the know' about the process, speaking to each other in legal language not readily understood by the people they represent. That is true for many people without disabilities, but it may well be of particular relevance to PWDs. The PWD may well become marginalised in the dynamic of the courtroom. Courts can attempt to make their proceedings more comprehensible to PWDs, but that is not easy, and it is not cheap. The object of the CRPD (and indeed arguably the MCA) is to move the PWD to the centre of the process; but court processes seem to do rather the reverse.

All this raises the obvious question of costs: lawyers do not come cheap. In many parts of the world, legal aid may not exist at all, or may be limited to the most minimal provision. Elsewhere, including in England, legal aid systems are often under serious pressure. Either way, this raises the question of access to justice for PWDs: who pays? Are we content that the rights are accessible only to those with sufficient financial means? Yes, the question of the price of justice is an old one, but that does not diminish its relevance.

One way forward, in theory, is to simplify the court processes, ideally to the point where professional legal representation is not required. The Law Commission proposals that led to the MCA had intended to adopt that approach: the Court of Protection would act in a 'relaxed and non-technical way' (Law Commission 1995: 10.25–26). The view was that the PWD would normally attend the court and speak directly to the judge, expert reports would only exceptionally be required, and the judge would be working directly with the litigants. That is not how things turned out. The *Court of Protection Rules 2017* run to 93 pages (plus explanatory notes), and in the silence of those rules, the regular court rules apply. Expert reports are routinely required, and the PWD is still absent from the hearing in a majority of cases. Indeed, it was initially questioned whether the court was permitted to meet and speak with the PWD (see, e.g., *CC v KK and STCC* [2012]; *Re SB (A Patient: Capacity to Consent to Termination)* [2013]; and generally Lindsey 2019). That obstacle has now been cleared by rules 1.2(1)(d) and 14.2(e) of the revised *Court of Protection Rules 2017*, but the Court of Appeal remains hesitant (*AD* [2021]). For the Court of Protection, judges are permitted to speak with the PWD who is the subject of an application before them only if procedural safeguards are in place to protect the interests of all parties to the litigation, and if appropriate professional support is available to assist the judge in interpreting the communications of the PWD. The reluctance of the Court of Appeal to allow, let alone encourage, direct conversations between the judge and the PWD is not merely out of kilter with the original vision of how courts would work under the MCA; it is also arguably inconsistent with the approach of the European Court of Human Rights (see, e.g., *Shtukaturov v Russia* 2008). It does serve as a reminder, however, that simplification of process may be met by considerable judicial resistance.

There are reasons for the way things have turned out. Often, the work done by the Court of Protection is legitimately legally and factually complex. It may involve disputes of fact, conflicting statutory interpretations of the MCA or conflicting or overlapping statutes. The Court of Protection seems to deal with the legal complexities notably well. As we move disabilities law into the community, where factual and legal universes are ever more complex and remedies may involve increasingly diverse actors in society, these difficulties can be expected to increase.

Further, the perception is that appropriate processes protect rights, and that human rights are sufficiently important that proper processes are required. Courts, including the Court of Protection, do find ways of tailoring processes when it is necessary to do so (for example, in cases of real urgency), but there is often a sense of scrambling around about such cases. They may well occur ex parte (ie, with only some of the relevant actors represented and without notice to other interested parties). Evidential standards may be compromised, with limited opportunity for testing of witness claims by opposing counsel (who may, as noted, be unaware even that the hearing is happening). Hearings may occur in suboptimal settings (as occurred in one Court of Protection case, with the judge hearing arguments by telephone from the back of a car, in the parking lot of Chester Zoo). No criticism of the court is implied here – in cases of urgency, what else are they to do? – but it is fair to ask whether this is the sort of procedural standard CRPD advocates want. We as lawyers may want to characterise these orders as merely 'interim', with the fig leaf that we can fix the mess with an extended process later, but often it is not obvious that a violation to the individual can be remedied down the road.

The approach of the Law Commission in its design of the MCA was to minimise the role of courts. In this they have at least arguably been successful. For matters relating to personal decision-making, the Court of Protection receives roughly 1,300 applications per year (Family Court Statistics Quarterly 2021: Table 21). The number of people within the scope of the MCA is not known, but for context, there are roughly 153,000 adults with learning disabilities receiving long-term support from local authorities in England (Public Health England 2021), and there are 676,000 people with dementia (NHS England 2016). Clearly, not all of these will be within the scope of the MCA, but a large number will, and the small number of court applications regarding personal decision-making is notable.

The difficulty with this minimal role for the courts however is that we know little of how decisions are being taken regarding PWDs outside the court's view. The best speculation is that family members, who are pivotal to much decision-making in the MCA system, are largely ignorant of the MCA provisions (House of Lords 2014: paras 95, 179–92). The limited evidence we have is that even professionals, where training has been provided by their professional organisations, have limited knowledge of the MCA, and are not reliably following its provisions. What all that means in terms of the rights of the PWD is at best speculative. If we really want to know that the laws are being followed, this does suggest that some more intensive legal processes and oversights are required (See discussion of regulatory systems by Diesfeld in Chapter 7, Dawson and Matthews in Chapter 8 and Katterl and Friel in Chapter 14 of this volume.)

The need for such enhanced oversight and process seems particularly convincing if the issue is characterised as relating to human rights, and the CRPD in particular. We tend to think of legal processes in terms of classic autonomous liberal subjects, who will launch legal proceedings in the event that they perceive their rights as violated. That model is problematic in much of human rights law and certainly in the case of a PWD. In at least some cases, it may not be sufficient to rely on the PWD to raise the alarm and press for the protection of his or her rights and the provision of a remedy, through the courts if necessary. It would be counterintuitive in the extreme, for example, to expect a PWD subject to violence, exploitation and abuse to whistleblow on his or her abusers, who may well be carers within their domestic environment or others with considerable practical power over the individual. The CRPD contains an ethos of support for the PWD. This suggests that there must, in some circumstances, be an obligation on the State Party to monitor situations and intervene in support of the individual when appropriate.

Mandatory processes create problems of their own, though, of which the deprivation of liberty safeguards (DoLS) introduced into the MCA in 2007 are illustrative. In response to litigation before the European Court of Human Rights (*HL v the United Kingdom* 2004), processes were introduced in England and Wales to ensure the propriety of all 'deprivations of liberty' of people lacking capacity (*Mental Health Act 2007*). For people detained in hospitals or registered care homes, this was done through an inspection process; for people detained elsewhere – in other institutions or in their own home – it was to be done by court order (see also Dawson and Matthews in Chapter 8 of this volume).

Both of these proved problematic. Abysmal legislative drafting and a failure to adequately resource the systems did not help, and the overarching sense was that this was introduced because we had to do it, not because it had a real potential benefit for PWDs (see Bartlett 2014 and Donnelly in Chapter 2 of this volume). That is unfortunate, as the statistics would suggest that the applications to detain were not approved for a significant number of people subject to the scheme; although statistics can mask a variety of factual situations,[2] at least arguably, their human rights were being violated. Nonetheless, moves are now afoot to 'simplify' the protections (see *Mental Capacity*

(Amendment) Act 2019, not yet in force). This provides a salient example of a point to be raised later in this chapter: if the politicians and professionals do not understand and support the importance of the changes to be introduced, it is unlikely that they will be successful.

Equally problematic is the court scheme. It is not merely that it is expensive to the state, although it certainly is. It is also that the process creates unanticipated consequences. The case of *London Borough of Brent v SL* [2017] brings together some of the difficulties. SL had been detained under mental health legislation and was being discharged into sheltered accommodation with a care plan that was sufficiently restrictive as to constitute a deprivation of her liberty. This was not a care home, so a court order was required. She did not want to be in the accommodation proposed, but was a woman with some means, and did not want her savings to go to hiring lawyers to contest the case. In the result, she was in an impossible position: because court hearings were required to protect against human rights abuses (a laudable aim), she could not drop the case, as a non-disabled litigant would be able to do, and the court rules required her to be represented (and for her to pay for the representation out of her savings). She could have reduced her financial exposure by applying to be removed as a party, as the court rules allowed, but this seems a bizarre outcome when she clearly had strong views as to what should happen.

None of these issues will surprise socio-legal scholars. While the nuances and twists will be specific to a mental disability context, the overall questions of access to justice have been understood for decades. Indeed, it is perhaps fair to ask how different the situation of the PWD enforcing their CRPD rights is to any other litigant of modest means, who finds the legal process alienating and rights difficult to enforce. That in turn raises the question of how non-discrimination is to be understood under the CRPD. If the point really is that the CRPD creates 'no new rights', should a PWD have better rights to legal process than other disadvantaged persons? Most of us who are advocates of the CRPD would I suspect want to argue that additional support is appropriate and indeed required by the CRPD, but it is not obvious how that argument works, if we take the non-discrimination point critically. PWDs do not have a monopoly on historic or grinding oppression.

The Persistence of Professionals

The CRPD is not a libertarian document – indeed, quite the reverse. It is a treaty that requires an active state that provides services to PWDs, from support for decision-making, to protection from exploitation, to a range of support services in the community, to inclusive education, to rights to habilitation and rehabilitation, to provision of health services, to public housing . . . the list goes on. Those will all be animated by professionals, and professionals will thus be central to the form that CRPD implementation takes.

That is consistent with the MCA implementation experience. For reasons related to the specific history of the MCA project, the Law Commission did address medical decision-making specifically, and did discuss doctors' involvement in that, but beyond this, professionals were largely absent from the discussion. That is not how it turned out. Professionals (medical and social work, primarily) became involved in a wide array of decision-making regarding people under the MCA, and quickly came to provide the key evidence before the Court of Protection.

Professional involvement is not without its advantages. If we want PWDs to get good medical advice, it is going to need to come from doctors. Planning for life in the community for at least some PWDs will require a set of specialist knowledges relating to housing, social care and support, and practical mechanisms for community integration (and how all of those services, provided often by different organisations, can be integrated together) that lay people may well not possess. Social workers and similar professionals will therefore be needed. Good professionals are likely to be vital to the success of the CRPD project, and the training of those professionals will require PWDs and their representative organisations to work with the relevant professional bodies.

That already raises challenges for CRPD implementation, however. PWDs and their representative organisations spoke with considerable passion during the negotiation process leading to the CRPD and since about the injustices they have experienced at the hands of medical and social care professionals. They have a point: the history of the 'care' of PWDs does not inspire confidence. Indeed, the reason that a new human rights convention was viewed as necessary for PWDs is precisely because their rights had been subject to manifest and systematic violation both in the past and in an ongoing basis. The culture that gave rise to that flows not just from politicians, but also from the relevant professionals and professional bodies. Good intentions they may often have had, but the need for the CRPD speaks to the disconnect between the professional values and the human rights of PWDs (see also Arstein-Kerslake in Chapter 12 of this volume).

The involvement of professionals in CRPD implementation may well therefore create something of a storm with PWDs and their organisations. They will argue, not unreasonably, that a good deal of the point of the CRPD is the re-orientation of disability away from the 'medical model', with its ethos of disability as a problem within the individual that is to be 'fixed' by the professional, to the 'social' model, where disability is meant to involve social changes to structures and environments so that they can accommodate PWDs. The PWDs might reasonably ask how that shift is to occur, if professionals with their 'old paradigm' values are viewed as central to implementation.

Recent history in England supports their concern. Notwithstanding years of encouraging language from professional bodies, academic research, and social care and medical governance organisations, shifts away from the dominance of expert values to an enhanced voice for the PWD have been remarkably slow to take effect on the ground. There is certainly some excellent practice under the MCA and in related fields in England that does acknowledge the centrality of the PWD, and it would be wrong to say that no progress has been made. At the same time, the shift from expertise as a truth imposed by the professional onto the PWD, to expertise as a resource that the PWD can mine to further his or her life goals and objectives, is proving slow indeed. Professions, be they law, social work, medicine or any other, are self-perpetuating groups of people who believe in their own expertise. It is difficult to change their values, and particularly difficult to do so from the outside. This is where the rubber hits the road in CRPD implementation, and attainment of that shift will perhaps be the greatest challenge if the CRPD is to make a real difference in the lives of PWDs (see also Jayakody and Perera in Chapter 15 of this volume).

That is the ideological battle. The sociology of the professions raises a range of more practical issues that lead to yet more scepticism as to how this will all pan out in a CRPD context. In short, just as courts behave like courts, professionals are likely to behave like professionals, and if CRPD implementation is going to be successful, those characteristics need to be taken into account.

I do not claim expertise in these areas but would make a few comments to start discussion.

The first is that professionals are part of systems, and the systems have sets of values and pressures of their own (see Clough 2022). That has been known for decades, but the rise in new systems of management and professional governance, all in the names of 'efficiency', 'evidence-based practice' and 'accountability', have ratcheted the tensions to new heights. Professionals of all stripes are increasingly subject to 'targets', codes of practice and conduct, 'governance', restrictions imposed by block service contracts and systems of professional audit that often bear little resemblance to the professional ideals which they are meant to espouse, let alone the priorities of those served or the values of the CRPD. How exactly is a GP meant to have a meaningful discussion with a PWD about their care, if the doctor is expected to see six patients per hour, the current NHS standard in England? How is the 'patient voice' really to be heard if the appropriate approach is governed by 'care pathways', determined according to the statistically average patient? How is individualised social service provision to be achieved in a universe of block contracts and administrative controls on variations from standard budget items? The focus of health and social care policy and ethics may be centred on the person using the service, but the administrative practice is centrally defined and top-down. Through no fault of the practitioners, it does seem to be the latter that carries the day.

The problems of professionalisation do not lie solely with health and social care professionals. Advocates (both lawyers and lay) are also subject to pressures that can work against what in CRPD terms would be understood as 'good' advocacy. It is not merely that the body commissioning the advocacy service may well be the body the advocate is arguing against (although that is certainly a common concern). It is also that for the maintenance of the advocate's credibility, he or she will not want to be known as the person promoting what the decision-maker may view as 'hopeless cases'. The advocate may temper his or her arguments accordingly. We as advocates justify that to ourselves on the basis that it does not help our future clients if our submissions are tainted by our reputation, and that may well be correct. It does, however, undercut the 'fearless advocate' image, and from the perspective of the individual client whose views are not being represented it must feel profoundly disempowering. This example is significant for present purposes because it does not flow from a policy imposed from higher up the hierarchy; it flows from the inherent nature of the system and how it operates.

Systemic consequences may also come into play between systems. It was noted earlier that the number of Court of Protection hearings relating to personal decision-making was about 1,300 per year. The comparable number of applications relating to property and financial affairs is somewhat over 20,000, and almost 15,000 of those involve long-term appointment of someone to make decisions the PWD is unable to make, a process used very rarely indeed for personal decision-making (Family Court Statistics Quarterly 2021: Table 22). The reasons for the differential are unclear. There is little difference between personal and property decisions in the statute. Certainly, there is a more established and consistent history of making longer-term orders in property-related matters than for personal decision-making, but insofar as that is an explanation, it serves merely as a reminder that older systems overreach into newer systems. More to the point here, it is also arguable that the difference is caused at least in part by the different practices of business – banks being an obvious example – in their insistence on clear legal formalities being in place for property and financial transactions. Capitalism wants that sort of certainty and clarity, and hopes that it will move from that position may well be optimistic. The most obvious point of conflict with the CRPD is in Article 12(5), which gives PWDs the right to control property, have equal access to loans and mortgages, and control their own financial affairs. There is the risk of a clash with financial systems, and working out a way through those systems may be complex.

The Provision of Real Alternatives

CRPD rights will be relevant only if positive programmes are put in place so that PWDs have real choices. The legal status of these rights, and their judicial enforceability, may well differ according to criteria that make legal sense but no practical sense. As an obvious example, the right to liberty in Article 14 will be meaningful only if real community options are made available as envisaged by Article 19 and other CRPD provisions. The right to liberty is a civil right, and a statute implementing it will almost certainly be judicially enforceable. Article 19 (the right to live independently and be included in the community) by comparison is a social and economic right. While enforceability would depend on the relevant domestic statute, certainly in England, legislators have been reluctant to provide for rights of enforcement, and even when they do, the courts have been very reluctant to give life to those provisions (see, e.g., *R (Barry) v Gloucestershire* (1997) and subsequent litigation relying upon it).

That court reluctance is reflected in the MCA jurisprudence, as in the case of *A Clinical Commissioning Group v N* [2017], where the scope of MCA best interests was held to be restricted to the options the service provider was prepared to make available. While the obvious reason for services not being made available is financial, the court's reasoning is not restricted to that circumstance. That places the question of access to services squarely within a classic judicial review framework, with the judicial deference that such a framework entails. There is now jurisprudence that health care providers must keep their procurement policies up to date, with an eye to the most recent systemic evidence of efficacy (*R (Rose) v Thanet Clinical Commissioning Group* [2014]). But that is not at all the same as saying that services must be provided, and in any event harkens back to the top-down model of services based on centralised priorities and determinations of facts, rather than an individualised service based on the priorities of the PWD. Rights have also been provided in the NHS for patients to claim that they are exceptional cases that should receive treatments other than those within the standard procurement arrangements (see, e.g., *R (Ross) v West Sussex PCT* [2008]), but those have tended to focus on clinical divergence rather than differing priorities for care. Judicial reviews of social care decisions have also been of similarly limited effect (see, e.g., *R (Davey) v Oxfordshire County Council* [2017]). The courts do seem to be engaging in closer scrutiny than in the past, but at least so far this is not translating into actual remedies.

The services that would make a difference therefore lie in the gift of the funders – notably the politicians – rather than in the courts. This undercuts the civil and political rights the courts purport to uphold. The right to liberty is meaningless unless there is somewhere the person can go to upon release; otherwise, he or she will end up back in the institutional structure. The tens of thousands of people in social care homes in central Europe are an obvious example of that. Similar issues exist in England, however, as people successfully challenging their psychiatric detention through legal processes may remain detained because services are not made available to them in the community (see, e.g., *Kolanis v the United Kingdom* 2005; *Johnson v the United Kingdom* 1997).

While this seems unsatisfactory, it does need to be said that the CRPD itself is not wholly coherent on these issues. The distinction between immediate enforceability of civil and political rights and the progressive realisation of economic and social rights is expressly maintained in Article 4(2). At the same time, the text itself does not distinguish clearly between these. By way of example, freedom from discrimination is generally viewed as a civil right and thus is immediately enforceable. Reasonable accommodation, with its financial ramifications, sounds more like an economic and social right and therefore subject to progressive realisation. Failure to provide reasonable accommodation, however, is expressly stated to constitute discrimination, so has an economic and social right become a civil right through the back door (see Mégret 2008)?

In the background is the political question of how much is appropriate to spend on services, and on the processes to protect rights within social care systems. By way of illustration, the DoLS system in England was not properly funded when it was established in 2007. The Law Commission noted in 2016–17 that proper implementation of the system would cost £309 million per year (Law Commission 2017), a figure viewed by some as excessive. It was, however, only 1.3% of the adult social care budget at that time, and would have affected over 200,000 people. Is the cost too much or too little? That is a conversation that the body politic seems reluctant to have. Does a wish to provide human rights safeguards to PWDs 'on the cheap' at some point itself raise questions of discrimination, if notably less funding is provided to protect these rights than, say, criminal detentions? This sort of question may give legal ways into challenging limitations on funding of services, but they have not yet been tried and courts may be hesitant to engage in what may be seen as 'political' matters. At the same time, the failure to engage with issues of service provision may seriously limit the provision of rights.

The problem of limited enforceability of social and legal rights is certainly not unique to the disability arena; but it is a potentially serious problem, particularly among politicians who tend to see human rights more as photo opportunities than as essential elements of democracy and civil society, and the foundations of meaningful lives for disadvantaged people.

The Problem of Social Change

The point here is brief, but no less significant for that: the changes envisaged by the CRPD involve changing the views and practices not of professionals, but of a considerable proportion of society. The rights contained in the CRPD are not limited to specific institutional structures. If, for example, social inclusion is going to work, fundamental changes will be necessary in the attitudes of a great deal of the population, not just specific professionals.

The implementation of the MCA gives cause for concern here. The evidence base is not strong, but the briefs and witnesses to the House of Lords ad hoc Committee on implementation of the MCA suggested that significant pockets of professionals and service providers for whom the MCA was a significant element of their job did not really understand its use. Sometimes this could at least partly be attributed to transience in workforces. Care home staff are badly paid, and may move on fairly frequently, to be replaced by other low-skilled workers. Nuanced training, buttressed by practical feedback loops reflecting experiences of the trainees in implementation, is difficult in that environment. Other difficulties suggested barriers that were less obvious. It seemed frequent, for example, that incapacity would routinely be found when a diagnosis of dementia had been made, with little if any reference to the other (significant!) criteria in the statute. Those situations presumably hearken back to the questions of professional structures noted earlier in this chapter. This is already an important point. As discussed earlier, professional 'buy-in' to the

CRPD project is going to be essential if real and beneficial change is going to happen. Even where, as with the MCA, there appears to have been broad support for the changes in principle, actual change may be harder to arrive at. At least some of the CRPD objectives are controversial within those professional bodies; obtaining real change is likely to be problematic.

The MCA, like the CRPD, is not restricted to professionals nor to specific institutional structures. Just as the CRPD is meant to affect PWDs wherever they are, so the MCA was to apply to people lacking capacity to make a decision, whatever or wherever that decision was to be taken. The substantive focus (capacity) of the MCA is already a good deal more narrow than the substantive focus of the CRPD, but even that narrower focus raises serious questions about how the required knowledge and cultural shifts can be attained. The evidence to the House of Lords committee was admittedly often unsystematic, but it was consistent and unequivocal: whatever the issues regarding service providing professionals, people in the community more broadly had little or no knowledge or understanding of the Act. It is unclear how decisions are being taken about people under the MCA by families and other domestic carers, for example. It may or may not be the case that such a broad range of people would be sympathetic to the provisions of the MCA (that will presumably depend on the individual), but more than 15 years after the passage of the Act, its key provisions do not seem to have entered the public consciousness.

The problems the CRPD will encounter can be expected to be a good deal more profound. The MCA made significant changes to domestic law; the CRPD is meant to introduce a paradigm shift. That is a huge ask, and there is little experience in how to bring such cultural changes about. The CRPD itself speaks frequently about public education, and promotion of rights, but it is not obvious how successful those campaigns are. Large amounts of money have been spent in the UK on anti-stigma campaigns relating to mental health, for example; it is not obvious at all that these campaigns have had much long-term success.

That is certainly not to say that social change is impossible. The LGBTQI+ community/communities in England have seen profound attitudinal change for the better in the last few decades. That is an interesting comparator, since it was not driven by central policy (indeed, for some of that time government policy was openly hostile, and there were certainly no mass publicly-funded campaigns of support). Such change cannot be assumed, of course, as anyone following the situation of black people in England will be aware. The take-home message seems instead to be that we know very little about how social attitudes change and, more to the point, how we ensure that the changes required by the CRPD will come about. And we cannot assume, given the MCA experience, that it will just happen, even if the relevant legislative reforms occur.

Conclusion

The CRPD matters. It provides an occasion to re-visit and address so much of the past oppression and marginalisation of PWDs. It is, almost certainly, the most significant opportunity in my generation to change the lives of PWDs for the better. The status quo ante has gone on more than long enough.

A good deal of literature is appearing on CPRD requirements, but a good deal less on quite how the noble objectives are to be given form in individual States, and as this chapter has discussed, that brings with it practical problems. None of these should come as a surprise; all have been part of the law and society literature for decades. If we are to see the changes we need, though, we have to engage with the people who have experience in those socio-legal questions, and bring their knowledge to bear on the situation of PWDs. And we will have to work with people whom we sometimes find very difficult, with consequent political ruptures. That may be unpalatable, but it seems to be the only way forward, and it is better that we acknowledge that up front so that we can be aware of, reflect on and debate the manoeuvres as they occur.

Notes

1 Domestic procedure will, of course, be determined by domestic constitutional law. Some legal systems make international human rights treaties directly enforceable; more usually, some form of enacting legislation is required. Even absent such legislation, many systems (including common law systems) allow international conventions such as the CRPD to be considered by courts, even if they are not binding.

2 Of 216,005 applications completed in 2018–19, 99,065 were not granted, but 31,130 of these people had died (NHS Digital 2018–19: Applications tables 4 and 5). These figures also have their context: the mean time for dealing with applications was 147 days, but there was considerable variability. The mean time in three local authorities was greater than a year, and in nine others was greater than nine months. Some applications were not closed for some years (NHS Digital 2018–19: Timeline table 1). The death rate is therefore not entirely surprising, given the demographics of the population in question – roughly 75% of applications concern people over the age of 85 (NHS Digital 2018–19: Applications table 3).

References

Cases

A, B, and C v X and Y [2012] EWHC 2400 (COP).
A Clinical Commissioning Group v N [2017] UKSC 22.
AH [2021] EWCA Civ 1768.
CC v KK and STCC [2012] EWCOP 2136.
HL v the United Kingdom, 45508/99, judgment of 5 October 2004 (ECHR).
Johnson v the United Kingdom, 22520/93, judgment of 24 October 1997 (ECHR).
Kolanis v the United Kingdom, 517/02, judgment of 21 June 2005 (ECHR).
London Borough of Brent v SL [2017] EWCOP 5.
R (Barry) v Gloucestershire (1997) 2 All ER 1 (HL).
R (Davey) v Oxfordshire County Council [2017] EWCA Civ 1308.
Re SB (A Patient: Capacity to Consent to Termination) [2013] EWHC 1417 (COP).
R (Rose) v Thanet Clinical Commissioning Group [2014] EWHC 1182.
R (Ross) v West Sussex PCT [2008] EWHC 2252 (Admin).
Shtukaturov v Russia, 44009/05, judgment of 27 March 2008 (ECHR).

Legislation and Legislative Instruments

Court of Protection Rules 2017 (SI 2017 No 1035 (L.16))
Mental Capacity Act 2005
Mental Capacity (Amendment) Act 2019
Mental Health Act 2007

Books, Journal Articles and Other Texts

Bartlett, P. (2014) 'Reforming the Deprivation of Liberty Safeguards (DOLS): What is it Exactly that We Want?' *Web Journal of Current Legal Issues*, 20(3). Available http://eprints.nottingham.ac.uk/27970/1/465 (accessed 25 November 2022).

Bartlett, P. (2020) 'At the Interface Between Paradigms: English Mental Capacity Law and the CRPD', *Frontiers in Psychiatry*, 11: 570735. Available www.frontiersin.org/articles/10.3389/fpsyt.2020.570735/full (accessed 25 November 2022).

Bartlett, P. (2022) 'Re-thinking the Mental Capacity Act 2005: Towards the Next Generation of Law', *Modern Law Review*, 86(3): 659–700. Available https://doi.org/10.1111/1468-2230.12774 (accessed 13 December 2022).

Clough, B. (2018) 'New Legal Landscapes: (Re)constructing the Boundaries of Mental Capacity Law', *Medical Law Review*, 26(2): 246–75.

Clough, B. (2022) *The Spaces of Mental Capacity Law: Moving Beyond Boundaries*, London: Routledge.

Donnelly, M. (2017) 'Best Interests in the Mental Capacity Act: Time to Say Goodbye?' *Medical Law Review*, 24(3): 318–32.

Family Court Statistics Quarterly: July-September 2019–20 (2021) London: Ministry of Justice. Available www.gov.uk/government/statistics/family-court-statistics-quarterly-july-to-september-2020 (accessed 25 November 2022).

House of Lords (2014) *Mental Capacity Act 2005: Post-Legislative Scrutiny*, HL Paper 139, London: HMSO. Available https://publications.parliament.uk/pa/ld201314/ldselect/ldmentalcap/139/139.pdf (accessed 25 November 2022).

Law Commission (1995) *Mental Incapacity*, Law Com No 231, London: HMSO. Available www.lawcom.gov.uk/app/uploads/2015/04/lc231.pdf (accessed 25 November 2022).

Law Commission (2017) *Mental Capacity and Deprivation of Liberty Impact Assessment.* Available https://s3-eu-west-2.amazonaws.com/lawcom-prod-storage-11jsxou24uy7q/uploads/2017/03/lc372_mental_capacity_impact.pdf (accessed 25 November 2022).

Lindsey, J. (2019) 'Testimonial Injustice and Vulnerability: A Qualitative Analysis of Participation in the Court of Protection', *Social & Legal Studies*, 28(4): 450–69.

Martin, W., Michalowski, S., Stavert, J., Ward, A., Ruck Keene, A., Caughey, C., Hempsey, A. and McGregor, R. (2016) *Three Jurisdictions Report: Towards Compliance with CRPD Art. 12 in Capacity/Incapacity Legislation Across the UK*, Colchester: Essex Autonomy Project. Available https://autonomy.essex.ac.uk/wp-content/uploads/2017/01/EAP-3J-Final-Report-2016.pdf (accessed 25 November 2022).

Mégret, F. (2008) 'The Disabilities Convention: Human Rights of Persons with Disabilities or Disability Rights?' *Human Rights Quarterly*, 30(2): 494–516.

NHS England (2016) *Dementia.* Available www.england.nhs.uk/mental-health/dementia/ (accessed 25 November 2022).

Public Health England (2021) *Learning Disability Profiles*, London: Office for Health Improvement and Disparities. Available https://fingertips.phe.org.uk/profile/learning-disabilities/data (accessed 25 November 2022).

Series, L., Fennell, P., Doughty, J. and Mercer, A. (2017) *Welfare Cases in the Court of Protection: A Statistical Overview*, Cardiff: Cardiff University. Available https://orca.cardiff.ac.uk/id/eprint/118054/1/Series%20Fennell%20Doughty%202017%20Statistical%20overview%20of%20CoP.pdf (accessed 25 November 2022).

Part II

Regulating Coercion and Restrictive Practices

5 Who Approves the Use of Restrictive Practices in Australia? The Case for a Uniform Authorisation Process

John Chesterman

Introduction

Bernadette McSherry has long held great interest in reforming the regulation of restrictive practices, with the aim always of the eventual elimination of their usage (see also Preface and Wilson, Maker, Gooding and Walvisch in Chapter 1 of this volume). Her activity here, which has included multiple significant works (referenced throughout this book, including Melbourne Social Equity Institute 2014; McSherry 2017; McSherry and Maker 2021), probably reached a high point in her work as a commissioner from 2019–2021 in the Royal Commission into Victoria's Mental Health System, with the Royal Commission recommending significant reform.

In this chapter I look at the current amalgam of laws and rules that characterise restrictive practices regulation in the disability, mental health and aged care sectors in Australia. I go on to argue for a clearer and more uniform manner in which restrictive practices might in the future be regulated, and their use diminished.

In Part 1 I outline the practices to which I refer in this chapter. Part 2 considers the mixture of regulatory requirements that currently exist in the disability, aged care and mental health fields. Part 3 identifies the core regulatory challenge as I see it confronting restrictive practices regulation in Australia, which I articulate as amounting to the need to decide whether to adopt a 'consent' or 'authorisation' model. Part 4 looks at missteps that have recently occurred in aged care restrictive practices regulation, while the final section calls for a uniform 'authorisation' approach to restrictive practices regulation in Australia.

I write this chapter from the perspective of someone now working in Queensland (I am a statutory officer with the role of promoting and protecting the rights of Queensland adults with impaired-decision-making ability). Prior to this, I was the Deputy Public Advocate in Victoria.

What Are Restrictive Practices?

In using the term 'restrictive practices' I mean interventions – be they chemical, environmental, physical or mechanical – that seek to modify certain

DOI: 10.4324/9781003350644-7

behaviours of individuals which have in the past attracted the euphemistic title 'behaviours of concern'. In the context of chemical restraints, which are the most utilised of restrictive practices, certainly in the mental health and aged care sectors, it is important to distinguish between a restrictive practice and medication. Although this distinction is not universally agreed upon, those jurisdictions with stronger restrictive practices regulation do distinguish between pharmacological interventions that are used simply to modify behaviour (which are seen as restrictive practices) and those pharmacological interventions that are utilised therapeutically to treat an illness (which are not restrictive practices). Victoria has for many years had relatively strong restrictive practices regulation in disability services. Not unrelatedly, Victoria's key medical consent legislation (*Medical Treatment Planning and Decisions Act 2016*: section 3) defines 'medical treatment' in such a manner that it does not include chemical (or other) restrictive practices (see Freckelton in Chapter 6 in this volume for a discussion of the regulation of chemical restraint).

Current Approval Models

The regulation of restrictive practices in Australia occurs at both the Commonwealth and state and territory levels. It is essentially sector-specific, particularly in the aged care, disability and mental health fields (see McSherry and Maker 2021: 5).

There are two models of regulation in evidence in Australia: what I will term the 'consent' and 'authorisation' models. The 'consent' model involves a requirement for the person affected, or someone on their behalf (a substitute decision-maker), to agree to the use of a restrictive practice. The 'authorisation' model, on the other hand, is the term I use to describe a requirement that a statutorily empowered person or body has oversight of an approval process, which usually involves other regularity and quality assurance requirements. This includes such requirements as the development of a 'behaviour support plan' that identifies strategies that will be used when a restrictive practice is being considered (see, for instance, parts 6A, 6B and 7 of the *Disability Act 2006* (Vic)).

In aged care the consent paradigm is foremost, while in the mental health field the authorisation model is in force. Both approaches are in force in the disability sector in different states and territories.

Disability

The *National Framework for Reducing and Eliminating the Use of Restrictive Practices in the Disability Service Sector* was adopted by Commonwealth, state and territory Disability Ministers in March 2014 (Department of Social Services 2014). It provided high-level commitments to ensure that by 2018 a series of strategies would be in place to reduce restrictive practices usage. While the national framework identified the need for the principles articulated in it to apply across Australia, it did not identify the need for any particular authorisation approach or mechanism to apply across the sector.

As noted earlier, currently in Australia both the consent and authorisation models are in force in the disability field. In Victoria, for instance, one kind of authorisation model is in place whereby a senior government official – the Senior Practitioner – oversees the appointment of 'authorised program officers' who can approve the non-emergency use of restrictive practices that are described in a behaviour support plan that is lodged with the Senior Practitioner (there are special allowances for emergency situations). This model in Victoria also sees the Senior Practitioner responsible for approving particularly incursive practices such as seclusion (*Disability Act 2006* (Vic): parts 6A, 6B and 7). A variation on this model exists in the Australian Capital Territory (*Senior Practitioner Act 2018* (ACT)), where 'panels' are appointed by the Senior Practitioner to approve behaviour support plans (which outline the need for, and detail proposed restrictive practice usage).

This model is to be contrasted with the 'consent' model which is in force, for instance, in the disability sector in Queensland. Here adult recipients of 'disability services' who are subject to non-emergency restrictive practices are able to have those approved on their behalf by a 'guardian for a restrictive practice' (*Guardianship and Administration Act 2000* (Qld): chapter 5B). Queensland legislation does also put in place some elements of an authorisation model, for restrictive practices usage by disability services, in enabling the head of the relevant government department to authorise some restrictive practices for short periods of time (*Disability Services Act 2006* (Qld): part 6). Also the Queensland Civil and Administrative Tribunal retains responsibility for authorising containment and seclusion (note that the Public Guardian can approve containment and seclusion for a period of up to six months; *Guardianship and Administration Act 2000* (Qld): chapter 5B).

It is worth noting that a review is currently underway in Queensland concerning the way in which restrictive practices are regulated in disability services. It is quite feasible that a 'Senior Practitioner' authorisation model will be adopted (see Queensland Government 2022). Until that happens, however, a consent model continues to apply in the Queensland disability sector.

The different approval mechanisms that exist for restrictive practice usage in the disability field survived the introduction of the National Disability Insurance Scheme (NDIS). The arrival of the NDIS saw new national regulatory requirements overlaying existing (or, in the case of some jurisdictions, non-existent) approval regimes.

When the NDIS came into operation, existing state and territory restrictive practices approval regimes (where they existed) remained in place, but new requirements were introduced regarding the registration of behaviour support providers, and the provision of monthly reports on restrictive practices usage to the NDIS Quality and Safeguards Commission (*National Disability Insurance Scheme Act 2013* (Cth): sections 73B and 181H; *National Disability Insurance Scheme (Restrictive Practices and Behaviour Support) Rules 2018* (Cth)). If evidence was needed of the poor state of restrictive practices regulation in Australia, the NDIS Quality and Safeguards Commission (2021: 5; see also Henriques-Gomes 2021) reported more than 1 million instances of 'unauthorised use of restrictive practices' in the year to June 2021.

Mental Health

In the mental health field, state and territory legislation provides requirements for the use of restrictive practices on in-patients. The criteria for their use do not generally require a person's (or a substitute decision-maker's) consent. Rather, legislation tends to empower clinical staff to authorise restrictive practice usage within certain constraints. These include limits on the period for which constraints can be used, and requirements to observe the person being restrained.

For instance, Victoria's *Mental Health Act 2014* (sections 3, 105, 110 and 113) enables the use of 'restrictive interventions', including 'bodily restraint' and seclusion, in particular circumstances in order 'to prevent imminent and serious harm'. Although the *Mental Health and Wellbeing Act 2022* (Vic) (MHWB Act 2022) has overtaken the 2014 Act, it does not come into operation until 1 September 2023 (MHWB Act 2022: section 2).

I note here that the Royal Commission into Victoria's Mental Health System, in which Bernadette McSherry was a commissioner, recommended (2021: 90, recommendation 54) significant changes in Victoria, namely that the state:

- 'act immediately to reduce the use of seclusion and restraint in mental health and wellbeing service delivery, with the aim to eliminate these practices within 10 years';
- 'regulate the use of chemical restraint through legislative provisions in the new Mental Health and Wellbeing Act'; and
- ensure the development of 'a strategy to reduce the use of seclusion and restraint'. (For further background and discussion of the Victorian Royal Commission see also Donnelly in Chapter 2 and Weller in Chapter 3 of this volume.)

The MHWB Act 2022 (Vic) is intended to implement the recommendations of the Victorian Royal Commission. At present, many of the provisions regarding restrictive interventions are largely similar to the 2014 Act, although the MHWB Act 2022 acknowledges that restrictive interventions have 'no inherent therapeutic benefit' (section 81), confirms the goal set by the Victorian Royal Commission of eliminating seclusion and restraint 'within 10 years' (section 12(c)(IX)(B)), and for the first time seeks to regulate the use of chemical restraint (section 3 defines chemical restraint as a restrictive intervention and section 139 regulates 'chemical restraint during transport') (see also Freckelton in Chapter 6 of this volume). Restrictive interventions are currently the subject of ongoing consideration by an Independent Review due to report to the Victorian Government in October 2023 whose recommendations are likely to form the basis of further reforms to the MHWB Act 2022 (Victoria 2022).

Other states and territories regulate restrictive practices in mental health settings in broadly the same manner through their mental health and associated legislation. Queensland's *Mental Health Act 2016* (chapter 8, sections 246, 256 and 270), for instance, provides specific requirements in relation to the use of mechanical restraint, physical restraint and seclusion. Queensland's *Forensic Disability Act 2011* (sections 50, 56 and 61), meanwhile, enables in particular circumstances the use of restraint, seclusion and 'behaviour control medication'.

Aged Care

Until relatively recently, aged care was a sector with no specific legislative requirements concerning restrictive practices approval and usage. That changed after considerable outcry and astonishment greeted the revelations concerning the routine usage of chemical restraints in the sector (see e.g. Royal Australian and New Zealand College of Psychiatrists 2019). However, reliable data here is hard to identify (Royal Commission into Aged Care Quality and Safety 2019: 11–13), as indeed it is in other settings (see e.g. Sara 2020: 194).

That outcry accompanied other contemporaneous scandals, such as revelations about the outrageous treatment of residents at the Oakden Older Persons Mental Health Service in South Australia (see Lander 2018; McSherry 2021 and Diesfeld in Chapter 7 of this volume).

In 2018 the Royal Commission into Aged Care Quality and Safety was established by the Commonwealth Government, which heard about the high use of restrictive practices in aged care settings. This led to new regulatory requirements in the aged care sector that adopted the consent approval model, which I shall discuss shortly.

Other Settings

Other sectors, such as hospital and educational settings, have tended to be devoid of legislated approval regimes for restrictive practice usage. Here professional norms and standards, industry-wide guidelines in some cases and institution-based policies have tended to constitute the regulation of restrictive practices.

I draw attention here briefly to a debate that exists in health settings. Sometimes a restrictive practice is so closely associated with a particular treatment that its approval might fairly be considered to form part of a medical treatment decision; sometimes, however, that nexus does not exist, and a separate approval process is warranted. The use of a sedative in the lead-up to surgery is an obvious example of the former. The use of a low-stimulation environment for someone who has experienced an acquired brain injury – and the requirement that the person not leave that environment for days or even weeks – likely constitutes the latter.

Regulatory Challenge

Restrictive practice usage in Australia is surprisingly widespread (see e.g. NDIS Quality and Safeguards Commission 2021). The regulatory challenge here is to establish a meaningful authorisation scheme while ensuring that restrictive practice usage is exceptional and not normalised. The principal challenge is to see restrictive practice usage dropping; the mere development of a sound authorising environment is not enough.

As I have indicated earlier in this chapter, the two models of restrictive practices regulation are what I have termed the consent (and substitute consent) model and the authorisation model.

My work in the disability sector in Victoria has led me to the strong view that the authorisation model is far superior to the consent model. The reasons for this were developed in an article I co-authored with Michael Williams and Richard Laufer (2014), and were further elaborated upon in a 'reform options' paper I released after moving to Queensland to take up my current role (Public Advocate Queensland 2021).

As I argued in the reform options paper, there are three problems with the consent model.

The first problem is the obvious philosophical one; it is somewhat bizarre to ask a person to agree to their own restrictive practice, and even more odd to hold them to that in situations when they no longer agree with it. Yet this is what is envisaged by enabling a person, or someone on their behalf (a substitute decision-maker), to consent to a restrictive practice. Preventing a person from leaving a building, for instance, on the basis that they previously agreed that they could be prevented from leaving the building, is simply odd (especially when they are actively trying to leave the building), since it effectively inhibits people from changing their mind. The term 'Ulysses pact' is sometimes applied to this kind of 'pre-agreement'.

Usually, of course, it is substitute consent that is envisaged by the 'consent' model, not the person's own consent. This is equally problematic, effectively for the same reason. As I argued in the reform options paper (Public Advocate Queensland 2021: 3; see also Australian Law Reform Commission 2014: 11–13, recommendation 3):

> Modern human rights developments are increasingly requiring any substitute decision-makers to make decisions that the person themselves would likely have made. This means, in the context of restrictive practices authorisation, substitute decision-makers should only consent to restrictive practices that the person themselves would likely have consented to.

The second problem is the invidious position in which the 'consent' model places substitute decision-makers. Ordinarily a substitute decision-maker is acting with the sole intention of improving the life and situation of the person on whose behalf they are making decisions. Indeed increasingly, such decision-makers are being required by human rights-informed legislative developments to make decisions that accord with what the person themselves would want to have happened (see e.g. *Guardianship and Administration Act 2000* (Qld): section 11B). Restrictive practices, however, are often utilised in order to negate a risk posed by the person concerned to others (or to themselves). Asking a substitute decision-maker to approve a restrictive practice suddenly requires them to consider not just the person's interests, but the interests and safety of others.

The third problem concerns the expertise of substitute decision-makers, especially people who are in the role only occasionally (and not professionally). A person who, for instance, is appointed to be the guardian for a family member in Queensland, with the power to consent to restrictive practices, will be highly unlikely to have clinical knowledge in the field of behaviour management, and cannot be expected to know about less restrictive mechanisms for changing behaviour than the use of restrictive practices. They will be hard-pressed to meaningfully query the advice they are receiving, or to object to the giving of their imprimatur. As I argued in the reform options paper (Public Advocate Queensland 2021: 3):

> It would be rare for a person on whom a restrictive practice is proposed, or for their substitute decision-maker (especially in the case of private guardians and attorneys), to have the clinical expertise to identify other less restrictive means of dealing with the circumstances that have given rise to the request to use a restrictive practice.

Recent Aged Care Regulatory Missteps

In this next section I will detail developments over the past four years in the regulation of aged care restrictive practices, because these developments show the challenges involved in creating a sector-specific, and Commonwealth-led, approach to this complex regulatory topic. They also show, I hope, the flaws in the consent model.

In discussing these developments, I identify at the outset three weaknesses in the general approach that has been taken (see Chesterman 2022).

The first is the unfortunate adoption of the consent model by which restrictive practice usage is approved. The second is the undue focus that has been placed on seeing restrictive practices as a 'health' intervention, rather than an intervention on a person's rights. The third, which is related to the second, is that there has been a repeated failure to distinguish restrictive practices from medical treatment.

In 2019 the Quality of Care Principles, made under the *Aged Care Act 1997* (Cth), contained a new requirement that physical restraints could only be used where 'the approved provider has the informed consent of the consumer or the consumer's representative to the use of the restraint, unless the use of the restraint is necessary in an emergency' (Quality of Care Principles 2014, compilation 6, 1 July 2019: sections 15F(1) and 15G). The use of chemical restraint, meanwhile, required a medical practitioner's approval, with the person's representative needing only to be advised that the restraint was being used.

This was a curious foray by the Commonwealth into the regulation of restrictive practices. Among the shortcomings of this approach was the fact that physical restraints could be consented to on a person's behalf by their 'representative', who was someone who could be appointed by the person or who indeed could self-nominate, so long as the aged care provider agreed with the person playing that role. Chemical restraints – which for reasons outlined earlier are distinct from medical intervention – could be provided with a medical practitioner's approval (Quality of Care Principles 2014, compilation 6, 1 July 2019: sections 5 and 15G).

Failing to identify the distinction between restrictive practices and medical treatment, a note was added to the next iteration of the Quality of Care Principles 2014 (compilation 7, 29 November 2019: note 2 following section 15G(1)), outlining that the states and territories had their own laws detailing who can provide substitute 'consent to the prescribing of medication'. The problematic implication however conveyed by the very inclusion of this note was that chemical restraints are always a form of medical treatment, which, of course, they are not.

In its final report the Royal Commission into Aged Care Quality and Safety addressed the important need to regulate the use of restrictive practices in aged care settings, but unfortunately it endorsed the consent approval model, recommending (2021: recommendation 17) that:

> The *Quality of Care Principles 2014* (Cth) should be amended . . . to provide that the use of restrictive practices in aged care . . . should . . . only be used . . . in accordance with relevant State or Territory laws and with the documented informed consent of the person receiving care or someone authorised by law to give consent on that person's behalf.

In 2021 new provisions were inserted into the *Aged Care Act 1997* (Cth) obliging the Quality of Care Principles to 'require that informed consent is given to the use of a restrictive practice in relation to a care recipient' (*Aged Care and Other Legislation Amendment (Royal Commission Response No. 1) Act 2021* (Cth): section 3, inserting section 54.10(1)(f) into the *Aged Care Act 1997* (Cth)).

Further changes were then made to the Quality of Care Principles in July 2021 (Quality of Care Principles 2014, compilation 9, 1 July 2021: sections 4, 15FA(1)(f)) requiring 'informed consent' to be given to any restrictive practice usage by the person or, where the person was unable to do so, by 'the restrictive practices substitute decision-maker'. This term was defined to mean:

> a person or body that, under the law of the State or Territory in which the care recipient is provided with aged care, can give informed consent to:
>
> a. the use of the restrictive practice in relation to the care recipient; and
> b. if the restrictive practice is chemical restraint – the prescribing of medication for the purpose of using the chemical restraint.

Later reforms then required the preparation of behaviour support plans in relation to restrictive practices usage (Quality of Care Principles 2014, compilation 10, 1 September 2021: part 4A, division 5).

The July 2021 changes did two things. First, they raised an immediate question of who could claim to be a 'restrictive practices substitute decision-maker', as this required knowing who, under state and territory laws, had power to consent generally to restrictive practice usage (a complex question in some jurisdictions, as I shall discuss).

Second, these changes sought in effect to officially identify chemical restraints as a form of medical treatment by seeming to empower medical treatment decision-makers to authorise chemical restraint usage.

On this second point, the change gave rise to the odd, legally questionable and very confusing scenario wherein some individuals, whose status and powers stem from state and territory legislation, suddenly had these powers broadened by federal delegated legislation. This change suggested that a medical treatment decision-maker under state or territory law, whose powers may not have extended to the ability to authorise the use of chemical restraints, was suddenly being given such power in relation to chemical restraint usage in aged care facilities. The legal and practical implications of this scenario are discussed using examples from Queensland and Victoria in the next section.

Who is the 'Restrictive Practices Substitute Decision-Maker'?

This new requirement that the consent of a 'restrictive practices substitute decision-maker' is needed before a restrictive practice can be used in non-emergency situations (where the person themselves is unable to consent to the restrictive practice) begged an immediate question: who, according to the law in a particular state or territory, has the power to play that role? In Queensland, for instance, the matter is complex and unclear.

Queensland's *Guardianship and Administration Act 2000* (chapter 5B, part 3 and section 80R) enables guardians to be appointed for restrictive practices, but only in relation to the receipt of 'disability services' by 'an adult with an intellectual or cognitive disability'. While that power clearly would not extend to restrictive practices in aged care settings, guardians can also be appointed (section 12, schedule 2) to make decisions concerning 'personal' matters, which are defined by reference to a broad non-exclusive list of possible matters, which does not specify restrictive practices generally (outside of usage in disability services). Likewise, attorneys under the *Powers of Attorney Act 1998* (Qld) (section 32, schedule 2) can be appointed to make decisions about 'personal matters', which similarly are defined by reference to a broad non-exclusive list that does not include reference to restrictive practices.

The legal question generated by the Commonwealth's changed requirements for the use of restrictive practices in aged care settings was this: does the power of guardians and attorneys in Queensland to make decisions about 'personal' matters extend to the authorisation of restrictive practices?

A similar question arose in Victoria as to whether an attorney, under an enduring power of attorney with power to make decisions about 'personal matters', or a guardian appointed by the Victorian Civil and Administrative Tribunal with power to make decisions about 'personal' matters, thereby had power to authorise restrictive practices (including in residential aged care settings). Neither the *Powers of Attorney Act 2014* (Vic) nor the *Guardianship and Administration Act 2019* (Vic) specifically enable attorneys or guardians to authorise restrictive practices, but the question was whether the category of 'personal matters' stretches that far. Similar to the situation in Queensland, the Victorian definition of 'personal matters' is accompanied by a non-exclusive list of examples which does not include reference to restrictive practices (*Powers of Attorney Act 2014* (Vic): sections 3 and 22; *Guardianship and Administration Act 2019* (Vic): sections 3 and 30).

An important decision of the Victorian Civil and Administrative Tribunal (VCAT) in early 2022 found that the power of guardians who are appointed to make decisions about 'personal' (as opposed to financial) matters does not extend to the power to authorise the use of 'restraints'. The restraints in this particular case were physical restraints that were considered to be necessary in order for the person in question to be provided with medical treatment. VCAT found in *HYY (Guardianship)* (2022: para 206) that a 'guardian's power to make decisions about medical treatment . . . does not extend to making decisions authorising forcible physical restraint in order to overcome resistance to medical treatment', although the tribunal noted that the provision of a regular anaesthetic would be a different matter (paras 47 and 106). The tribunal did ultimately decide, however, that it could authorise the use of restraints in cases such as the one before it, in order to ensure a person's compliance with a guardian's medical treatment decision.

The main outcome from this case was the finding that a guardian with power to make decisions about 'personal' matters under the *Guardianship and Administration Act 2019* (Vic) does not have the power to authorise restrictive practices. Central to the tribunal's reasoning was the consideration that other earlier Victorian legislation (in the disability and mental health fields) specifically created approval mechanisms for restrictive practices; the fact that the subsequent guardianship legislation did not do likewise suggested that parliament had not envisaged that restrictive practices could be authorised under it. In addition, the tribunal drew in its reasoning from the Victorian *Charter of Human Rights and Responsibilities Act 2006*, finding in *HYY (Guardianship)* (2022: para 175) that 'it is not the most Charter compatible reading of the definition of "personal matter" to say that it can include the imposition of forcible physical restraint'.

There are potential implications from this case for a jurisdiction such as Queensland, which similarly enables guardians to make decisions about 'personal' matters and which also has similar human rights legislation in the form of the *Human Rights Act 2019* (Qld). However, as noted earlier, one difference in Queensland is that the guardianship legislation does specifically enable the appointment of guardians for restrictive practices in relation to disability services. This leads to a question of whether the Queensland Parliament, in not specifying that guardians can consent to aged care restrictive practices, meant for guardians not to have this power, or whether the legislature merely had not given the matter any thought.

The legally dubious circumstance of having Commonwealth delegated legislation purport to broaden the powers of individuals appointed under state and territory laws was curiously sought to be resolved by a further amendment to the *Aged Care Act 1997* (Cth). This amendment was proposed in a bill introduced prior to the 2022 federal election (*Aged Care and Other Legislation Amendment (Royal Commission Response No. 2) Bill 2021* (Cth): section 1) and was ultimately included in legislation that was passed following the election (*Aged Care and Other Legislation Amendment (Royal Commission Response) Act 2022* (Cth): schedule 9). It enables the Quality of Care Principles to 'make provision for, or in relation to, the persons or bodies who may give informed consent to the use of a restrictive practice in relation to a care recipient if the care recipient lacks capacity to give that consent'.

This change, in essence, ostensibly makes specific the power of the Commonwealth to identify who can consent to restrictive practices.

The problem with this whole approach (current at the time of writing in August 2022) is that the Commonwealth, in consistently attempting to identify and authorise substitute decision-makers who can authorise aged care restrictive practices, is in effect seeking to provide additional powers to people exercising roles that have been created under state or territory legislation (such as medical decision-makers, guardians and attorneys). In other words, the Commonwealth is effectively seeking to give more powers to some substitute decision-makers than they actually have under the state and territory laws that create their roles. In addition to the confusion that this causes, it will lead to all sorts of odd developments, such as requiring that people be told that their automatic or appointed medical decision-makers may also have the power to approve them being confined to a room if they are living, one day, in an aged care facility.

A Uniform Approach?

It is worth considering the difficult path the Commonwealth has trodden in the attempt to regulate restrictive practices in aged care. I am hopeful it will demonstrate both the pitfalls of Commonwealth regulation in this area, and of the consent model, as well as make the case for more uniform requirements. Such uniform requirements need to occur at state and territory level, since it is at this level of government that most substitute decision-making laws exist.

In my reform options paper published in October 2021 (Public Advocate Queensland 2021) I called for a uniform approach to restrictive practices regulation in Queensland, utilising the 'Senior Practitioner' model of restrictive practices authorisation.

To my mind the preferred version of the Senior Practitioner model is the one I discussed earlier that operates in the disability field in Victoria and the Australian Capital Territory (ACT) (*Disability Act 2006* (Vic): parts 6A, 6B and 7; *Senior Practitioner Act 2018* (ACT)). This sees a state or territory official (the Senior Practitioner) appointed who oversees the selection of authorised program officers (in Victoria) or an authorisation panel (in the ACT), which are typically located at the service provider level. Restrictive practices, outside emergency situations, can only be approved when they are included in a behaviour support plan that is lodged with the Senior Practitioner. The Senior Practitioner exercises clinical governance and oversight functions by, among other things, reviewing and auditing behaviour support plans, and in monitoring the approval of restrictive practices.

This model could quite easily be adapted for non-disability environments, including in aged care, education and out-of-home child protection settings. It could also be applied, with some modifications, in mental health settings, where 'emergency' restrictive practices usage is more typical than in other settings (see Melbourne Social Equity Institute 2014: 164–66, for a call for 'uniformity' of restrictive practices regulation within the mental health sector). This might involve expansion of the regulatory powers of state and territory Chief Psychiatrists to oversee restrictive practice approvals by clinical staff.

The mere use of a Senior Practitioner model does not automatically, of course, mean that restrictive practice usage will fall. For it to work effectively, the Senior Practitioner's office needs to be adequately resourced. In addition, the Senior Practitioner needs to have sufficient independence and authority to enable a reasonably wide array of important roles and functions to be performed. These ideally include the following: practice leadership generally in forcing down restrictive practice usage; rigorous auditing of behaviour support plans; the provision of expert advice on alternative strategies to restrictive practice usage; the overriding of inappropriate authorisations of particular restrictive practices; the taking of administrative and other action (including deregistration) where there has been inappropriate approval given to restrictive practice usage; and the making of referrals (including to police where this is warranted).

The general appeal of this model is that it ensures that clinical expertise can be brought to bear on the judgments of those individuals who are approving, and those who are implementing, restrictive practices. As one staff member at a disability service provider put it to me, when I was discussing this model, it enables someone with clinical expertise to go 'toe to toe' with the provider on the rationale for the restrictive practice usage (something one could not expect a non-expert person in a substitute consenting role to be able to do).

It is important also to note that moving from a consent model does not mean that the individual concerned, and their supporters, suddenly do not have to be involved in discussing any restrictive practice usage. Quite the contrary, they should be informed at every stage, and they should be informed in such a manner that promotes their understanding of the concerns that have led to a restrictive practice being proposed, and engages any ideas the person or their supporters may have about how to address those concerns less restrictively than through usage of a restrictive practice. Indeed, one improvement to existing versions of the Senior Practitioner model would be to build in a more effective way of ensuring the oversight of people around the individual to what is occurring (so that they can advocate and seek reviews of the use of particular restrictive practices where they consider this to be warranted). Suffice it to say, the model also requires, for it to be effective, simple and cost-free review mechanisms (which include empowering the person concerned, or their supporters, to take matters to the state or territory civil and administrative tribunal where the Senior Practitioner's judgment itself is being questioned).

In this reform process we must continually remind ourselves, as Bernadette McSherry has always reminded us, that the goal here is not just the clearer approval process for the use of restrictive practices. That is merely one of the important mechanisms through which we can advance toward the actual ultimate goal; namely the reduction and eventual elimination of restrictive practice usage.

References

Australian Law Reform Commission (2014) *Equality, Capacity and Disability in Commonwealth Laws*. Available www.alrc.gov.au/publication/equality-capacity-and-disability-in-commonwealth-laws-alrc-report-124/ (accessed 8 November 2022).

Chesterman, J. (2022) 'Stopping the Inappropriate Use of Restrictive Practices', *Australian Ageing Agenda*, 17 May. Available www.australianageingagenda.com.au/tag/restrictive-practices/ (accessed 8 November 2022).

Department of Social Services (2014) *National Framework for Reducing and Eliminating the Use of Restrictive Practices in the Disability Service Sector*. Available www.dss.gov.au/our-responsibilities/disability-and-carers/publications-articles/policy-research/national-framework-for-reducing-and-eliminating-the-use-of-restrictive-practices-in-the-disability-service-sector (accessed 8 November 2022).

Henriques-Gomes, L. (2021) 'NDIS Providers Used Unauthorised Restraints on Clients Over a Million Times in 12 Months', *The Guardian*, 10 November. Available www.theguardian.com/australia-news/2021/nov/10/ndis-providers-used-unauthorised-restraints-on-clients-over-a-million-times-in-12-months (accessed 8 November 2022).

HYY (Guardianship) (2022) VCAT 97.

Lander, B. (2018) *Oakden: A Shameful Chapter in South Australia's History*, Independent Commissioner Against Corruption. Available www.icac.sa.gov.au/publications/published-reports/oakden (accessed 8 November 2022).

McSherry, B. (2017) 'Regulating Seclusion and Restraint in Health Care Settings: The Promise of the Convention on the Rights of Persons with Disabilities', *International Journal of Law and Psychiatry*, 53: 39–44.

McSherry, B. (2021) 'The Intractable Use of Restraint, Organisational Culture and "Othering": Lessons from the Oakden Scandal', in B. McSherry and Y. Maker (eds) *Restrictive Practices in Health Care and Disability Settings: Legal, Policy and Practical Responses*, Abingdon: Routledge, 219–35.

McSherry, B. and Maker, Y. (2021) 'Restrictive Practices: Options and Opportunities', in B. McSherry and Y. Maker (eds) *Restrictive Practices in Health Care and Disability Settings: Legal, Policy and Practical Responses*, Abingdon: Routledge, 3–15.

Melbourne Social Equity Institute (2014) *Seclusion and Restraint Project: Report*, University of Melbourne. Available https://socialequity.unimelb.edu.au/__data/assets/pdf_file/0017/2004722/Seclusion-and-Restraint-report.PDF (accessed 8 November 2022).

Mental Health Act 2014 (Vic).

Mental Health and Wellbeing Act 2022 (Vic).

NDIS Quality and Safeguards Commission (2021) *Activity Report 1 July 2020 to 30 June 2021*. Available www.ndiscommission.gov.au/media-centre/ndis-commission-releases-12-monthly-activity-report (accessed 8 November 2022).

Public Advocate Queensland (2021) *Improving the Regulation of Restrictive Practices in Queensland: A Way Forward*. Available www.justice.qld.gov.au/__data/assets/pdf_file/0004/697729/20211005-opa-restrictive-practices-reform-options-paper.pdf (accessed 8 November 2022).

Queensland Government (2022) *Restrictive Practices Review*. Available www.dsdsatsip.qld.gov.au/our-work/disability-services/disability-connect-queensland/positive-behaviour-support-restrictive-practices/restrictive-practices-review (accessed 8 November 2022).

Royal Australian and New Zealand College of Psychiatrists (2019) *Misuse of Restrictive Practices in Aged Care Deeply Concerning Say Psychiatrists*. Available www.ranzcp.org/news-policy/news-archive/news-archive-2019/misuse-of-restrictive-practices-in-aged-care-deepl (accessed 8 November 2022).

Royal Commission into Aged Care Quality and Safety (2019) *Background Paper 4 – Restrictive Practices in Residential Aged Care in Australia*. Available https://agedcare.royalcommission.gov.au/publications/background-paper-4-restrictive-practices-residential-aged-care-australia (accessed 8 November 2022).

Royal Commission into Aged Care Quality and Safety (2021) *Recommendations*. Available https://agedcare.royalcommission.gov.au/sites/default/files/2021-03/final-report-recommendations.pdf (accessed 8 November 2022).

Royal Commission into Victoria's Mental Health System (2021) *Final Report, Summary and Recommendations*. Available https://finalreport.rcvmhs.vic.gov.au/ (accessed 8 November 2022).

Sara, G. (2020) 'Showing Restraint: The Uses and Limitations of Data in Supporting Restraint Reduction', in B. McSherry and Y. Maker (eds) *Restrictive Practices in*

Health Care and Disability Settings: Legal, Policy and Practical Responses, Abingdon: Routledge, 188–202.
Victoria (2022) *Parliamentary Debates*, Legislative Assembly, 23 June (James Merlino, Deputy Premier, Second Reading Speech of Mental Health and Wellbeing Bill).
Williams, M., Chesterman, J. and Laufer, R. (2014) 'Consent Versus Scrutiny: Restricting Liberties in Post-Bournewood Victoria', *Journal of Law and Medicine*, 21(3): 641–60.

6 Chemical Restraint Use and Reform in Health Care and Disability Settings

Ian Freckelton

Introduction

The 2017 report into the provision of care at the Oakden Older Persons Mental Health Service in Adelaide thrust into Australia's public gaze many uncomfortable issues about how persons in congregate care are managed and cared for. Among these was the use of excessive levels of sedating medication polypharmacy that was not clinically justified, and a variety of forms of restrictive intervention, including physical, mechanical and chemical restraint, as well as the use of seclusion (Groves et al. 2017). However, it is apparent that comparable issues exist in relation to what is often termed 'chemical restraint' (the definition of which is discussed later) in many settings other than aged care residences.

Debates about the unnecessary or excessive use of chemical restraint have occurred in multiple contexts, including emergency management scenarios in ambulance transport by paramedics (Cheney et al. 2006; Weiss et al. 2012; Burnett et al. 2015); care provided in hospital accident and emergency departments (Cannon, Sprivulis and McCarthy 2001; Weiss et al. 2012); and medication responses in settings for persons with mental illness (Muir-Cochrane, Grimmer et al. 2020; Maker and McSherry 2019; Danda 2020), persons with intellectual disability (McGillivray and McCabe 2004; Matson and Boisjoli 2009; Edwards et al. 2020), persons with brain injuries (Williamson et al. 2016a, 2016b) and persons living in aged care residences (Lee et al. 2021; Robins et al. 2021; Peisah, Jessop and Breen 2020; Maker 2022).

The role of restrictive interventions has become internationally controversial over the past two decades. Bernadette McSherry and her colleagues at the Melbourne Social Equity Institute have been at the forefront of working toward elimination of such interventions (Melbourne Social Equity Institute 2014), their work culminating in the leading international work on the subject, *Restrictive Practices in Health Care and Disability Settings* (McSherry and Maker 2021a). In addition, McSherry was a commissioner on the Royal Commission into Victoria's Mental Health System (2021) which endorsed the impetus toward such reform. In turn, the *Mental Health and Wellbeing Act 2022* (Vic) (MHWB Act 2022), which implemented the Royal Commission's

DOI: 10.4324/9781003350644-8

recommendations, has resulted in a new level of oversight in relation to chemical restraint as part of a package of reforms directed toward eliminating all forms of restrictive interventions in mental health and wellbeing services (section 161(1)(g)–(h)). (See also the discussion of reforming restrictive interventions by Chesterman in Chapter 5 of this volume.)

Inhibitions on freedom of movement and autonomy by way of restrictive interventions take place in both an acute and a chronic setting, but most critical attention has been given to the chronic setting, leaving something of a policy disjunction between the approaches used in the two categories of settings. However, the purported objective of restrictive interventions in all environments is compassionate and by way of the exercise of a duty of care to the person and those in their vicinity – to reduce the potential for dangerousness of a person to themselves or to others, namely fellow detainees or residents, visitors and staff (see e.g. MHWB Act 2022: section 127; *Mental Health Act 2016* (Qld): sections 247, 249 and 250). Thus, from the perspective of those with obligations toward staff and others in a number of workplaces, the usage of restrictive interventions arises at least in part from the discharge of occupational health and safety responsibilities which extend to all persons present in workplace settings.

The issues raised by the use of chemical restraint are significant both by reason of the number and diversity of persons affected and the importance of the human rights involved (Jessop and Peisah 2021; Maker and McSherry 2019; Breen 2019; McSherry and Gooding 2013; McSherry 2008). For instance, about half of those in residential aged care facilities and up to 80% of persons with dementia have been identified as being prescribed psychotropic medications (Peisah and Skladzien 2014; see also Banerjee 2009), many of them for the purpose of modifying behaviour that is considered antisocial or dangerous to the person or others, including staff providing them with care.

A significant reform movement has gathered international momentum to eliminate or at least substantially reduce the use of mechanical and physical restraints and of seclusion (McSherry and Maker 2021a; World Health Organization 2019; Human Rights Council 2017). In Germany, this has found expression in a decision by its Constitutional Court that the use of mechanical restraint in patients for more than 30 minutes requires a judge's immediate decision (Flammer, Hirch and Steinert 2021). In Australia, the National Mental Health Commission (Australian and New Zealand College of Psychiatrists 2021) and the Royal Commission into Victoria's Mental Health System (2021) have endorsed the impetus toward reduction and ultimate elimination of restrictive interventions. However, until latterly, chemical restraint has not been the focus of reform. In some respects, this is surprising, as the use of prescribed medications to inhibit the risks of problematic behaviour in care environments has long been widespread, in part so as to avoid the use of other forms of restrictive intervention.

This chapter focuses upon the usage of chemical restraint, also called 'rapid tranquillisation' in some literature (Nadkarni et al. 2015; Dickinson and Clark

2020; Cookson 2018; Hirsch and Steinert 2019), which is defined as the administration of pharmaceutical drugs to control a person's behaviour, rather than to provide treatment. A distinctive contribution of this chapter is that it reflects on the impetus toward eliminating, or at least substantially reducing, the incidence of chemical restraint across a variety of settings. These include the transport of patients to hospital by paramedics, the emergency department setting, residential aged care and inpatient mental health wards. It also identifies common forms of pharmacotherapy restraint; grapples with the 'dual purpose conundrum'; and considers definitional issues in respect of what constitutes chemical restraint. It then reviews the recommendations for reform from the Royal Commission into Victoria's Mental Health System and the Commonwealth Royal Commission into Violence, Abuse, Neglect and Exploitation of People with Disability, before making observations about the trajectory of likely future reforms.

Common Forms of Chemical Restraint and Their Consequences

The term 'chemical restraint' is value-laden as it connotes the usage of 'chemicals' introduced involuntarily into a person's body (often against their will) to manage their conduct or for 'organisational convenience' (Robins et al. 2021). The deployment of chemical restraint as a 'compeller of the peace' or as a management tool has a history of some duration – in the past, bromides, chloral, hyoscine, paraldehyde, morphine and later barbiturates have all fulfilled this function, by a combination of heavy sedation and partial anaesthesia (Shorter 1997). It is controversial because of the fact that it inherently constitutes the use of force against a distressed person. By reason of it depriving individuals of autonomy and on occasions dignity, it has multiple ethical and human rights ramifications (Kumble and McSherry 2010) and can have significant counter-therapeutic effects (Gallagher 2016). It has the potential to be counter-productive in terms of its adverse impact upon constructive therapeutic relationships with clinical teams; it can erode the assumption of personal responsibility for actions on the part of subjects; and, by reason of being experienced as an assault, can generate anger, feelings of powerlessness, betrayal, fear (Greenberg, Moore-Duncan and Herron 1996; Mayers et al. 2010; Yap et al. 2017) and even post-traumatic stress disorder. There can also be adverse effects in terms of trauma and damage to morale and therapeutic relationships for staff who have authorised or supervised it (Chieze et al. 2019). Another aspect of chemical restraint is that it can render people additionally vulnerable to abuse because of their inability to resist physically or communicate what has happened to them, including while under the effects of medication (Chief Psychiatrist of Tasmania 2017).

There are six major categories of medications that can be used to control behaviour. Each also has the potential to be used for therapeutic purposes. They are:

- antipsychotic medications, such as Olanzapine and Risperidone;
- benzodiazepine medications, such as Diazepam and Nitrazepam;

- mood stabilisers, such as Clonazepam and Lithium carbonate;
- anaesthetic agents, such as ketamine;
- antidepressants, such as Fluoxetine and Sertraline Hydrochloride; and
- hormonal medications, such as Cyproterone acetate (New South Wales Department of Communities and Justice 2021; see also Royal Commission into Violence, Abuse, Neglect and Exploitation of People with Disability 2021: 15).

Although relatively little has been documented in the clinical literature about the adverse effects of chemical restraint (de Bruijn et al. 2020), what is known is that the usage of agents that have the potential to operate as chemical restraint is extensive across a variety of contexts and can be experienced as oppressive and distressing by patients (Edwards et al. 2020), although staff may regard the option as 'more kind' than mechanical restraint (Trivedi, Shelly and Park 2009). For instance, censuses of the residential and nursing home population in Leicestershire, England, disclosed a prevalence of the prescription of antipsychotic medication of between 29.1% and 30.7% between 1990 and 1997 (Lindesay, Matthews and Jagger 2003). A 2006 study of 12 nursing homes across three English cities found 48% of residents to be taking a psychotic medication (Fossey et al. 2006). Subsequently, Banerjee (2009: 5) conducted a review of the use of antipsychotic medications for people with dementia and concluded that 'these drugs appear to have only a limited positive effect in treating . . . symptoms but can cause significant harm to people with dementia'. She acknowledged that there are groups, including persons for whom there is severe and complex risk, where there may be value in the use of antipsychotic medications, but expressed concern that 'they are too often used as a first-line response to behavioural difficulty in dementia rather than as a considered second-line treatment when other non-pharmacological approaches have failed' (Banerjee 2009: 5).

Views about chemical restraint differ, in part depending on the category of person consulted. In an extensive survey, published in 2017, for instance, attitudes amongst clinicians, carers and consumers were elicited and compared. Only a small minority of clinicians stated that they believed that it was feasible to eliminate chemical restraint (13%) and, compared with clinicians, both carers and consumers were significantly more likely to believe that elimination of chemical restraint was both desirable and feasible (Kinner et al. 2017: 539).

In *An NHS Trust v ST (Refusal of Deprivation of Liberty Order)* (2022: para. 37) Justice MacDonald provided a judicial perspective. He expressed significant concerns about the use of chemical restraint in relation to a minor with Autism Spectrum Disorder:

> The hospital takes the view that without this chemical sedation ST's behaviour would now be unmanageable. Whilst it is said that this tranquilising medication is being administered in accordance with internal guidance provided by the relevant internal medication protocol, I remain to be convinced that this is an appropriate course of action

> without authorisation of the court in circumstances where the purpose of the medication is plainly one of restraint, and hence, arguably, the deprivation of ST's liberty.
>
> (see also Tingleff et al. 2017)

It has been asserted that the threat of chemical and other restraint is itself used on occasion as a management tool by those running detention environments in order to secure compliance (see assertions made on behalf of the complainant in *LB v AJ* 2021; See also Weller in Chapter 3 of this volume). It has also been found that chemical restraint has been utilised for collateral and impermissible purposes, such as to obtain a blood sample from a patient (*College of Nurses of Ontario v Theodossiou* 2020). On occasions, too, the agents utilised for chemical restraint, particularly older generation anti-psychotic medications, can generate adverse reactions, such as Parkinsonian or dystonic reactions, as well as psychological distress (see e.g. *Conway v Jaques* 2005: para. 25). The process of administration of chemical restraint against a person's will can involve significant infliction of physical force (see e.g, *LB (Re)* 2010), which in turn can have traumatic consequences.

The Dual Purpose Conundrum

There is often ambiguity as to the purposes for which chemical restraint is prescribed and administered by clinicians (McSherry and Tellez 2016; Hu et al. 2019: 21). Three Western Australian decisions illustrate the issue. For instance, in *Re Application for Guardianship Order (BCB)* (2002) the Guardianship and Administration Board of Western Australia was asked to determine whether the use of chemical and physical restraint on BCB, an elderly man with dementia who resided in an aged care facility, constituted medical treatment. The Board was required to draw upon the prevailing definition of chemical restraint, namely, 'the intentional use of medication to control a person's behaviour when no medically identified condition is being treated, where the treatment is not necessary for the condition or amounts to overtreatment for the condition'. BCB was intermittently agitated and physically aggressive. He was given the anti-psychotic Serenace as a 'calmative' and to control his delusions.

The Board concluded that a clear distinction could not be made between the usage of medication for behaviour and control of symptomatology:

> In relation to chemical restraint it may be arguable that a medical practitioner may prescribe drugs for a particular person to control inappropriate behaviour relating to an underlying medical condition and when the drug is being used for that purpose, it is treatment. However, if the drug is used for behaviour management for the convenience of staff it would fall outside that category.
>
> (*Re Application for Guardianship Order (BCB)* 2002: 347)

It determined that the relevant purpose needed to be decided on a case-by-case basis (see also *Re BTO* 2004).

Six years after the *BCB* decision, the State Administrative Tribunal in Western Australia was required to consider a comparable scenario in relation to a 59-year-old man with an acquired brain injury, JP, who resided in an aged care facility (*Re JP* 2008). It rejected the argument advanced by the Public Advocate that an antipsychotic medication, olanzapine (Zyprexa), for suppression of his more aggressive behaviour, and another older generation antipsychotic, Largactil, prescribed to reduce his delusions, was not a restraint. The tribunal was critical of the definition of 'chemical restraint,' observing that 'the definition refers to the use of medication as a way of controlling a person's behaviour when that intervention is indicated only by a perceived need to control the behaviour' (*Re JP* 2008: para. 63). The tribunal reasoned that 'if the purpose is to intentionally control a person's movement or behaviour (other than the treatment of a diagnosed mental illness), it is my view that the intervention is properly characterised as restraint and not treatment' (*Re JP* 2008: para. 66).

Employing similar reasoning, when the same tribunal considered whether ADP, a man with frontal and temporal lobe dementia who was living in a nursing home and was being administered olanzapine in his food without his knowledge, was receiving the medication as a treatment or to address his behaviour, it found that the medication was to 'keep him settled': 'The amount given is at the lower end of the recommended dosage but on the evidence available indicates some level of restraint is intended' (*Re ADP* 2005: para. 27).

The three decisions are illustrative of the difficulty of disentangling the purposes for the administration of antipsychotics, especially to the elderly, where it is common that prescription and administration have interconnected dual purposes (Chandler, White and Willmott 2017; Sara 2021).

Use of Chemical Restraint in Different Settings and the Impetus Toward Reduction

Use of Chemical Restraint in the Pre-hospital Setting

The clinical literature contains many expressions of concern by paramedics about the risks of assault posed to them, as well as to their patients, when patients manifest significant agitation prior to being conveyed to hospital (see e.g. Cheney et al. 2006; Weiss et al. 2012). An aspect of this has been the escalation in community use of crystal methamphetamine and associated drugs (Jones, Usher and Woods 2019; Willacy 2015; Hagan 2013).

A number of analyses have been conducted of the intra-muscular use of chemical restraint options such as the hypnotic-sedative, midazolam (Weiss et al. 2012); the anaesthetic, ketamine (Cheney et al. 2006; Hick and Ho 2005; Burnett et al. 2015; Katkhuda 2021); and the antipsychotic, haloperidol (Macht 2014), a significant percentage of the time in conjunction with physical restraint during transport of patients to hospital (Weiss et al. 2012). Cheney et al. (2006) reported a 28% correlation between use of chemical restraint and assaults on emergency services personnel. Much of the paramedic literature focusses on the combination of occupational health and safety issues and the risks posed by patients to themselves, when combative, distressed or agitated (Maguire et al. 2014; Losonczi and Hanis 2022), including as a result of ingestion of substances and/or mental illness. There is comparatively little international impetus in this setting to reduce the use of chemical restraint, with the principal focus in the clinical literature being upon risks posed to paramedics by patients.

Use of Chemical Restraint in the Emergency Department Setting

Persons who are mentally ill and/or affected by drugs such as crystal methamphetamine present regularly to accident and emergency departments, whether conveyed to them by paramedics, police or otherwise. They pose risks of disruption, injury and distress to staff and patients, as well as physical damage to the environment. Although the conduct that is the focus of attempts at mitigation or remediation can have a number of aetiologies, it is often termed in the accident and emergency context 'acute severe behavioural disturbance' (Australian and New Zealand College of Anaesthetists 2019).

As long ago as 2001, a study of 116 emergency departments in Australasian hospitals found that chemical restraint was used in not just some but all departments (Cannon, Sprivulis and McCarthy 2001). The commonest agents used were haloperidol (93%), midazolam (82%) and diazepam (53%) (compare Richards, Derlet and Duncan 1998). The study found that manual restraint (87%) was frequently used as a prelude to chemical or, less frequently, mechanical restraint (69%). Seclusion was used in 23% of Australasian emergency departments. The authors identified little formal training in, or documentation or audit of, pharmacological restraint in such contexts, despite the important clinical, occupational health and medico-legal issues associated with it. Studies in other countries have made similar findings and identified lack of knowledge and reflection about chemical restraint (see e.g. Cunha et al. 2016).

In the intervening years, controversies have grown in relation to the use of psychotropic agents in emergency department settings (Currier 2003; Stefan 2006). In a 2020 meta-synthesis, for instance, it was identified that there had been a reduction in the use of chemical restraint in emergency department settings, but a need for more standardised data exists so as to enable better comparisons to be made between health care settings and countries (Muir-Cochrane, Oster et al. 2020). However, also in 2020 a study was published about the security calls for unarmed threats ('Code Greys') in Victorian emergency departments during 2016 (Knott et al. 2020). Details were analysed in relation to 494 persons who had been admitted, with chemical restraint being used for 78.5% of patients ($n = 388$), physical restraint for 33.4% ($n = 165$) and mechanical restraint for 59.9% ($n = 296$). What was particularly pronounced was the frequent use of sedation, often in conjunction with other forms of restrictive intervention.

The 'Statement on the Use of Restrictive Practices in Emergency Departments' by the Australasian College for Emergency Medicine (2022) notes that the term 'chemical restraint' refers to the administration of medication for the primary aim of controlling behaviour, rather than providing safe care. It states that chemical restraint should not occur in an emergency department but pointedly creates a key exception: 'The use of medication to allow the safe assessment and treatment of the patient in the ED is not considered chemical restraint'. It requires the adoption of a minimally restrictive approach when medications are administered for safe assessment, with a person being invited to consent to such medication 'in a manner without pressure or coercion' and staff aiming 'to collaborate with the person where possible':

> The aim of safe assessment is never to render the patient unconscious, but to reduce their level of arousal in order to safely assess and care for them. The person must be placed in an area of the department with access to appropriate staffing, monitoring, and resuscitation equipment to maintain a safe level of sedation.
>
> (Australasian College for Emergency Medicine 2022: 4)

Two considerations are apparent in the emergency unit setting – the significant prevalence of mental illness alongside illegal drug use, and high levels of the use of chemical restraint to reduce the risk of injury and to render the environment more therapeutically viable in terms of effective provision of assessment and treatment.

Use of Chemical Restraint in the Residential Aged Care Setting

The Oakden report precipitated a fresh focus on the use of chemical restraint amongst persons in Australian residential aged care (Groves et al. 2017). The Australian Law Reform Commission (ALRC) completed its report on elder abuse later in 2017 and recommended regulation of the use of 'restrictive practices' in aged care, adopting the existing definition of the Australian Government from its *National Framework for Reducing and Eliminating the Use of Restrictive Practices in the Disability Service Sector* (Department of Social Services 2014) – which defined them broadly as 'any practice or intervention that has the effect of restricting the rights or freedom of movement of a person with disability, with the primary purpose of protecting the person or others from harm' and explicitly incorporated chemical restraint as a form of restrictive intervention. The ALRC found that the use of restrictive practices had the potential to amount to elder abuse and recommended a consistent approach to regulation of restrictive practices between the aged care and disability services sectors 'as a matter of principle and pragmatism' (Australian Law Reform Commission 2017: 143).

The Commonwealth Government then commissioned a review of aged care quality regulatory processes. The review recommended compliance with guidelines limiting the use of restraint and antipsychotic medication, as well as the creation of an independent statutory complaints commissioner (Carnell and Paterson 2017). In turn this led to the *Quality of Care Amendment (Reviewing Restraints Principles) Principles 2019* (Cth) which, amongst other things, amended the *Quality of Care Principles 2014* (Cth) to require chemical restraint only to be used as a last resort.

By 2021 the Royal Commission into Aged Care Quality and Safety (2021: Volume 1, 93) identified the use of restrictive practices as an area requiring immediate attention, stating:

> The overuse of restrictive practices in aged care is a major quality and safety issue. Restrictive practices impact the liberty and dignity of people receiving care. Urgent reforms are necessary to protect older people from unnecessary, and potentially harmful, physical and chemical restraints.

It recommended amendment of the *Quality of Care Principles 2014* (Cth) to provide that the use of restrictive practices in aged care be based on an assessment by an independent expert and subject to ongoing monitoring and reporting, with a behaviour support plan lodged with the Quality Regulator. In addition, it recommended:

> Restrictive practices should only be used where alternative strategies to meet the person's needs have been tried and found unsuccessful. Any exception that applies if a restrictive practice is necessary in an emergency should only apply for a short period, for as long as needed to prevent significant harm.
>
> (Royal Commission into Aged Care Quality and Safety 2021: Volume 1, 93)

Together these changes have the potential to reduce the use of chemical restraint substantially. (See also discussion of restraint in aged care by Chesterman in Chapter 5 of this volume.)

Use of Chemical Restraint on Inpatient Mental Health Wards

Many concerns have been expressed about the usage of chemical restraint in relation to the management of persons on mental health wards, especially in emergency settings (Danda 2020; Muir-Cochrane, Grimmer et al. 2020; Maker and McSherry 2019; Kinner 2017). It is clear that there needs to be standardised data-collection and consistency of definitions, in order to evaluate differences in approach across countries.

A 2019 study of the use of chemical restraint on South Australian adult psychiatric inpatient units provided an important insight into the phenomenon in Australia (Hu et al. 2019). What were classified as 'chemical restraint events' over a 12-month period were analysed. There were 166 such chemical restraint events involving 11 consumers. The highest prevalence was 28.78 events per 1,000 occupied bed days. More males (n = 69, 57.5%) were the subject of chemical restraint than females. This contrasted with a study across 12 European countries that identified that it was more common for women to be chemically restrained than men (Nawka et al. 2013) and a Norwegian study that found no significant gender differential.

In the South Australian study schizophrenia, schizotypal and delusional disorders were the most common diagnoses in the context of administration of chemical restraint and most events occurred during three time blocks: 14:00–14:59, 16:00–16:59 and 21:00–21:59. The mean age of persons restrained was 33 years. The two most common medications used for restraint were the antipsychotic, olanzapine, and the benzodiazepine, clonazepam. However, the study did not provide many indications of the likely precipitants to the use of chemical restraint. In contrast, a 2018 German study found that predictors of the experience of coercion related to the prescribed antipsychotic medication of forensic psychiatric inpatients with schizophrenia and related disorders were potentially influenceable variables, such as insight into illness or attitude towards medication (Horvath, Steinert and Jaeger 2018). However, the South Australian study did record that the most commonly stated reason for administration of chemical restraint was 'intrusive behaviour, verbal abuse or disruption' (n = 115, 42.6%), followed by 'actual, threat of physical aggression' (n = *60*, 22.2%), 'aggression or damage to property' (n = 38, 14.1%) and to administer involuntary treatment under mental health legislation (n = 31, 11.5%).

The presence of security guards was reported to assist with the administration of medications in most chemical restraint events (n = 123, 74.1%), followed by seclusion/environment (n = 65, 39.2%). In only 21 events were counselling or de-escalation skills listed and in over two thirds of cases injections were administered without any indication that an oral route was first offered. 'Disruptive behaviour, verbal aggression or disruption' was the most frequent form of problematic behaviour involved in chemical restraint events, prompting the authors to observe: 'Since all the involved disruptive behaviours were at low severity levels, it may also raise a concern about a lack of solution seeking for alternatives to restraint, a low tolerance to problematic behaviour, and a low threshold to medicate' (Hu et al. 2019: 20).

The authors of the South Australian study also observed that it was likely that nurses understood

> that the medication is for behavioural control but are also aware that the medications prescribed also have a treatment effect. This duality continues to be problematic in the definition and use of chemical restraint, and this study provides useful insights into this form of restrictive intervention.
>
> (Hu et al. 2019: 21)

Definitional Issues in Respect of 'Chemical Restraint'

It is apparent that the use of chemical restraint and other forms of pharmacotherapy to address emotional distress resulting in behavioural disturbance is common over a variety of contexts. This has been the subject of increasingly concerted measures in an attempt to reduce its incidence. Generally, such steps have been taken on the basis of regulation or even preclusion where the purpose of such administration of pharmacotherapy has been to control behaviour and ease the stress of the therapeutic domain, rather than to treat a person's symptoms of illness.

In the first mental health legislation in Australia to regulate the use of chemical restraint, 'chemical restraint' was defined by section 3 of the *Mental Health Act 2013* (Tas) to mean:

> medication given primarily to control a person's behaviour, not to treat a mental illness or physical condition.

In 2022 this was substantially replicated by section 3(1) of the MHWB Act 2022 (Vic), which defines chemical restraint as

> the giving of a drug to a person for the primary purpose of controlling the person's behaviour by restricting their freedom of movement but does not include the giving of a drug to a person for the purpose of treatment or medical treatment.

In South Australia, although the *Mental Health Act 2009* (SA) does not specifically address the use of chemical restraint, in 2015 the state government published policy guidelines governing the use of restraint and seclusion in mental health services (Office of the Chief Psychiatrist 2015). In addition, under section 145(1) of the *Disability Services Act 2006* (Qld), chemical restraint of an adult with an intellectual or cognitive disability is defined to mean:

> the use of medication for the primary purpose of controlling the adult's behaviour in response to the adult's behaviour that causes harm to the adult or others.

The provision notes that '[h]arm to a person includes physical harm to the person and a serious risk of physical harm to the person'. Section 145(2) of this Queensland legislation provides that the following are not chemical restraint:

(a) using medication for the proper treatment of a diagnosed mental illness or physical condition;
(b) using medication, for example a sedative, prescribed by a medical practitioner to facilitate or enable the adult to receive a single instance of health care under the *Guardianship and Administration Act 2000* (Qld).

In general, chemical restraints cannot be used in Queensland in relation to an adult with an intellectual or cognitive disability, unless the person is assessed by an appropriately qualified person, such as a medical practitioner, psychiatrist, psychologist or behaviour analyst. The assessment involves making findings about the nature, intensity, frequency and duration of the behaviour of the person that causes harm to themselves or others; developing theories about factors contributing to the adult's behaviour; and making recommendations about appropriate strategies to improve the adult's capabilities and quality of life, and to reduce and manage the behaviour.

Rule 6 of the *National Disability Insurance Scheme (Restrictive Practices and Behaviour Support) Rules 2018* (Cth) (the Rules) imposes regulations on all registered National Disability Insurance Scheme (NDIS) providers who use restrictive practices in the course of delivering NDIS supports, in relation to the use of seclusion, chemical restraint, mechanical restraint, physical restraint and environmental restraint. Chemical restraint is defined at rule 6(b) of the Rules as:

> the use of medication or chemical substance for the primary purpose of influencing a person's behaviour. It does not include the use of medication prescribed by a medical practitioner for the treatment of, or to enable treatment of, a diagnosed mental disorder, a physical illness or a physical condition.

From 2021 the use of chemical restraint as a regulated restrictive practice has needed to be a part of a positive behaviour support plan which will introduce skills and strategies to work towards reducing the regulated restrictive practice. All staff are obliged to be aware of possible side-effects of medications that may be prescribed (National Disability Services 2021: 10). The Rules specify conditions that limit the circumstances in which a registered NDIS provider may use restrictive practices or provide specialist behaviour support services. The conditions include the following:

- if a state or territory prohibits the use of a restrictive practice, a registered NDIS provider providing supports or services to participants in that jurisdiction must not use the restrictive practice;
- if a state or territory has an authorisation process in relation to the use of a regulated restrictive practice, the registered NDIS provider's use of the restrictive practice must be authorised in accordance with that process, and the provider must lodge evidence of such authorisation with the NDIS Commission;
- where a state or territory does not require authorisation for the use of a restrictive practice, the registered NDIS provider must take all reasonable steps to facilitate the development of a behaviour support plan;
- where it is likely that a regulated restrictive practice will be used on an ongoing basis, a registered NDIS provider must take all reasonable steps to

facilitate the development of a behaviour support plan by a 'specialist behaviour support provider' that covers the use of the restrictive practice. The plan must be developed in accordance with any authorisation process that applies in the state or territory in which the restrictive practice will be used; and
- the restrictive practice may only be used in accordance with the behaviour support plan. Plans must be lodged with the NDIS Commission and are subject to review arrangements (*National Disability Insurance Scheme (Restrictive Practices and Behaviour Support) Rules 2018* (Cth): rules 8, 9,11, 12, 13, 10, 22 and 24).

The Rules have broad application. Thus, for instance, a 'restrictive practice' is defined under section 3 of the *Disability Act 2006* (Vic) to mean any practice or intervention that 'has the effect of restricting the rights or freedom of movement of a person with a disability or of an NDIS participant,' and a 'regulated restrictive practice' has the same meaning as in the *NDIS (Restrictive Practices and Behaviour Support) Rules*. This is part of a suite of reforms to the *Aged Care Act 1997* (Cth) and the *Quality of Care Principles 2014* (Cth) to change the culture of over-ready resort to restraints, including chemical restraints, and reduce the extent of use of restrictive practices in aged care. However, as yet it is not known how much the new measures have reduced the amount of prescription and administration of antipsychotic medications to persons in aged care or whether prescribers have continued their practices and rebadged them as provided for the purpose of treatment.

The Recommendations of Victoria's Mental Health Royal Commission

In February 2021 the Royal Commission into Victoria's Mental Health System (2021) delivered its five-volume final report. Its recommendation 54 was that the Victorian Government act immediately to reduce the use of seclusion and restraint in mental health and wellbeing service delivery, with the aim of eliminating these practices within ten years and that it regulate the use of chemical restraint through legislative provisions. It recommended that a Mental Health and Wellbeing Commission provide oversight over current use and help drive reduction in restraint. It noted that four Australian states had already taken steps to regulate chemical restraint:

- in 2013 the Tasmanian Government introduced a definition of chemical restraint as part of the *Mental Health Act 2013* (Tas);
- in 2016 the Queensland Government introduced provisions in the *Mental Health Act 2016* (Qld) relating to the inappropriate use of medication;
- in 2017 the South Australian Government amended the *Mental Health Act 2009* (SA) to add chemical means to the forms of restraint covered by the legislation; and
- in 2020 New South Wales Health updated its policy directive on using seclusion and restraint (in all health settings) to include a definition of chemical restraint.

The Royal Commission into Victoria's Mental Health System (2021: Volume 4, 335) concluded that defining and regulating the use of chemical restraint would protect consumers and enable the practice to be appropriately monitored. In implementation of the Royal Commission's recommendations, section 127 of the *Mental Health and Wellbeing Act 2022* (Vic) provides that chemical restraint is a form of 'restrictive intervention' and is only able to be used '(a) to prevent imminent and serious harm to that person or another person; (b) in the case of bodily restraint – to administer treatment or medical treatment to the person'. In addition, section 128 provides that a restrictive intervention can only be used on a person if it is necessary to achieve a section 127 purpose and cannot be used 'unless all reasonable and less restrictive options have been tried or considered and have been found to be unsuitable' (see also Sara 2021).

The Analysis by the Disability Royal Commission

In 2021 another Royal Commission, the Royal Commission into Violence, Abuse, Neglect and Exploitation of People with Disability (2021) (Disability Royal Commission), established by the Commonwealth Parliament, published its public hearing report into the use of psychotropic medication. The report noted that previously the Committee on the Rights of Persons with Disabilities (2013: para. 35) expressed concern that in Australia:

> persons with disabilities, particularly those with intellectual impairment or psychosocial disability, are subjected to unregulated behaviour modification or restrictive practices such as chemical, mechanical and physical restraints and seclusion, in various environments, including schools, mental health facilities and hospitals.

Accordingly, it recommended that Australia 'take immediate steps to end such practices' (Committee on the Rights of Persons with Disabilities 2013: para. 36).

However, the Disability Royal Commission found that:

> Despite the absence of reliable statistical data and taking into account the higher prevalence of mental illness among people with cognitive disability, the evidence establishes that psychotropic medication is over-prescribed to people with cognitive disability. In particular such medication is over-prescribed and over-used as a response to behaviours of concern by people with cognitive disability.
>
> (Royal Commission into Violence, Abuse, Neglect and Exploitation of People with Disability 2021: 61)

It noted that if medications are nominally prescribed for treatment of a mental disorder but in fact are prescribed to control behaviours of concern, 'the extent to which medications are used as chemical restraints will be underestimated. It follows that the extent to which psychotropic medications are over-used or misused for people with cognitive disability will also be underestimated' (Royal

Commission into Violence, Abuse, Neglect and Exploitation of People with Disability 2021: 62). This is problematic as people with cognitive disability are significantly more likely to experience mental illness than the general population. The Royal Commission concluded that the distinction drawn in existing Commonwealth and Queensland disability services legislation between prescription of medication to treat people with cognitive disability and to control behaviours of concern is problematic in practice for three reasons:

- the boundary between treatment for a mental illness and administration of a chemical restraint is unclear and the notion of mutually exclusive categories does not come to grips with the nuances and complexity of the issues associated with addressing 'challenging behaviour';
- medical practitioners are not bound by the rules governing the use of psychotropic medication as a chemical restraint so that it is difficult to control inappropriate prescribing of psychotropic drugs;
- in any event, many medical practitioners either do not have the training or experience to distinguish between using psychotropic medication to treat mental illness and using chemical restraints as a means of addressing challenging behaviours or alternatively, reject the distinction (Royal Commission into Violence, Abuse, Neglect and Exploitation of People with Disability 2021: 65).

It noted the absence of clear data on the extent to which psychotropic medication is prescribed to people with a cognitive disability and the reasons for such prescription, in particular whether it is prescribed for treatment of a diagnosed medical illness or to respond to behaviours of concern (Royal Commission into Violence, Abuse, Neglect and Exploitation of People with Disability 2021: 67). However, it recognised that gathering such data will not be straightforward because 'most psychotropic medications to address behaviours of concern in people with cognitive disability are prescribed "off-label"'. The Commission committed to further exploration of the issue and, in particular to further consideration of whether:

- changes should be made to the PBS [Pharmaceutical Benefits Scheme] reporting systems to enable data to be disaggregated by disability status and a diagnosis of mental illness; and
- mechanisms should be created to collect data on 'off-label' prescriptions of psychotropic drugs for people with cognitive disability (Royal Commission into Violence, Abuse, Neglect and Exploitation of People with Disability 2021: 68).

The Commission identified as themes from the evidence adduced before it the need for medical practitioners prescribing psychotropic medications for persons with cognitive disability to take into account the risks of doing so before prescribing the medication and the importance of persons with disability, their families and their supporters understanding the potential adverse effects of such medication, and the need for monitoring for such adverse effects. It also highlighted the need for regular reviews of persons for whom psychotropic medications are prescribed to prevent adverse consequences arising from the use of such medications (Royal Commission into Violence, Abuse, Neglect and Exploitation of People with Disability 2021: 70–71). Evidence before the Commission identified the risk of extrapyramidal (ie, involuntary movement) side-effects from such medications, neuroleptic malignant syndrome, antidepressant-induced mania, reduced cognitive functioning, impotence, weight gain, increased risk of Type II diabetes, osteoporosis and the development of Parkinsonian symptoms. At a more subtle level the evidence also identified reduced capacity of persons with disabilities to communicate, boredom and lack of stimulation which in turn can be precipitants for engagement in behaviours of concern.

The Commission found that:

- people with cognitive disability may experience more side effects, including atypical effects, of psychotropic medication than people without disability;
- the adverse effects of psychotropic medication can lead to people with cognitive disability displaying more and more varied behaviours of concern; and
- the adverse effects of psychotropic medication are compounded for many people with cognitive disability, given the prevalence of polypharmacy amongst that population (Royal Commission into Violence, Abuse, Neglect and Exploitation of People with Disability 2021: 75).

It committed to further exploration of ways of mandating regular reviews of the prescription and administration of psychotropic medications to persons with disability and the most appropriate means of ensuring that medical practitioners closely supervise the process of reducing the dosage of such medication (Royal Commission into Violence, Abuse, Neglect and Exploitation of People with Disability 2021: 80). It observed that the over-use and misuse of psychotropic medication in relation to people with cognitive disability requires multidisciplinary collaboration to address it and expressed concern that

> the absence of a nationally consistent definition of 'chemical restraint' has militated against a shared understanding between the health and disability sectors as to the circumstances in which it is appropriate for psychotropic medication to be prescribed and administered to people with cognitive disability who display behaviours of concern.
>
> (Royal Commission into Violence, Abuse, Neglect and Exploitation of People with Disability 2021: 83)

While the Commission accepted that in the short term, in some circumstances, the sedative effects of psychotropic medication may reduce behaviours of concern displayed by persons with cognitive disability, it found limited evidence that use of psychotropic medications alone constitutes an effective response and concluded that it is unlikely to address the cause of behaviours of concern (Royal Commission into Violence, Abuse, Neglect and Exploitation of People with Disability 2021: 86). The Royal Commission considered the role of positive behaviour support plans (PBSPs), which, as noted earlier, are required under the *National Disability Insurance Scheme (Restrictive Practices) Rules 2018* (Cth) where a registered NDIS provider uses a 'regulated restrictive practice' in relation to a person with disability. It found that PBSPs, when designed and implemented carefully, reduce the incidence of behaviours of concern among people with cognitive disability and also reduce the use of psychotropic drugs as a chemical restraint. However, it concluded that waiting times are unduly lengthy for the preparation of such plans and that they 'are often not of a satisfactory quality' (Royal Commission into Violence, Abuse, Neglect and Exploitation of People with Disability 2021: 93). It proposed to investigate measures necessary to improve the skills of those preparing PBSPs and resources required for the plans to be prepared in a timely way and in accordance with best practice, including how to provide information about alternatives to psychotropic medication in managing behaviours of concern.

The Commission expressed concern that people with cognitive disability who have the most complex needs often do not receive assistance from appropriately skilled and experienced behaviour support practitioners (Royal Commission into Violence, Abuse, Neglect and Exploitation of People with Disability 2021: 117), increasing the likelihood of resort to prescription of psychotropic medication. It urged the NDIS Commission to collect data identifying complaints relating to the use of restrictive practices, in particular the use of chemical restraint (Royal Commission into Violence, Abuse, Neglect and Exploitation of People with Disability 2021: 124). It also observed that environmental factors, including lack of choice in accommodation, unsuitable living arrangements and social isolation, have a propensity to increase behaviours of concern and can have long-term adverse effects on the health and wellbeing of persons with disability.

The Road Toward Future Reforms

The Disability Royal Commission has significantly advanced knowledge and awareness in Australia in relation to the phenomenology of the use of chemical restraint. While its focus has been principally upon the use of psychotropic medications for persons with cognitive disability, it is likely that much of its analysis can be extrapolated to other categories of persons in congregate care who may be being prescribed such medication principally as a means of behaviour control.

While data about the use of chemical restraint is growing, much remains unknown about the use and misuse of psychotropic medications for persons who are conveyed to hospital by paramedics; persons who receive treatment in accident and emergency departments; and persons who live in aged care facilities, mental health wards, rehabilitation facilities and locations where persons with cognitive disabilities reside. The attempt by the Disability Royal Commission to assemble such data has the potential to generate a better-informed understanding about the extent of the use of pharmacotherapies and polypharmacy and the kinds of symptoms and behaviours that are prompting both prescription and administration of sedating agents. Assembling comparable data in other contexts would be very constructive to provide an empirical base for practice reform.

It is apparent that there is no bright line distinction between use of pharmacotherapies for treatment of mental health conditions as against their use for behavioural management. This is problematic as most current legislative definitions of 'chemical restraint' are based upon an unrealistic dichotomy between treatment and behavioural management. Often the two intersect and commonly it is not easy for the one to be disentangled from the other. In addition, it is easy (and tempting for clinicians) to prescribe and administer psychotropic medication that is rationalised as being principally for treatment, with a corresponding advantage for management of the person. In a context in which behaviours of concern amongst persons in congregate care often occur in the context of distress, disorientation, boredom and environmental stress, the relationship between conduct and cause is frequently complex. It may be, however, that the exigencies of paramedic intervention and provision of care in busy accident and emergency departments constitute a relevantly different forum.

Traditionally, the voices of persons subject to restrictive interventions have been heard and listened to inadequately. Currently, persons with a human rights perspective and activists in relation to the *Convention on the Rights of Persons with Disabilities* are playing an influential role in practice reform. (See Cameron in Foreword, Katterrl and Friel in Chapter 14 and Jayakody and Perera in Chapter 15 of this volume.) It is important too that the perspective of persons who work on a daily basis caring for those who may be subject to chemical restraint be attended to as they also have important insights and entitlements. It is they who have the responsibility for caring for people in difficult environments, often with few resources and inadequate training, who can behave in ways that are dangerous to themselves and others and whose conduct can erode workers' right to a workplace that is safe. Amongst other things, as a matter of law, this is a challenging occupational health and safety issue. (See also discussion of the role of professionals by Bartlett in Chapter 4 of this volume.)

It is unlikely that the complete elimination of chemical restraint is a feasible aspiration. However, the Disability Royal Commission has highlighted steps that can be taken on an empirically informed basis to reduce the use of psychotropic medications whose effects have a foreseeable suite of adverse consequences for persons in congregate care. Similarly, the Royal Commission into Victoria's Mental Health System highlighted a range of options other than chemical restraint. Much depends on resourcing and skill-building, as well as the creation of an environment conducive to calm and meaningful interactions. In addition, considerable skills in managing diverse challenges and crises are needed by clinicians. Even de-escalation of persons whose behaviour from time to time is highly challenging and frightening for workers requires strategies and commitments to avoidance of coercive measures, when there is always the temptation for the short- and longer term fix provided by the use of sedating medication – quiet and calm patients are easy patients.

Evidence before the Disability Royal Commission, and research evidence from other service settings, identified that there can be a range of precipitants to behaviours of concern that may give rise to the perception that chemical restraint needs to be used and that a focus on eroding these can go a long way toward reducing the need for psychotropic medications. This is feasible for persons who are residents in congregate care settings for more than a few days. Part of this in the ongoing context of care is construction of individualised behaviour management plans, and their adjustment in accordance with changes in people's needs and behaviours. However, these need to be individualised and translated from concept into action. They require investment of time and resources, as well as involvement of the persons about whom they are written to optimise the potential for their being effective. (See also Chesterman in Chapter 5 of this volume.)

Another realistic and pragmatic contribution of the Disability Royal Commission has been the proposed consolidation of accountability mechanisms for the administration of 'chemical restraint'. A similar approach has been adopted by the MHWB Act 2022. Erection of barriers for both one-off and serial prescription of chemical restraint is likely to exercise a deterrent effect on clinicians and to provide a fillip for encouraging exploration of other solutions to address both symptoms of distress and challenging behaviours. Similarly, the incorporation of reporting requirements and demanding preconditions for the use of chemical restraints, as well as other forms of restrictive intervention, has the potential to improve therapeutic cultures and environments. Therapeutic jurisprudence scholarship has highlighted that reduction in the use of coercion in a therapeutic context, including by the administration of unwanted pharmacotherapy, has the prospect of reducing trauma, resentment and anger, as well as to enhance the quality of therapeutic relationships (Winick 1997).

The aim of the efforts to reform the use of restrictive interventions has been to enhance the rights of persons with disability and to improve the quality of life of persons whose circumstances are generally out of public view. The work of McSherry and the Melbourne Social Equity Institute at the University of Melbourne has played a vital role in bringing the issues into more sensitised scholarly attention. The Disability Royal Commission, utilising its powers to assemble evidence from diverse sources, has built constructively on the available evidence base and the analysis of what has the potential to be done to minimise the use of coercion in the care environment. What has become apparent is that there is a lack of accurate data on the use of chemical restraint in its various acute and chronic contexts, but there exists an emerging awareness of the medical and quality of life consequences that can flow from all forms of restrictive intervention, including chemical restraint. There may well be gender (Maker 2021, 2022) and ethnicity (Nash et al. 2021) issues too which need to be explored further.

For the present, what can be said is that chemical restraint carries the potential for disempowerment, trauma and demoralisation that has already been identified with mechanical and physical restraint, as well as seclusion (Australian and New Zealand College of Psychiatrists 2021), but it also runs the risk of becoming a chronic mechanism for controlling problematic behaviours while other forms of restrictive intervention are being phased out. Case notes referring to dangerous incidents have the potential to be reframed into histories of violence and, with easy resort to 'cutting and pasting,' can be recycled without rigorous analysis of factors that may have precipitated behaviours of concern. Such factors can include traumatic experiences, abuse within the care environment, as well as covert issues such as experience of pain, boredom and distress that cannot be expressed in other ways. A danger with chemical restraint is that apparently impulsive and dangerous conduct can be attributed to pathology and regarded as a source of ongoing risk requiring psychotropic medication without sufficient inquiry as to other measures that might mitigate it and enable de-escalation. Sedation can render a person of reduced risk but results in hopelessness, disempowerment and an impoverished capacity to enjoy stimuli and to communicate about feelings and wishes. (See Cameron in Foreword in this volume.)

The Melbourne Social Equity Institute, spearheaded by Bernadette McSherry, the *National Framework for Reducing and Eliminating the Use of Restrictive Practices in the Disability Service Sector* (Department of Social Services 2014), the Royal Commission into Victoria's Mental Health System and, in particular, the Royal Commission into Violence, Abuse, Neglect and Exploitation of People with Disability have all constructed an important base for fundamental clinical and cultural change, supported by law reform and requirements to adhere to human rights-respecting mechanisms of accountability. The new impetus for considering alternative mechanisms for discouraging and inhibiting violent behaviours in congregate and emergency care settings (Breen 2019) constitutes the potential for developing a conceptual framework for substantial reduction in the use of chemical restraints.

As McSherry and Maker (2021b: 300) have fittingly observed, 'ultimately it will only be through reform endeavours on multiple fronts that the Noble Dream of eliminating restrictive practices inches closer to reality'.

References

Cases

An NHS Trust v ST (Refusal of Deprivation of Liberty Order) [2022] EWHC 919 (Fam).
College of Nurses of Ontario v Theodossiou, 2020 CanLII 456 (ON CNO). Available https://canlii.ca/t/j8lx6 (accessed 29 December 2022).
Conway v Jaques (2005) 250 DLR (4th) 178.

LB (Re), 2010 CanLII 21401 (ON CCB). Available www.canlii.org/en/on/onccb/doc/2010/2010canlii21401/2010canlii21401.html (accessed 29 December 2022).
LB v AJ, 2021 CanLII 5858 (ON HPARB). Available www.canlii.org/en/on/onhparb/doc/2021/2021canlii5858/2021canlii5858.html (accessed 29 December 2022).
Re ADP [2005] WASAT 131.
Re Application for Guardianship Order (BCB) (2002) 28 SR (WA) 338.
Re BTO, unreported, Guardianship and Administration Board (WA), 14 October 2004.
Re JP [2008] WASAT 3.

Books, Journal Articles and Other Texts

Australasian College for Emergency Medicine (2022) *Statement on the Use of Restrictive Practices in Emergency Departments*. Available https://acem.org.au/getmedia/2f351ebe-c139-4f8b-b8e5-a7578561e0d4/S817_Restrictive-Practices-ED-Statement (accessed 29 December 2022).
Australian and New Zealand College of Anaesthetists (2019) *Guideline for Patients Sedated in Health Care Facilities for Behavioural Disturbance*. Available www.anzca.edu.au/getattachment/eccd42fd-1463-4964-9059-d49396d10472/PS63-Guideline-for-safe-care-for-patients-sedated-in-health-care-facilities-for-acute-behavioural-disturbance (accessed 29 December 2022).
Australian and New Zealand College of Psychiatrists (2021) *Minimising and, Where Possible, Eliminating the Use of Seclusion and Restraint*. Available https://www.ranzcp.org/clinical-guidelines-publications/clinical-guidelines-publications-library/minimising-the-use-of-seclusion-and-restraint (accessed 19 June 2023).
Australian Law Reform Commission (2017) *Elder Abuse – A National Legal Response, ALRC Report 131*. Available www.alrc.gov.au/publication/elder-abuse-a-national-legal-response-alrc-report-131/ (accessed 29 December 2022).
Banerjee, S. (2009) *The Use of Antipsychotic Medication for People with Dementia: Time for Action, Report for the Minister of State for Care Services*. Available www.aph.gov.au/DocumentStore.ashx?id=48340346-1dbd-4e37-920b-0e724229047b (accessed 29 December 2022).
Breen, J. (2019) 'Chemical Restraint Has No Place in Aged Care, But Poorly Designed Reforms Can Easily Go Wrong', *The Conversation*, 26 February. Available https://theconversation.com/chemical-restraint-has-no-place-in-aged-care-but-poorly-designed-reforms-can-easily-go-wrong-112218 (accessed 29 December 2022).
Burnett, A.M., Panchal, D., Peterson, B., Ernest, E., Griffith, K., Frascone, R.J. and Engebretsen, K. (2015) 'The Administration of Pre-hospital Ketamine for Restraint Does Not Prolong On-scene Times Compared to Haloperidol Based Sedation', *Australasian Journal of Paramedicine*, 12(1): 1–6.
Cannon, M.E., Sprivulis, P. and McCarthy, J. (2001) 'Restraint Practices in Australasian Emergency Departments', *Australian and New Zealand Journal of Psychiatry*, 35(4): 464–67.
Carnell, K. and Paterson, R. (2017) *Review of National Aged Care Quality Regulatory Processes*. Available www.health.gov.au/sites/default/files/review-of-national-aged-care-quality-regulatory-processes-report.pdf (accessed 29 December 2022).
Chandler, K., White, B. and Willmott, L. (2017) 'What Role for Adult Guardianship in Authorising Restrictive Practices?' *Monash University Law Review*, 43(2): 492–529.
Cheney, P.R., Gossett, L., Fullerton-Gleason, L., Weiss, S.J., Ernst, A.A. and Sklar, D. (2006) 'Relationship of Restraint Use, Patient Injury, and Assaults on EMS Personnel', *Prehospital Emergency Care*, 10(2): 207–12.

Chief Psychiatrist of Tasmania (2017) *Clinical Guideline 10: Chemical Restraint*. Available www.health.tas.gov.au/sites/default/files/2021-12/CFP_Clinical_Guideline_10_Chemical_Restraint_DoHTasmania.pdf (accessed 29 December 2022).

Chieze, M., Hurst, S., Kaiser, S. and Sentissi, O. (2019) 'Effects of Seclusion and Restraint in Adult Psychiatry: A Systematic Review', *Frontiers in Psychiatry*, 10: 491.

Committee on the Rights of Persons with Disabilities (2013) *Concluding Observations on the Initial Report of Australia*, 10th sess, UN Doc CRPD/C/AUS/CO/1. Available https://documents-dds-ny.un.org/doc/UNDOC/GEN/G13/476/80/PDF/G1347680.pdf (accessed 29 December 2022).

Cookson, J. (2018) 'Rapid Tranquillisation: The Science and Advice', *BJ Psych Advances*, 24(5): 346–58.

Cunha, M., Andre, S., Bica, I., Ribiero, O., Dias, A. and Andrade, A. (2016) 'Chemical and Physical Restraint of Patients', *Procedia – Social and Behavioral Sciences*, 217: 389–99.

Currier, G. (2003) 'The Controversy Over "Chemical Restraint" in Acute Care Psychiatry', *Journal of Psychiatric Practice*, 9(1): 59–70.

Danda, M. (2020) 'Putting Restraint on Chemical Restraint: Exploring the Complexity of Acute Inpatient Nurses' Experience of Chemical Restraint Interventions', *Witness: The Canadian Journal of Critical Nursing Discourse*, 2(2): 29–53.

de Bruijn, W., Daams, J.G., van Hinnik, F.J.G., Arends, A.J., Boelens, E.M., Meerveld, J., Roelands, B., van Munster, B.C., Verwey, B., Figee, M., de Rooij, S.E. and Mocking, R.J.T. (2020) 'Physical and Pharmacological Restraints in Hospital Care: Protocol for a Systematic Review', *Frontiers in Psychiatry*, 10: 921.

Department of Social Services (2014) *National Framework for Reducing and Eliminating the Use of Restrictive Practices in the Disability Service Sector*. Available www.dss.gov.au/our-responsibilities/disability-and-carers/publications-articles/policy-research/national-framework-for-reducing-and-eliminating-the-use-of-restrictive-practices-in-the-disability-service-sector (accessed 29 December 2022).

Dickinson, T. and Clark, L.L. (2020) 'Rapid Tranquillisation: An Issue for All Nurses in Acute Care Settings', *British Journal of Nursing*, 29(15): 880–83.

Edwards, N., King, J., Williams, K. and Hair, S. (2020) 'Chemical Restraint of Adults with Intellectual Disability and Challenging Behaviour in Queensland, Australia: Views of Statutory Decision Makers', *Journal of Intellectual Disabilities*, 24(2): 194–211.

Flammer, E., Hirsch, S. and Steinert, T. (2021) 'Effect of the Introduction of Immediate Judge's Decisions in 2018 on the Use of Coercive Measures in Psychiatric Hospitals in Germany: A Population-based Study', *Lancet Regional Health Europe*, 11: 100233.

Fossey, J., Ballard, C., Juszczak, E., James, I., Alder, N., Jacoby, R. and Howard, R. (2006) 'Effect of Enhanced Psychosocial Care on People with Severe Dementia: Cluster Randomised Trial Antipsychotic Use in Nursing Home Residents', *British Medical Journal*, 332(7544): 756–61.

Gallagher, M. (2016) 'No Means No, Or Does It? A Comparative Study of the Right to Refuse Treatment in a Psychiatric Institution', *International Journal of Legal Information*, 44(2): 137–72.

Greenberg, W.M., Moore-Duncan, L. and Herron, R. (1996) 'Patients' Attitudes Toward Having Been Forcibly Medicated', *Bulletin of the American Academy of Psychiatry and Law*, 24(4): 513–24.

Groves, A., Thomson, D., McKellar, D. and Procter, N. (2017) *The Oakden Report*. Available https://apo.org.au/sites/default/files/resource-files/2017-04/apo-nid76130.pdf (accessed 29 December 2022).

Hagan, K. (2013) 'Unpredictable Ice Users Put Paramedics in Fear', *The Age*, 1 October. Available www.theage.com.au/national/victoria/unpredictable-ice-users-put-paramedics-in-fear-20130930–2uosd.html (accessed 29 December 2022).

Hick, J.L. and Ho, J.D. (2005) 'Ketamine Chemical Restraint to Facilitate Rescue of a Combative "Jumper"', *Prehospital Emergency Care*, 9(1): 85–89.

Hirsch, A. and Steinert, T. (2019) 'The Use of Rapid Tranquillization in Aggressive Behavior', *Deutches Artzeblatt International*, 116(26): 445–62.

Horvath, J., Steinert, T. and Jaeger, S. (2018) 'Antipsychotic Treatment of Psychotic Disorders in Forensic Psychiatry: Patients' Perception of Coercion and its Predictors', *International Journal of Law and Psychiatry*, 57: 113–21.

Hu, F., Muir-Cochrane, E., Oster, C. and Gerace, A. (2019) 'An Examination of the Incidence and Nature of Chemical Restraint on Adult Acute Psychiatric Inpatient Units in Adelaide, South Australia', *International Journal of Mental Health Nursing*, 28(4): 909–21.

Human Rights Council (2017) *Mental Health and Human Rights: Report of the United Nations High Commissioner for Human Rights*, 34th sess, UN Doc A/HRC/34/32. Available https://documents-dds-ny.un.org/doc/UNDOC/GEN/G17/021/32/PDF/G1702132.pdf (accessed 29 December 2022).

Jessop, T. and Peisah, C. (2021) 'Human Rights and Empowerment in Aged Care: Restraint, Consent and Dying with Dignity', *International Journal of Environmental Research and Public Health*, 18(15): 7899.

Jones, R., Usher, K. and Woods, C. (2019) 'Crystal Methamphetamine's Impact on Frontline Emergency Services in Victoria, Australia', *Australasian Emergency Care*, 22(4): 201–5.

Katkhuda, F. (2021) 'The Risks and Benefits of Prehospital Use of Ketamine', *Roundtable Journal on Health Policy*, 3(2). Available https://roundtablejournal.org/2021/04/05/the-risks-and-benefits-of-prehospital-use-of-ketamine (accessed 29 December 2022).

Kinner, S.A., Harvey, C., Hamilton, B., Brophy, L., Roper, C., McSherry, B. and Young, J.T. (2017) 'Attitudes Towards Seclusion and Restraint in Mental Health Settings: Findings from a Large, Community-based Survey of Consumers, Carers and Mental Health Professionals', *Epidemiology and Psychiatric Sciences*, 26(5): 535–44.

Knott, J., Gerdtz, M., Dobson, S., Daniel, C., Graudins, A., Mitra, M., Bartley, B. and Chapman, P. (2020) 'Restrictive Interventions in Victorian Emergency Departments: A Study of Current Clinical Practice', *Emergency Medicine Australasia*, 32(3): 393–400.

Kumble, S. and McSherry, B. (2010) 'Seclusion and Restraint: Rethinking Regulation from a Human Rights Perspective', *Psychiatry, Psychology and Law*, 17(4): 551–61.

Lee, D-C.A., Robins, L.M., Bell, J.S., Srikanth, V., Mohler, R., Hill, K.D., Griffiths, D. and Haines, T.P. (2021) 'Prevalence and Variability in Use of Physical and Chemical Restraints in Residential Aged Care Facilities: A Systematic Review and Meta-analysis', *International Journal of Nursing Studies*, 117: 103856.

Lindesay, J., Matthews, R. and Jagger, C. (2003) 'Factors Associated with Antipsychotic Drug Use in Residential Care: Changes Between 1990 and 1997', *International Journal of Geriatric Psychiatry*, 18(6): 511–19.

Losonczi, P. and Hanis, J. (2022) 'Analysis of Occupational Risks in the Profession of a Paramedic', *Annals of Burns and Fire Disasters*, 35(1): 36–40.

Macht, M., Mull, A.C., McVaney, K.E., Caruso, E.H., Johnston, B., Gaither, J., Shupp, A.M., Marquez, K.D., Haukoos, J.S. and Colwell, C.B. (2014) 'Comparison

of Droperidol and Haloperidol for Use by Paramedics: Assessment of Safety and Effectiveness', *Prehospital Emergency Care*, 18(3): 375–80.
Maguire, B.J., O'Meara, P.F., Brightwell, R.F., O'Neill, B.J. and Fitzgerald, G.J. (2014) 'Occupational Injury Risk Among Australian Paramedics', *Medical Journal of Australia*, 200(8): 477–80.
Maker, Y. (2021) 'Beyond Restraint: Gender-sensitive Regulation of the Control of Women's Behaviour in Australian Mental Health and Disability Services', in B. McSherry and Y. Maker (eds) *Restrictive Practices in Health Care and Disability Settings: Legal, Policy and Practical Responses*, Abingdon: Routledge, 91–118.
Maker, Y. (2022) 'Ending Seclusion and Restraint Use in Victoria's Mental Health Services: The Implications for Women of the Royal Commission's Recommendations', *Alternative Law Journal*, 47(2): 150–56.
Maker, Y. and McSherry, B. (2019) 'Regulating Restraint Use in Mental Health and Aged Care Settings: Lessons from the Oakden Scandal', *Alternative Law Journal*, 44(1): 29–36.
Matson, J.L. and Boisjoli, J.A. (2009) 'Restraint Procedures and Challenging Behaviours in Intellectual Disability: An Analysis of Causative Factors', *Journal of Applied Research in Intellectual Disabilities*, 22(2): 111–17.
Mayers, P., Keet, N., Winkler, G. and Flisher, A.J. (2010) 'Mental Health Users' Perceptions and Experiences of Sedation, Seclusion and Restraint', *International Journal of Social Psychiatry*, 56(1): 60–73.
McGillivray, J.A. and McCabe, M.P. (2004) 'Pharmacological Management of Challenging Behaviour of Individuals with Intellectual Disability', *Research in Developmental Disabilities*, 25(6): 523–37.
McSherry, B. (2008) 'Protecting the Integrity of the Person: Developing Limitations on Involuntary Treatment', in B. McSherry (ed) *International Trends in Mental Health Law*, Sydney: Federation Press, 111–24.
McSherry, B. and Gooding, P. (2013) 'Torture and Ill-treatment in Health Care Settings: Lessons from the United Nations', *Journal of Law and Medicine*, 20(4): 712–18.
McSherry, B. and Maker, Y. (eds) (2021a) *Restrictive Practices in Health Care and Disability Settings: Legal, Policy and Practical Responses*, Abingdon: Routledge.
McSherry, B. and Maker, Y. (2021b) 'Regulating Restrictive Practices: Challenges and Possibilities', in B. McSherry and Y. Maker (eds) *Restrictive Practices in Health Care and Disability Settings: Legal, Policy and Practical Responses*, Abingdon: Routledge, 295–301.
McSherry, B. and Tellez, J.J. (2016) 'Current Challenges for the Regulation of Chemical Restraint in Health Care Settings', *Journal of Law and Medicine*, 24(1): 15–19.
Melbourne Social Equity Institute (2014) *Seclusion and Restraint Project: Report*. Available https://socialequity.unimelb.edu.au/__data/assets/pdf_file/0017/2004722/Seclusion-and-Restraint-report.PDF (accessed 29 December 2022).
Muir-Cochrane, E., Grimmer, K., Gerace, A., Bastiampillai, T. and Oster, C. (2020) 'Prevalence of the Use of Chemical Restraint in the Management of Challenging Behaviours Associated with Adult Mental Health Conditions: A Meta-synthesis', *Journal of Psychiatric Mental Health Nursing*, 27(4): 425–45.
Muir-Cochrane, E., Oster, C., Gerace, A., Dawson, S., Damarell, R. and Grimmer, K. (2020) 'The Effectiveness of Chemical Restraint in Managing Acute Agitation and Aggression: A Systematic Review of Randomized Controlled Trials', *International Journal of Mental Health Nursing*, 29(2): 110–26.
Nadkarni, P., Jayaram, M., Nadkarni, S., Rattehalli, R. and Adams, C.E. (2015) 'Rapid Tranquillisation; A Global Perspective', *BJ Psych International*, 12(4): 100–2.

Nash, K.A., Tolliver, D.G., Taylor, R.A., Calhoun, A.J., Auerbach, M.A., Venkatesh, A.J. and Wong, A.H. (2021) 'Racial and Ethnic Disparities in Physical Restraint Use for Pediatric Patients in the Emergency Department', *JAMA Pediatrics*, 171(12): 1283–85.

National Disability Insurance Scheme (Restrictive Practices and Behaviour Support) Rules 2018 (Cth).

National Disability Services (2021) *Recognising Restrictive Practices: Guide.* Available www.nds.org.au/images/zt/Recognising_Restrictive_Practices_Guide.pdf(accessed 29 December 2022).

Nawka, A., Kalisova, L., Raboch, J., Giacco, D., Chihal, L., Onchev, G., Karastergiou, A., Solomon, Z., Fiorillo, A., Del Vecchio, V., Dembinskas, A., Kiejna, A., Nawka, P., Torres-Gonzales, F., Priebe, S., Kjellin, L. and Kallert, T.W. (2013) 'Gender Differences in Coerced Patients with Schizophrenia', *BMC Psychiatry*, 13: 257–66.

New South Wales Department of Communities and Justice (2021) *Restrictive Practices Guidance: Chemical Restraint.* Available www.facs.nsw.gov.au/providers/deliver-disability-services/restrictive-practices-authorisation-portal/rpa-resources/resources/restrictive-practices-guidance-chemical-restraint (accessed 29 December 2022).

Office of the Chief Psychiatrist (2015) *Policy Guideline: Restraint and Seclusion in Mental Health Services.* Available www.sahealth.sa.gov.au/wps/wcm/connect/5dd2f58048f79928929df70e3d7ae4ad/Guideline_restraint+and+seclusion_july2015.pdf (accessed 29 December 2022).

Peisah, C., Jessop, T. and Breen, J. (2020) 'A Missed Opportunity to Improve Practice Around the Use of Restraints and Consent in Residential Aged Care: Limitations of the Quality of Care Amendment (Minimising the Use of Restraints) Principles 2019', *Australasian Journal of Ageing*, 39(3): 292–96.

Peisah, C. and Skladzien, E. (2014) *The Use of Restraints and Psychotropic Medications in People with Dementia, Report for Alzheimer's Australia.* Available www.dementia.org.au/sites/default/files/20140321_Publication_38_A4_print%20version_Web.pdf (accessed 29 December 2022).

Richards, J.R., Derlet, R.W. and Duncan, D.R. (1998) 'Chemical Restraint for the Agitated Patient in the Emergency Department: Lorazepam Versus Droperidol', *Journal of Emergency Medicine*, 16(4): 567–73.

Robins, L.M, Lee, D-C.A., Bell, J.S., Srikanth, V., Mohler, J., Hill, K.D. and Haines, T.P. (2021) 'Definition and Measurement of Physical and Chemical Restraint in Long-Term Care: A Systematic Review', *International Journal of Research in Public Health*, 18(7): 3639.

Royal Commission into Aged Care Quality and Safety (2021) *Final Report: Care, Dignity and Respect – Volume 1: Summary & Recommendations.* Available https://agedcare.royalcommission.gov.au/sites/default/files/2021-03/final-report-volume-1_0.pdf (accessed 29 December 2022).

Royal Commission into Victoria's Mental Health System (2021) *Final Report.* Available https://finalreport.rcvmhs.vic.gov.au/download-report/ (accessed 29 December 2022).

Royal Commission into Violence, Abuse, Neglect and Exploitation of People with Disability (2021) *Public Hearing Report: Psychotropic Medication, Behaviour Support and Behaviours of Concern.* Available https://disability.royalcommission.gov.au/publications/report-public-hearing-6-psychotropic-medication-behaviour-support-and-behaviours-concern (accessed 29 December 2022).

Sara, G. (2021) 'Showing Restraint: The Uses and Limitations of Data in Supporting Restraint Reduction', in B. McSherry and Y. Maker (eds) *Restrictive Practices in Health Care and Disability Settings: Legal, Policy and Practical Responses*, Abingdon: Routledge, 188–202.

Shorter, E. (1997) *A History of Psychiatry: From the Age of Asylum to the Era of Prozac*, London: John Wiley & Sons.

Stefan, S. (2006) *Emergency Department Treatment: Policy Issues and Legal Requirements*, Oxford: Oxford University Press.

Tingleff, E.B., Bradley, S.K., Gildberg, F.A., Munksgaard, G. and Hounsgaard, L. (2017) '"Treat Me with Respect": A Systematic Review and Thematic Analysis of Psychiatric Patients' Reported Perceptions of the Situations Associated with the Process of Coercion', *Journal of Psychiatric Mental Health Nursing*, 24(9–10): 681–98.

Trivedi, M., Shelly, M. and Park, G. (2009) 'Advances in Patient Comfort: Awake, Delirious, or Restrained', *British Journal of Anaesthesia*, 103(1): 2–5.

Weiss, S., Peterson, K., Cheney, P., Froman, P., Ernst, A. and Campbell, M. (2012) 'The Use of Chemical Restraints Reduces Agitation in Patients Transported by Emergency Medical Services', *Journal of Emergency Medicine*, 43(5): 820–28.

Willacy, M. (2015) '"Unpredictable, Superhuman Strength": Frontline Paramedics Facing Violence from Ice Users Say They Fear for Their Safety', *ABC News*, 21 June. Available www.abc.net.au/news/2015-06-21/paramedics-on-frontline-of-ice-epidemic-fear-for-safety/6549150 (accessed 29 December 2022).

Williamson, D.R., Frenette, A.J., Burry, L., Perreault, M.M., Charbonney, E., Lamontagne, F., Potvin, M-J., Giguere, J-F., Megta, S. and Bernard, F. (2016a) 'Pharmacological Interventions for Agitation in Patients with Traumatic Brain Injury: A Systematic Review', *BMJ Open,* 9(7): e029604.

Williamson, D.R., Frenette, A.J., Burry, L., Perreault, M.M., Charbonney, E., Lamontagne, F., Potvin, M-J., Giguere, J-F., Megta, S. and Bernard, F. (2016b) 'Pharmacological Interventions for Agitation in Patients with Traumatic Brain Injury: Protocol for a Systematic Review and Meta-analysis', *Systematic Reviews*, 5: 193.

Winick, B.J. (1997) 'Coercion and Mental Health Treatment', *Denver University Law Review*, 74(4): 1145–68.

World Health Organization (2019) *Strategies to End Seclusion and Restraint: WHO QualityRights Specialized Training*. Available www.who.int/publications/i/item/9789241516754 (accessed 29 December 2022).

Yap, C.Y.L., Knott, J.C., Kong, D.C.M., Gerdtz, M., Stewart, K. and Taylor, D.M. (2017) 'Don't Label Me: A Qualitative Study of Patients' Perceptions and Experiences of Sedation During Behavioral Emergencies in the Emergency Department', *Academic Emergency Medicine*, 24(8): 957–67.

7 Who Do We Turn To? Safeguarding Residents in Aged Care Settings From Abuse and Neglect in New Zealand

Kate Diesfeld

Introduction

In New Zealand, at least one in ten people over the age of 65 experiences some form of elder abuse (Waldegrave 2015). The definition from the World Health Organization (WHO) and the United Nations is commonly adopted; elder abuse is defined as 'a single, or repeated act, or lack of appropriate action, occurring within any relationship where there is an expectation of trust which causes harm or distress to an older person' (World Health Organization 2002). Age Concern New Zealand similarly defines elder abuse as 'an act, repeated act or an act of omission which causes harm or distress to an older person who is in a relationship of trust' (Bruce 2022: 1; Collins 2014). Elder abuse may occur in diverse settings, including aged care residences.

Of concern, many older people in New Zealand reside in settings that they have not chosen (Anderson-Bidois and Fisher 2018). They are admitted either under formal legal compulsion or informal arrangements and people subject to the latter do not have adequate independent oversight, legal protections or access to free legal representation (Anderson-Bidois and Fisher 2018; White 2018). This human rights dilemma is explored by John Dawson and Frances Matthews in Chapter 8 in this volume. Tragically, some residents are victims of abuse and neglect within these settings (Ministry of Social Development 2019).

As noted in Australia, abuse and neglect often occurs behind closed doors, without witnesses (Groves et al. 2017). Sometimes, maltreatment *is* observed but is normalised or ignored (Royal Commission into Aged Care Quality and Safety 2021). These settings may be described as closed environments, defined by Bronwyn Naylor and colleagues (2014: 1) as:

> any place where persons are, or may be, deprived of their liberty by means of placement in a public or private setting in which a person is not permitted to leave at will by order of any judicial, administrative or other order ... [including] closed mental health and disability units.

DOI: 10.4324/9781003350644-9

Two defining features are 'power imbalances between staff members and residents' and 'barriers to public scrutiny' (Stevens 2014: 231).

In closed environments, such as some aged care settings, residents are vulnerable to human rights violations due to their isolation and relative powerlessness. A human rights framework in such sites intends to promote dignified care and transparency (Naylor, Debeljak and Mackay 2014). Also, external scrutiny and monitoring create more 'permeable' sites that are 'less prone to the development of abusive practices' (Quirk, Lelliott and Seale 2006: 2114). It is vital that relatively 'unseen' people in positions of dependence receive protection and independent monitoring (McKay 2015: 618).

Efforts are underway abroad and in New Zealand (Baker 2014; Collins 2014; Age Concern New Zealand 2021) to promote older residents' human rights while preventing elder abuse. In this chapter, the deaths of two older men in residential care in 2016 and 2018, discussed later, are the platform for examining the legal protections that exist for older people in closed environments in New Zealand. This exploration acknowledges that most people in residential settings receive beneficial, therapeutic care. Their professional carers deserve thanks, particularly in recent years, given the difficult conditions that COVID-19 continues to pose. Also, this analysis does not claim that the evidence presented necessarily justifies a formal governmental inquiry into New Zealand's aged care regime. Rather, it examines New Zealand's complaints regime and Ombudsman's powers, to assess how they can be harnessed for greatest protective impact.

The Health and Disability Commissioner Complaints Regime and the Human Rights Review Tribunal

Before describing the two cases, an introduction to New Zealand's complaints regime and Human Rights Review Tribunal is described for context.

What Is the Health and Disability Commissioner?

The Health and Disability Commissioner (HDC) was established under the *Health and Disability Commissioner Act 1994* (NZ). The role is funded under the Monitoring and Protecting Health and Disability Consumer Interests Appropriation within Vote Health (HDC 2021: 7), with Vote Health being the main source of funding for New Zealand's health and disability system. The objectives of the HDC are: resolution of complaints; improved understanding of rights; better, safer and more equitable care; and provider accountability (HDC 2021: 8–9).

The HDC receives complaints regarding individual consumers and, in general, does not respond to issues regarding the systemic landscape. Under this regime, facilities that provide residents with health and disability services are obligated to comply with the Health and Disability Service Standards, which should provide assurances regarding facilities' quality of care. An Aged Care Commissioner was appointed within the Office of the HDC in 2022 and perhaps this will widen the HDC's scope to examine issues of systemic practices regarding older people across settings.

Residents of aged care facilities, as consumers of health and disability services, are entitled to the ten rights within the *Health and Disability Commissioner (Code of Health and Disability Services Consumers' Rights) Regulations 1996* (NZ). All health and disability service providers have corresponding duties. The HDC resolves complaints about rights breaches, holds service providers to account and uses the findings to improve the quality of services at the individual provider level and (reportedly) across the health and disability system (HDC 2021: 6; 2022). Again, there is potential for the Aged Care Commissioner to expand the HDC's scope to improving the quality of aged care facilities and human rights protections in future decades.

What Is the Human Right Review Tribunal?

The HDC and the Human Rights Review Tribunal (HRRT) sit within New Zealand's human rights framework (Baker 2008; Paterson 2015). The HRRT is an independent judicial body that 'performs an intrinsically important role in protecting human rights' (Anderson-Bidois and Hancock 2020: 370). Of relevance to this analysis, the HRRT considers claims relating to the *Health and Disability Commissioner Act 1994* (NZ) (HDCA) and adjudicates complaints about breaches of the Code. Proceedings may be brought against a provider if the HDC has established, after an investigation, that a breach of the Code has occurred. The right to bring proceedings lies with the Director of Proceedings (the Director). Only if the HDC has determined that a breach occurred but has not elected to refer the person to the Director, or a referral has been made but the Director declines or fails to take proceedings, may the aggrieved person bring proceedings themselves before the HRRT.

Remedies include a declaration that the defendant has breached the Code, an order for specific performance to redress any loss or damage suffered as a result of the breach, damages and such other relief as the HRRT sees fit. The range of damages includes compensation for pecuniary loss, loss of benefit, humiliation, loss of dignity, injury to feelings and any action that is in flagrant disregard of the aggrieved person's rights. Damages are limited to the same monetary level as that available to the District Court of New Zealand.

However, if any person has suffered a personal injury, within the meaning of the *Accident Compensation Act 2001* (NZ), then no other damages other than punitive damages may be sought from, or awarded by, the HRRT (HDCA 1994: section 52(2)).

Additionally, registered practitioners, such as nurses in rest homes, may be disciplined under the *Health Practitioners Competence Assurance Act 2003*

(NZ) (Kersey et al. 2017). Regardless of registration status, a provider may be criminally prosecuted. Also, registered practitioners may be both criminally prosecuted and disciplined by the Health Practitioners Disciplinary Tribunal (Surgenor et al. 2022). More detailed discussion of legal remedies for elder abuse, neglect and exploitation is available (Baker 2014).

Unfortunately, the two HDC and HRRT cases this chapter discusses were not isolated incidents. The HDC website details a range of breaches within aged care settings, and not all HDC opinions are published.

How Many Cases of HDC Rights Breaches in Aged Care Facilities Are Reported?

The most recent HDC Annual Report, ending 31 June 2021, documented a 130% increase in the *overall* number of cases being referred to the HDC Investigations Team, compared with the previous year (HDC 2021: 3). The HDC received 5,396 complaints, but only 123 were investigated, with a breach opinion in 106 cases (HDC 2021: 13).

This pattern of a low number of resulting investigations was historically critiqued, with a view to whether consumers do, in fact, have access to justice (Manning 2010, 2018). Commonly, an HDC breach results in an apology from the provider; the adequacy of only an apology for institutional neglect and abuse in New Zealand's psychiatric facilities has also attracted critique (Diesfeld 2012).

Consumers over the age of 65 were the second largest category of consumers for whom complaints were made (18%). This may be an underestimate, given that '26% declined to answer or their ages were unknown' (HDC 2021: 12). Analysis and advocacy on behalf of older persons is difficult when HDC opinions do not specify consumers' ages (Diesfeld 2011).

When all issues raised in HDC complaints were considered (not just 'primary' issues), the most common complaint issue categories in 2020-21 were care/treatment (71%) and communication (66%) (HDC 2021: 14). Importantly, aged care settings ranked *third* in the organisations that were most complained about, being the subject of 151 complaints overall (HDC 2021: 14). It is likely that more breaches occur, but remain unreported, given that some older people in positions of dependence are unable to self-advocate or navigate the complaints system. Of note, a complaint regarding one resident may be suggestive that other residents are at risk.

While not all complaints of neglect and abuse in residential settings are reported (Ministry of Social Development 2019; Naus 2022), the existing data from the HDC discussed earlier and further data from the Ministry of Social Development discussed later suggest that strong human rights advocacy is needed. While the HDC and HRRT hold providers accountable *after* a breach, *preventive* measures are vital. The deaths discussed below may have been prevented if such preventive strategies had been in place.

Revelations From HDC Opinions and HRRT Cases

The Case of Oceania's Resident

In the first case, Mr A was 80 years old when he was admitted to a rest home owned by Oceania Care Company Limited (Oceania) (*Director of Proceedings v Oceania Care Company Ltd* 2022). Mr A had many complex health conditions. At the time of his admission, Mr A had frontal lobe dementia, T4 paraplegia, chronically low blood pressure, a catheter and a colostomy. For 26 years, Mr A's wife had been his primary carer. But while a resident of the rest home in 2018, he developed serious pressure wounds and required hospitalisations for urinary tract infections. Six months after his admission to the rest home, Mr A died.

Mr A's son filed a complaint with the HDC (*Opinion 18HDC01049* 2021). In the opinion of the Deputy HDC, Oceania breached right 4(1) of New Zealand's Code of Health and Disability Services Consumers' Rights (the Code), contained within the *Health and Disability Commissioner (Code of Health and Disability Services Consumers' Rights) Regulations 1996* (NZ). Right 4(1) provides '[e]very consumer has the right to have services provided with reasonable care and skill'. Oceania breached right 4(1) for inadequacies in: assessment and care planning; documentation and evaluation of Mr A's wound progress; fluid balance monitoring which resulted in Mr A's urinary tract infections; and staff compliance with Oceania's policies and procedures.

According to the HDC, Oceania did not ensure that its services complied with the New Zealand Health and Disability Service Standards. The facility had primary responsibility for the patterns of unsatisfactory care Mr A received from multiple staff members. Also, the HDC did express an adverse comment regarding Registered Nurse C. Given Mr A's paraplegia, he was unlikely to be able to reposition himself while restrained in a recliner chair and this contributed to his pressure injuries. The nurse approved this restraint practice (reclining arm chair), which was not aligned with Oceania's policy.

The matter was referred to the Director of Proceedings, who brought the case before the HRRT. Concurring with the finding of the Deputy HDC, the HRRT declared that right 4(1) was breached by Oceania in this case (*Director of Proceedings v Oceania Care Company Ltd 2022*).

The Case of Karadean Court's Resident

There are similarities between Mr A's situation and the second case this chapter examines. (Both men were actually referred to as 'Mr A' in the respective cases. However, to distinguish the two names in this chapter, the name 'Mr B' will be inserted.) Mr B was 87 years old at the time of the relevant events (*Director of Proceedings v Ultimate Care Group Limited* 2022). He had resided at Ultimate Care Karadean Court (Karadean Court) for hospital-level care since 2009. His complicated health conditions included vascular dementia, a history of heart attack, atrial fibrillation, Type II diabetes, hypertension, stroke, hypothyroidism and ischemic heart disease. On 21 August 2016, Mr B was transferred to Christchurch Hospital when attempts to administer antibiotics for a parotid gland obstruction were unsuccessful. Mr B passed away three days later due to septicaemia and facial cellulitis. The matter was referred to the HDC (*Opinion 17HDC00352* 2020).

Almost six years later, the HRRT issued a declaration that Karadean Court breached right 4(1) (*Director of Proceedings v Ultimate Care Group Limited* 2022). The breach involved 14 factors, from inadequate continence plans and podiatric reviews, to unacceptable management of Mr B's diabetes, pressure injuries and pain. Regarding staffing, medical advice from a general practitioner was not sought in a timely manner. Also, there was a lack of leadership and too few nurses available for supervision of junior staff.

Insights From the Cases

These cases illustrate how breaches that result in residents' deaths may progress to the HRRT. In both, the outcome was simply a declaration of breach. The tribunal may award damages for breaches of the Code, but neither case reported that damages were sought or awarded. In the second case, there was a delay of almost six years between the resident's death and the outcome of the hearing. The shortcomings of this scheme, where few cases are referred to the Director (and fewer prosecuted), as well as unreasonable delays and limited remedies, has been widely criticised (Manning 2010, 2018; Diesfeld, Surgenor and Rychert 2020).

One might ask whether the deficient care could qualify as elder abuse, based upon the definition used by the World Health Organization and Age Concern New Zealand (World Health Organization 2002; Collins 2014). There was a lack of appropriate action within a relationship of trust that harmed both older men.

Of note, restraint in its multiple forms is of international concern. (See also Chesterman in Chapter 5 of this volume.) The Oceania resident described earlier was intentionally positioned in a reclining chair as restraint resulting in severe pressure sores, and this constituted a breach of his rights. Lessons from Australia inspired recommendations for regulating the use of restraints (Maker and McSherry 2019; McSherry 2021). Other forms of restraint are pervasive in aged care facilities, as detailed in a 2017 South Australian report (the Oakden Report) on the Oakden Older Persons Mental Health Service in South Australia (Groves et al. 2017). For example, chemical or pharmaceutical restraint is often justified by staff to manage complex behaviours, but how staff manage this 'dual use conundrum' is often highly problematic, as analysed by Ian Freckelton in Chapter 6 in this volume. The Oakden Report will be discussed in more detail later.

Reflecting upon this type of scholarship and recent HRRT cases in New Zealand raises a number of questions.

Are These Isolated Cases?

One might ask whether this type of breach of the residents' rights is rare. Reportedly, it is not. Across New Zealand, according to Witton (2022: 2):

> Older people are dying sooner in aged residential care homes, the nurses union says, as a significant increase in complaints over short-staffing prompts serious concerns basic care is being compromised. . . . The sector is short about 1000 nurses around the country, as an ageing population with more complex needs adds to pressure. . . . The shortfall means staff aren't always able to provide basic care, which impacts a patient's quality of life. It is also behind a rise in complaints to the Health and Disability Commissioner. . . . The Ministry of Health has been notified of 2192 instances of short-staffing, health and safety risks to patients, deaths and police investigations across aged care providers for just the first six months of this year [2022], compared with 2794 for the whole of last year. This is up from 1842 for 2020.

The staff shortages have escalated, with some staff reportedly working 24-hour shifts (Theunissen 2022). Undoubtedly this pattern impacts upon the services delivered to residents.

As noted by the Ministry of Health, the HDC and the HRRT, additional staffing issues contribute to the standard of care. Concern regarding the types and levels of staffing was echoed by the recently appointed Aged Care Commissioner for the HDC, Carolyn Cooper:

> One of the common issues seen on assessment of the more serious complaints HDC receives about aged residential care facilities is the skills mix of staff does not always reflect the growing complexity and acuity of older people needing care.
>
> (Witton 2022: 4)

The impact of staff shortages and insufficient access to specialist care for older residents was concerning, even prior to the COVID-19 pandemic (Kersey et al. 2017). However, the HDC has primarily focused on individual complaints, as illustrated in the aforementioned cases.

What Does Age Concern New Zealand (ACNZ) Reveal About Elder Abuse?

The ACNZ Elder Abuse Response Service (EARS) is another source of information regarding abuse in aged care. Funded by the Ministry of Social Development, EARS is 'the largest coordinated national programme responsible for delivering non-crisis response services to those experiencing, or at risk of experiencing, abuse' (Ministry of Social Development 2019: 16). EARS intervention ranges from 'advocacy, safety and social support' to provision of maintenance services (Ministry of Social Development 2019: 19). An overview of the EARS process and the major response activities, such as referrals and intervention, was published by the Ministry of Social Development (2019). Referrals are made to the HDC when abuse is within the HDC's jurisdiction.

The Ministry of Social Development has 21 contracted EARS providers, and 14 are led by Age Concern members (Ministry of Social Development 2019: 16). Approximately 32 full-time equivalent roles deliver EARS across the nation. Even prior to the pandemic, resources were stretched. 'In 2019, 4,204 people were referred to EARS, which was 30 percent above contracted volumes' (Ministry of Social Development 2019: 22). Thus, the service that investigates elder abuse is itself over-burdened.

ACNZ defines institutional abuse as 'a policy or accepted practice within an organisation that disregards a person's rights or causes harm and distress' (Naus 2022). Examples included: services and routines that do not respect the person's values or needs; inadequate levels of treatment that care residents required (e.g. for skin integrity and mobility); restrictions on hygienic services (e.g. provision of adequate continence products and showering); and limited visitation unless approved by the resident's Enduring Power of Attorney (Naus 2022).

New Zealand's data on institutional abuse is important, given that international research indicated 'that 64.2% of staff admitted to elder abuse' but 'caution is needed when interpreting the estimates from staff self-report'; these rates of elder abuse and neglect perpetrated by staff are merely a partial picture and 'do not indicate the overall prevalence of abuse in the institution' (Yon et al. 2019: 61). Thus, the two recent cases alert us to the need for vigilance with, and on behalf of, residents in aged care settings.

Some recent complaints to ACNZ's EARS related to restrictions during the pandemic (from February 2020 onwards). Examples included 'no visitation' and restrictive telephone policies, containment to bedrooms and barring residents from exiting the premises, regardless of residents' conditions or availability of support people (Naus 2022). Thus, the challenges posed by the pandemic resulted in additional rights issues.

Explanations About ACNZ Statistics

The vast majority of elder abuse cases reported by ACNZ involved people 65 years of age or older, but approximately 4% were under 65. ACNZ could not correlate 'age' with 'types of abuse' in its statistical analysis. However, given that most people in residential care were in older age groups, presumably only a small percentage of the institutional abuse cases would involve people under 65 (Naus 2022).

According to ACNZ's 2020–2021 cycle of reporting for all types of complaints, '1186 over-65s accessed elder abuse and neglect assistance' and '477 vulnerable older people were supported with case management' (ACNZ 2021: 4). Not all lived in aged care settings.

Regarding institutional abuse, there may be some difficulties in interpreting the ACNZ statistics. ACNZ's definition of institutional abuse is broad, encompassing any agency that offers services to older people (e.g. support within the person's own home). However, the vast majority of institutional abuse that ACNZ dealt with occurred in residential care facilities (Naus 2022).

Another complexity related to the nature of residential facilities. Many residential complexes have retirement villages with rest homes on site (Naus 2022). Differentiating the rights of those who have paid for their units (retirement villages with the 'right to occupy') from those in residential care becomes problematic. One example was the difficulty of determining whether COVID-19 lockdown restrictions applied to both categories. Likewise, some misconduct against residents was not categorised as institutional abuse because it was perpetrated by *family* members, such as their refusal to release funds for residents' haircuts, toiletries, clothes and outings (Naus 2022).

Of note, the ACNZ statistics did not include the Bay of Plenty and Wellington regions; the number of abuse cases presumably would be higher if these regions were included. Also, ACNZ could not definitively identify the causes for variation in the statistical pattern in the years reported in the following paragraphs; small changes may have been attributable to COVID-19 factors (Naus 2022).

Finally, all abuses in residential care were not necessarily reported to ACNZ. Some were managed through internal processes or within the owners' (regional or national) management structure. Also, some complaints were filed with other government agencies such as the HDC or District Health Boards.

Over a three-year period, there were 334 reported cases of institutional abuse. The following refers to *individual* years:

> From July 2018 through June 2019, 2420 cases were reported and investigated. Of these cases, *5% (133) included institutional abuse.* (Of these, 54% reported it was the 'main type of abuse'.)
>
> From July 2019 through June 2020, 2411 cases were reported and investigated. Of these cases, *5% (118) included institutional abuse.* (Of these, 64% reported it was the 'main type of abuse'.)
>
> From July 2020 through June 2021, 2452 cases were reported and investigated. Of these, *3% (83) included institutional abuse.* (Of these, 66% reported it was the 'main type of abuse'.)
>
> (Naus 2022)

Thus, the numbers of reported cases were broadly similar with an increased percentage of complaints with institutional abuse portrayed as the 'main form of abuse'. While the numbers may seem low, they may be suggestive of additional residents at risk. This information is one valuable method to assess New Zealand's protections for older people in aged care.

More recently, the Ministry of Social Development released a proposed future strategy for EARS in December 2020. It prioritises: supporting older people to live abuse free; serving the needs of an ageing population; supporting providers to deliver best-practice services; giving regions support to deliver an integrated response and recognising elder abuse services as a key family violence service (Ministry of Social Development 2020). This strategy holds potential for coordinating New Zealand's elder abuse regime but does not establish a specified statutory body for elder abuse response. For prevention, we may also look to other bodies.

What Is the Chief Ombudsman's Role?

The role of the Chief Ombudsman (the Ombudsman) holds great potential for the protection of older residents. New Zealand has made an international commitment to ensure that 'detained' people are treated humanely and are living in a humane environment. The Ombudsman has a vital role in safeguarding people in such settings. As an independent Officer of Parliament, the Ombudsman is independent of government, the health and disability sector, and private interests. With a focus on prevention of rights breaches, he does not have the power to investigate *individual* complaints (Ombudsman New Zealand 2019).

Rather, the role focuses on prevention. The Ombudsman examines and monitors the treatment and conditions of people who are detained in health and disability facilities, including privately run aged care facilities. To meet international obligations, they assess the conditions and treatment of detained people to determine if there are any risks, poor practices or systemic problems in the facility that could result in a human rights violation. Their team inspects facilities where people are not free to leave at will, including settings such as dementia and psychogeriatric units.

This preventive activity is a form of human rights protection. New Zealand is a signatory to the *Optional Protocol to the Convention against Torture and other Cruel, Inhuman or Degrading Treatment or Punishment* (OPCAT), an international human rights agreement. Under OPCAT, the Ombudsman aims to prevent torture and other cruel, inhuman or degrading treatment or punishment through monitoring.

In July 2019, the New Zealand Parliament funded the Ombudsman to develop and implement a new inspection programme over three years. Pursuant to section 26 of the *Crimes of Torture Act 1989* (NZ), the Ombudsman's monitoring scope extends to persons held securely in *privately* run aged care facilities (New Zealand Gazette 2020). This provides Parliament and the public with an independent overview of how some of our most vulnerable people are treated and what, if any, improvements need to be made to meet existing human rights standards.

The physical inspections of facilities are sometimes unannounced. Inspectors also review relevant paperwork, policies and procedures. They hold discussions with staff, residents (where possible) and residents' family, *whānau*, or representatives. The criteria for these inspections focus on:

- how residents are treated, including any allegations of ill-treatment, the use of isolation, force or restraint;
- the facility's protection measures, such as information provided to residents on admission, complaint processes, registers and record-keeping;
- residents' living conditions;
- residents' activities, such as contact with their family and others outside the facility, outdoor exercise, education and leisure activities;
- residents' access to health care; and
- the facility's staffing levels, staff conduct and staff training.

Reports include affirmations of good practice and areas for improvement, with recommendations. There is a process for monitoring compliance with the recommendations (Ombudsman New Zealand 2019).

During New Zealand's COVID-19 lockdown periods, the Ombudsman remotely monitored facilities, primarily through information gathering and selective (announced) on-site inspections. Inspections focused on COVID-19 issues (Boshier 2020). The Ombudsman reported that several aged care facilities experienced clusters of the disease and, sadly, a number of people died. They specifically examined whether the facilities 'were doing all they could to prevent the virus spreading to those most at risk, and that steps were being taken to ensure the basic human rights of residents were protected' (Boshier 2020: 4).

Six secure aged care facilities were inspected between 17 April and 8 May 2020 during a COVID-19 'lockdown' at Alert Levels 3 and 4. One method to assess robustness is to inquire whether sufficient number of sites are inspected and the depth of the inspections. Another is to examine the nature of the Ombudsman's findings. With regards to *disability* rights, the Chief Ombudsman reported that all facilities were physically accessible for residents. In one, they noted there was 'some conflation between mental health needs and intellectual disability' (Boshier 2020: 13). Therefore, they recommended that the facility more appropriately meet the needs of the specific and diverse groups. With regards to hearing aids, the Ombudsman was not persuaded by one facility's claim that it was 'not practicable' to provide the devices in the dementia unit because they were often lost or needed repairs. They noted that hearing difficulties could be exacerbated when staff are wearing masks (Boshier 2020: 13).

Regarding cultural responsiveness, inspectors were told by one facility that meeting residents' cultural needs was a priority. For example, when a resident complained that other residents behaved in a culturally inappropriate fashion, training was provided for prevention and de-escalation, with advice regarding 'cultural norms' (Boshier 2020: 14). These are examples of the content of the reports. However, advocates may inquire whether the Ombudsman's OPCAT inspections have thrown the human rights net widely enough, utilising all strands of human rights protections.

How Is the United Nations *Convention on the Rights of Persons With Disabilities* (CRPD) Relevant to Residents of Aged Care Settings?

The Ombudsman's early inspections of aged care residences fleetingly referred to matters of concern to people with disabilities, as indicated earlier. In turn, we might ask whether a more robust application of the CRPD by the Ombudsman would make a difference for people in aged care.

The Ombudsman has obligations to monitor the rights of people in aged care facilities *as well as* disabled people. New Zealand is a signatory to the CRPD. New Zealand thereby expresses commitment to ensuring disabled persons have full and equal enjoyment of all human rights and fundamental freedoms. With regards to CRPD monitoring, the Ombudsman does have two partners under New Zealand's Independent Monitoring Mechanism (IMM) – the Human Rights Commission and the Disabled People's Organisations Coalition. The IMM promotes, protects and monitors the implementation of the CRPD, reports to Parliament, the public and the United Nations on the implementation of the CRPD, and provides advice on legislation, policy and practice affecting disabled people.

The CRPD is highly relevant for protecting older aged care residents. It is another tool for prevention of rights violations. Many, but not all, residents may have or acquire conditions that qualify for the CRPD's protection. Examples include physical, neurological, mental health and sensory impairments.

Mr A and Mr B both had conditions that would qualify as disabilities and attract the protection of the CRPD. New Zealand's ratification of OPCAT and the CRPD provides a potentially potent framework for the protection of these, and similar, residents. As observed in Australia:

> OPCAT provides a unique opportunity to spotlight the torture and ill-treatment of people with disability. . . . OPCAT provides the opportunity to challenge specific practices of institutional violence against people with disability, such as the use of restraint and seclusion.
>
> (Lea et al. 2018: 71)

While the Ombudsman referred to physical accessibility and hearing devices in their report, greater scrutiny of aged care settings through the lens of the CRPD would further protect residents. Future inspections could be informed by the human rights research conducted within New Zealand (White 2019) and focused on older people in closed environments (Anderson-Bidois and Fisher 2018). Vital lessons from abroad regarding optimum enforcement of the CRPD in aged care can guide practice in New Zealand (Bartlett and

Sampson 2021; Breen 2021). One example is the human rights critique of restraints (McSherry and Maker 2021; McSherry 2021; see also Chesterman in Chapter 5 and Freckelton in Chapter 6 of this volume). Given the fatal impact of restraint in a recliner chair in our first case involving Mr A, this form of advocacy is overdue in New Zealand.

What Lessons Might We Learn From Australia?

Insights from Australia are instructive. The neglect of an older resident of a health facility at Oakden in South Australia was the catalyst for a breadth of national initiatives to safeguard older people within its borders. Australia's initiatives are particularly timely, given New Zealand's current investigation into historical abuse in state care.

The Inquiry into the Oaken Older Persons Mental Health Service was published in 2017. In response, the Royal Commission into Aged Care Quality and Safety was established in 2018 by the Australian Government. Both recommended safeguards that are of relevance to New Zealand and other jurisdictions.

Oakden Older Persons Mental Health Service in South Australia

Mr. Robert Spriggs was an Australian who was reliant upon a facility for his daily care, like the residents in the two New Zealand cases. In 2015, Mr. Spriggs had Parkinson's disease and Lewy Body Disease. He was admitted to the Oakden Older Persons Mental Health Service in a suburb of Adelaide, South Australia. His family saw his condition rapidly deteriorate (Gage 2017). Due to very significant, unexplained bruising to Mr Spriggs' hip, in February 2016 he was admitted to the Royal Adelaide Hospital with severe dehydration and malnutrition, pneumonia and evidence of overmedication (Senate Community Affairs References Committee 2018: 12–13). At the age of 66, Mr. Spriggs died in July 2016. The investigation of Mr. Spriggs' death inspired a national movement in Australia to safeguard elders in aged care.

An investigation into Mr. Spriggs' treatment revealed that on three consecutive days, staff had administered ten times the prescribed dose of his antipsychotic medication (Senate Community Affairs References Committee 2018: 12–13). It was probable that Mr. Spriggs' bruising was caused by being restrained with straps in a chair (Senate Community Affairs References Committee 2018: 12–13). Mr. Spriggs' family reported their concerns regarding his treatment at Oakden and ultimately the Chief Psychiatrist of South Australia conducted an external, independent review of Oakden's clinical care of *all* consumers (Groves et al. 2017). The Chief Psychiatrist is a statutory role with powers and functions relating to the administration of the *Mental Health Act 2009* (SA) and the standard of mental health care in South Australia (Office of the Chief Psychiatrist South Australia 2022).

Over decades, many other residents were subjected to diverse, serious abuses in this isolated environment (Senate Community Affairs References Committee 2018). As the authors of the review reported:

> For Oakden the world has stood still. The impact of being a stand-alone service, away from the scrutiny of peers, believing one has been cast adrift, and repeatedly faced with evidence of having a limited future with no one championing the cause for change cannot be underestimated.
>
> (Groves et al. 2017: 115)

In response, the review addressed multiple factors, all important for our scrutiny of aged care and regardless of jurisdiction. First, the review asked why Oakden had not designed, endorsed or adopted a modern model of therapeutic care (Groves et al. 2017: 27). The review emphasised that residents were entitled to a robust model to 'address the State's obligation to provide high quality care' (Groves et al. 2017: 38). The void impacted the employees' attitudes, with many believing that residents would remain at Oakden for the duration of their lives. This belief became a self-fulfilling prophecy when employees neglected to attend to residents' complex behaviours.

Reportedly, Oakden operated 'like a mental institution from the middle of the last century' (Groves et al. 2017: 57). In response, the review recommended that the facility be fully de-commissioned and that a new purpose-built facility be constructed.

Next, the review critiqued Oakden's staffing model, echoing the deficiencies detected within the two New Zealand cases. The review called for mandatory staff training on rights, elder abuse prevention and reporting. The 'optimal mix of the full range of members of a multi-disciplinary service' was required (Groves et al. 2017: 72), including expertise from the fields of social work, geriatric medicine, psychology and clinical pharmacy. (It was noted that the delivery of the model of care was made more complex by Australia's funding scheme, which utilised a mixed model of federal, state and local funding.)

Disturbing numbers of consumers' injuries were reported. In ten files examined by the review, *all* consumers had sustained injuries. 'Challenging behaviour' was dealt with through extensive use of medication and mechanical restraints and seclusion, with inadequate reporting (Groves et al. 2017). The review critiqued Oakden's restrictive practices, finding it unlikely that there were only four instances of restraint between 2009 and 2013, as had been reported. There was a 'significant failure to appreciate the seriousness of restraint as stated by the UN and as agreed in Australia both in [the] CRPD and also as a National Safety priority in mental health' (Groves et al. 2017: 105). The review concluded that staff were inadequately trained to understand the appropriate use, required limitations and monitoring of restrictive measures (Groves et al. 2017).

Oakden's toxic culture included verbal abuse, seclusion, restraint and 'rough handling practices' (Groves et al. 2017: 97) that was shrouded in secrecy. 'Poor performing' nurses were disciplined with a transfer to Oakden (Groves et al. 2017: 97). Preventable staff conflict escalated over insufficient resources, equipment and devices. The review called for appointment of senior leadership staff who promoted the 'core principles and the values of dignity, respect, care and kindness' for both consumers and staff (Groves et al. 2017: 102).

In addition to the closure of Oakden, the review recommended that the new services be informed by contemporary principles of best practice, such as Trauma Informed Care strategies. To ensure that the failings of Oakden never recur, the review recommended a new direction for *all* Specialist Older Person Mental Health Services in South Australia (Groves et al. 2017). Subsequently, an Independent Review of Commonwealth aged care regulatory processes was completed (Carnell and Paterson 2017).

Australian Royal Commission Into Aged Care Quality and Safety

The concerns raised in the Oakden Review and other reports of abuse and poor conditions in aged care led to a wider investigation. In October 2018, the Australian Government established a Royal Commission into Aged Care Quality and Safety (RCACQS). The RCACQS examined the quality of aged care services and whether those services were meeting the needs of the Australian community. The scope encompassed care for older people: living at home; living with dementia; and living in residential aged care (including younger people with disabilities) (RCACQS 2018).

According to Commissioner Lynelle Briggs, at least one in three consumers of residential aged care and home care services have experienced unsatisfactory care (RCACQS 2021: 72). Disturbing conclusions included that:

- the incidence of assaults may be as high as 13–18%;
- there is a clear overuse of physical and chemical restraint;
- some 47% of people have concerns about staff, including understaffing, unanswered call bells, high rates of staff turnover, and agency staff not knowing the residents and their needs; and
- substandard care has become normalised in some sectors so that older people have low expectations of the quality of their care (RCACQS 2021: 72).

Also, the RCACQS was concerned about the impact of life in institutions upon older people:

> Good design in residential aged care, particularly for people living with dementia, usually involves smaller, lower-density congregate living arrangements rather than larger, more institutional settings. . . . Large, noisy institutional environments can worsen the adverse consequences of dementia.
>
> (RCACQS 2021: 105)

The prospect of large institutions may be of concern to New Zealanders, as our ageing population grows. We should be mindful of the benefits of customised care in smaller aged care settings, and the dangers of institutional facilities with lower staffing, regimented routines and reduced privacy.

The Final Report of the RCACQS identified the need for a robust rights protection system. The constellation of protections included:

> the right to freedom from degrading treatment, or any form of abuse; the right to liberty; the right of autonomy and to make decisions about their care; the right to fair and non-discriminatory treatment; and the right to voice opinions and make complaints.
>
> (RCACQS 2021: 80)

These rights are equally valued in New Zealand where consumers are entitled to protection through the HDC under the Code of Health and Disability Services Consumers' Rights and international human rights, as examined later.

Also, according to this report, the *compulsory* reporting scheme in aged care within Australia was unsatisfactory. Only a limited scope of incidents were required to be reported and the resulting information was 'not used effectively' (RCACQS 2021: 140). However, in July 2021, a Serious Incident Response Scheme was implemented that mandates reporting of a much wider spectrum of incidents in aged care services subsidised by the Australian Government (Aged Care Quality and Safety Commission 2022a, 2022b). Now, both residential aged care and flexible care providers must take reasonable action to prevent incidents and to protect consumers' safety, health, wellbeing and quality of life. Aged care providers must notify the police when criminal conduct occurs and Australia's Aged Care Quality and Safety Commission when eight types of incidents occur:

- unreasonable use of force;
- unlawful sexual contact or inappropriate sexual conduct;
- neglect of a consumer;
- psychological or emotional abuse;
- unexpected death – where reasonable steps were not taken by the provider to prevent the death, the death is the result of care or services provided by the provider or a failure by the provider to provide care and services;
- stealing or financial coercion by a staff member;
- inappropriate use of restrictive practices; and
- unexplained absence from care (Aged Care Quality and Safety Commission 2022a, 2022b).

Non-compliance may result in regulatory action (Aged Care Quality and Safety Commission 2022a). A similar regime, if adopted in New Zealand, would provide clarity for aged care providers and greater safety for residents. However, for effective safeguards, responsive strategies must be accompanied by preventive strategies.

The Royal Commission's Final Report (RCACQS 2021) called for the creation of a new, independent Australian Aged Care Quality and Safety Commission. As noted earlier, in February 2022, New Zealand did appoint its inaugural Aged Care Commissioner within the Office of the HDC to address systemic change and to ensure older consumers will be empowered to 'speak up, be heard, and receive a timely response' (Verrall 2022).

The Australian experience is informative because it focused on older people. While there have been comparable recent initiatives to investigate and prevent abuse in diverse settings in New Zealand, these have not specifically focused on *older* people in residential settings.

What Is New Zealand's Royal Commission of Inquiry Into Abuse in Care Revealing?

Currently, New Zealand's Royal Commission of Inquiry into Abuse in Care, or Abuse in Care Royal Commission (ACRC), is exposing a range of historical misconduct. The findings may provide potent lessons for older people within closed environments. The New Zealand Government established the ACRC to comprehensively investigate abuse and neglect, in both state care and in faith-based settings (ACRC 2018). Survivors include young people and vulnerable adults who were in care between 1950 and 1999 (although the Commission examines experiences outside those dates). After the inquiry's investigations are completed in June 2023, the ACRC will make recommendations to the Governor-General of New Zealand on recommendations for prevention and improved redress systems (ACRC 2020a, 2020b).

Contexts for the ACRC range from short term care (such as police cells) to institutional and community-based services, where some people reside for the duration of their lives. The review encompasses care funded directly or indirectly by the state. The hearings focus on: Māori and Pacific peoples' experiences; youth justice care; children's state psychiatric care; disability settings; and state and faith-based care settings including any group connected by a 'spiritual belief system' (ACRC 2020a).

The New Zealand inquiry does not specifically focus on aged care residents. However, it does encompass vulnerable adults, for example in psychiatric institutions. We cannot definitively state that older residents of aged care facilities, such as rest homes, were subject to abuse and neglect during the relevant timespan. Presumably very few residents of aged care facilities during the 1950 to 1999 inquiry scope are alive to participate in the Royal Commission hearings. However, the inquiry did recognise that survivors who are now older persons require swift consideration.

Urgency is needed for the Minister for the Public Service to publish the Crown's initial response to the report's recommendations, with a timetable and plan for 'giving priority and urgency to claims from elderly or seriously ill survivors', including making interim payments where appropriate (ACRC 2021a: 133). So, although the inquiry is not probing for abuse in aged care settings, its findings across sectors are instructive as we plan future human rights safeguards.

We do know that between 1950 and 2019, approximately 655,000 children young people and vulnerable adults went through some of the care settings within the Royal Commission's terms of reference and up to 250,00 may have been abused (ACRC 2020a). Thus, it is likely the Royal Commission's final report will understate the number of survivors. Racism and discrimination by authorities and the public impacted upon admission to services and treatment. Like the Australian Oakden Report findings, New Zealand facilities had a lack of staff training and vetting, poor complaints systems and retaliation for reporting. For many, redress processes caused enduring trauma.

The inquiry has revealed residents' extreme vulnerability in closed environments. A spectrum of harrowing maltreatment, including horrific physical and sexual abuse, was reported. 'There was psychological and emotional abuse, discrimination because of race or disability, isolation, and improper use of medical procedures as punishment. Much of this was criminal, and some of it was torture' (ACRC 2021a: 6). This extensive abuse suggests that residents in other closed environments, including elders, require protection.

For the next stage of progress, the Royal Commission has adopted te Reo (Māori). It will address:

> the tūkino, or abuse, harm and trauma, that has occurred to [survivors], restore their mana and heal and grow in ways that allow them to achieve 'utua kia ea' or restoration and balance. [The inquiry has] proposed the establishment of a new puretumu, or holistic redress, scheme.
>
> (ACRC 2021b: 6)

The inquiry reminds us of the characteristics of the thousands of dependent people who were victimised, across sectors:

> Society was also in denial, despite calls over the decades for an inquiry into abuse in care – abuse that was going on in hospitals, boarding schools, orphanages, foster *and other care homes*, homes for unmarried mothers and churches. The denial was fostered by the common and negative social attitudes of the time about race, gender, disability, mental health and the place of children, Deaf and disabled people. Many of those in care came from already disadvantaged or marginalised parts of the community.
>
> (ACRC 2021b: 5) [emphasis added]

Equally, we must ask whether negative social attitudes in New Zealand towards *older* people currently place them at risk. New Zealand's survivors were socially isolated and undervalued while dependent on their carers. If our older residents share these risk factors, we must strengthen our preventive and monitoring systems to avert abuse. The ACRC's activities are dovetailing with other preventive initiatives, more specifically designed for older residents, such as the international human rights preventive mechanisms.

Who Do You Turn To?

In some respects, New Zealand's human rights regime protects older people in residential settings. New Zealand does have a constellation of domestic legal protections, such as the HDC's complaint system, the Code and the HRRT. Arguably, Age Concern New Zealand's EARS elder abuse service provides a measure of protection. But these safeguards are called upon after the mistreatment and neglect occurs.

New Zealand does have a preventive mechanism for protecting the human rights of people in detention, under our Ombudsman's regime. To address the human rights of residents across sectors, the Ombudsman now inspects both public and *private* aged care facilities. OPCAT is one strand of protection. But for older residents with impairments, the CRPD's potential is currently untapped. Coordination across sectors, with fully funded adult protective services and a stronger reporting mandate for aged care providers would certainly demonstrate New Zealand's renewed commitment to the human rights of people in aged care settings.

Our Royal Commission of Inquiry into Abuse in Care is revealing the mistreatment of people, of all ages, who did not enjoy the human rights protections that we have in 2023. The specific experience of older people as aged care residents is unlikely to be deeply scrutinised by the inquiry. However, the lessons from this inquiry, and from Australia, can inform our future human rights strategies. With New Zealand's appointment of the inaugural Aged Care Commissioner, and the Ombudsman's recently expanded scope of monitoring, we should expect greater safeguards. With New Zealand's commitment to OPCAT and the CRPD, there is great potential to protect older people. And there is hope that very soon residents like Mr A and Mr B in New Zealand can confidently turn to a coordinated, fully resourced network to safeguard their rights.

References

Cases

Director of Proceedings v Oceania Care Company Ltd [2022] NZHRRT 8 (25 February 2022). Available www.justice.govt.nz/assets/Documents/Decisions/2022-nzhrrt-8-director-of-proceedings-v-oceania-care-company-ltd.pdf (accessed 30 December 2022).

Director of Proceedings v The Ultimate Care Group Ltd [2022] NZHRRT 17 (8 April 2022). Available www.justice.govt.nz/assets/Documents/Decisions/2022-NZHRRT-17-DoP-v-The-Ultimate-Care-Group-Ltd-Redacted.pdf (accessed 30 December 2022).

Opinion 17HDC00352 (2020) 'The Ultimate Care Group Limited (trading as Ultimate Care Karadean Court) – A Report by the Deputy Health and Disability Commissioner', 30 June, Case 17HDC0035, Health and Disability Commissioner. Available www.hdc.org.nz/media/6231/17hdc00352.pdf (accessed 30 December 2022).

Opinion 18HDC01049 (2021) 'Oceania Care Company Limited – A Report by the Deputy Health and Disability Commissioner', 19 February, Case 18HDC01049, Health and Disability Commissioner. Available www.hdc.org.nz/media/6006/18hdc01049.pdf (accessed December 2022).

Books, Journal Articles and Other Texts

Age Concern New Zealand (ACNZ) (2021) *Annual Report 2020–2021*. Available www.ageconcernauckland.org.nz/media/website_pages/resources/Age-Concern-Auckland-Annual-Report-2020–2021.pdf (accessed 30 December 2022).

Aged Care Quality and Safety Commission (2022a) *Non-compliance Register*. Available www.agedcarequality.gov.au/aged-care-performance/non-compliance-register (accessed 30 December 2022).

Aged Care Quality and Safety Commission (2022b) *Serious Incident Response Scheme*. Available www.agedcarequality.gov.au/sirs (accessed 30 December 2022).

Anderson-Bidois, J. and Fisher, M. (eds) (2018) *This Is Not My Home: A Collection of Perspectives on the Provisions of Aged Residential Care Without Consent*, New Zealand Human Rights Commission. Available https://cfnhri.org/wp-content/uploads/2020/01/HRC_This_is_not_my_Home.pdf (accessed 30 December 2022).

Anderson-Bidois, J. and Hancock, J. (2020) 'Human Rights', in T. Gibbons and M. Duggal (eds) *New Zealand Tribunals: Law and Practice*, Wellington: Thomson Reuters, 339–70.

Baker, T. (2008) 'The Human Rights Review Tribunal and the Rights of Health and Disability Consumers in New Zealand', *Journal of Law and Medicine*, 16(1): 85–102.

Baker, T. (2014) 'Legal Protections and Remedies for Elder Abuse, Neglect and Exploitation', in K. Diesfeld and I. McIntosh (eds) *Elder Law in New Zealand*, Wellington: Thomson Reuters, 477–507.

Bartlett, P. and Sampson, S. (2021) 'Human Rights and Rapid Tranquilisation', in B. McSherry and Y. Maker (eds) *Restrictive Practices in Health Care and Disability Settings: Legal, Policy and Practical Responses*, Abingdon: Routledge, 41–67.

Boshier, P. (2020) *OPCAT COVID-19 Report: Report on Inspections of Aged Care Facilities Under the Crimes of Torture Act 1989*, Office of the Ombudsman Tari o te Kaitiaki Mana Tangata. Available www.ombudsman.parliament.nz/resources/opcat-covid-19-report-report-inspections-aged-care-facilities-under-crimes-torture-act (accessed 30 December 2022).

Breen, J. (2021) 'Psychotropic Use in Australian Aged Care Homes', in B. McSherry and Y. Maker (eds) *Restrictive Practices in Health Care and Disability Settings: Legal, Policy and Practical Responses*, Abingdon: Routledge, 219–35.

Bruce, A. (2022) 'Almost Half of Elder Abuse Inflicted by Adult Children', *Otago Daily Times*, 27 June. Available www.odt.co.nz/regions/central-otago/almost-half-elder-abuse-inflicted-adult-children (accessed 30 December 2022).

Carnell, K. and Paterson, R. (2017) *Review of National Aged Care Quality Regulatory Processes*. Available health.gov.au/resources/publications/review-of-national-aged-care-quality-regulatory-processes-report (accessed 30 December 2022).

Collins, L. (2014) 'Elder Abuse and Neglect Prevention', in K. Diesfeld and I. McIntosh (eds) *Elder Law in New Zealand*, Wellington: Thomson Reuters, 553–77.
Diesfeld, K. (2011) 'Analysis of Legal Cases for Prevention of Elder Abuse: Decisions from New Zealand', *Journal of Law and Medicine*, 18(4): 737–48.
Diesfeld, K. (2012) 'Apology in New Zealand's Mental Health Context: An Enigmatic Juxtaposition', *Waikato Law Review*, 20: 50–66.
Diesfeld, K., Surgenor, L. and Rychert, M. (2020) 'Breaches of New Zealand's Health and Disability Services Consumers' Rights: Human Rights Review Tribunal Decisions', *Journal of Law and Medicine*, 27(3): 679–92.
Gage, N. (2017) 'Spriggs Family Searches for Answers After Father Was Overmedicated at Oakden Mental Health Facility', *ABC News*, 18 January. Available www.abc.net.au/news/2017-01-18/sa-father-overmedicated-at-oakden-mental-health-family-says/8191428 (accessed 30 December 2022).
Groves, A., Thomson, D., McKellar, D. and Proctor, N. (2017) *The Oakden Report*. Available https://apo.org.au/sites/default/files/resource-files/2017-04/apo-nid76130.pdf (accessed 30 December 2022).
Health and Disability Commissioner (HDC) (2021) *Pūrongo ā-Tau – Annual Report for the Year Ended June 2021*. Available www.hdc.org.nz/media/6046/hdc-annual-report-2021.pdf (accessed 30 December 2022).
Health and Disability Commissioner (HDC) (2022) *The Code and Your Rights*. Available www.hdc.org.nz/your-rights/the-code-and-your-rights/ (accessed 30 December 2022).
Kersey, K., Diesfeld, K., Surgenor, L. and Ip, M. (2017) 'Professional Discipline of the New Zealand Nursing Residential Care Workforce: A Mixed Method Analysis of HPDT Decisions 2004–2014', *Journal of Law and Medicine*, 24(4): 803–20.
Lea, M., Beaupert, F., Bevan, N., Celermajer, D., Gooding, P., Minty, R., Phillips, E., Spivakovsky, C., Steele, L., Wadiwel, D.J. and Weller, P. (2018) 'A Disability Aware Approach to Torture Prevention? Australian OPCAT Ratification and Improved Protections for People with Disability', *Australian Journal of Human Rights*, 24(1): 70–96.
Maker, Y. and McSherry, B. (2019) 'Regulating Restraint Use in Mental Health and Aged Care Settings: Lessons from the Oakden Scandal', *Alternative Law Journal*, 44(1): 29–36.
Manning, J. (2010) 'Access to Justice for New Zealand Health Consumers', *Journal of Law and Medicine*, 18(1): 178–94.
Manning, J. (2018) '"Fair, Simple, Speedy and Efficient?" Barriers to Justice in the Health and Disability Commissioner's Complaints Process in New Zealand', *New Zealand Law Review*, 4: 611–56.
McKay, C. (2015) 'Human Rights in Closed Environments', *Sydney Law Review*, 37(4): 617–34.
McSherry, B. (2021) 'The Intractable Use of Restraint, Organisational Culture and "Othering"', in B. McSherry and Y. Maker (eds) *Restrictive Practices in Health Care and Disability Settings: Legal, Policy and Practical Responses*, Abingdon: Routledge, 219–35.
McSherry, B. and Maker, Y. (eds) (2021) *Restrictive Practices in Health Care and Disability Settings: Legal, Policy and Practical Responses*, Abingdon: Routledge.
Ministry of Social Development (2019) *Elder Abuse in Aotearoa: The Role and Current State of MSD's Elder Abuse Response Services*. Available www.msd.govt.nz/documents/about-msd-and-our-work/work-programmes/initiatives/family-and-sexual-violence/elder-abuse-in-aotearoa.pdf (accessed 30 December 2022).

Ministry of Social Development (2020) *Elder Abuse in Aotearoa: The Proposed Future Strategy for Elder Abuse Response Services.* Available www.msd.govt.nz/documents/about-msd-and-our-work/work-programmes/initiatives/family-and-sexual-violence/2020–07-elder-abuse-in-aotearoa-the-proposed-future-strategy-for-elder-abuse-response-services.pdf (accessed 30 December 2022).

Naus, H. (2022) *Personal Communications from Professional Educator: Elder Abuse and Neglect Prevention*, Age Concern New Zealand, 17 March. On file with author.

Naylor, B., Debeljak, J. and Mackay, A. (2014) 'Introduction: Implementing Human Rights in Closed Environments', in B. Naylor, J. Debeljak and A. Mackay (eds) *Human Rights in Closed Environments*, Alexandria, NSW: Federation Press, 1.

New Zealand Gazette (2020) *Designation of National Preventive Mechanisms*, 2 July. Available www.gazette.govt.nz/notice/id/2020-go2845 (accessed 30 December 2022).

Office of the Chief Psychiatrist (2022) *Office of the Chief Psychiatrist South Australia.* Available www.chiefpsychiatrist.sa.gov.au (accessed 30 December 2022).

Ombudsman New Zealand (2019) *Fact Sheet: Aged Care Monitoring.* Available www.ombudsman.parliament.nz/resources/fact-sheet-aged-care-monitoring (accessed 30 December 2022).

Paterson, R. (2015) 'The Code of Patients' Rights', in P. Skegg and R. Paterson (eds) *Health Law in New Zealand*, Wellington: Thomson Reuters, 22–66.

Quirk, A., Lelliott, P. and Seale, C. (2006) 'The Permeable Institution: An Ethnographic Study of Three Acute Psychiatric Wards in London', *Social Science & Medicine*, 63: 2105–17.

Royal Commission into Aged Care Quality and Safety (RCACQS) (2018) *Terms of Reference.* Available https://agedcare.royalcommission.gov.au/about/terms-reference (accessed 30 December 2022).

Royal Commission into Aged Care Quality and Safety (RCACQS) (2021) *Final Report: Summary.* Available https://agedcare.royalcommission.gov.au/sites/default/files/2021-03/final-report-executive-summary.pdf (accessed 30 December 2022).

Royal Commission of Inquiry into Abuse in Care (ACRC) (2018) *Terms of Reference – Ngā Tikanga Whakahaere.* Available www.abuseincare.org.nz/our-progress/library/v/3/terms-of-reference (accessed 30 December 2022).

Royal Commission of Inquiry into Abuse in Care (ACRC) (2020a) *Tāwharautia: Pūrongo o te Wā – Interim Report, Volume 1.* Available www.abuseincare.org.nz/assets/Uploads/Abuse-in-Care-Volume-One.pdf (accessed 30 December 2022).

Royal Commission of Inquiry into Abuse in Care (ACRC) (2020b) *Tāwharautia: Pūrongo o te Wā – Interim Report, Volume 2 Survivor Voices.* Available www.abuseincare.org.nz/assets/Uploads/Abuse-in-Care-Volume-Two.pdf (accessed 30 December 2022).

Royal Commission of Inquiry into Abuse in Care (ACRC) (2021a) *He Purapura Ora, he Māra Tipu – From Redress to Puretumu Torowhānui: Volume 1, Executive Summary.* Available www.abuseincare.org.nz/our-progress/reports/from-redress-to-puretumu/from-redress-to-puretumu-4/he-karakia-3 (accessed 30 December 2022).

Royal Commission of Inquiry into Abuse in Care (ACRC) (2021b) *He Purapura Ora, he Māra Tipu – From Redress to Puretumu Torowhānui: Shortform Version.* Available www.abuseincare.org.nz/assets/Uploads/Documents/He-Purapura-Ora-he-Mara-Tipu-Vol_1-ShortForm.pdf (accessed 30 December 2022).

Senate Community Affairs References Committee (2018) *Effectiveness of the Aged Care Quality Assessment and Accreditation Framework for Protecting Residents from Abuse and Poor Practices and Ensuring Proper Clinical and Medical Care Standards Are Maintained and Practised – Interim Report.* Available www.aph.gov.

au/Parliamentary_Business/Committees/Senate/Community_Affairs/AgedCare Quality/Interim report (accessed 30 December 2022).

Stevens, J. (2014) 'Changing Cultures in Closed Environments: What Works?' in B. Naylor, J. Debeljak and A. Mackay (eds) *Human Rights in Closed Environments*, Alexandria, NSW: Federation Press, 228.

Surgenor, L., Diesfeld, K., Rychert, M., Kelly, O. and Kersey, K. (2022) 'Criminal Convictions of Disciplined Health Practitioners in New Zealand', *Journal of Law and Medicine*, 29(1): 117–28.

Theunissen, M. (2022) '"24 Hour Shifts": Aged Care Sector Staff Shortages at Crisis Point', *Radio New Zealand*, 22 July. Available www.1news.co.nz/2022/07/22/24-hour-shifts-aged-care-sector-staff-shortages-at-crisis-point (accessed 30 December 2022).

Verrall, A. (2022) 'First Aged Care Commissioner Appointed', 14 February. Available www.beehive.govt.nz/release/first-aged-care-commissioner-appointed (accessed 30 December 2022).

Waldegrave, C. (2015) *Measuring Elder Abuse in New Zealand: Findings from the New Zealand Longitudinal Study of Ageing (NZLSA)*, Family Centre Social Policy Research Unit. Available https://officeforseniors.govt.nz/assets/documents/our-work/elder-abuse/Elder-abuse-technical-report.pdf (accessed 30 December 2022).

White, M. (2018) 'Aged Residential Care Without Consent: A Human Rights Perspective', in J. Anderson-Bidois and M. Fisher (eds) *This Is Not My Home: A Collection of Perspectives on the Provisions of Aged Residential Care Without Consent*, Wellington: Human Rights Commission, 51–58.

White, M. (2019) 'The Role and Scope of OPCAT in Protecting Those Deprived of Liberty: A Critical Analysis of the New Zealand Experience', *Australian Journal of Human Rights*, 25(1): 44–65.

Witton, B. (2022) 'Older People are Dying More Quickly in Aged Care with Sector in Crisis', *Stuff*, 2 July. Available www.stuff.co.nz/national/politics/129146272/older-people-are-dying-more-quickly-in-aged-care-with-sector-in-crisis (accessed 30 December 2022).

World Health Organization (2002) *Missing Voices: Views of Older Persons on Elder Abuse*, UN Doc WHO/NMH/VIP/02.1. Available https://apps.who.int/iris/bitstream/handle/10665/67371/WHO_NMH_VIP_02.1.pdf (accessed 30 December 2022).

Yon, Y., Ramiro-Gonzalez, M., Mikton, C.R., Huber, M. and Sethi, D. (2019) 'The Prevalence of Elder Abuse in Institutional Settings: A Systematic Review and Meta-Analysis', *European Journal of Public Health*, 29(1): 58–67.

8 Some Concerns About Arbitrary Detention of Elderly People in Secure Rest Home Care

John Dawson and Frances Matthews[1]

Introduction

This chapter illustrates certain situations in which elderly people who are considered to lack the mental capacity to make decisions about their living arrangements might be arbitrarily detained in secure rest home care. In particular, we examine a number of situations in which the legal authority relied on to justify such detention, or the procedures governing it, may not be adequate. We offer these thoughts as a way of showing our respect and admiration for the outstanding contributions made by Bernadette McSherry to the fields of mental health and disability law, particularly her contributions to scholarship on civil detention and restrictive practices in health and care settings.

The main focus of the chapter will not be on the powers provided by mental health legislation (or 'the Mental Health Act'), under which people's detention, when it occurs, usually takes place in a hospital (see Donnelly in Chapter 2 and Arstein-Kerslake in Chapter 12 in this collection). Instead, it will be on the authority and procedures provided by certain other legal regimes, especially the common law of necessity and adult guardianship (or mental capacity) legislation, because it is these latter sources of authority that are more commonly used to justify the detention of elderly people in community-based facilities (see also Bartlett in relation to lessons which can be learnt from the implementation of English mental capacity legislation in Chapter 4 of this volume). Our primary concern is for the law to protect the right of elderly people not to be arbitrarily detained.

The precise requirements set by human rights law in this field are not easily summarised. With regard to the legal requirements in different national jurisdictions, these requirements will vary somewhat depending on the range of human rights instruments to which the particular state is a party under international law, and the weight these international instruments carry in its domestic legal system. It will also depend on the manner in which personal liberty is protected within a nation's constitution and legislation, and probably on elements of judge-made law, including principles of interpretation. There is little doubt, however, that the right of persons of any age not to be arbitrarily

DOI: 10.4324/9781003350644-10

detained is firmly protected under both international law and most domestic legal systems.

That '[n]o-one shall be subjected to arbitrary . . . detention' is affirmed by Article 9 of the *Universal Declaration of Human Rights* (UDHR), promulgated in 1948. It is also enshrined in Article 9(1) of the *International Covenant on Civil and Political Rights* (1966) (ICCPR), which says:

> everyone has the right to liberty and security of person. No one shall be subjected to arbitrary arrest or detention. No one shall be deprived of his liberty except on such grounds and in accordance with such procedures as are established by law.

In addition, regarding the procedures required to prevent arbitrary detention, Article 9(4) of the ICCPR declares that any detained person:

> shall be entitled to take proceedings before a court, in order that that court may decide without delay on the lawfulness of his detention and order his release if the detention is not lawful.

The *Convention on the Rights of Persons with Disabilities* (CRPD) (2007: Article 14) adds that all persons with disabilities shall enjoy the right to liberty 'on an equal basis with others', and 'the existence of a disability shall in no case justify a deprivation of liberty'.

Equivalent entitlements are protected by international human rights instruments operative within certain regions of the world. Article 5 of the *European Convention on Human Rights* (1950: Article 5(1)) (ECHR), for example, declares that no one shall be deprived of liberty, except on certain 'lawful' grounds (which are listed), and 'in accordance with a procedure prescribed by law'. The ECHR also specifies that every detained person must be permitted 'to take proceedings by which the lawfulness of his detention shall be decided speedily by a court and his release ordered if the detention is not lawful' (Article 5(4)).

A state's national constitution may contain equivalent guarantees concerning personal liberty. The fifth amendment to the *Constitution of the United States* (1788), for example, provides that '[n]o person shall be . . . deprived of . . . liberty . . . without due process of law' and section 7 of the *Canadian Charter of Rights and Freedoms* (1982) declares: 'everyone has the right to . . . liberty . . . and the right not to be deprived thereof except in accordance with the principles of fundamental justice'. Rights of that kind may be invoked to challenge arbitrary detention as contrary to domestic constitutional law.

In some jurisdictions, legislation of a national parliament is to similar effect, or incorporates the international human rights guarantees into domestic law. The *Human Rights Act 1998* (UK), for instance, has the effect of incorporating the provisions of the ECHR into UK law, making it enforceable in the domestic courts, including the provisions of Article 5 (discussed earlier) concerning unlawful deprivation of liberty. Similarly, New Zealand's statutory bill of rights, the *New Zealand Bill of Rights Act 1990*, that was specifically enacted to give effect to the ICCPR within New Zealand law, declares that '[e]veryone has the right not to be arbitrarily . . . detained' (section 22).

Thus, at both the international level, and often within national law, a powerful human rights norm can be said to exist that can be described, in general terms, as the right of every person not to be arbitrarily detained. The importance of this norm has been explored by Bernadette McSherry in relation to post-sentence preventive detention laws (McSherry and Keyzer 2011) as well as civil detention laws relating to suspected terrorists and people diagnosed with severe mental illness (McSherry 2014).

What this norm requires specifically of a state's legal system must then be extrapolated, partly from the detailed terms (where they exist) of the relevant human rights instruments by which the state is bound, and partly from the declarations concerning the meaning of those instruments issued by the committees, tribunals and courts responsible for the enforcement of those instruments on the international and national plane.

The Core Principles of the Right Not To Be Arbitrarily Detained

At the risk of generalisation, what protection of this right requires of a legal system, at least in relation to a person not currently charged with a criminal offence (which will usually be the case with an elderly person), might be summed up in three core principles (ICCPR 1966; Macken 2005; United Nations Human Rights Committee 2014; Sifris 2011; McSherry 2014: chapter 7; Chandler 2021).

First, some form of clear legal authority must exist for the detention, to prevent it being arbitrary. If it is not authorised by law, it will be both unlawful and arbitrary. As the United Nations Human Rights Committee (2014: para 11) (UNHRC) puts it, in its General Comment No. 35 on the meaning of Article 9 of the ICCPR, 'detention that lacks any legal basis is . . . arbitrary'.

Second, the grounds for detention must not be arbitrary. This requirement has many facets, because the grounds for detention could be considered arbitrary in many different senses. The UNHRC says the notion of arbitrariness in the grounds can cover 'inappropriateness, injustice, lack of predictability, . . . reasonableness, necessity and proportionality' (UNHRC 2014: para 12). These concern, variously, the substance of the grounds for detention ('injustice'); the availability of less invasive means of achieving the state's legitimate objectives ('necessity' and 'proportionality'); fitness for purpose ('appropriateness'); and 'sufficient precision to avoid overly broad or arbitrary interpretation or application' ('predictability') (UNHRC 2014: para 22).

Third, there is the need for effective procedural protections to govern all forms of detention, the aim being to prevent unlawful or arbitrary detention occurring (ICCPR 1996: Article 9; UNHRC 2014: Part V; ECHR 1950:

Article 5(2)–(4)). There should be a process established by law through which those responsible for a person's detention must show reliably that the relevant legal criteria are met. All detained persons must have effective and prompt access to a court (or independent tribunal) for the review through a fair process of the lawfulness of their detention, with that court having the power to order their release. The detained person must have adequate assistance in that process, so the lawfulness of their detention can be effectively challenged. Regular reassessment must occur as to whether the criteria for their detention continue to be met. And the law must protect people against wrongful detention by third parties, not only detention by agents of the state.

These might be described as the general requirements set by human rights law for compliance with the right not to be arbitrarily detained, particularly in the case of persons not currently subject to the criminal process.

In the field of mental health, the relevant requirements imposed by the ICCPR are summarised by the UNHRC (2014) in its General Comment No 35. Having noted that the 'existence of a disability shall not in itself justify a deprivation of liberty', the UNHRC writes (2014: para 19):

> any deprivation of liberty must be necessary and proportionate, for the purpose of protecting the individual in question from serious harm or preventing injury to others. It must be applied only as a measure of last resort and for the shortest appropriate period of time, and must be accompanied by adequate procedural and substantive safeguards established by law. The procedures should ensure respect for the views of the individual and ensure that any representative genuinely represents and defends the wishes and interests of the individual. . . . Deprivation of liberty must be reevaluated at appropriate intervals with regard to its continuing necessity. The individuals must be assisted in obtaining access to effective remedies for the vindication of their rights, including initial and periodic review of the lawfulness of their detention.

Elderly people, including those living with dementia, are obviously entitled to the benefit of these guarantees; and, when held behind closed doors in a rest home or similar environment, without having provided valid consent to that arrangement, or their movements are fully and effectively controlled by others, they are undoubtedly detained.

It may be hard to enforce all the relevant guarantees in some states' domestic legal systems, if the rights invoked are based exclusively on international legal sources which are not recognised as directly enforceable in the state's domestic courts. Nevertheless, in the remainder of this chapter, we draw attention to certain situations – using New Zealand's legal arrangements as the primary example – in which detention of elderly people in secure rest home care could be considered arbitrary and therefore contrary to human rights norms. In particular, we consider situations in which the detention might be arbitrary in the first and third senses discussed earlier: that is, arbitrary because the detention is not governed by any clear legal authority, or not subject to an adequate legal process.

Some of the *grounds* commonly invoked to justify detention of elderly people might also be challenged as arbitrary, on the basis that they are vague or unpredictable in application. Detention based on broad notions of 'incapacity' and 'best interests' might be vulnerable on that basis, particularly given human rights concerns regarding the need to distinguish legal capacity from mental capacity (McSherry 2012). We leave those matters, including interpretive disagreements about the matter between the UNHRC and the CRPD Committee (Martin and Gurbai 2019), for another day.

The Adequacy of the Legal Authority Invoked to Justify the Detention of Elderly People in Secure Rest Home Care

In this section, we start from the assumption that there are situations in which people – especially elderly people – are detained, or deprived of their liberty, when placed in secure rest home care. It seems uncontroversial to say they are detained when held behind locked doors that will not be opened to permit them to leave, and, even if the doors are not locked, when they are actually prevented from leaving by staff.

Whether a person is detained, in the relevant legal sense, is not always clear. The doors of a rest home may not be locked, for example, and the person whose detention is in question may not (yet) have shown any intention to leave. But the staff may have firmly decided that they will not permit the person to leave, should they try to go. Is that person detained already, or are they only detained when actually stopped from leaving? As was shown by the disagreement between the judges on the matter in the House of Lords, in *R v Bournewood* (1999), the legal position on this point can be unclear.

Nevertheless, in many parts of the world, significant numbers of elderly people who are considered to lack the mental capacity to make decisions about their living arrangements are held behind locked doors, in rest homes or equivalent facilities, or prevented from leaving by staff (see also Chesterman in Chapter 5 and Diesfeld in Chapter 7 of this volume). There is little doubt that, in those circumstances, they are detained, under the usual principles of human rights law.

What we propose to explore, in the following section, are certain situations in which there are doubts as to whether detention of this kind is adequately authorised by law. If it is not, it will be arbitrary and contrary to human rights law.

Some Areas of Doubt as to the Scope of the Authority to Detain

In most parts of the common law world, at least, several different forms of legal authority, quite distinct from mental health legislation, might be thought to cover detention of this kind. The question is whether these forms of authority really are sufficient to cover it, on a proper interpretation of the law.

The forms of authority upon which we wish to focus are, first, the common law principle of necessity, which may still be invoked in many parts of the common law world to justify a person's detention in these circumstances; and, second, various forms of authority provided by what is usually called adult guardianship (or mental capacity) legislation (see also discussion of the difficulties of implementing English mental capacity legislation by Bartlett in Chapter 4 of this volume).

The Common Law Justification of Necessity

In many jurisdictions whose legal system has English roots, the common law principle of necessity (provided it has not been abolished or superseded by statute) can be relied upon to justify the restraint or detention of a person who is at grave risk of harm, at least in emergency situations (*Bournewood* 1999). Nevertheless, the question remains: for *how long* can this common law principle be relied upon to justify a person's detention? Can it be relied upon *beyond* the duration of an immediate emergency, when the procedures established by some statutory scheme, such as an adult guardianship scheme, might be set in motion to justify the detention, and that scheme would provide greater procedural protections for the person detained?

In practice, some elderly people may seem to be placed in secure care without any obvious legal foundation for it. They might simply be admitted, for instance, to the closed ward of a hospital or rest home, following arrangements made, or an agreement reached, between their relatives and the staff of that facility, without any apparent legal formality. Or they may be moved by staff from the 'open' to the 'closed' side of a facility, leading to their detention, without their having provided valid consent to it, and without any obvious form of legal authority being invoked.

Nevertheless, if challenged, the staff of the facility responsible for the person's detention may argue that the common law principle of necessity can justify detention in these circumstances. The common law has long provided certain grounds upon which such detention may take place. It may justify a person's detention, for instance, when: they are considered to lack the mental capacity to make decisions about their place of residence and the arrangements for their care; their placement in secure care is considered 'necessary' to ensure their safety (or perhaps the safety of others); there is no less restrictive way to manage the situation; and no other person with the power to authorise their detention is reasonably available to approve it at the time (*Bournewood* 1999; Dawson 1999). Detention in these circumstances would not then be arbitrary on the basis that there was no lawful justification for it, as the relevant justification would have been established by the common law. Nevertheless, there is still the question of how long such a common law justification can be relied upon, if Parliament has deliberately enacted an alternative statutory scheme, with its own process, that could be used to justify the detention, and there has been a reasonable opportunity to set that process in motion – such as the process established by adult guardianship legislation.

A great weakness of the common law of necessity, as identified by the European Court of Human Rights (ECtHR), in the *HL v United Kingdom* (2005) case, is that it merely establishes certain *grounds* upon which the restraint or detention of a person may take place, for reasons of safety. The common law does not go further, to establish any automatic or readily available *process* for reviewing a person's detention, to ensure those grounds are met. This was the reason why, in *HL*, the ECtHR held that the common law of necessity, in England, did not prevent violation of Article 5 of the ECHR, because it provided no adequate procedure for review of detention on the basis of the grounds prescribed.

What this also suggests, therefore, is that, where an alternative statutory scheme is available, which contains an adequate review process, and could be relied upon to justify the detention, then that scheme should be invoked, as soon as reasonably practical, if a continuing lawful justification for the detention is to exist. Reliance on the common law of necessity may be legitimate in some urgent circumstances – as was considered to be the case, by the House of Lords, regarding HL's emergency admission to hospital in the *Bournewood* case (1999). But where Parliament has deliberately enacted a statutory scheme that provides greater procedural protections against arbitrary detention, and there has been a reasonable opportunity to set that process in motion, those responsible for the detention should invoke that process, if an adequate justification for the detention is to be maintained.

The decision of the House of Lords in *B v Forsey* (1988) is instructive on this point. There, a man had been detained in hospital under Scotland's mental health legislation, but the clinicians decided not to take the necessary steps under the statute to renew the authority for his detention for a further period of time. The statutory authority for his detention therefore lapsed. But his condition suddenly deteriorated, so he was not released. He then claimed to be unlawfully detained. In response, the hospital authorities argued that his continued detention could be justified, not by the statute, but by the common law of necessity, which they could rely upon instead.

The House of Lords rejected that argument, finding, in effect, that where a person has initially been detained under a statute that specifies a certain process to be followed if the authority for their detention is to be maintained, then the authorities cannot substitute a common law justification in its place – one that provided fewer procedural protections for the person's rights.

The House of Lords did not reject the possibility that a common law justification for detention might survive around the margins of the statutory scheme, provided its operation was not inconsistent with that scheme. As Lord Keith put it, in urgent circumstances, the common law justification might operate 'until a statutory warrant . . . could be obtained' (*B v Forsey* 1988: 575). But it would not operate thereafter.

Obviously, that conclusion is particularly compelling when the person has been initially detained under a statutory scheme that requires a certain process to be followed in order to maintain the authority for a person's detention. Nevertheless, we suggest that the general conclusion still applies: that where a statutory scheme containing procedural protections against arbitrary detention exists, and could properly be invoked to justify a person's detention, the common law of necessity should be viewed as superseded as soon as a reasonable opportunity exists to invoke that statutory process. That approach provides the best protection against arbitrary detention.

By way of an example: New Zealand's adult guardianship legislation – the *Protection of Personal and Property Rights Act 1988* (the PPPR Act) (Diesfeld and McIntosh 2014; Reuvecamp and Dawson 2019) – says nothing expressly about abolition or supersession of the common law of necessity as a justification for intervention. Nor does it say that the statutory adult guardianship scheme constitutes a full codification of the relevant powers. Nevertheless, if the procedural aspects of the right not to be arbitrarily detained are to be given effect, then the additional procedural protections provided by such a statutory scheme should be set in motion, when its criteria for intervention apply, in order to provide the necessary authority for any continuing detention, as soon as there is a reasonable opportunity to do so. If, on the other hand, that step is not taken, any detention lawfully commenced under the common law should be viewed as having become unlawful and therefore arbitrary.

The Scope of the Authority for Detention Provided by an Adult Guardianship Scheme

There is still the question of the scope of the authority for a person's detention that an adult guardianship scheme provides, on its proper interpretation. Does the scheme really authorise *detention* – specifically?

A comprehensive adult guardianship scheme usually provides several distinct mechanisms that permit substitute decisions to be made about the personal care of a person considered to lack the mental capacity to make their own decisions about the matter. First, it will usually provide that a court or tribunal may assume the power to make such decisions. Second, it will provide that a specific individual – often a family member – may be appointed to act for them (taking on a role that may be described as that of an adult guardian). And third, it will provide that a person with mental capacity may nominate in advance their own substitute decision-maker, who will assume the authority to act for them should they later lose the requisite capacity – via the execution of an enduring power of attorney (EPOA).

Under such legislation, a range of parties – either a court, tribunal, adult guardian, or enduring attorney – might be thought to acquire the authority to direct, or give a substitute consent to, the placement in secure rest home care of an elderly person who is considered to lack the mental capacity to decide on their own living arrangements. Nevertheless, there can still be doubt as to whether the scope of their authority really covers *detention*, as an aspect of those arrangements. (See also discussion by Chesterman in Chapter 5 of this volume about whether guardianship legislation authorises substituted consent to restrictive interventions.)

What if the relevant provisions of the legislation that authorise the court to act do not mention detention, or deprivation of liberty, or confinement, specifically; or the terms of appointment of the adult guardian or enduring attorney do not do so? Perhaps because parliament viewed the legislation it was enacting as 'protective' of elderly (or disabled) people's rights, the provisions may contain no express reference to detention. Instead, it may be expressed in rather vague or euphemistic terms. Alternatively, the provisions may use other specific concepts, such as 'residential placement', 'entry into an institution', or 'provision of care and treatment', to indicate the scope of the powers conferred. Should the power to make decisions about those matters be viewed as also entailing a power to decide that a person should be detained? Or are more specific terms of empowerment required when the right to personal liberty is at stake? These questions go directly to the issue of arbitrary detention, because, if a person's detention is not adequately authorised by law, it will be arbitrary under human rights law.

Where the provisions are of that kind, a critical matter will be the correct interpretive approach. In light of the prohibition of arbitrary detention, what is the right approach to take to the interpretation of non-specific empowering clauses that might, on a certain reading, authorise detention, but not do so in direct terms?

Two general interpretive approaches are likely to suggest themselves: a purposive approach, that might be more pragmatic in application, and a stricter rights-driven approach.

A purposive approach might give the relevant powers a broad reading, to 'make the whole scheme workable' (as it is often put). The carers of an elderly person may reasonably believe, for instance, that it is necessary, to protect that person's health or safety, that they be detained, and that protecting vulnerable people's health and safety in this way is a major purpose of the legislation.

Alternatively, a rights-driven approach may be advocated. This can be expressed in terms of a duty to interpret legislation, where possible, in a manner consistent with human rights norms, protected either under international or domestic law. Or it can be expressed in terms of a presumption that parliament should not be intended to abrogate fundamental rights unless the legislation makes this abundantly clear.

In the English, Australian, and New Zealand legal systems, which do not contain an entrenched bill of rights, ideas of this kind are often referred to under the (rather vague) name of the 'principle of legality' (Meagher and Groves 2017). This principle, effectively, gives common law expression to the rights-driven approach. Lord Hoffmann gave a much-quoted statement of the principle in the House of Lords where he wrote (*R v Secretary of State for the Home Department; Ex parte Simms* [2000] 2 AC 115 at 131):

> Fundamental rights cannot be overridden by general or ambiguous words. This is because there is too great a risk that the full implications of their unqualified meaning may have passed unnoticed in the democratic process. In the absence of express language or necessary implication to the contrary, the courts therefore presume that even the most general words were intended to be subject to the basic rights of the individual.

In addition, a rigorous test has been set by the House of Lords for drawing a 'necessary implication' from a statute, in such circumstances. The implication must be one that (*R v Special Commissioner and Another, ex parte Morgan Grenfell and Co Ltd* [2002]: 45):

> necessarily follows from the express provisions of the statute construed in their context. It distinguishes between what would have been sensible or reasonable for Parliament to have included, or what Parliament would, if it had thought about it, probably included and what is clear that the express language of the statute must have included.

The question, then, is how these principles apply to the interpretation of general or insufficiently specific empowering clauses in adult guardianship legislation, that might seem, on a certain reading, to authorise a person's detention in a rest home, but do not authorise detention in direct terms.

An Example of an Interpretive Dilemma

Consider, for instance, the terms in which the power to make a 'personal order' concerning the care and welfare of a person who lacks the mental capacity to make certain decisions is conferred on the New Zealand Family Court by section 10(1) of the *PPPR Act*. The Court is granted the power to order:

(d) that the person shall enter, attend at, or leave an institution specified in the order, not being a psychiatric hospital;
(e) that the person be provided with living arrangements of a kind specified; and
(f) that the person is provided with medical advice or treatment of a kind specified.

None of these clauses expressly confers a power to order a person's *detention* in an institution or rest home. Nor is it impossible for the actions contemplated there to be carried out without detention. People can 'enter' or 'attend' institutions (or rest homes), or be provided there with 'living arrangements' or 'medical advice or treatment', without their being detained. Nothing in these clauses demands the implication that, under the aegis of such powers, a person can be detained.

Nor is any indication given in the legislation as to who exactly would enjoy any power to detain a person in a rest home, if such a power were impliedly conferred. There is no reference to the staff of any facility having a power of detention, or to the police (or anyone else) having the power to detain a person and return them to the facility should they leave. Parliament could have given the court an express power to order a person 'to be detained in such an institution', and specified who could 'enforce' that order, but it did not.

It is true that the New Zealand Parliament conferred on the court a further power, under section 10(4) of the *PPPR Act*, to 'make such orders and give such directions as may be necessary or expedient to give effect, or better effect, to' any personal order made by the court under section 10(1). That power to give directions can therefore be used to supplement a personal order (or set of orders) – directing a person's 'entry' into an institution, for instance, or specifying the 'living arrangements' or 'medical treatment' they should receive there – to give such an order 'better effect'. Even so, it seems unlikely that a power of ***detention*** could be conferred on that basis, when no express power to order detention is conferred by section 10(1). The power to give directions seems merely supplementary to the power to make a parent order. It is doubtful that it could be used to expand, in such a fundamental manner, the scope of the parent power.

This was the general conclusion reached by the New Zealand Law Commission (2002: 14) when it considered the matter:

> The terms of s.10(1)(d), (e), (f) and (g) suggest that while the statute's framers must have known *au fond*, that in some cases there would be a need for compulsion, they shrank, in a statute which from its long title is expressed in terms of rights, from any adequately forthright acknowledgement of the existence of this need.

The Commission rejected the idea that a power of compulsion was implicit:

> the power to make an order that "the person be provided with medical advice or treatment" . . . does not amount to an authority to compel submission to the treatment, and we doubt whether . . . a power expressed in such general terms comes anywhere near furnishing clear authority for physical restraint.
>
> (New Zealand Law Commission 2002: 13)

> We very much doubt whether, in the statute we are discussing, any of the statutory powers are clear enough to justify physical restriction. Provision of living arrangements, for example, as provided by section 10(1)(e) falls a long way short of compelling their use.
>
> (New Zealand Law Commission 2002: 12)

In these passages, the Commission clearly favoured a rights-driven approach. It was unwilling to conclude that a power to order detention can be drawn by implication from section 10 as a whole. The Commission therefore recommended in its report that the *PPPR Act* should be amended to explicitly confer such a power of coercion on the court. That recommendation has never been taken up by the New Zealand Parliament, however, and, to this day, the powers of the court to make personal orders under section 10 remain those just quoted.

In practice, the New Zealand Family Court has issued court orders under section 10 that seem to authorise detention. It made the following orders, for instance, in *Loli v MWY* (2011: 24), in relation to a man with brain damage caused by excessive alcohol use:

(1) That Mr Y shall enter and reside at Anne Maree Gardens Rest Home or . . . such other appropriate dementia unit including a dementia unit offering a more secure level of care.
(2) That reasonable force may be used, including by the police, if necessary, to transport or return Mr Y to a residential care facility identified in order (1).

Should a court really consider it has the power to make such a coercive order, on the basis of an empowering provision that says nothing specifically about detention or the powers of the police? As long ago as 1765, Lord Campden, the Chief Justice of England, said, in *Entick v Carrington*:

> Such is the power, and therefore one should expect that the law to warrant it should be clear in proportion as the power is exorbitant. . . . If it is the law, it will be found in our books. If it is not to be found there, it is not law. . . . What would the Parliament say, if the judges should take upon themselves to mould an unlawful power into a convenient authority. . . . That would be, not judgment, but legislation.

This approach requires Parliament to take full responsibility for placing limits on fundamental rights – under the glare of the Opposition, the public, and the media, in the legislative process.

This is merely one example. The broad interpretation of many other legal provisions could be questioned in the same way, particularly provisions conferring powers on adult guardians or enduring attorneys to make decisions about elderly people's care and welfare, and those conferring powers on health professionals to provide health or disability services without consent. Are the powers conferred by the legislation to make decisions about 'care and welfare', or about providing 'health and disability services', sufficient to confer a power to detain? If not, any such detention may be unlawful and arbitrary.

Decisions of the Courts in Analogous Cases

Further guidance on these matters can be drawn from decisions of courts in cases concerning powers to detain people in community facilities under the authority of mental health legislation. In both New Zealand and England, the courts have had to decide whether the community treatment powers conferred by a Mental Health Act extend to authorising a compulsory patient's detention in a community facility, such as a boarding house or group home, when – in the view of the responsible clinician – the patient could only be safely treated in the community if they were detained in such a facility.

In New Zealand, the leading case concerns whether such a power to detain a compulsory patient in a community facility is conferred under the (civil) Community Treatment Order (CTO) regime (*Department of Health v D* (1999)). The relevant provisions of New Zealand's legislation declare that a compulsory patient under the CTO regime can be required to 'accept' such 'treatment for mental disorder' as the responsible clinician shall direct; can be required to 'attend' at a specified place to receive such treatment; can be recalled swiftly to hospital by the responsible clinician if their continued treatment in the community is no longer considered viable; and police assistance is available in that recall process (*Mental Health (Compulsory Assessment and Treatment Act 1992* (NZ): sections 29, 40, 41, and 59).

In the court's view, none of those powers – even collectively – was sufficient to authorise the detention of the patient (known as D) in a hostel that was specified by the responsible clinician as the place where he must 'accept treatment'. The court considered no such power of community detention was conferred by the CTO regime, even though D had previously gone 'absent without leave' from the hostel; 'smoked cannabis regularly and abused alcohol', exacerbating his condition; and been suspected of raping an elderly woman at another hostel – as a result of which the responsible clinician thought he could only be safely treated in the community if he was 'at all times . . . subject to 24 hours supervision' at the hostel (*Department of Health v D* (1999): 235, 238, and 240). The court was particularly influenced by the fact that no power to 'enforce' detention at a community hostel was conferred by the legislation, other than the general power to recall the patient to hospital.

Similar issues arose in a pair of cases heard by the UK Supreme Court. One concerned the existence of a power of detention in a community facility under the 'conditional discharge' scheme established under the *Mental Health Act 1983* (UK) for forensic patients (*MM v Secretary of State for Justice* [2018]). The other concerned the existence of an equivalent power under the CTO regime, for civilly committed patients (*Welsh Ministers v PJ* [2018]). Both patients, MM and PJ, were being considered by their responsible clinician for discharge from a secure ward of a psychiatric hospital, with the idea that their detention would continue at a community facility running a special programme for men in their position.

In MM's case, the requirement that he be detained in the community facility was to be imposed under the generally-worded power to require a forensic patient receiving conditional discharge from hospital to 'comply with such conditions (if any) as may be imposed at the time of discharge by the tribunal or . . . by the Secretary of State' (*Mental Health Act 1983* (UK): section 73). The UK Supreme Court had little difficulty concluding that no community detention condition could be imposed under the aegis of that broad power – citing Lord Hoffman's formulation of the principle of legality quoted above in *Simms* (2000). A general power to impose conditions on a patient's discharge from hospital was not sufficiently clear or explicit to have that effect.

In PJ's case, the question concerned the power to set the conditions upon which a patient would be released from hospital under a CTO. The relevant provision permitted the responsible clinician to set such conditions for the CTO as were 'necessary or appropriate' for certain purposes, including 'ensuring that the patient receives medical treatment'; 'preventing risk of harm to the patient's health or safety'; or 'protecting other persons' (*Mental Health Act 1983* (UK): section 17B(2)). Here again, even though the community detention condition imposed on PJ may have satisfied one of those purposes – particularly 'protecting other persons' – the Court held that a general power to impose conditions was inadequate to authorise detention in a community facility, especially when the statutory scheme provided no obvious powers to enforce the detention.

The Supreme Court of New Zealand also recently held that no power to order community detention was conferred by a provision authorising a court to impose 'special conditions' on an offender as part of a community-based criminal sentence – even though the relevant power was pitched in 'very permissive terms' (*Woods v New Zealand Police* [2020]: para 63). The Court declared (para 62, fn 46) that the principle that statutes should be interpreted in favour of liberty 'has been part of the common law for centuries', and that (para 68):

> If an unrestricted power to order such detention were intended, then it could have been expected that Parliament would have spoken directly to confer that power. But there is no express power to detain set out.

Furthermore, no criteria had been specified to determine the suitability of any residence in which the offender might be detained, and no process had been established for regulating detention in that environment – both counting against recognition of that power (*Woods* 2020: para 72).

These judicial decisions at the highest level clearly support the notion that only statutory provisions expressed in the most explicit terms will be effective to confer a power of detention in a community facility. There seems no reason why these principles would not apply to the detention of elderly people in rest home care.

Procedural Arbitrariness

We turn now more directly to the question of procedure. Generally speaking, any form of detention can be considered arbitrary if no adequate procedure is established by law to govern it. This could be called the prohibition of procedural arbitrariness. It would seem to apply to the detention of elderly people in rest home care. So, what procedures would be required to prevent their detention being arbitrary?

Guidance can be found in the detailed provisions of the international human rights instruments, in the UN Human Rights Committee's (2014) General Comment No. 35 on Article 9 of the ICCPR, and in the jurisprudence of the ECtHR (Bartlett, Lewis and Thorold 2007). These materials suggest, firstly, that the relevant procedures must be set 'by law': most likely by a statutory scheme. Then, there must be an independent and automatic process, involving proper professional input, for scrutinising the necessity for a person's detention, around the time it occurs. As the UN Human Rights Committee (2014: para 14) puts it, all regimes involving deprivation of liberty must 'be accompanied by procedures that prevent arbitrary detention'.

This indicates the primary aim of the procedures: to *prevent* improper detention. A process will not be sufficient, therefore, that merely permits detained people taking steps to challenge their detention in a court (by seeking a writ of habeas corpus, for instance) after their detention has occurred, because, as the ECtHR held in *HL* (2005), such ex post facto rights are not sufficient to prevent unlawful detention occurring.

Moreover, the responsibility for activating the process should be imposed on the authorities or staff engaged in the person's detention. The person detained should not be required to activate the process, as they will not usually be in a good position to set a legal process in motion. The position should be that, unless those responsible for the person's detention follow the specified process, the authority for the detention will lapse. This provides the necessary incentive for those responsible to set the process in motion.

In the well-known *Winterwerp v Netherlands* decision (1979), the ECtHR set the minimum procedural requirements, under the ECHR (1950), for detention of a person for mental health purposes. These requirements can be adapted to the current context. They would seem to require, at least, independent verification, by suitably qualified professionals, of the fact that the elderly person, whose detention is contemplated, lacks the mental capacity to decide on their own need for secure care; such a restrictive form of care is necessary, for compelling reasons; and there is no less restrictive way of managing the situation. The process of 'certification' or 'sectioning' of a person, conducted by two independent health professionals, against the criteria for compulsion established by mental health legislation, provides a prototype, as do the procedures for independent assessment of the need for a person to be deprived of their liberty under the *Mental Capacity Act 2005* (UK) – though perhaps a somewhat less rigorous process, involving one, rather than two, independent professionals, may suffice, where no one objects. What is required above all is a rigorous independent professional assessment, free of conflict of interest, of the need for the person to be detained, conducted against the criteria for such detention established by law – to be conducted before, or shortly after, the person has been detained, and then again, at regular intervals, to ensure the necessary justification is maintained.

Moreover, this process is intended to supplement, not replace, the right of access to a court. Every detained person must also have an effective right of access to a court (or tribunal or similar body), and that body must be empowered to determine the lawfulness of the person's detention, and, in appropriate cases, order their release. The detained person must have the right to appear in person in those proceedings, or appear via a representative, plus a right to legal representation (to effectively challenge the detention decision). The UN Human Rights Committee (2004: para 19) says: 'the procedures should ensure respect for the views of the individual and ensure that any representative genuinely represents and defends the wishes and interests of the individual'. The proceedings must also be heard 'speedily' (ECHR 1950: Article 5(4)) or 'without delay' (ICCPR 1966: Article 9(4)), to avoid the detention becoming arbitrary. These seem to be the minimum procedural requirements set by international law for scrutinising the need for a person's detention on health or welfare grounds.

The typical 'needs assessment' exercise, to determine whether a person requires rest home care, which is usually conducted by a qualified professional, such as a social worker or nurse, against appropriate professional standards, can certainly contribute to such a process, especially if the 'needs assessor' is sufficiently independent to avoid conflicts of interest. But that process alone, even if required by law, is unlikely to suffice, mainly because the typical 'needs assessment' process is not specifically focused on whether the legal criteria for a person's detention are met. Indeed, such an assessment often has the rather different purpose of determining whether the person meets the criteria for funding of their rest home care (as under the *Care Act 2014* (UK)).

Ensuring Adequate Review of Detention at the Time It Occurs

A major concern, therefore, is whether the law establishes an adequate process for determining whether proper grounds exist for a person's detention, at the time it occurs, and on a regular basis thereafter.

Where a person's detention is directly ordered by a court (or tribunal), under an adult guardianship scheme, the legislation will usually specify an adequate process. This would usually involve a hearing before the court, at least if the matter is contested. The person whose detention is contemplated would have counsel to represent them (appointed, if necessary). They would be entitled to participate in the hearing. The burden would lie on those advocating detention to produce sufficient evidence to show the legal criteria are met. There would be a right of appeal, at least on matters of law, and so on. Such a process would probably satisfy the requirements of human rights law.

More questions are likely to arise about the adequacy of the process when the person's detention is not ordered by a court but proceeds on the basis of the approval of an adult guardian or enduring attorney, appointed to act on the person's behalf. What procedures would be then required to prevent arbitrary detention?

It may seem that the procedures that surrounded the initial appointment of an adult guardian or enduring attorney would be sufficient to prevent arbitrary detention taking place. But would those procedures, surrounding the initial appointment, really be sufficient to prevent arbitrary detention occurring at a later time – perhaps years later – when the guardian or attorney so appointed actually comes to make the decision to approve the detention in a community facility of the person for whom they act?

In some instances, the adult guardian may have been appointed by a court, under what seems to be an adequate process. Similarly, an adequate process may seem to govern the initial appointment of an enduring attorney. A person executing an enduring power of attorney, for instance, will usually be advised by a lawyer at that time. They may even be advised in addition by a second lawyer, to ensure they receive advice from a lawyer who is not also advising the attorney who will be appointed (in order to avoid the conflicts of interest involved in a single lawyer advising both parties). Moreover, a person executing an EPOA can choose whom they will appoint as their attorney; they can influence the terms in which the attorney's appointment is made; and they must have the necessary capacity to make the appointment, at the time. Adequate protections may therefore seem to surround their initial appointment.

Moreover, under the terms of their appointment, an adult guardian or enduring attorney may seem to have acquired the necessary authority to consent to the detention in a rest home of the person for whom they act. The terms of their appointment may say, for instance, that they are authorised to make decisions regarding 'all matters of care and welfare' for that person. And the legislation may also say that decisions properly made by a guardian or attorney, in this manner, are deemed to take effect 'as if they were decisions of the person for whom they act' (or something of that kind) (e.g. *PPPR Act* (NZ): sections 19(1) and 98(5)). Such broad terms of appointment might seem to permit the guardian or attorney to consent to the detention of the person for whom they act, and that consent may then seem to provide a lawful justification for it.

Nevertheless, even broad terms of appointment of that kind would not, we suggest, permit a guardian or attorney to consent to the *arbitrary* detention of the person for whom they act, especially when a guardian or attorney is usually under a duty to promote that person's 'best interests' (e.g. *PPPR Act* (NZ): sections 18(3): 98A; *Mental Capacity Act 2005* (UK): section 4). It could hardly be in a person's 'best interests' to be arbitrarily detained.

What seems to be required is a set of procedures to govern the detention of a person via the substitute consent of a guardian or attorney that is sufficient to prevent the person's detention being arbitrary, when the person comes to be detained. Adequate procedures for appointing the guardian or attorney in the first place are not sufficient for that purpose, particularly because the appointment process will not usually be focused on the question of a proper justification for any subsequent detention decision: that is, ensuring the person's detention via the substitute consent of a guardian or attorney is necessary, proportionate, for an appropriate purpose, the least restrictive approach and so on. Those matters that go directly to the justification for detention can only be determined on the basis of information available at the time the detention occurs. The conclusion is therefore hard to resist that, even if proper procedures governed the guardian or attorney's initial appointment, those procedures should not be considered sufficient to prevent arbitrary detention occurring at a later time.

Nor would a process be sufficient that merely provided a person with a right to challenge in a court the decision of a guardian or attorney to approve their detention, where such a process operates only after detention has occurred, and at the initiative of the person who is detained. This is because such a process will not usually operate with sufficient speed, and because it is not realistic to expect the process to be activated by a person who is detained (especially one assessed as lacking mental capacity to make decisions about their own care) – as the ECtHR held in *HL* (2005). Such a process is no substitute for a contemporaneous process of review, which must be set in motion by those responsible for the detention, which is designed to prevent arbitrary detention, in every case.

The Deprivation of Liberty Safeguards (DoLS) regime (Jones and Piffaretti 2018) was enacted by the UK Parliament to address this procedural deficit, following the decision of the ECtHR in *HL* (2005); and in a sign of the turbulent impact of the regime, DOLS has now been abolished and superseded by the Liberty Protection Safeguards (LPS), introduced in the *Mental Capacity (Amendment) Act 2019* (UK). The Code of Practice and the Regulations for the LPS scheme are being developed at the time of writing, indicating the unresolved questions that remain about establishing ideal legal responses to deprivation of liberty in care settings (see Series 2022). The need for adequate procedural protections of this kind now needs to be addressed with the same seriousness in many other jurisdictions, to prevent arbitrary detention, in these circumstances.

Conclusions

This chapter has illustrated a range of situations in which the legal arrangements governing the detention of elderly people in secure rest home care may not be sufficient to prevent it being arbitrary. Similar concerns may apply to the position of other people detained in community facilities. The position of elderly people has been used to illustrate the arguments because, in many jurisdictions, they are the group most likely to be subject to detention of this kind.

We have emphasised specific elements of the general prohibition of arbitrary detention under human rights law, including the fact that this prohibition applies with full force to the detention of elderly people. Particularly, we have focused on the need for abundantly clear sources of legal authority to justify detention, and the dangers of (what can be called) procedural arbitrariness – especially where detention occurs via the apparent consent of a substitute decision-maker, such as an adult guardian or enduring attorney, rather than via the order of a court. We have stressed the need to consider carefully the character of relations between common law and statutory sources of authority for people's detention, especially when the statutory sources contain more extensive procedural protections for liberty. Following that approach, we have called into question the adequacy of the common law of necessity, as a justification for detention, in anything but the short-term.

We have also sought to draw attention to certain principles of interpretation, particularly the importance of the rights-driven approach to the interpretation of the sources of authority for detention. We have emphasised how that rights-driven approach is reinforced, in some jurisdictions, by the older common law principle of legality, which encourages us to take the view that parliament does not intend its legislation to limit fundamental rights unless it has made that intention abundantly clear in the law.

As can be seen, plenty of guidance is available as to the legal measures needed to avoid arbitrary detention. It can be found in the detail of the international human rights instruments, and in the decisions of both international tribunals and domestic courts. This guidance should inform the efforts of legislatures everywhere, as they seek to make good the commitment that their state has entered, on ratifying the relevant international human rights instruments, to bring their laws into line with the requirement that no one should be arbitrarily detained.

Note

1 This chapter draws on material from the PhD thesis of Frances Matthews, 'Are People in Secure Dementia Care in New Zealand Arbitrarily Detained?' (University of Otago 2021), available https://ourarchive.otago.ac.nz/handle/10523/12869 (accessed 26 November 2022).

References

Cases

B v Forsey 1988 SLT 572.
Department of Health v D (1999) 18 FRNZ 233.
Entick v Carrington (1765) 19 Howell's State Trials 1029; 95 ER 807 (KB).
HL v United Kingdom (2005) 40 EHRR 32.
Loli v MWY (unreported) FAM-2009-004-1877, 14 January 2011, Auckland Family Court.

MM v Secretary of State for Justice [2018] UKSC 60.
R v Bournewood and Community Mental Health NHS Trust; Ex parte L [1999] 1 AC 458.
R v Secretary of State for the Home Department; Ex parte Simms [2000] 2 AC 115.
R v Special Commissioner and Another; Ex parte Morgan Grenfell and Co Ltd [2002] UKHL 21.
Winterwerp v Netherlands 6301/73 [1979] ECHR 4.
Woods v New Zealand Police [2020] NZSC 141.

Legislation and International Instruments

Canadian Charter of Rights and Freedoms (1982) Enacted by the Canada Act 1982, c 11 (proclaimed in force 17 April 1982).
Constitution of the United States (1788).
Convention on the Rights of Persons with Disabilities (2007) Opened for signature 13 December 2515 UNTS 3 (entered into force 3 May 2008).
European Convention for the Protection of Human Rights and Fundamental Freedoms (European Convention on Human Rights) (1950) Opened for signature 4 November 1950, ETS 5 (entered into force 3 September 1953).
Human Rights Act 1998 (UK).
International Covenant on Civil and Political Rights (1966) Opened for signature 16 December, 999 UNTS 171 (entered into force 23 March 1976).
Mental Capacity Act 2005 (UK).
Mental Capacity (Amendment) Act 2019 (UK).
Mental Health Act 1983 (UK).
Mental Health (Compulsory Assessment and Treatment) Act 1992 (NZ).
New Zealand Bill of Rights Act 1990 (NZ).
Protection of Personal and Property Rights Act 1988 (NZ).
Universal Declaration of Human Rights (1948) GA Res 217A(III), 3rd sess, 183rd plen mtg, UN Doc A/810.

Books, Journal Articles and Other Texts

Bartlett, P., Lewis, O. and Thorold, O. (2007) *Mental Disability and the European Convention on Human Rights*, Leiden: Martinus Nijhoff.
Chandler, K. (2021) 'The Regulation of Restrictive Practices on People with Intellectual Impairment: The Challenges and Opportunities Posed by a Rights-based Approach', in B. McSherry and Y. Maker (eds) *Restrictive Practices in Health Care and Disability Settings: Legal, Policy and Practical Responses*, Abingdon: Routledge, 68–90.
Dawson, J. (1999) 'The Law of Emergency Psychiatric Detention', *New Zealand Law Review*, 2: 275–303.
Diesfeld, K. and McIntosh, I. (eds) (2014) *Elder Law in New Zealand*, Wellington: Thomson Reuters.
Jones, R. and Piffaretti, E. (2018) *Mental Capacity Act Manual*, 18th edn, London: Sweet and Maxwell.

Macken, C. (2005) 'Preventive Detention and the Right of Personal Liberty and Security Under the International Covenant on Civil and Political Rights 1966', *Adelaide Law Review*, 26(1): 1–28.
Martin, B. and Gurbai, S. (2019) 'Surveying the Geneva Impasse: Coercive Care and Human Rights', *International Journal of Law and Psychiatry*, 64: 117–28.
McSherry, B. (2012) 'Legal Capacity under the Convention on the Rights of Persons with Disabilities', *Journal of Law and Medicine*, 20(1): 22–27.
McSherry, B. (2014) *Managing Fear*, New York: Routledge.
McSherry, B. and Keyzer, P. (2011) '"Dangerous" People: The Road Ahead for Policy, Prediction and Practice', in B. McSherry and P. Keyzer (eds) *Dangerous People: Policy, Prediction and Practice*, New York: Routledge, 251–54.
Meagher, D. and Groves, M. (eds) (2017) *The Principle of Legality in Australia and New Zealand*, Annandale, NSW: Federation Press.
New Zealand Law Commission (2002) *Protections Some Disadvantaged People May Need, R80*, Wellington: NZLC. Available www.lawcom.govt.nz/sites/default/files/projectAvailableFormats/NZLC%20R80.pdf (accessed 26 November 2022).
Reuvecamp, I. and Dawson, J. (eds) (2019) *Mental Capacity Law in New Zealand*, Wellington: Thomson Reuters.
Series, L. (2022) *Deprivation of Liberty in the Shadows of the Institution*, Bristol: Bristol University Press.
Sifris, R. (2011) 'An International Human Rights Perspective on Detention Without Charge or Trial', in B. McSherry and P. Keyzer (eds) *Dangerous People: Policy, Prediction and Practice*, New York: Taylor and Francis, 13–24.
United Nations Human Rights Committee (2014) *General Comment No. 35 – Article 9 (Liberty and Security of Person)*, 112th sess, UN Doc CCPR/C/GC/35.

Part III

Improving Access to Justice and the Criminal Law

9 Whydunnit?

Causal Explanations in Sentencing Offenders With Mental Health Problems

Jamie Walvisch, Andrew Carroll, Tim Marsh and Jaydip Sarkar

Introduction

Throughout her distinguished career, Bernadette McSherry has sought to ensure justice for individuals with mental health problems in both civil and criminal contexts. To achieve this goal, she has aimed to 'integrate the expertise of international and Australian mental health experts from a range of disciplines' to develop model frameworks that are supported by evidence and comply with international human rights (McSherry 2008: 2). In doing so, she has clarified many of the underlying legal principles in the area and has provided guidance on the appropriate roles of the various participants. It is in this spirit that this chapter is written. It draws on the expertise of a legal academic, a barrister and two forensic psychiatrists to address two key issues that arise when a person with mental health problems is convicted of a criminal offence: how should legal practitioners, mental health experts and judges understand the relationship, if any, between their mental health problems and their offending conduct? And what impact should that relationship have on the sentence imposed?

Before beginning our analysis of this complex issue, we think it is important to make clear that most individuals with mental health problems, including those with severe mental disorders, do not commit crimes. This was emphasised in the Final Report of the Royal Commission into Victoria's Mental Health System (2021), to which Bernadette McSherry served as a commissioner, which stated that:

> The existing body of research on mental illness and offending can be summarised in this way: 'most people with mental illnesses are not violent, most violent offenders are not mentally ill, and the strongest risk factors for violence (e.g. past violence) are shared by those with and without mental illnesses'.
>
> (Volume 3, 354, citing Skeem, Peterson and Silver 2011: 113)

The relationship between mental health problems and crime is highly complex (McSherry 2020: 573). It has been suggested that whether or not an

DOI: 10.4324/9781003350644-12

individual's mental health problems create an additional risk of offending behaviour

> depends upon the type of diagnosis, the nature and severity of the symptoms present, whether the person is receiving treatment and care, if there is a past history of violence by the individual, the co-occurrence of antisocial personality disorder and substance misuse and the social, economic and cultural context in which an individual lives.
>
> (Thornicroft 2006: 139)

Although most people with mental health problems never engage in criminal offending, many convicted offenders have experienced mental health problems at some point during their lives (see e.g. Fazel and Seewald 2012). In common law countries such as Australia, England and Wales, the presence of mental health problems at the time of the offence or sentencing currently plays a key role in determining what penalty to impose on convicted offenders.[1] This makes it essential to ensure that the part (if any) that is played by mental health problems in an individual's offending behaviour is properly understood by all participants in the criminal justice system and is addressed in a principled manner. Not only will this help ensure the just outcomes that are central to McSherry's work, but it will also help to achieve the rehabilitative aims of the sentencing process, by providing judges with information that can assist them to properly tailor a sentence to the needs of the offender and the community. It is for this reason that we have written this chapter.

It is important to note that our focus is on the sentencing process. We are looking at individuals who have been convicted of one or more offences and who are going to have a penalty imposed upon them. This differs from two other matters which often arise when an individual with mental health problems comes into contact with the criminal justice system: whether they should be held responsible for their criminal conduct at all, which relates to the availability of the 'insanity' defence or its jurisdictional equivalent;[2] and whether they are fit to stand trial, which focuses on their capacity to understand and participate in the trial proceedings.[3] We note that Professor McSherry has addressed both of these related matters in her writings (see e.g. Carroll et al. 2008; Hopper and McSherry 2001; Gooding et al. 2017).

There are five parts to this chapter. Part One examines the ways in which Australian, English and Welsh sentencing courts currently assess the relationship between mental health problems and offending conduct, focussing in particular on the determination of the offender's culpability. While the connection between the offender's mental health and the offence they committed may also be important to other aspects of the sentencing determination – such as the judge's assessment of the offender's rehabilitative prospects, the appropriateness of imposing a deterrent sentence or the need to protect the community from the offender (see e.g. Walvisch 2018a) – it is in the culpability context that this connection assumes a central role.

Part Two considers the 'psycho-legal challenge' that arises whenever the courts place reliance on evidence from mental health experts in the sentencing context: the task of bridging the two worlds of 'sentencing law' and 'mental health science'. It addresses two aspects of the challenge that are especially relevant to criminal sentencing: the role played by moral evaluative considerations in determining the causal relationship between mental health problems and offending behaviour; and the relevance of 'indirect' causal factors.

Part Three focuses on the type of explanation that should be given to help courts determine whether an offender's mental health problems and offending behaviour are related, and if so how they are related. It suggests that experts should give 'possibility explanations' rather than 'necessity explanations' (Walker 1980) and explores the consequences of this suggestion for the form, content and limits of the evidence that is given. Part Four outlines a framework that experts can use to describe the strength of the causal relationship. Part Five concludes the chapter by considering the roles that legal practitioners and the courts should play in assessing the causal issue.

Part One: Current Approaches to Assessing the Causal Relationship

Various mechanisms have been put in place to try to limit the number of individuals with mental health problems who are tried and convicted in the ordinary way (Walvisch 2018b: 160). For example, where it appears that an individual with a mental health problem has committed a crime, the police may issue a caution rather than charge them. In some cases, they may qualify for a diversion programme (see e.g. Richardson and McSherry 2010). If they are charged, the individual may be found unfit to stand trial or not guilty on the basis of the 'insanity' defence. These measures are, however, only of limited effect: most individuals with mental health problems stand trial in the ordinary way and may be convicted or plead guilty. Where this occurs, the sentencing judge needs to determine how (if at all) the offender's mental health problems should affect the sentencing determination.

The Australian Approach

Across Australia, this matter is largely governed by the '*Verdins* principles' (see Walvisch, Carroll and Marsh 2021). These principles, which were enunciated by the Victorian Court of Appeal in the landmark case of *R v Verdins* (2007) (*Verdins*), hold that mental health problems can be relevant to sentencing in at least six ways. They can:

- reduce the offender's moral culpability, thereby affecting the punishment that is just in the circumstances and the importance of denunciation as a sentencing consideration;
- influence the kind of sentence that should be imposed, or the conditions under which it should be served;

- moderate or eliminate the need for general deterrence as a sentencing consideration;
- moderate or eliminate the need for specific deterrence as a sentencing consideration;
- make a sentence weigh more heavily on the offender than on a person in normal health, thereby affecting the determination of a proportionate sentence; or
- create a serious risk of imprisonment having a significant adverse effect on the offender's mental health, suggesting the need to reduce the sanction.

The principles apply to any proceeding in which 'the offender is shown to have been suffering at the time of the offence (and/or to be suffering at the time of sentencing) from a mental disorder or abnormality or an impairment of mental function' (*Verdins*: 271). There is no need for an offender to have a diagnosable mental disorder, or for that condition to be of a particular level of gravity, for the principles to apply (although in practice a diagnosable disorder is almost invariably required). What matters is 'what the evidence shows about the nature, extent and effect of the mental impairment experienced by the offender at the relevant time' (*Verdins*: 271). In particular, sentencing courts need to consider 'how the particular condition (is likely to have) affected the mental functioning of the particular offender in the particular circumstances – that is, at the time of the offending or in the lead-up to it – or is likely to affect him/her in the future' (*Verdins*: 272).

In the years since the *Verdins* decision was handed down, these principles have been accepted in all Australian jurisdictions, as well as in New Zealand (Walvisch and Carroll 2017). They have been cited in over 1,000 cases, most of which have focussed on *Verdins* Principle 1: the reduction of the offender's moral culpability. The Court in *Verdins* (275) offered further guidance on this principle, stating that an offender's moral culpability may be reduced if, at the time of the offence, their mental condition had any of the following effects:

(a) impairing the offender's ability to exercise appropriate judgment;
(b) impairing the offender's ability to make calm and rational choices or to think clearly;
(c) making the offender disinhibited;
(d) impairing the offender's ability to appreciate the wrongfulness of the conduct;
(e) obscuring the intent to commit the offence;
(f) contributing (causally) to the commission of the offence.

This list essentially describes ways in which the courts' general assumption that 'a person who commits a criminal offence is a rational agent who calculates the benefits and costs of criminal behaviour and then makes a considered choice to commit a criminal offence' (Edney 2006: 253) can be challenged by the effects of a mental health problem. While the list was stated to be non-exhaustive, these '*Verdins* effects' have been the focus of almost all subsequent cases that have addressed *Verdins* Principle 1 (Walvisch 2010: 191).

In the current context, point (f) is of particular significance, as it focuses on the *causal link* between the offender's impairment and the commission of the offence. In explicating this point, courts have held that an offender's moral culpability will only be reduced if 'the disorder was operative at the time of the offence and . . . it contributed to, in some way is connected to or explains the offending' (*Arthars v R* (2013): 614).

For the *Verdins* principles to apply, there needs to be specific expert evidence about the nature, extent and effects of the offender's mental health problems (*O'Connor v R* [2014]: para 65). However, such evidence must be thoroughly scrutinised by the judge, having regard to matters such as the witness's expertise and the information upon which it was based (*Ross v R* [2015]). It is for the judge to determine whether to accept the evidence and how to use it.

The English Approach

A similar approach has been taken to sentencing offenders with mental health problems in England and Wales. In October 2020, the Sentencing Council for England and Wales' (Sentencing Council) guideline on *Sentencing Offenders with Mental Disorders, Developmental Disorders, or Neurological Impairments* came into effect (the 'sentencing guideline').[4] This guideline states that '[c]ulpability may be reduced if an offender was at the time of the offence suffering from an impairment or disorder (or combination of impairments or disorders) such as those listed in Annex A' (Sentencing Council for England and Wales 2020: para 9). Annex A lists various mental disorders, neurological impairments and developmental disorders, such as schizophrenia, bipolar disorder, intellectual disability, autism spectrum disorder, substance use disorder, personality disorders and the dementias.

The sentencing guideline states that '[c]ulpability will only be reduced if there is sufficient connection between the offender's impairment or disorder and the offending behaviour' (Sentencing Council for England and Wales 2020: para 11). It goes on to list a number of questions that courts may find to be a 'useful starting point' in assessing an offender's culpability, such as whether the offender's impairment or disorder impaired their ability to exercise appropriate judgment, make rational choices, or understand the nature and consequences of their actions; or whether it caused them to behave in a disinhibited way (Sentencing Council for England and Wales 2020: para 15).

The guideline makes it clear that the decision about culpability is for the sentencer to make, after careful analysis of all of the circumstances of the case and all relevant materials (Sentencing Council for England and Wales 2020: paras 12–13). While expert evidence on the issue may be very valuable, and must be considered, 'it is the duty of the sentencer to make their own decision, and the court is not bound to follow expert opinion if there are compelling reasons to set it aside' (Sentencing Council for England and Wales 2020: para 14).

Similarities and Differences Between the Australian and English Approaches

The similarities between the Australian and English approaches are readily apparent. In both jurisdictions there is:

- an acknowledgment of the possibility that an offender's mental health problems may reduce their culpability for the offence;
- a requirement that there be a relationship between the offender's mental health problems and their offending behaviour;
- an illustration of the various ways in which this relationship may be manifest, such as through the impact of the offender's mental health problems on their cognitive or volitional capacities; and
- a division of labour between the role of the expert witness and the sentencer, with the final determination falling within the sentencer's purview.

There is, however, one key difference between the jurisdictions. Although the English guideline acknowledges that it is for the sentencer to determine whether the offender's mental health problems reduced their culpability, English courts allow mental health experts to directly opine on this issue (Hallett 2020). By contrast, Australian courts have repeatedly emphasised that mental health experts should not comment on moral culpability, as it is a legal issue and thus outside their area of expertise (see e.g. *Wright v R* [2015]). In Victoria, this has been reinforced in the Supreme Court Practice Note on *Sentencing Hearings: Expert Reports on Mental Functioning of Offenders*, which explicitly states that it is beyond an expert witness's scope to comment on this matter (Supreme Court of Victoria 2017: section 7.3). In our view, this division of responsibility makes sense: culpability is a value-laden construct, influenced by a range of factors that go well beyond clinical expertise (Walvisch and Carroll 2022: 130).

Part Two: The 'Psycho-Legal Challenge' in Assessing the Causal Relationship

There is a 'psycho-legal challenge' whenever the courts place reliance on evidence from mental health experts (generally forensic psychiatrists or psychologists) in the sentencing context: the task of bridging the two worlds of 'sentencing law' and 'mental health science', with their quite distinct aims, histories and epistemological frameworks.[5] Communication across the gap that separates those worlds is often suboptimal – beset by misunderstandings and consternation on both sides. In this section we briefly consider two aspects of this challenge that are especially relevant to criminal sentencing: the role played by moral evaluative considerations in determining the causal relationship between mental health problems and offending behaviour; and the relevance of 'indirect' causal factors.

The Role of Moral Evaluative Considerations

One of the court's key foci when sentencing offenders with mental health problems is their *moral culpability*. It is important to distinguish this from their *legal responsibility*. Unlike individuals who are found not guilty by reason of 'insanity', individuals who face the sentencing process have been held legally responsible for their behaviour.[6] They have been found guilty and are to be punished for their crime in some way. However, due to their mental health problems, they may not be considered as blameworthy for their behaviour as they would have been had their mental functioning not been impaired. Consequently, the court may not consider it appropriate to punish them as harshly as other offenders.

The Victorian Court of Appeal explained the concept of moral culpability, and its relationship with mental health conditions, in *DPP v Weidlich* [2008] (para 15):

> Generally, the measure of culpability of an offender under the criminal law rests upon the extent to which the individual can be seen to be personally responsible for both the prohibited acts and their consequences. Little thought is required to appreciate that the greater the level of insight and understanding possessed by him or her concerning the act and its potential harm, the higher becomes the level of culpability for then deliberately engaging in the conduct involved. The Court in . . . Verdins recognised that sometimes as a consequence of the contribution made to the commission of an offence by a mental disorder from which a perpetrator was suffering at the time, it would be unjust to attribute to the offender a full measure of personal responsibility.

It can be seen from this passage that for an offender's culpability to be reduced, there needs to be *some kind of connection* between their mental health problem(s) and their offending behaviour. Without such a connection they will be equally as blameworthy as other offenders, despite the existence of any mental disorder. This does not, however, mean the same sanction should be imposed on them: as noted earlier, there are various other ways in which an offender's mental health problems may properly affect the sentencing determination. For example, an offender's sanction may be reduced if, due to their mental health problems, they would experience imprisonment as disproportionately burdensome, even if there is no relationship between their mental health problems and their offending behaviour.

Although not made clear by the courts, their determination that an offender's mental health condition was (or was not) a relevant 'cause' of their offending behaviour seems to be based on moral evaluative considerations. This can be clearly seen in a case such as *Paparone v R* [2000], in which the offender pleaded guilty to possessing and manufacturing amphetamines. He had been diagnosed with attention deficit disorder, and as outlined in the appellate judgment, his counsel argued that 'the attention deficit disorder had resulted in the [offender] taking drugs on a self-help basis for the purpose of alleviating the symptoms of his disorder and that this had resulted in the circumstances leading to the offences' (para 10). This argument was rejected by the original sentencing judge, who held that 'the disorder had no necessary connection with the manufacture or possession of illicit drugs' (para 10). The majority of the Western Australian Court of Appeal agreed, holding (para 54, italics added):

> There was no causal link *of the required kind* between the applicant's attention deficit disorder and his offending behaviour. He did not commence to manufacture, consume and sell amphetamines because he suffered from the disorder, but by reason of his deliberate choice, initially taken to obtain relief from the symptoms of the disorder. There was never any suggestion that the disorder precluded him from seeking treatment and the prescription of appropriate medication.

In reaching this conclusion, the court has rejected a purely fact-based (or 'but for') approach to causation. It has not accepted that the offender's mental disorder caused the offending behaviour because the offence would not have happened in its absence (as *but for* the attention deficit disorder he would not have needed the drugs for self-help purposes, and so would not have manufactured or possessed them). Instead, the court has *evaluated* the various factors that contributed to his behaviour, and has decided that it was his choice to take illicit drugs, rather than to seek treatment, which was the most significant factor. It has consequently labelled this decision the 'cause' of his actions. The phrase 'of the required kind' is a tacit acknowledgment of the evaluative nature of the decision-making.

A similar approach can be seen in *Carroll v R* [2011], in which the Victorian Court of Appeal stated (para 20, italics added):

> Where reliance is placed on proposition 1 [of *Verdins*], concerning moral culpability, the question for the Court is whether the evidence establishes – on the balance of probabilities – that the impairment of mental functioning did contribute to the offending *in such a way as to render the offender less blameworthy* for the offending than he/she would otherwise have been. Very often, this question is approached as one of causation. Did the evidence establish a causal connection between the impairment of mental functioning and the offending for which sentence is to be imposed?

The moral evaluative nature of legal determinations regarding causation has been commented on by Jane Stapleton, who observes that we use the term causation when addressing 'transitions' that have occurred in the world. She notes that while such transitions may have been the result of a myriad of factors, the courts must decide 'which of the factors that, it is agreed, brought about the transition seem important in the context of a legal dispute about responsibility' (Stapleton 2002: 18). Furthermore, '[w]here, as in law, the purpose at hand is the moral or policy evaluation of human conduct, this . . . inquiry can never be reduced to a question of fact. Indeed, it is only reached after the facts have been agreed or decided' (Stapleton 2002: 18).

Once the evaluative nature of causal determinations is accepted, it becomes clear that the conventional legal 'but for' test of causation will not be sufficient to fully meet the needs of the court when assessing the connection between mental health problems and offending behaviour. The issue the court is seeking to address is whether the offender *should* be considered less blameworthy for their behaviour because of their mental health problems – a moral evaluative question, the answer to which may be heavily influenced by broader public policy concerns. This requires consideration of various other factors such as the cause of the condition, the nature and strength of its impact on the offender's cognitive and volitional capacities, the offender's insight into their condition, and the opportunities the offender had to address the condition prior to offending (including the social and economic circumstances that shaped those opportunities) (Walvisch 2023).

This has consequences for the role that expert mental health evidence should play in a sentencing hearing. In our view, matters of moral evaluation sit outside a mental health expert's field of expertise and hence should not be directly opined on (contrary to the approach that is currently taken in England and Wales). Expert mental health evidence on this issue should be limited to clarifying the ways in which an offender's moral reasoning and self-control may have been affected by impaired mental functioning, such as by way of the '*Verdins* effects'. It is for the judge to determine whether, in light of that evidence, the connection was of the right kind to reduce the offender's blameworthiness.

The Relevance of 'Indirect' Causal Factors

When providing an explanation of offending behaviour, mental health experts ideally employ the clinical skill of 'formulation': an attempt at explaining that behaviour, to the degree possible, on the basis of evidence-based biopsychosocial variables (including mental disorder) in the context of the individual's whole life. Such formulations may take various forms (Weerasekera 1993), but generally involve:

- exposition of symptoms of mental disorder and how they have varied over time;

- description of interactions – often involving bidirectional and synergistic causal relationships – between
  - the effects of 'comorbid' mental disorders diagnosed in the same person (for example, interactions between a mood disorder, substance use disorder and personality disorder); and
  - situational factors (such as interpersonal stress and environmental context) and the effects of mental disorders; and
- description of the effects of enduring psychopathology (such as personality disorder or neurocognitive disorder) that act as predisposing/vulnerability factors for certain adverse outcomes, including offending behaviour.

Inevitably, a significant degree of hypothesising and reasoned speculation is involved in this task, given the inherent limits on what we can ever know about past events (Sadler 2002).

The ways in which the interaction between enduring 'background' personality-based variables and temporary situational factors can influence the court's determination of moral culpability is well illustrated in the following passage, in which the judge is passing sentence on a young woman who killed a previously unknown man, Mr Rathod:

> It is abundantly clear from all of the evidence that you have a profound personality disorder and impaired mental functioning particularly when you are in an aroused state. . . .
>
> The prosecution submitted that whilst *Verdins* principles can apply in an appropriate case, there is no realistic connection or causal link in your case. I disagree with the proposition that there is no realistic connection or causal link.
>
> I am satisfied that the disorder and its profound psychological deficits were active at the time of the offending and significantly impaired your mental functioning. . . .
>
> In your case, once you had reached an acute level of anger and were in an aroused state, your emotional dysregulation made it extremely difficult for you to control the impulse to act out that anger so that while you were aware that strangling Mr Rathod was wrong and you knew what you were doing and could in fact organise the steps that led to the actions which caused Mr Rathod's death, I am satisfied that your cognitive state (that is your capacity to think clearly and logically about your actions) was likely to have been severely impaired, particularly at the time of the doing of the act. Furthermore, your reduced capacity to experience and express empathy meant that you were not sufficiently responsive to Mr Rathod's distress to stop.
>
> In all the circumstances, your moral culpability for the offending is significantly reduced by reason of your severe personality disorder, which relevantly impaired your mental functioning at the time. As a result your sentence must be significantly moderated.
>
> (*R v Dolheguy* [2020]: paras 54–59)

As noted earlier, expert formulations should not seek to usurp the court's role in determining whether the causal connection was of a kind that is appropriate to reduce the offender's culpability. Nonetheless, expert opinions should be of practical utility to the courts – an aim that is facilitated by clarity about what factors the court may consider to be relevant.

It has been made clear that the impairment does not need to have been the *sole* cause of the offence. Instead, it must be shown that there was a 'realistic' (*R v Vuadreu* [2009]: para 37) or 'sufficient' (Sentencing Council for England and Wales 2020: para 11) connection between the impairment and the offending, or that the impairment 'contributed to' (*DPP v Patterson* [2009] VSCA 222) the offending in some way. Unfortunately, the law has not always provided consistent or clear guidance about the requisite nature and extent of this connection.

Some cases have suggested that moral culpability will not be reduced where the impairment only formed the 'background' to the commission of the offence (see e.g. *Bowen v R* [2011]), or where its contribution was 'indirect' (see e.g. *R v Surtees* [2022]): that *direct* causation of offending is required. For example, where an offender with a mental disorder was under the influence of drugs at the time of the offence, defence counsel may argue that their mental disorder predisposed them to use drugs, the effects of which in turn resulted in offending behaviour. Courts have consistently refused to mitigate on this basis, due to the 'indirect' contribution made by the mental disorder (see e.g. *Johnston v R* [2013]).

The argument that indirect causes do not count for mitigation seeks to distinguish between:

- direct causation: manifestations of mental disorder → offending behaviour; and
- indirect causation: manifestations of mental disorder → consequences (in terms of behavioural choices, such as ingestion of illicit drugs or in terms of other enduring vulnerabilities) → offending behaviour.

It is not clear, however, why the indirect nature of the contribution should preclude mitigation. The fact that the cause of an offender's conduct was indirect does not mean that it lacked significance. It will often be the case that an offender's mental disorder will greatly increase their vulnerability to choose to engage in offending behaviour, playing a crucial, but indirect, causative role in the offence. Examples of such indirect relationships would include:

- Post Traumatic Stress Disorder (PTSD) → Hypervigilance to threat → increased vulnerability to serious reactive violence if threatened;
- Major Depression → Reduced impulse control and fragile self-esteem → increased vulnerability to angry aggression if humiliated;
- Intellectual Disability → Reduced capacity for consequential thinking → increased vulnerability to reckless substance use → increased vulnerability to offending due to intoxication.

In the context of systems science, when analysing adverse outcomes such as aviation accidents, best practice is to take into account enduring background factors ('latent conditions') that confer vulnerability to future adverse outcomes when the system is under stress (Reason 2000). If we analogise this approach to the current context, offending behaviour can be considered to be an adverse outcome arising in a complex 'system' represented by an offender with an enduring mental disorder attempting to function in society. Their disorder can be seen as a 'latent condition' that renders the person vulnerable to the adverse outcome of offending. It makes sense to take such a disorder into account when analysing the offending behaviour, even if its impact is indirect: an explanatory framework that simply ignores the role of such factors because of their indirect nature is diminished.

Whilst there may be valid *policy* grounds for deciding, for example, that moral culpability is not reduced where the offender's mental disorder predisposed them to use drugs, this is a policy decision about the usage of illicit drugs rather than about the significance of the mental disorder to, or its direct relationship with, the offending behaviour. To limit mitigation *a priori* to those cases where there are no intervening mediating variables between symptoms of the disorder and the offending also seems to be contrary to the spirit of *Verdins*, a decision that nowhere sought to set such a limitation.

Hence, rather than focussing on whether the causal connection was direct or indirect, it would be preferable for sentencing judges to focus on whether the connection was *sufficient* to reduce the offender's moral culpability. As noted earlier, that is a moral evaluative question, appropriately influenced by social policy concerns. It not only requires a nuanced consideration of the relationship between the mental health condition and the offending behaviour, but also a consideration of the various factors mentioned in the previous section, such as the aetiology of the condition and the nature and strength of its impact on the offender's cognitive and volitional capacities. In the next section we consider the type of causal explanation that should be given to help the judge make this determination.

Part Three: Using 'Possibility Explanations' to Explain the Causal Relationship

Nigel Walker's (1980) distinction between 'necessity explanations' and 'possibility explanations' provides a useful starting point for addressing the way in which mental health experts should explain the causal relationship (if any) between mental health problems and offending behaviour. 'Necessity explanations' answer the question 'why is or was that *necessarily* so?' and apply when a particular set of circumstances *necessarily* leads to certain consequences. Such explanations are the foundation of the physical sciences: an example from the realm of chemistry is elemental sodium being added to water, which *necessarily* results in an exothermic reaction releasing heat and light.

Such causal pathways have several characteristics:

- they are readily replicated: one can be confident that a repetition of the addition of sodium to water will *necessarily* have the same outcome;
- the causal explanation can be given in terms of a clear, well-established mechanism (in this case, electron exchange with consequent energy release);
- there is a direct relationship between the antecedent variables and the consequential outcome that can be summarised in equation form ($2Na + 2H_20 \rightarrow 2NaOH + H_2$); and
- the causal explanation is 'values free' – unaffected by potential cultural biases and other peculiarities of perspective of the person doing the explaining, and existing outside of any moral framework. For example, it would be absurd to blame the chemical ingredients of a bomb for the deaths inflicted by a terrorist.

By contrast, 'possibility explanations' answer the question 'how was that *possible*?' Such explanations are appropriate where the variables involved, and the interrelationships between them, are not replicable and are so complex that a simple, linear, equation-like assertion, directly linking antecedent conditions to consequent effects, will not be satisfactory. In such circumstances it is not possible to assert that a certain outcome was *inevitable*: the most that can be achieved is an account which adequately explains how that result *could* have occurred.

Walker (1980) notes that the complexity of human behaviour – including criminal behaviour – makes 'necessity explanations' for human conduct (including offending) impossible. Thus, the challenge of explaining, and hence linking potential causal variables to offending behaviour is akin to the challenge faced by a historian in explaining the outbreak of a war, not the challenge faced by a chemist in explaining an explosive reaction. All that can be realistically provided by a forensic mental health expert is a possibility explanation that explains how the relevant mental health problems could have contributed to the offending behaviour in the circumstances. This has implications for the form, content and limits of mental health evidence, as outlined in the following sections.

Form

Possibility explanations need to be presented in narrative form (Walker 1980). Unlike chemical reactions, the variables involved and the complex interrelationships between those variables are such that linear, equation-like assertions are not feasible.

In the sentencing context, this means that mental health experts should endeavour to construct a narrative account of the relationship between mental health problems and offending (if present) which is clinically convincing, best fits the known facts and is held together by a clear logical thread: the path of reasoning. Ideally, the result will be a persuasive formulation built with empathy and clinical logic; consistent with the agreed factual foundation, but a *story*, rather than the ultimate complete version of 'the true cause' of the offence. Such stories can help to meet the psycho-legal challenge by focussing on factors such as the likely aetiology of any condition, any opportunities the offender may have had to address the condition prior to offending and the offender's insight into their condition, alongside evidence concerning the nature and strength of the impairment. The task is akin to creating a movie – developing a longitudinal, multi-perspectival account based on the collateral materials available to the forensic expert and the offender's lived experiences – rather than merely providing a snapshot of the cross-sectional variables at play at the time of the offence itself.

It is rare for such accounts to be simple. Unlike the necessity explanations underpinning chemical processes, possibility explanations of criminal offending generally involve multiple elements interacting in complex ways. Consequently, courts should be suspicious of one-dimensional explanations proffered by counsel which seek to oversimplify the story.

Content

While providing a possibility explanation necessarily involves an element of speculation, this does not give licence to the expert to be vague or unconstrained in their opinion. Notwithstanding the fact that forensic experts are dealing with states of affairs that are not replicable and are delivering opinions that are narrative rather than equation-like in form, the task must nonetheless be undertaken with scientific rigour. The story that is told about the *individual* offender must be built upon a solid foundation of empirical knowledge, based on evidence derived from group-based data. The way in which the expert's evidence draws out the causal relationship between the offender's mental health problems and their offending behaviour must be consistent with the evidence base – the underlying 'framework evidence' (Faigman, Monahan and Slobogin 2014) – regarding the relevant variables. For example, evidence regarding the relationship between delusions of infidelity and serious violence (Mullen 1995) may support an account in which morbid jealousy plays an important causal role in the commission of a specific violent offence.

Limits

Unlike necessity explanations, possibility explanations are not susceptible to scientific falsifiability; the relevant concatenation of circumstances can never be repeated. Consequently, a persuasive possibility explanation concerning mental health problems and offending behaviour will clarify the limits about what can and cannot be meaningfully asserted.

Persuasiveness will hinge on consistency with what is known, both about the accepted facts of the case itself and about the relevant underlying framework evidence. In some cases, this constraint may set limits on the extent to which any given offence can be satisfactorily explained to the courts at all. A logical pathway of reasoning is key, and specious claims of certainty are unlikely to help meet the psycho-legal challenge. It is preferable to acknowledge the broad confidence limits inherent in possibility explanations.

One key limitation arises from the fact that possibility explanations, unlike necessity explanations, are not underpinned by well-established mechanistic processes. We know next to nothing about the psychophysiological processes spanning and bridging the gap between, for example, a disrespectful insult and the decision to throw a punch towards a victim. The best that can be generally hoped for is a resort to common sense 'folk' psychological processes, bolstered by relevant framework evidence. These limits are intrinsic to the nature of the causal explanation itself and not indicative of inadequate expert skills.

Another limitation of possibility explanations arises from their subjective and plural nature. Just as different historians have emphasised diverse variables as being central to the genesis of World War One (Stone 2009), different mental health experts may legitimately emphasise diverse factors as being causally relevant to a particular offence. This similarity between the work of mental health experts and historians was commented on by John Z Sadler (2002: 55), who noted how mental health experts seeking to explain a past event by drawing upon a range of evidentiary materials 'must *select* and *order* the priority, importance or salience of such materials, a core task of history-writing, lawyering or doctoring that is inherently subjective'. Sadler (2002: 55) asserts that this process of selection and prioritisation is not 'arbitrary or whimsical', and it is not the case that 'just *any* conclusions about cases can be drawn'; nonetheless, 'more than one set of potential conclusions may exist within the discipline's set of methodological constraints'. In light of this, mental health experts should acknowledge (at least to themselves) that their opinions, however honest and evidence-based, will be influenced by their own personal, subjective values.

Part Four: Describing the Strength of the 'Causal Relationship'

While it is not the role of a mental health expert to determine whether the relationship between mental health problems and offending behaviour is sufficient to warrant mitigation, experts should provide a clear and cogent opinion regarding the strength and nature (if any) of the causal connection. In practice, given that we are dealing with states of affairs that are not replicable, providing such an opinion requires the forensic expert to engage in a mental exercise that involves a degree of hypothesising and speculation; this includes conducting a counterfactual 're-run' of the events and conditions antecedent to the offending *in the absence* of the mental disorder of concern. To the extent

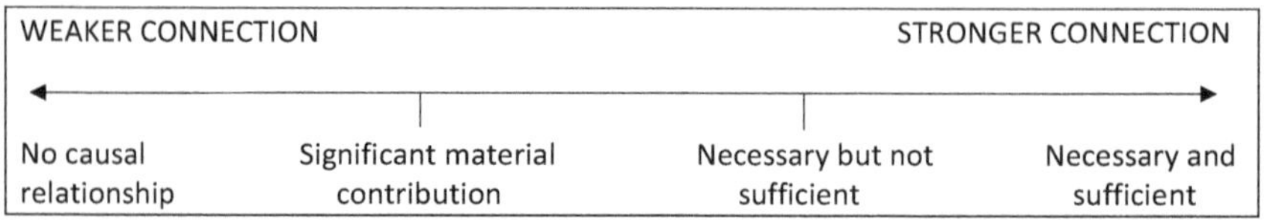

Figure 9.1 Spectrum of causal relationships

that the offending remains explicable in the absence of that mental disorder, the causal connection between the disorder and the offending can be considered to be correspondingly weaker.

Although there is often a complex interplay between multiple mental disorders diagnosed within the same offender, in practice courts sometimes require an expert to opine on the strength of *each* disorder's relationship to the offending behaviour. This is particularly likely to be the case where one of the disorders is a substance use disorder, due to the different policy considerations raised by such disorders (see earlier). This mental exercise may therefore need to be carried out more than once.

The strength of the causal relationship exists on a continuous spectrum, from no causal relationship to a necessary and sufficient relationship (see Figure 9.1). However, there is practical utility in delineating four distinct degrees of 'strength of causal relationship': no causal relationship; significant material contribution; necessary but not sufficient; necessary and sufficient. Descriptions of these categories are presented next. It is important to note, however, that while such categories may help mental health practitioners to explain the connection between an offender's mental health problems and their offending behaviour, they should *not* be taken as directly mapping onto any particular *legal* outcomes (such as justifying a particular degree of mitigation): that is a judicial determination that will depend on the sentencing judge's interpretation of the specific details of the case.

No Causal Relationship

At one end of the spectrum, there will be cases where an expert concludes that there is no causal relationship between the alleged mental disorder and the offending behaviour. This may be because, in their view:

- the offender did not have a mental disorder at the time of the offence; or
- the offending still would have occurred even in the absence of mental disorder; or
- the offending and the mental disorder simply co-occurred due to a common third factor, such as voluntary drug use; or
- there is no plausible mechanism to link the disorder with the offending.

The case of *R v Hayes* [2010] provides a useful illustration. The offender in that case had been diagnosed with borderline personality disorder, which a mental health expert considered was likely to make her 'reckless and dangerously impulsive' and to act 'without thinking first about the consequences'; she was also diagnosed with an adjustment disorder. However, the offending in question – a series of systematic fraud offences – was not impulsive in nature and clearly required premeditation and planning. Consequently, there was not found to be any causal connection between her disorders and the offending.

Significant Material Contribution

Moving along the spectrum, there will be cases in which an expert does not find an adequate basis to confidently assert that the mental disorder was a *necessary* part of the causal matrix that explains the offending behaviour, but concludes that the disorder made a significant material contribution to that behaviour. The concept of 'material contribution' has long been accepted as grounds for a causal relationship in the realm of civil tort law: see e.g. *Bonnington Castings v Wardlaw* [1956]. In these cases, the offending *may* still have occurred even in the absence of the mental disorder; however, the disorder made a significant contribution that made the offending more likely.

Many cases that come before the courts fall within this category. This includes cases in which mental disorder is a background, 'indirect' vulnerability factor, rather than a source of symptoms that 'directly' drove the offending behaviour. The case of *DPP v Missen* [2019] provides an illustration. In that case, the offence – the murder of a father by his adult son – occurred in the context of complex household dynamics, described by the judge as 'like a tinderbox' (para 12). Although the offence was not directly driven by any identifiable psychiatric symptom, it was found that the offender's propensity for serious violence had been influenced by a range of background mental health conditions (major depressive disorder, methamphetamine use disorder and post-traumatic stress disorder) acting in a mutually synergistic fashion and 'contributing to the episode of rage that erupted' at the time of the killing (para 60).

Necessary but Not Sufficient

Moving further along the spectrum, there will be cases in which a mental health expert concludes that the offending would not have occurred in the absence of the mental disorder, but that other causal factors were also involved. In such cases, the mental disorder can be considered to be a necessary, but not sufficient, causal factor.

The case of *DPP v Brown* [2020], in which the offender engaged in repeated acts of arson, provides an illustration. While it was accepted that the offender's severe personality disorder was a necessary element in explaining her repeated fire-setting, her instrumental goal of wanting to live in a custodial environment was also considered to be an essential part of the causal explanation for the offending.

Necessary and Sufficient

There will be some cases in which an expert concludes that the offending would not have occurred in the absence of the mental disorder, and that no other factors of more than negligible causal significance were present. In many, but not all, such cases, a defence of 'insanity' or its equivalent may be viable. Where the defence is not available, or where an individual chooses not to avail themselves of the defence,[7] their disorder will need to be taken into account in sentencing.

The case of *DPP v UA* [2018] provides an illustration. In that case the offender experienced a schizophrenic illness characterised by emotionally laden delusions regarding family members. In the midst of an acute relapse, she stabbed and killed her young daughter. While she could have raised the defence of mental impairment (Victoria's version of the 'insanity' defence), she chose to plead guilty to infanticide. In sentencing her for this offence, it was accepted that the offending would not have occurred in the absence of her mental disorder, and that there were no other significant factors underlying her conduct.

Part Five: The Role of Legal Practitioners and the Court in Addressing Causation

Assessing the causal relationship between an offender's mental health problems and offending behaviour is not an easy task. In most cases, the causal matrix will be complex. A mental disorder experienced by an offender is likely to:

- have a multiplicity of effects on their state of mind and behavioural propensities; and
- impact upon, and be impacted by:
    - situational factors (such as interpersonal relational dynamics or availability of psychiatric treatment);
    - behavioural choices (such as substance use or decisions to seek psychiatric treatment); and
    - comorbid disorders, impairments and disabilities – whether physical or psychological (and including enduring disorders that act as vulnerability factors).

The relationships between mental disorders and the preceding factors may involve complex bidirectional processes. Given this complexity, it is almost always possible to argue, where a diagnosis has been made, that there is at least *some* causal connection (in the broad sense) between an offender's mental health problems and the offending behaviour. Conversely, it is also generally possible to argue that it was 'really' something *other* than the mental disorder that *caused* the offending behaviour.

In an adversarial system, such as exists in countries like Australia, England and Wales, the participants' role in the system will influence the way in which they deal with this complexity. It is the sentencing judge's role to determine the strength of the connection. In doing so, they may find the spectrum presented in Part Four to be a useful tool. As noted earlier, however, the strength of the causal relationship is not determinative of the issue: sentencing judges must also make a moral evaluation of whether that relationship was of the appropriate kind to mitigate the offender's culpability. This may involve consideration of various factors such as the offender's conduct prior to the offence (for example, the use of illicit drugs) and the opportunities the offender had to address their mental health condition (Walvisch 2023).

The role of prosecuting and defence counsel is to assist the judge to make these assessments. They should do this by presenting expert evidence that addresses the relevant issues and by constructing a narrative that suits their forensic goals. Defence counsel's role is to present the strongest mitigating arguments on their client's behalf. Where the offender has mental health problems, the greatest mitigating force will be offered by demonstrating that the offender's circumstances fall within one or more of the established categories of mitigation (such as those set out in *Verdins* or the sentencing guideline). Consequently, the primary task of defence counsel should be to relate the available expert evidence to those categories.

As noted in Part One, there are various bases on which a sanction may be reduced due to the presence of mental health problems. For example, a judge may decide that there is less need for a deterrent sentence, or that a lesser sentence should be imposed due to the likelihood that imprisonment will be more burdensome simply because of the presence of a mental disorder. The case law in this area indicates, however, that the biggest sentencing reduction tends to flow from establishing that there was a strong causal relationship between the offender's mental health problems and their offending behaviour, and consequently that their moral culpability was substantially reduced. Defence counsel should therefore seek to locate the causal relationship as far to the right of the spectrum described in Part Four as is supported by the evidence.

Where the proximate cause of the offending seems to have been a factor unrelated to the offender's mental health problems, defence counsel may seek to develop a narrative that explains how the offender's mental health problems contributed in a contextual fashion to the offender being in a situation that was productive of the offending (thereby demonstrating that they made a significant material contribution to the offending behaviour). For example, it may be argued that a diagnosis of a mental disorder in early adulthood led to the offender's estrangement from their family, an unstable housing situation and a drug addiction, which in turn led to the offending behaviour.

The narrative should be constructed in a way that appeals to both the mental health-specific sentencing principles and a more generalised assessment of the offender's moral blameworthiness. This is because even if a case does not fall within the scope of the *Verdins* principles or the sentencing guideline, the presence of mental health problems may nonetheless be relevant to a sentencing judge's global assessment of the offender's culpability. It may help to explain who the individual is as an offender, and how they have come to be in their current situation (see e.g. *DPP v O'Neill* (2015)). Presenting this evidence to the court can help to ensure that the offender is sentenced in a manner that gives full weight to who they are as an individual.

A useful illustration of this is provided by *Alexopolous v R* [2022] before the Victorian Court of Appeal. In that case the offender had been diagnosed with attention deficit hyperactivity disorder early in his life. While he had initially received psychiatric support, this was removed and he declined 'into a cycle of drug abuse, offending and court appearances' (para 42). Although the sentencing judge did not mitigate the offender's sentence on *Verdins* grounds, his psychiatric history was nonetheless considered mitigating because it helped explain his use of drugs and offending behaviour. On appeal, it was held that:

> Acceptance of this explanation was logically capable of permitting the judge to reason that [his] offending on this occasion was less the manifestation of wilful disobedience of the law than it was the product of drug addiction that had its genesis in a particular troubled background and psychological profile.
>
> (para 43)

Defence counsel should also seek to address the moral evaluative issue. Where it is arguable on the evidence, they may present a narrative which asserts that it was the offender's mental health problems, rather than any other relevant factors, which largely or even wholly explain the offending behaviour. In this regard, the decision of an offender to disengage from treatment or engage in drug use will often be highlighted by prosecuting counsel as examples of how it was the offender's poor decision-making, rather than the presence of the underlying condition, that led to the offending. In such cases, the ability of the defence advocate to anchor the decision to spurn pharmacotherapy or take recreational drugs within the ambit of the offender's underlying condition will be critical to the causal relationship being given full weight by the court.

Although the role of prosecuting counsel is sometimes presented as being the opposite of defence counsel, this is not the case. Their role is not to seek the heaviest sentence possible, but rather to make submissions addressing their views on the seriousness of the offence and the offender's circumstances. In doing so, they will often place an emphasis on different aspects of the causal matrix than defence counsel. For example, they may seek to make much of the fact that the offender's mental disorder did not necessitate the offending behaviour, since most people with that disorder do not offend. They may also present a narrative that emphasises the role of morally culpable choices made by the offender or may seek to amplify the significance of other factors such as voluntary drug use.

In presenting their competing narratives, prosecuting and defence counsel will often seek to push a mental health expert in the direction of greater or lesser degrees of certainty, as suits their forensic goals. In doing so, they may diminish the complexity of the mental health expert's possibility explanation. It is critical that expert witnesses resist being browbeaten into accepting an overly simple explanation of the causal relationship and present a full and nuanced account of the complex causal matrix.

In reaching their final determination, sentencing judges must comply with an increasingly complex web of restrictions: sentencing statutes around the common law world now prescribe various offence categories, limitations on available sentences and frameworks for evaluating the weight to be given to certain factors (see e.g. *Sentencing Act 1991* (Vic)). These structures make it seem as if the sentencing process is a rational, almost algorithmic process. However, this chapter has shown that it continues to involve an instinctive, values-based assessment: the sentencing judge must make a moral evaluation of the extent to which the offender should be held to be individually responsible for their conduct. Different judges are likely to attach different levels of significance to certain behaviours, such as an offender's decision to cease taking anti-psychotic medication. One judge may see this decision as existing within the framework of the offender's disorder, secondary to the lack of 'insight' that is a very common core element of severe mental disorder; another may see it as a rational decision made in acceptance of the possible consequences. Judges may reach these conclusions despite the absence of evidence bearing directly on the issue. To ensure rigour in their assessment, judges should acknowledge, at least to themselves, that they are making a values-based decision, and consider the ways in which their own background and experience may be influencing their determination.

Conclusion

Bernadette McSherry's (2008: 2) goal of integrating the expertise of the various participants in the criminal justice system is an important one. All participants – lawyers, judges and mental health experts – have a key role to play, and if just outcomes are to be achieved it is essential that we understand how these roles fit together. In this chapter we have considered the roles that the various participants should play in the sentencing context, when addressing the connection between an offender's mental health problems and their offending behaviour.

We have argued that the current focus on the *directness* of the connection is misplaced, as the mere fact that the cause of an offender's conduct was indirect does not mean that it lacked significance. We have suggested that it would be preferable for sentencing judges to instead focus on whether the connection was *sufficient* to reduce the offender's moral culpability. This is a moral evaluative question, appropriately influenced by social policy concerns. It requires judges to consider not only the relationship between the offender's mental health condition and their offending behaviour, but also factors such as the aetiology of the condition and the nature and strength of its impact on the offender.

To assist judges in making this determination, we have recommended that mental health experts use 'possibility explanations' to explain how the offender's mental health problems could have contributed to the offending behaviour in the circumstances. This has implications for the form, content and limits of the evidence that is given. One of the key issues that mental health experts will frequently need to address is the strength of the relationship between the offender's mental health problems and their offending behaviour. We have provided a framework for describing the strength of this relationship that they may find helpful in undertaking this task. We have also provided guidance for defence counsel, prosecuting counsel and sentencing judges who need to address the causal issue.

The psycho-legal challenges that are raised when assessing the connection between mental health problems and offending behaviour are complex. We are hopeful that the tools provided in this chapter can assist mental health experts, legal practitioners and sentencing judges to adopt a principled, rigorous and just approach to the task.

Notes

1 We note that views differ on whether an individual's mental health problems should be taken into account in assessing their responsibility or culpability for their criminal behaviour. For example, Minkowitz (2015) has argued that differentiating between individuals due to their mental health problems is discriminatory and that the criminal law should be reformed to remove such distinctions. We do not address this issue in this chapter. We proceed on the basis that mental health problems currently play a key role in sentencing determinations and are likely to continue to do so in the future. In light of this fact, our aim is to develop a principled approach to the way in which mental health problems are addressed by legal practitioners, expert witnesses and courts.

2 While the requirements for this defence vary, it will generally be established by proving that, at the time they committed the relevant act, the individual had a 'disease of the mind' that caused them either to not understand the nature and quality of their conduct, or to not know that their conduct was wrong: see e.g. *R v M'Naghten* (1843); *Crimes (Mental Impairment and Unfitness to be Tried) Act 1997* (Vic) section 20. In some jurisdictions it can also be established by proving that the individual could not control their behaviour: see e.g. *Criminal Code 1995* (Qld) section 52. While in England and Wales this defence is still referred to as the 'insanity' defence, it has been given different names in other jurisdictions. For example, in Victoria it is called the defence of 'mental impairment', while in New South Wales it is referred to as the 'mental disorder' defence. For the sake of simplicity, it will be referred to as the 'insanity' defence throughout this chapter. The word 'insanity' will be enclosed in inverted commas to make clear that this is technical legal terminology, rather than an endorsement of the term.

3 While the fitness to stand trial requirements vary from jurisdiction to jurisdiction, an individual will generally only be deemed unfit to stand trial where, at the time of the trial, they were unable to do one or more of the following: understand the charges; understand the potential consequences of the proceedings; understand the trial process; participate in the trial process; or communicate with counsel: see e.g. *Crimes (Mental Impairment and Unfitness to be Tried) Act 1997* (Vic) section 6(1); *Criminal Procedure (Insanity) Act 1964* (UK) chapter 84, section 4; *R v Pritchard* (1836).

4 While this guideline applies to courts in both England and Wales, for simplicity this chapter refers to it as the English approach.

5 See Walvisch (2017) for a discussion of the different aims of law and mental health science, as well as a consideration of some of the limitations of the current psychiatric framework.

6 In passing we note that the 'insanity' defence does not raise the same concerns that we address in this chapter, as it does not hinge upon the strength of the causal relationship between an individual's mental disorder and their offending behaviour. It depends upon the impact of the individual's mental health problems on their ability to know the nature and quality or wrongfulness of their conduct, or (in some jurisdictions) on their ability to control their impulses. Attempts to tether the defence to causal relationships by way of a causal 'product rule' have historically proven to be problematic (see e.g. *United States of America v Archie W Brawner* (1972)).

7 An individual may choose not to raise the 'insanity' defence, even if it is available, due to the potential consequences. Depending on the jurisdiction, these may include being detained (possibly in prison) or subjected to supervision for a longer period than had they been found guilty of the offence, possibly in conditions worse than prison, or being subjected to compulsory treatment. In order to avoid these prospects, some individuals may prefer to instead plead guilty and seek more advantageous dispositions at the sentencing stage.

References

Cases

Alexopolous v R [2022] VSCA 145.
Arthars v R (2013) 39 VR 613.
Bonnington Castings v Wardlaw (1956) 1 All ER 615.
Bowen v R [2011] VSCA 67.
Carroll v R [2011] VSCA 150.
Director of Public Prosecutions (DPP) v Brown [2020] VCC 196.
Director of Public Prosecutions (DPP) v Missen [2019] VSC 32.
Director of Public Prosecutions (DPP) v Patterson [2009] VSCA 222.
Director of Public Prosecutions (DPP) v UA [2018] VSC 423.
Director of Public Prosecutions (DPP) v O'Neill (2015) 47 VR 395.
Director of Public Prosecutions (DPP) v Weidlich [2008] VSCA 203.
Johnston v R [2013] VSCA 362.
O'Connor v R [2014] VSCA 108.
Paparone v R [2000] WASCA 127.
Ross v R [2015] VSCA 302.
R v Dolheguy [2020] VSC 704.
R v Hayes [2010] QCA 96.
R v M'Naghten (1843) 8 ER 718.

R v Pritchard (1836) 7 C&P 303.
R v Surtees [2022] VSC 124.
R v Verdins (2007) 16 VR 269.
R v Vuadreu [2009] VSCA 262.
United States of America v Archie W Brawner, 471 F 2d 969 (DC Cir, 1972).
Wright v R [2015] VSCA 88.

Books, Journal Articles and Other Texts

Carroll, A., McSherry, B., Wood, D. and Yannoulidis, S. (2008) 'Drug-Associated Psychoses and Criminal Responsibility', *Behavioural Sciences & the Law*, 26(5): 633–53.

Edney, R. (2006) 'Models of Understanding Criminal Behaviour and the Sentencing Process: A Place for Criminological Theory?' *Journal of Criminal Law*, 70(3): 247–71.

Faigman, D., Monahan, J. and Slobogin, C. (2014) 'Group to Individual (G2i) Inference in Scientific Expert Testimony', *University of Chicago Law Review*, 81(2): 417–80.

Fazel, S. and Seewald, K. (2012) 'Severe Mental Illness in 33,588 Prisoners Worldwide: Systematic Review and Meta-Regression Analysis', *British Journal of Psychiatry*, 200(5): 364–73.

Gooding, P., Arstein-Kerslake, A., Andrews, L. and McSherry, B. (2017) 'Unfitness to Stand Trial and the Indefinite Detention of Persons with Cognitive Disabilities in Australia: Human Rights Challenges and the Proposals for Change', *Melbourne University Law Review*, 40(3): 816–65.

Hallett, N. (2020) 'To What Extent Should Expert Psychiatric Witnesses Comment on Criminal Culpability?' *Medicine, Science and the Law*, 60(1): 67–74.

Hopper, S. and McSherry, B. (2001) 'The Insanity Defence and International Human Rights Obligations', *Psychiatry, Psychology and Law*, 8(2): 161–73.

McSherry, B. (2008) *Rethinking Mental Health Laws: Developing Model Frameworks*, Criminal Justice Research Consortium Seminar, Monash Law Chambers, Melbourne, 19 February. Available www.monash.edu/medicine/cjrc/activities/seminars/rethinking-mental-health-laws (accessed 24 November 2022).

McSherry, B. (2020) 'Preventing Harm to Others as a Criterion for Compulsory Treatment: An Overview of Criticisms and Current Research', *Journal of Law and Medicine*, 27(3): 570–73.

Minkowitz, T. (2015) 'Rethinking Criminal Responsibility from a Critical Disability Perspective: The Abolition of Insanity/Incapacity Acquittals and Unfitness to Plead, and Beyond', *Griffith Law Review*, 23(3): 434–66.

Mullen, P. (1995) 'Jealousy and Violence', *Hong Kong Journal of Psychiatry*, 5: 18–24.

Reason, J. (2000) 'Human Error: Models and Management', *BMJ*, 320(7237): 768–70.

Richardson, E. and McSherry, B. (2010) 'Diversion Down Under – Programs for Offenders with Mental Illnesses in Australia', *International Journal of Law and Psychiatry*, 33(4): 249–57.

Royal Commission into Victoria's Mental Health System (2021) *Final Report*. Available https://finalreport.rcvmhs.vic.gov.au/ (accessed 11 November 2022).

Sadler, J.Z. (2002) 'What Can We Ever Know About the Past? A Philosophical Consideration of the Assessment of Retrospective Mental States', in R. Simon and D. Shuman (eds) *Retrospective Assessment of Mental States in Litigation: Predicting the Past*, Washington, DC: American Psychiatric Publishing, 47–71.

Sentencing Council for England and Wales (2020) *Sentencing Offenders with Mental Disorders, Developmental Disorders, or Neurological Impairments.* Available www.sentencingcouncil.org.uk/overarching-guides/magistrates-court/item/sentencing-offenders-with-mental-disorders-developmental-disorders-or-neurological-impairments (accessed 24 November 2022).

Skeem, J., Peterson, J. and Silver, E. (2011) 'Toward Research-Informed Policy for High Risk Offenders with Serious Mental Illness', in B. McSherry and P. Keyzer (eds) *Dangerous People: Policy, Prediction, and Practice*, New York: Routledge, 111–21.

Stapleton, J. (2002) 'Scientific and Legal Approaches to Causation', in I. Freckelton and D. Mendelson (eds) *Causation in Law and Medicine*, Aldershot: Ashgate Publishing Co, 14–37.

Stone, N. (2009) *World War One: A Short History*, New York: Basic Books.

Supreme Court of Victoria (2017) *Practice Note Sc Cr 7: Sentencing Hearings: Expert Reports on Mental Functioning of Offenders.* Available www.supremecourt.vic.gov.au/areas/legal-resources/practice-notes/sc-cr-7-expert-reports-on-mental-functioning-of-offenders (accessed 24 November 2022).

Thornicroft, G. (2006) *Shunned: Discrimination Against People with Mental Illness*, Oxford: Oxford University Press.

Walker, N. (1980) *Behaviour and Misbehaviour: Explanations and Non-Explanations*, Oxford: Wiley-Blackwell.

Walvisch, J. (2010) 'Sentencing Offenders with Impaired Mental Functioning: Developing Australia's "Most Sophisticated and Subtle Analysis"', *Psychiatry, Psychology & Law*, 17(2): 187–201.

Walvisch, J. (2017) 'Defining "Mental Disorder" in Legal Contexts', *International Journal of Law and Psychiatry*, 52: 7–18.

Walvisch, J. (2018a) 'Mandated Treatment as Punishment: Exploring the Second Verdins Principle', in C. Spivakovsky, K. Seear and A. Carter (eds) *Critical Perspectives on Coercive Interventions: Law, Medicine and Society*, Abingdon: Routledge, 185–98.

Walvisch, J. (2018b) '"Mental Disorder" and Sentencing: Resolving the Definitional Problem', *Journal of Law and Medicine*, 26(1): 159–69.

Walvisch, J. (2023) 'Sentencing Offenders with Self-Induced Mental Disorders: Towards a Theory of Meta-Culpability', *Psychiatry, Psychology & Law*, 30(1): 12–32.

Walvisch, J. and Carroll, A. (2017) 'Sentencing Offenders with Personality Disorders: A Critical Analysis of DPP v O'Neill', *Melbourne University Law Review*, 41(1): 417–44.

Walvisch, J. and Carroll, A. (2022) 'An Australian Perspective', in M. van der Wolf (ed) *Safeguarding the Quality of Forensic Assessment in Sentencing: A Review Across Western Nations*, New York: Routledge, 121–45.

Walvisch, J., Carroll, A. and Marsh, T. (2021) 'Sentencing and Mental Disorder: The Evolution of the Verdins Principles, Strategic Interdisciplinary Advocacy and Evidence-based Reform', *Psychiatry, Psychology and Law*, 29(5): 731–51.

Weerasekera, P. (1993) 'Formulation: A Multiperspective Model', *Canadian Journal of Psychiatry*, 38: 351–58.

10 Finetuning a Jurisprudence of Risk

Christopher Slobogin

Introduction

Bernadette McSherry's contributions to the literature on risk assessment, culminating in her book *Managing Fear: The Law and Ethics of Preventive Detention and Risk Assessment* (McSherry 2014), are well known. I'd like to use this commemoration of McSherry to look at this vein of her work through the prism of my own work in the area, much of which appears in a recently published book, *Just Algorithms: Using Science to Reduce Incarceration and Inform a Jurisprudence of Risk* (Slobogin 2021). In particular, this chapter will discuss what I consider to be three essential components of any coherent 'jurisprudence of risk' – the term I use to describe the principles that should govern the use of risk assessment as a basis for depriving people of liberty. The first principle has to do with 'fit,' the requirement that risk assessments answer the questions that the law asks, which in turn requires that the law specify the questions it wants answered. The second principle focuses on 'validity,' the straightforward idea that risk assessments should be good at what they purport to do. Finally, the 'fairness' principle requires that risk assessment be attentive to equality, dignity, transparency and voice concerns.

Legislatures and courts have for the most part ignored or simply waved at these three issues. In *Managing Fear*, McSherry very capably surveys the theories that justify the use of risk, the instruments used to assess it, the laws that govern it, and the human rights and ethical issues raised by risk assessment endeavours. In the course of doing so, she devotes considerable attention to the fit, validity and fairness issues. Here, I use her work as a springboard in setting forth my take, from an American perspective, on these difficult topics, after briefly describing why I think assessment of risk is an important component of the justice system.

Why Risk Assessment Is Important

Risk assessment – the effort to evaluate the risk of future offending – and risk management – the effort to reduce risk – have always been significant features of both the criminal and civil justice systems. On the criminal side,

DOI: 10.4324/9781003350644-13

they have informed pretrial detention and sentencing decisions. On the civil side, they are even more crucial in making determinations about involuntary hospitalisation and post-sentence detentions of sex offenders and others considered dangerous. In *Managing Fear*, McSherry (2013: chapter 4) describes how the risk assessment agenda has expanded beyond these settings to include preventive detention and community control of suspected terrorists, registration and notification requirements for sex offenders, and antisocial behaviour orders and related community-supervision orders governing the lives of individuals released from confinement. She also details the advent of 'risk assessment instruments' that rely on statistically derived risk factors to assign individuals to high, medium and low risk categories (McSherry 2013: chapter 3).

The overall tone of academic commentary on these developments, including McSherry's, is one of scepticism. Many commentators go further, arguing that risk assessment instruments are racist, de-humanising and antithetical to the central tenets of criminal justice (see e.g. Harcourt 2015; Eubanks 2018). These writers believe that these tools should be banned, and many also believe the entire risk assessment enterprise should be shut down and play no role in the justice system.

I too am concerned about the potential for risk assessment instruments to subvert fundamental values and the potential net-widening effects of modern preventive efforts. At the same time, in *Just Algorithms* (Slobogin 2021) I caution against a precipitous prohibition of risk-oriented decision-making in the criminal and quasi-criminal domains (I do not address their use in the civil commitment process). The argument of the book, very briefly stated, is of the 'compared-to-what' variety. At sentencing, for instance, the primary alternative to considering risk in fashioning dispositions is to base sentences entirely on assessments of blame, which are notoriously disparate, impossible to falsify and often harsh. Thus, within broad retributively defined guideposts, sentences calibrated according to risk may be the lesser of two evils. In a similar vein the book argues that, assuming risk is a legitimate consideration, banning risk assessment instruments is likely counterproductive, because it will leave evaluations of risk in the hands of judges and clinicians who are both less accurate and more likely to let biases creep into the analysis.

The primary reason I feel the need to defend risk as a legal criterion and risk assessment instruments as a methodology stems from a desire to do something significant about a peculiarly American phenomenon, albeit one from which the United Kingdom and Australia are not immune – mass incarceration. The United States puts vastly greater numbers of people in prison per capita than any other Western country, and in raw numbers, even more than China, which has four times its population (Walmsley 2018: list 6, table 2). Pretrial detention numbers in the US are also through the roof (Subramanian et al. 2015). Many policymakers, from both the left and the right of the political spectrum, think this is not a good thing, for a variety of reasons. But to date there has been no effective response to it. Most reforms aimed at reducing incarceration – decriminalisation, abolition of mandatory minimum sentences, elimination of cash bail – have been largely unsuccessful. These reforms have not worked because they only go after low-hanging fruit, such as people who commit minor, non-violent crime who rarely end up in prison for a long time anyway, or because they give decision-makers discretion to ignore them, which decision-makers routinely do, on the assumption that many of the people they confront are dangerous and need to be locked up (O'Hear 2017: xvii).

In fact, however, most people who have offended are not likely to commit serious crimes. The base rate for violence among pretrial detainees is less than 8% (Baughman 2017: 198). The base rate for homicide, rape, robbery and any type of assault among those released from federal prison is less than 30%, and most of that reoffending is for assault (Durose, Cooper and Snyder 2016: table 2). If we could identify those who are not likely to commit violent crime, and provide effective violence-reduction programmes for those who *are* likely to do so, we could release a large percentage of people much earlier than we currently do, and in many cases perhaps avoid imprisonment altogether. Importantly, the public would probably be on board with that approach. For instance, one poll of citizens from Wisconsin, a 'purple' swing state, found that people were willing to reduce the sentences of offenders by half for both non-violent *and* violent offenders if the offender could demonstrate he was no longer a threat to society (O'Hear and Wheelock 2015: 279).

Back before the 1970s, governments in the US were much more willing to do that kind of thing. Most states had parole boards, which often released individuals before their sentence expired on the ground that they had been rehabilitated and were no longer a threat to society. Although parole boards were rightly subject to serious criticism, they did serve as a safety valve. Kevin Reitz (2006: 1974), among others, has argued that this was not true – that this sort of indeterminate sentencing regime resulted in sentences as long or longer than sentences in determinate sentencing states. But this assertion is based on data collected after the 1970s. In fact, the same punitive attitudes that, in the past 50 years, brought mandatory minimum sentences, habitual offender laws that impose life sentences on three-time felons, and truth in sentencing statutes that require offenders to serve most of their term, also decimated the parole systems of those states that still had them, by significantly changing parole eligibility rules. Today, for instance, the four biggest state carceral machines with parole boards – Texas, Georgia, Oklahoma and Louisiana – have reduced the percentage of prisoners eligible for parole to, respectively, 55%, 39%, 17% and 7% (Renaud 2019). Thus, the fact that sentences in modern 'indeterminate' sentencing regimes are just as long as those in determinate sentencing jurisdictions doesn't reflect the impact of a truly indeterminate regime. Rather, it is an artifact of the move to determinacy and 'just desert' sentencing. Indeed, Reitz's (2020: 2745) more recent research has found that the states that are leading the current decarceration charge in the US are all states with meaningfully functioning parole boards.

At the same time, as I've already suggested, most of those released early during the recent decarceration surge have been low-hanging fruit. If we are to attack mass incarceration successfully, we need some means of figuring out whom, among those who today remain in prison or jail, could be released on conditions or released entirely. Unfortunately, while social scientists have devoted considerable energy to that project, the law has been reticent about endorsing it. In part, that's because over the past 50 years we have become very ambivalent about dangerousness as a legal criterion. Retributivists – who have dominated much of the policy-making – have usually been downright hostile to it. As observed by Michael Tonry (2020: 177), 'predictive sentencing is . . . incompatible with mainstream retributive punishment theories'. After all, these critics say, the state should not be able to punish or detain people for something they haven't done. Even many with a more utilitarian bent are prone to think that we are so bad at assessing risk that we shouldn't even try, especially given the potential for racial bias, which is always possible any time the law allows discretionary decision-making (Tonry 2020: 160–62).

Despite this pushback, which is very strong, the law has yet to reject risk as a legitimate consideration. Dangerousness permeates the common law of crimes, both in terms of crime definition and sentencing criteria (Loewy 1988). Although many jurisdictions have moved toward determinate sentencing that purportedly does not consider risk, some still have not (Frase 2005). And the US Supreme Court in *Jurek v Texas* (1976) has said that risk is a permissible consideration even in capital cases. A small number of scholars, many of whom purport to be retributivists, are willing to contemplate some role for risk assessment (see e.g. Frase 2013), as do the new Model Penal Code (2017: § 6.06(2)(a)) sentencing provisions, despite their overall desert-orientation. These 'limiting retributivists' endorse a system in which just desert sets the range of a sentence, while risk helps determine its precise duration. So dangerousness is definitely not off the table as a legal criterion.

If that is the case, the law should – and, I argue in *Just Algorithms*, *must* – develop what I've called a jurisprudence of risk, or a jurisprudence of dangerousness (Slobogin 2021). Given the potential of risk assessment to address the incarceration crisis, I think this jurisprudence is the most important substantive criminal justice issue today. Unfortunately, despite the efforts of people like McSherry, this jurisprudence barely exists. We have mountains of case law, statutory law and commentary on *mens rea*, *actus reus* and the defences, and scholars and advocates often claim that any imprecision that occurs in these areas violates the principle of legality. Yet we routinely enhance sentences, refuse to grant parole and consign individuals to indeterminate commitments based on unanchored pronouncements that the person is a threat to society, using extremely vague terminology. We can do much better than that.

Fit

The most important thing the law can do is define risk more precisely. Just as there are elements of crime, there ought to be elements of risk. Specifically, the law ought to make clear what *probability* of what *outcome* over what *period of time* in the absence of what *intervention* justifies a risk designation. If legislatures and courts do not define these terms, experts and the people who develop risk assessment instruments will do so *de facto*, an opaque process that may not reflect societal values.

In *Just Algorithms*, I go into detail about how the probability, outcome, duration and intervention criteria might be formulated (Slobogin 2021: chapter 2). Here, instead, I simply want to emphasise how poor a job the law has done on this score. In *Managing Risk*, McSherry (2013: 67) confirms that view, pointing out that 'there is little case law on what is meant by such terms . . . [as] the likelihood of harm to others'.

Consider, first, the nonchalance of American law on the probability issue, even in cases where a risk assessment could support the ultimate penalty of death. In Texas, a person convicted of capital murder may be sentenced to death if the jury finds beyond a reasonable doubt that there is 'a probability that the individual will commit criminal acts of violence that constitute a continuing threat to society' (*Texas Code of Criminal Procedure*: art 37.071(b)(2)). Although occasionally Texas courts have permitted the parties to stipulate that 'probability' means more likely than not (see e.g. *Varga v State* (2003): 4), the Texas Court of Criminal Appeals has explicitly and repeatedly refused to define the word (*Long v State* (2009): 3). At one time, that stance might have been defensible. When the only evidence about dangerousness was clinical in nature, saying anything about the risk of reoffending other than that it should be 'significant' or more than a 'possibility' might have seemed disingenuous. But now that risk assessment instruments can provide numerical estimates of reoffending, the obstacle to quantification of the required probability has disappeared and courts should provide more guidance.

Nor have the Texas courts been willing to define the word 'violent' – the outcome variable – used in the state's death penalty statute. Admittedly, the US Supreme Court's decision in *Jurek v Texas* (1976) upheld this language against a vagueness challenge. But since then, the Supreme Court has decided *Johnson v United States* (2015), which held that the residual clause of the *Armed Career Criminal Act of 1984* (*US Code:* Title 18 § 924(e)) that enhances sentences for a 'violent felony' is void for vagueness, because it could apply to virtually any crime, including witness tampering, failing to stop after seeing a police officer's signal and attempted burglary. The same reasoning should require legislatures and courts fashioning or interpreting preventive detention statutes to do a much better job answering the question 'risk of *what*?'

A similar point can be made with respect to the duration issue, the third risk element. In the bail context, given speedy trial limitations (see e.g. *US Code*: Title 18 § 161(b)(c), requiring in federal cases a presumptive period between arrest and trial of 100 days), we should only care about an offender's risk over a three- to six-month period. That significantly limits the degree of risk posed by individuals in the pretrial setting. Similarly, at sentencing, if a statutory maximum is three years, that should be the relevant risk period, not something longer. Yet some of the risk assessment instruments in use today were validated using follow-up periods of seven to ten years (Hilton et al. 2021: 131–36).

Finally, and most importantly, an individual's risk of reoffending can vary enormously depending on the law's response to the risk. Fifty years ago, the US Supreme Court decided *Jackson v Indiana* (1972), involving a successful challenge to the prolonged detention of an individual who had been found permanently incompetent to stand trial. In concluding that Jackson's detention was unconstitutional, the Court declared that the Due Process Clause requires that the 'nature and duration of commitment bear some reasonable relation[ship] to [its] purpose' (*Jackson v Indiana* (1972): 738). This pronouncement, repeated in several subsequent Supreme Court decisions (*Seling v Young* (2001): 265; *Youngberg v Romeo* (1982): 324), is echoed in the *Convention on the Rights of People with Disabilities* and decisions by the European Court of Human Rights, as McSherry emphasizes in *Managing Fear* (2013: 182). It has at least three implications for any sentence based on a risk (Slobogin 2021: 138–42).

First, *Jackson* can be read to require that any government deprivation of liberty in the name of prevention be the least drastic means of achieving the state's preventive aim. That would mean, for instance, that alternatives to incarceration should always be a consideration to the extent risk is the issue. While imprisonment might substantially reduce risk, it may not be any more effective at doing so than placement in a substance abuse treatment programme in the community, a vocational training programme in a halfway house or a job-release programme coupled with an ankle monitor. *Jackson*'s parsimony principle requires consideration of these types of options.

Second, *Jackson* means that the government *must* provide rehabilitative services if they will reduce the length of the intervention. Otherwise, once again, the disposition is not the least restrictive way of accomplishing the state's preventive aim. It is unlikely that this principle could be transformed into an affirmative duty on the part of the state to create treatment services. But it could create an incentive to provide at least those services that are available, because the state will know release is the only alternative. In *Kansas v Hendricks* (1997: 366–67), the Supreme Court held that where incapacitation is the goal, treatment need not occur if it is not 'available' or 'possible'. But it strongly implied that if available treatment is *not* offered, continued preventive detention would violate due process. In *Seling v Young* (2001: 265), the Court explicitly made the same point.

Finally, *Jackson*'s reasonable relationship requirement means that any confinement that occurs should be proportionate to the risk, and that the longer the intervention extends, the greater the proof of risk that must be shown (a precept that could be called risk proportionality, analogous to desert proportionality). This principle should mean that individuals considered to be low risk or at risk of committing only minor crimes should never be detained solely for preventive purposes. Even individuals considered to be high risk could not be confined for prolonged periods of time without increasingly higher showings of risk.

Validity

The second area in which the law needs to do more work is with respect to assuring the accuracy of risk assessment. As a matter of legal precedent in the United States, the validity inquiry is most sensibly framed under the Federal Rules of Evidence (2019: rule 702) and analogous rules in virtually every state, which require experts to use 'reliable principles and methods' that are 'reliably applied.' While to a social scientist 'reliable' means replicability rather than accuracy, these rules use the term the way the Supreme in *Daubert v Dow Chemical Co* (1993) did, to mean accuracy or validity as well as reliability. Thus, consistent with the Supreme Court's rulings in *Daubert* and subsequent cases, these rules tell courts to ensure that the basis of expert testimony has been subjected to some type of verification process, such as empirical testing, the generation of error rates and peer review through publication in accepted journals. Unfortunately, most jurisdictions hold that Rule 702 and the *Daubert* criteria are inapplicable to the post-conviction, pretrial and commitment settings – where most preventive detention decisions are made – because they were devised as rules of evidence meant to apply at criminal and civil trials (see e.g. *United States v Field* (2007). But, to put it bluntly, this makes no sense; if the *Daubert* test must be met before evidence can be presented in a tort suit (the context of the *Daubert* case), it should certainly apply where weeks, months or years of jail, prison or hospital time are at stake.

If *Daubert* or something similar did apply, the nature of risk assessment would have to change. In Texas back in the 1970s and 1980s, the psychiatrist Dr James Grigson was famous for testifying – in over 100 capital sentencing cases, always for the prosecution – that the offender was dangerous and thus met an aggravating circumstance justifying the death penalty (Washington Times 2003). In *Barefoot v Estelle* (1983) he actually said there was a 110% chance the offender would commit acts of violence if not executed. The basis for his judgments? In one case, a half-hour interview (*Estelle v Smith* (1981)); in *Barefoot* itself, no interview at all, but simply facts provided through a hypothetical question! As McSherry (2013; citing Perlin 2012: 5) points out in her survey of the law, this slipshod approach to expert testimony amounts to making decisions based on the 'problematic notion of "common sense" reasoning' that often reflects 'irrational prejudice'. (For discussion of rigorous expert testimony see Walvisch et al. in Chapter 9 and Gooding and Maker in Chapter 13 of this volume.)

Whatever might have been permissible in the early 1980s, today, with the advent of sophisticated risk assessment instruments, Grigson-type testimony should never be permitted in any proceeding, much less a capital sentencing hearing. Yet the Texas courts still allow it. In *Nenno v State* (1998) the expert offered no research in support of his opinion and admitted that he did not follow any particular methodology for determining dangerousness. While he claimed his opinion was based on his experience in dealing with hundreds of cases, he, of course, had no information on whether his opinions in those cases were right or wrong. The Texas Court of Criminal Appeals in *Nenno* (1998: 562) nonetheless permitted Grigson's testimony, stating that predictions of violence are inherently a product of soft social science that may not be amenable to 'hard science methods of validation, such as assessing the potential rate of error or subjecting a theory to peer review'. Four years later, the US Fifth Circuit Court of Appeals found this position of the Texas court rejecting the need for hard science to be so clearly supported by state precedent that it characterised as 'frivolous' any objection to such testimony (*Johnson v Cockrell* (2002): 254).

Yet the assertion that risk assessments cannot be subject to scientific testing is dead wrong. Today there are literally scores of statistically sophisticated risk assessment instruments available to experts and to the courts. Study after study has shown that the traditional manner of evaluating risk – seat of the pants assessments by judges, or the types of opinions offered by mental health professionals like Dr Grigson – are much worse, and more biased, than these risk assessment instruments. Research also shows that these research assessment instruments, which henceforth I will call 'RAIs,' can better facilitate matching offenders with treatment programmes; they can help pinpoint whether someone needs cognitive therapy, vocational training, substance treatment or some other programme when the goal is to reduce risk (see e.g. Viljoen, Cochrane and Jonnson 2018).

Most importantly, because RAIs are based on statistical analysis of risk factors and can produce risk scores that are associated with specific probabilities of reoffending, courts can demand concrete evidence about whether: (1) the probabilities the instrument generates are stated with an acceptable level of confidence (what is usually called calibration validity); (2) the RAI does a passable job at distinguishing high risk from low risk individuals (discriminant validity); (3) the RAI is validated on a population similar to the population in question (external or local validity); (4) the RAI has satisfactory inter-rater agreement (in social science terms, reliability); and (5) information about all of these factors is periodically updated (current validity).

In *Just Algorithms*, I devote an entire chapter to fleshing out these various aspects of validity (Slobogin 2021: chapter 3). Here I want to make four simpler points. First, notice that the preceding description of validity's components does not require perfection in any of these areas ('acceptable' level of confidence, 'passable job' at discrimination, 'similar' validation sample, 'satisfactory' reliability and 'periodic' updating). Certainty is simply not possible in the risk assessment area. Policymakers will need to think hard about how much uncertainty we should be willing to tolerate.

Second, the most important measure of validity from a legal perspective is calibration, the extent to which a given risk group identified by an RAI recidivates at the predicted rate (see Helmus and Babchishin 2016). Experts using RAIs should be able to indicate, with a high degree of confidence, that a person is within a group, X% of which engage in the relevant outcome within the relevant period in the absence of intervention (cf. *R v Peta* 2007: para 53, where the New Zealand Court of Appeal held the use of categories such as 'high, moderate or low risk should be qualified by probability statements that give corresponding re-offence rates for groups of similar offenders and the numbers of offenders in each category should be specified'). Measures of discriminant validity – usually measured by something called Area Under the Curve (see Helmus and Babchishin 2016), where this value measures the extent to which an RAI does better than chance – are often given prominence by social scientists in discussions of RAI validity. However, for the legal purpose of deciding whether to deprive someone of liberty, calibration accuracy – determining whether a person is, say, within a group only 5% of whom recidivates or instead within a group over 30% of whom recidivate – is most important. Furthermore, if limited in this way, predictions can sidestep the debate, alluded to by McSherry (2013: 48–49) in *Managing Fear*, over whether nomothetic information is 'relevant' to an individual prediction; a well-calibrated prediction instrument assigns an individual to a risk group rather than trying to make the either-or decision about whether he or she will reoffend.

A third point has to do with the role RAIs should play in reaching conclusions about risk. In *Just Algorithms* I take the position that, if an RAI is considered valid in the various ways set out earlier and its use in a particular case survives the adversarial process discussed later, its results should be given presumptive effect. Judges and parole boards should not be able to second-guess those results unless empirically based information is presented about risk and protective factors that are not already considered in developing the instrument. Otherwise, there is no point in using the instrument in the first place. Unfortunately, judges routinely ignore the results of RAIs, or blithely state that those results are just one of many variables to consider in evaluating risk, apparently assuming that they know best. Research comparing actuarial and clinical decision-making indicates otherwise (Eckhouse et al. 2019: 186; Slobogin 2021: 67 and 76), and research also suggests that when judges do depart from RAI results, they tend to do so in an upward direction – sometimes, for instance, based on criminal history that has already been incorporated into the statistical risk assessment (Slobogin 2021: 79).

Finally, with the exception of the fourth type of validity – which is a measure of whether a valid instrument was reliably applied in a given case – the validity of an RAI can and should be evaluated on a jurisdiction-wide basis. In practice, a state entity or a university can perform the analysis required to measure calibration, discriminant, external and current validity. That would take a significant burden off the shoulders of judges and parole boards, which would then need merely ensure that the evaluator was well-trained in risk assessment and correctly identified the relevant risk factors and combined them correctly.

With the advent of RAIs, it is now possible to make meaningful judgments about the relative accuracy of risk assessment. Thus, policymakers and courts have a duty to engage in that judgment. Failing to do so is a gross abdication of responsibility.

Fairness

Even if RAIs answer the law's questions in a reasonably accurate fashion, they can encounter at least three objections about their fairness, which focus on what I call egalitarian justice, retributive justice and procedural justice. These justice issues have triggered intense criticism of risk algorithms, to the effect that they are racially biased, antithetical to the tenets of the criminal justice system and dehumanising. Most dramatic in this regard was a letter signed in 2020 by 2,500 academics, 'demanding' that Springer Publishing Company issue a statement 'condemning' the use of statistics to predict criminality and that it no longer publish works that rely on such data (Coalition for Critical Technology 2020).

Egalitarian Injustice

With respect to the egalitarian injustice claim, the argument that has received the most publicity builds on a ProPublica article that showed that, under one of the most widely used RAIs, black persons are much more likely to be falsely identified as high risk than white persons (Angwin et al. 2016). The developers of the instrument did not dispute this claim, but pointed out that, under their instrument, black people and white people with the same risk score recidivated at the same rates, which they argued should be what RAIs try to do (Corbett-Davies et al. 2016). Others pointed out that the higher black false positive rate was inevitable as a statistical matter, if in fact the crime rate among people of colour is higher than the white crime rate, which the data from the Propublica article indicated was in fact the case (Corbett-Davies et al. 2016). When black defendants have a higher rate of reoffending, a well-calibrated algorithm will classify a greater proportion of black defendants as high risk, and thus a greater proportion of black defendants who ultimately do not reoffend will be classified as high risk. (The same phenomenon would occur, for instance, with age and sex; because young people and males commit more crimes, a well-calibrated RAI will produce more false positives at each score among youth and men than among older people and women.)

Of course, if there is a differential in crime rates between races, that could very well be the result of structural or systemic racism. But then RAIs are not the real problem; rather the entire criminal justice system is. One solution – which has become increasingly popular among academics – is to abolish that system (including police, prisons and prosecutors) and start from scratch. But assuming that is not going to happen soon, RAIs can be part of the solution. For instance, the law should make sure that RAIs do not use biased outcome measures. Given the impact of racialised policing, it is very possible that an RAI that purports to predict *arrests* – as opposed to convictions – for *any* crime – as opposed to serious crimes – significantly misrepresents how often people of colour actually engage in the type of crime that should be of interest; rather these RAIs merely report how often people are arrested for petty crimes, which could easily be the result of biased and discriminatory police decisions (Matthews 2013). As Sandra Mayson (2019: 2264) has said, in New Orleans, where she used to practice, a black person with three low level arrests was not a major concern, but a white person with three arrests 'was really bad news!' If so, RAI developers should adjust their outcome measures accordingly. They might also consider developing separate instruments for black people and white people, given the differing base rates involved (and, by the way, developing separate RAIs for women as well).

Note that this discussion about inequality and risk factors is only possible when risk assessment is a product of an RAI. If instead a risk assessment is the product of human judgment, figuring out whether a given decision is biased, and then figuring out what ameliorative action to take, would be much more difficult. Even with implicit bias training, humans are often heavily influenced by race or race proxies. And even with a requirement that reasons for acting be documented, human intuitive predictions of reoffending are opaque, which makes them difficult to challenge. In contrast, an RAI displays its stereotyping assumptions on its face. Thus, compared to human-driven risk assessment, RAIs allow bias to be more easily discovered. And because of that transparency, RAIs can take racial biases into account. For example, using the Post-Conviction Risk Assessment tool (a federal probation instrument) and large samples, Jennifer Skeem and Christopher Lowenkamp (2020) have shown a number of ways race can be used in constructing a well-calibrated RAI that reduces significantly the 'proxy effect' of race. These types of efforts illustrate the fact that, as Sendhil Mullainathan (2019) has noted, 'biased algorithms are easier to fix than biased people'. One role of the independent body described earlier would be to look for algorithmic bias and make sure any biases that are discovered are fixed.

Retributive Injustice

The second fairness objection – the retributive injustice claim – is the idea that, to the extent risk factors on an RAI consist of anything other than prior criminal behaviour, its use is antithetical to the entire premise of the criminal justice system, which is that people should only be punished for blameworthy behaviour. There is much to this criticism. It is related to the larger debate about whether it is ever permissible to base punishment, or any other deprivation of liberty, on something a person has not yet done (and may never do). But the focus here is not whether risk is a legitimate legal consideration – an issue I have addressed elsewhere (Slobogin 2006: chapter 4; Slobogin 2011) – but rather whether, in considering risk, only those risk factors that sound in blameworthiness may be considered. Andrew Von Hirsch (1985: 11) put it this way: 'unless the person actually made the wrongful choice he was predicted to make, he ought not to be condemned for that choice – and hence should not suffer punishment for it'. That view might permit risk-oriented punishment based on prior crimes as well as the crime of conviction. But, as applied to RAIs, it would prohibit not only risk factors that do not consist of conduct like age and gender, but also factors based on conduct that is not criminally blameworthy, such as choices about substance use or employment. Thus, it would put an end to most modern risk assessment tools, which rely on these types of risk factors.

One response to this criticism is practical: if we take out risk factors that are not related to blameworthy conduct – like age, gender and diagnosis – not only will accuracy suffer, but discrimination will result, especially against women and older people, who have lower base rates of recidivism. For instance, a young male with psychopathic tendencies and one prior crime represents a much higher risk than an older female suffering from anxiety who has committed the same crime. Yet, under a crime-only approach, both would be treated identically in terms of risk.

A more conceptual rebuttal to the retributive injustice claim is that a person's risk categorisation *is* closely associated with blameworthy choices, in two ways. First, risk assessment is, in large part, an evaluation of what a person has chosen to do. People make decisions not only about whether to engage in antisocial conduct, but about their friends and acquaintances, family life, education and work; the places they frequent; the amount of drugs or alcohol they ingest; and whether to seek treatment for emotional problems such as anger and impulsivity – all of which are examples of precisely the types of activities captured in the most sophisticated RAIs. If these choices combine to make one's character high risk, they could be said to be blameworthy, even if individually they do not involve criminal activity.

Of course, this kind of analysis alone does not justify using risk factors that have nothing to do with choice, such as age, gender and diagnosis. But the ultimate argument against the retributive injustice claim is that, viewed properly, risk factors – whether or not they are the product of choice – are not the *reason* for a high-risk offender's sentence. Rather, they are merely *evidence* of what a person will decide to do in the future, in the same way that a finding of blameworthy choice in the past may rely on various facts that are not culpable in themselves, like being married to the victim, presence near the scene of the crime or possession of a weapon. Risk assessments try to predict future culpable choices, just as circumstantial evidence about actus reus and mens rea tries to postdict culpable choices.

Procedural Injustice

The final fairness issue is the procedural injustice claim, which is that even if RAIs are pretty good at answering the law's questions in a way that does not trench on equality and just desert, we should not be converting people into risk categories. Doing so cuts against the idea that the justice system should treat people with dignity, and as humans, not as numbers. There is much to this concern as well (see O'Hear 2020: 195–96). But imposition of several procedural requirements would help mitigate the impact of legal reliance on quantified, statistically derived risk evaluations.

First, as McSherry (2020: 30) argues, RAIs should be transparent, as 'the lack of transparency in the development of such risk assessment tools is troubling because any limitations in the operation of such tools can have deleterious consequences for a person's human rights'. (See also Gooding and Maker in Chapter 13 of this volume.) Many modern RAIs were developed by private companies that claim trade secret protection of their work product. But, even if, as suggested earlier, the validity of the instrument has been vetted by an independent body, transparency is needed to help individuals understand and contest the reasons for their specific risk score, and to make sure that, under the presumption scheme I outlined earlier, the decision-maker does not 'adjust' the risk score based on factors that have already been considered in the development of the RAI. In *Just Algorithms*, I argue that, for these and other reasons, it should be unconstitutional to deprive someone of liberty without the ability to find out about the risk factors considered and the weight they are accorded (Slobogin 2021: 102–10). The Supreme Court's decision in *Gardner v Florida* (1977: 361) makes the point nicely: 'our belief that debate between adversaries is often essential to the truth-seeking function of trials requires us also to recognize the importance of giving counsel an opportunity to comment on facts which may influence the sentencing decision'. Although *Gardner* was a capital case, its logic applies to any type of case in which deprivations of liberty can occur. (See also Walvisch et al. in Chapter 9 of this volume.)

Gardner's reference to counsel signals a second way of grappling with the procedural injustice claim. RAIs should only be used in fully adversarial proceedings, in which lawyers can contest the accuracy of the risk factors the person supposedly has and ensure that the risk assessment was properly conducted. Many of the proceedings in which risk assessment evidence is presented – including capital sentencing proceedings – are not as formal as a trial. In *Just Algorithms* I argue that must change. As Judge Appel of the Iowa Supreme Court stated in *State v Guise* (2018: 34), 'one thing is clear: if the state intends to offer risk assessments for the court to rely upon in sentencing, the defendant has a right to an adequate opportunity to attack it'. McSherry (2013: 198) is in accord: 'where preventive detention and supervision regimes are considered lawful, the right to a fair hearing can operate as an effective check on the procedures used within those regimes'. None of this can occur without counsel. Unfortunately, while there is a right to counsel at sentencing, in the US there is no automatic right to a lawyer at parole or pretrial detention proceedings. At the same time, the US Supreme Court *has* held in *Gagnon v Scarpelli* (1973: 788) that, even at a parole hearing, defendants are entitled to counsel when 'a disputed issue can fairly be presented only by a trained advocate'. That is surely the case when a risk assessment is involved.

As a third way of improving procedural justice, RAIs should incorporate as many 'dynamic' risk factors as empirical investigation warrants. In contrast to static factors, dynamic factors – such as substance abuse, impulsivity or gang membership – describe traits or situations the person can do something about. As McSherry (2014: 45) notes in *Managing Fear*, 'many risk assessment scales do not consider current clinical variables (such as response to treatment or motivation), protective factors (such as stable employment), or variables that reduce the risk of reoffending (such as physical illness or frailty)'. Structured professional judgment instruments like the HCR-20 and Legal Services Inventory-Revised, in contrast, include such factors, and can be very useful in structuring risk management programmes. For that reason, in later work McSherry (2020) calls such instruments the 'least worst option' among RAIs (see also Gooding and Maker in Chapter 13 of this volume). Most importantly from the procedural justice perspective, inclusion of dynamic factors in RAIs can help convince offenders that they are not the victim of robot justice and can change their risk score.

Some have suggested that a final way procedural justice could be enhanced is through community participation in the development and application of risk assessment instruments. As Okidegbe (2021: 45) puts it, 'the exclusion of communities [of colour] within algorithmic governance operates to reinforce and legitimize the barriers that already impede these communities' ability to challenge or gain control over the very criminal justice institutions responsible for their oversurveillance, overcriminalization, and over incarceration'. It remains unclear how this participation would be implemented – for instance, it would need to be determined who would represent the 'community' and whether these people would be able to veto use of particular RAIs or risk factors, or whether instead their input would be considered but not made dispositive. In any event, if the community is to be involved, it should be fully informed about the alternatives to RAIs and the various types of restrictions that, consistent with this chapter, should be imposed on their use.

Conclusion

This chapter has only briefly touched on the jurisprudence of risk that both Professor Bernadette McSherry and I have tried to develop in our work. Risk assessments can play a crucial role in reducing incarcerated populations, and risk assessment instruments, strenuously regulated in terms of fit, validity and fairness, can improve accuracy, impartiality and racial fairness. Unless policymakers consciously and carefully develop a jurisprudence of risk, however, the cure could be worse than the disease.

References

Cases

Barefoot v Estelle, 463 US 880 (1983).
Daubert v Dow Chemical Co, 509 US 579 (1993).
Estelle v Smith, 451 US 454 (1981).
Gagnon v Scarpellli, 411 US 778 (1973).
Gardner v Florida, 430 US 360 (1977).
Jackson v Indiana, 406 US 715 (1972).
Johnson v Cockrell, 306 F 3d 249 (5th Cir, 2002).
Johnson v United States, 576 US 591 (2015).
Jurek v Texas, 428 US 262 (1976).
Kansas v Hendricks, 521 US 346 (1997).
Long v State, 2009 WL 960598 (Tex Crim Ct App, 2009).
Nenno v State, 970 SW 2d 549 (Tex Crim Ct App, 1998).
R v Peta, (2007) 2 NZLR 627.
Seling v Young, 531 US 250 (2001).
State v Guise, 921 NW 2d 26 (Iowa 2018).
United States v Field, 483 F 3d 313 (5th Cir, 2007).
Varga v State, 2003 WL 21466926 (Tex Crim Ct App, 2003).
Youngberg v Romeo, 457 US 307 (1982).

Legislation and Legislative Instruments

Armed Career Criminal Act of 1984, 18 USC.
Federal Rules of Evidence (2019) Available www.uscourts.gov/sites/default/files/federal_rules_of_evidence_-_dec_1_2019_0.pdf (accessed 23 November 2022).
Model Penal Code: Sentencing (2017) Available https://robinainstitute.umn.edu/publications/model-penal-code-sentencing-proposed-final-draft-approved-may-2017 (accessed 23 November 2022).
Texas Code of Criminal Procedure.
United States Code.

Books, Journal Articles and Other Texts

Angwin, J., Larson, J., Mattu, S. and Kirchner, L. (2016) 'Machine Bias', *ProPublica*, 23 May. Available www.propublica.org/article/machine-bias-risk-assessments-in-criminal-sentencing (accessed 23 November 2022).
Baughman, S.B. (2017) *The Bail Book: A Comprehensive Look at Bail in America's Criminal Justice System*, Cambridge: Cambridge University Press.
Coalition for Critical Technology (2020) *Abolish the #TechToPrisonPipeline*, 30 June. Available https://medium.com/@CoalitionForCriticalTechnology/abolish-the-techtoprisonpipeline-9b5b14366b16 (accessed 23 November 2022).
Corbett-Davies, S., Pierson, E., Feller, A. and Goel, S. (2016) *What Makes an Algorithm Fair?* 28 October. Available https://medium.com/soal-food/what-makes-an-algorithm-fair-6ad64d75dd0c (accessed 23 November 2022).
Durose, M.R., Cooper, A.D. and Snyder, H.N. (2016) *Recidivism of Prisoners Released in 30 States in 2005: Patterns from 2005 to 2010 – Supplemental Tables: Most Serious*

Commitment Offense and Types of Post-release Arrest Charges of Prisoners in 30 States in 2005, Washington, DC: US Department of Justice Office of Justice Programs. Available https://bjs.ojp.gov/content/pub/pdf/rprts05p0510_st.pdf (accessed 23 November 2022).

Eckhouse, L., Lum, K., Conti-Cook, C. and Ciccolini, J. (2019) 'Layers of Bias: A Unified Approach for Understanding Problems with Risk Assessment', *Criminal Justice and Behavior*, 46(2): 185–209.

Eubanks, V. (2018) *Automatic Inequality: How High-Tech Tools Profile, Police, and Punish the Poor*, New York: St. Martin's Press.

Frase, R.S. (2005) 'State Sentencing Guidelines: Diversity, Consensus and Unresolved Policy Issues', *Columbia Law Review*, 105(4): 1190–232.

Frase, R.S. (2013) *Just Sentencing: Principles and Procedures for a Workable System*, Oxford: Oxford University Press.

Harcourt, B. (2015) 'Risk as a Proxy for Race: The Dangers of Risk Assessment', *Federal Sentencing Reporter*, 27(4): 237–43.

Helmus, L.M. and Babchishin, K.M. (2016) 'Primer on Risk Assessment and the Statistics Used to Evaluate Accuracy', *Criminal Justice and Behavior*, 44(1): 8–25.

Hilton, N.Z., Rice, M.E., Harris, G.T., Judd, B. and Quinsey, V.L. (2021) 'Actuarial Guides for Apprising the Risk of Violent Reoffending Among General Offenders, Sex Offenders and Domestic Assaults', in K.S. Douglas, P. Zapf and R.K. Otto (eds) *Handbook of Violence Risk Assessment*, 2nd edn, New York: Routledge, 131–55.

Loewy, A. (1988) 'Culpability, Dangerousness and Harm: Balancing the Factors on Which Our Criminal Law is Predicated', *North Carolina Law Review*, 66(2): 283–314.

Matthews, D. (2013) 'The Black/White Marijuana Arrest Gap, in Nine Charts', *Washington Post*, 4 June. Available www.washingtonpost.com/news/wonk/wp/2013/06/04/the-blackwhite-marijuana-arrest-gap-in-nine-charts (accessed 23 November 2022).

Mayson, S.G. (2019) 'Bias In, Bias Out', *Yale Law Journal*, 128(8): 2218–300.

McSherry, B. (2014) *Managing Fear: The Law and Ethics of Preventive Detention and Risk Assessment*, New York: Routledge.

McSherry, B. (2020) 'Risk Assessment, Predictive Algorithms and Preventive Justice', in J. Pratt and J. Anderson (eds) *Criminal Justice, Risk and the Revolt against Uncertainty*, Cham: Palgrave Macmillan, 17–42.

Mullainathan, S. (2019) 'Biased Algorithms Are Easier to Fix Than Biased People', *New York Times*, 6 December. Available www.nytimes.com/2019/12/06/business/algorithm-bias-fix.html (accessed 23 November 2022).

O'Hear, M. (2017) *The Failed Promise of Sentencing Reform*, Santa Barbara: Praeger.

O'Hear, M. (2020) 'Actuarial Risk Assessment at Sentencing: Potential Consequences for Mass Incarceration and Legitimacy', *Behavioral Sciences and the Law*, 38(3): 193–206.

O'Hear, M. and Wheelock, D. (2015) 'Imprisonment Inertia and Public Attitudes Toward "Truth-in-Sentencing"', *Brigham Young University Law Review*, 2: 257–306.

Okidegbe, N. (2021) 'The Democratizing Potential of Algorithms?' *Connecticut Law Review*, 53(4): 739–86.

Perlin, M. (2012) *International Human Rights and Mental Disability Law: When the Silenced Are Heard*, Oxford: Oxford University Press.

Reitz, K. (2006) 'Don't Blame Determinacy: Incarceration Growth Has Been Driven by Other Forces', *Texas Law Review*, 84(7): 1787–802.

Reitz, K. (2020) 'Prison Release Reform and American Decarceration', *Minnesota Law Review*, 104: 2741–79.
Renaud, J. (2019) *Grading the Parole Release Systems of All 50 States*, Northampton: Prison Policy Initiative. Available www.prisonpolicy.org/reports/grading_parole.html (accessed 23 November 2022).
Skeem, J. and Lowenkamp, C. (2020) 'Using Algorithms to Address Trade-Offs in Predicting Recidivism', *Behavioral Sciences and the Law*, 38(3): 259–78.
Slobogin, C. (2006) *Minding Justice: Laws that Deprive People with Mental Disability of Life and Liberty*, Cambridge, MA: Harvard University Press.
Slobogin, C. (2011) 'Prevention as the Primary Goal of Sentencing: The Modern Case for Indeterminate Dispositions in Criminal Cases', *San Diego Law Review*, 48(4): 1127–72.
Slobogin, C. (2021) *Just Algorithms: Using Science to Reduce Incarceration and Inform a Jurisprudence of Risk*, Cambridge: Cambridge University Press.
Subramanian, R., Delaney, R., Roberts, S., Fishman, N. and McGarry, P. (2015) *Incarceration's Front Door: The Misuse of Jails in America*, New York: Vera Institute of Justice. Available www.vera.org/downloads/publications/incarcerations-front-door-report_02.pdf (accessed 23 November 2022).
Tonry, M. (2020) *Doing Justice, Preventing Crime*, New York: Oxford University Press.
Viljoen, J.L., Cochrane, D.M. and Jonnson, M.R. (2018) 'Do Risk Assessment Tools Help Manage and Reduce Risk of Violence and Reoffending? A Systematic Review', *Law and Human Behavior*, 42(3): 181–214.
von Hirsch, A. (1985) *Past or Future Crimes: Deservedness and Dangerousness in the Sentencing of Criminals*, New Brunswick, NJ: Rutgers University Press.
Walmsley, R. (2018) *World Prison Population List – 12th Edition*, London: Institute for Criminal Policy Research. Available www.prisonstudies.org/sites/default/files/resources/downloads/wppl_12.pdf (accessed 23 November 2022).
Washington Times (2003) 'Texas "Dr. Death" Retires After 167 Capital Case Trials', 20 December. Available www.washingtontimes.com/news/2003/dec/20/20031220-113219-5189r/ (accessed 23 November 2022).

11 The Rights of Persons With Sensory Disabilities to Participate in Juries

Lisa Waddington and Paul Harpur

Introduction

This edited collection draws inspiration from the career of Professor Bernadette McSherry. Amongst her many roles, Professor McSherry is a commissioner of the Victorian Law Reform Commission (VLRC). The Commission has been tasked with considering the changes to legislation and practices that should be made to enhance access for people who are deaf, hard of hearing, blind or have low vision, who wish to serve as jurors in Victoria. The Commission published a Consultation Paper, *Disability Inclusive Juries*, in December 2020. This chapter pays attention to the VLRC's work on inclusive juries, and analyses how international and European law grants persons with sensory disabilities an equal right to be a juror.

Juries play a pivotal role in criminal justice systems in common law jurisdictions, including Australia, and many civil law systems. However, as evidenced in the literature review included in this chapter, persons with disabilities have been routinely excluded from serving or working as jurors. While persons who are blind or have low vision, and persons who are deaf or have a hearing impairment, are not the only persons with disabilities to have been denied the possibility to be jurors, their situation has attracted particular attention from academics, courts and, in recent years, (quasi-)judicial bodies. This attention has been brought into focus by the UN *Convention on the Rights of Persons with Disabilities* (CRPD). The CRPD represents a tipping point in how persons with disabilities are regulated and treated by society (Harpur and Stein 2022a), and has precipitated a new emphasis on participation of persons with disabilities in society (Harpur and Stein 2022b: 75). The Committee on the Rights of Persons with Disabilities (CRPD Committee), which is tasked with interpreting and monitoring the implementation of the CRPD (see Lord and Stein 2020), has issued individual communications in two cases involving deaf individuals who were denied the possibility to serve as jurors in Australia (*Beasley v Australia* 2016; *Lockrey v Australia* 2016). Meanwhile, the issue of jury participation by a person who is blind under European law has also been addressed by the Court of Justice of the European Union (CJEU) (*TC and UB v Komisia za zashtita ot diskriminatsia and VA* 2021).

DOI: 10.4324/9781003350644-14

The opening of this chapter presents an overview of the literature which explores the scope for persons with hearing or visual impairments to be a member of a jury in several jurisdictions, as well as the (legal) barriers to jury participation. Next, we analyse the two communications of the CRPD Committee, as well the recent 2021 judgment of the CJEU. Both institutions have addressed the conditions under which such individuals can serve as jurors and have paid particular attention to the role reasonable accommodations can play in this respect. The chapter then concludes by briefly engaging with the work of the VLRC on inclusive juries. This chapter uses international human rights law to illustrate how the right to jury participation of persons with sensory disabilities should be operationalised.

Jury Membership and Persons With Sensory Disabilities – An Overview

Persons who are blind or have low vision, and persons who are deaf or hearing impaired, can face legal barriers to participating in a jury. False assumptions further reduce the possibility of persons with sensory disabilities to be jurors. Barriers to persons with sensory disabilities acting as jurors can and should be removed.

Legal Barriers to Jury Participation

Persons with sensory disabilities can face various hurdles when it comes to being selected as a potential juror. In common law jurisdictions, where jury service is a civic responsibility, individuals are usually randomly selected from pre-existing lists or databases, such as lists of holders of a driver's license and/or the electoral register (Benson 2018: 439). However, persons with visual impairments will not be included in the former list, and there is some evidence that persons with disabilities are less likely to be on the electoral register than other citizens (Bleyer, McCarty and Wood 1995a: 250).

A further legal barrier relates to the presence of an additional person in the room where the jury is deliberating (Spencer et al. 2017: 334; Napier et al. 2019: 243–44). Some argue that this violates the sanctity of the deliberation in common law jurisdictions, including Australia (Boyle 2011: 17; McEwin 2015). Jurors who are deaf or hard of hearing may require a sign language interpreter or transcriber, while jurors with a visual impairment may require a reader. Such jurors can only effectively carry out their tasks when this assistance is present throughout the proceedings, including during the deliberation process. Some English courts have excluded interpreters from the jury room (Boyle 2011: 10), while contrastingly, some US and New Zealand judges have allowed an interpreter to be present (Boyle 2011: 19; see also Law Reform Commission (Ireland) 2013: chapter 4; Majid 2007). As observed by Dickhute (1998: 868):

> courts have consistently feared that an interpreter or reader in a jury room would: (1) fail to interpret the evidence correctly; (2) offer opinions to

the aided juror or the group; (3) disrupt the deliberations; or (4) ultimately interfere with a vigorous and candid discussion of the issues.

In some jurisdictions, persons with sensory disabilities who have been selected for potential jury service may be excused from jury service by a judge (Bleyer, McCarty and Wood 1995a: 250), or removed following challenges for removal for cause or peremptory strikes (Benson 2018: 441; Crehan 1998; Boyle 2011: 35–38). There is no explanatory requirement when potential jurors are removed from the relevant jury pool via peremptory strikes (Kaiser 1984: 193). Benson (2018: 439) has argued:

> Peremptory strikes of disabled jurors serve as an additional, discretionary way in which the disabled are discouraged from serving on juries, even when a particular juror's disability does not actually preclude him or her from carrying out the duties of jury service, and they have not been eliminated at the for-cause removal stage.

Weis (1997: 5), writing some 20 years before Benson, argued that 'peremptory challenges remain the final and ultimate bastion of prejudice, segregation, and exclusion preventing jury service by "qualified" people with physical and mental impairments'.

Lastly, in terms of legal barriers, while legislation prohibiting disability discrimination now exists in many jurisdictions, it does not always extend to jury service or participation (Bleyer, McCarty and Wood 1995a: 250). As such, there may be no legal right for a person with sensory impairments to be protected from different forms of discrimination, including direct discrimination and the unjustified failure to provide a reasonable accommodation or adjustment, in the context of being a juror. Moreover, even when legislation does cover this area (see e.g. *American with Disabilities Act 1990* (US): Title II; see also Budworth, Ryan and Bartels (2017): 36–41), discrimination can be difficult to prove. Additionally, in some jurisdictions, persons with some disabilities are barred from participating in a jury through practice (McEwin 2015), or by law, with Bleyer, McCarty and Wood (1995a: 250) noting some US states exclude from jury service those deemed incompetent 'by reason of physical or mental ability to render satisfactory service'.

False Assumptions Regarding the Ability of Persons With Sensory Disabilities

Many of the concerns regarding the capacity of jurors with sensory disabilities to perform jury tasks are based on false assumptions or can be addressed through appropriate remedial action.

One perceived concern identified in the literature relates to the ability of jurors with sensory disabilities to assess demeanour, credibility and evidence (Boyle 2011), or to comprehend proceedings (McEwin 2015: 25). Bleyer, McCarty and Wood (1995a) note how US courts initially perceived blind or deaf persons as being unable to assess the credibility of witnesses. However, since 1993 a line of judgments has taken a different view, and courts have noted how such jurors must also assess credibility in their everyday life, so are, in principle, able to do this in the courtroom. Deaf jurors, for example, are able to evaluate demeanour through sign language interpretation and by observing the witness (Bleyer, McCarty and Wood 1995a: 251). Moreover, Boyle (2011: 23) notes how the Australian High Court has warned against placing too much emphasis on the truthfulness or reliability of testimony based on the appearance of witnesses (*Fox v Percy 2003*: 129). She argues that a juror who focuses only on facts is actually better than a juror who is influenced by the appearance or demeanour of a witness (Boyle 2011: 23), while Kaiser (1984: 199) has argued that in the case of a blind juror 'the absence of visual signs can remove sources of distractions to understanding and objectivity'.

While the ability to assess visual or aural evidence is indeed vital in some cases, the importance of this skill can be overestimated. Visual content can be described for those jurors who cannot see, while interpretation – either through sign language or written text – can facilitate understanding by people with hearing impairments. Moreover, in many cases, the content of visual or auditory evidence will not be contested, and jurors will not be called upon to interpret this kind of evidence. Crehan (1997: 106) argues that in most cases in US state courts 'the majority of evidence [is] testimonial, with the primary issues being credibility and weight of the evidence', meaning that there are few documents to study, and identification, or visits to the scene of an incident, are often not required of the jury. Nevertheless, there will be some cases where jurors must observe, assess and interpret visual or aural evidence. It has been argued that, in such cases, jurors lacking the relevant sensory capacities should be excluded, but this should happen on a case by case basis, and not result in a blanket exclusion of such jurors (Boyle 2011: 2). Crehan (1997: 110) argues that exclusion should not be automatic even in such cases for blind jurors and that a 'judge should require further inquiry as to the other skills the juror brings to the proceedings' before granting a challenge for cause to such a juror in a case in which visual identification is an issue. This position arises from an empirical study conducted by Crehan (1997: 108) where he reported that some blind people who had served as jurors in the US indicated that they would be able to serve on a case which required them to 'compare a person's physical appearance with other evidence'. Jurors from Crehan's (1997: 108) study stated that they 'would listen and evaluate testimony relating to the identification and rely on the other jurors to describe the actual physical attributes of the person being identified'. Crehan (1997: 110) does conclude, though, '[d]epending on the expected evidence in a case, there may be a reason to sustain the challenge of a person who is blind'. Similarly, Dickhute (1998: 857) argues '[w]ith reasonable accommodations, blind jurors can serve in virtually every case where visual cues, used for interpreting evidence, can be substituted for other equally reliable sensory cues'.

In the context of deaf jurors, Lee (1989) has considered four potential bases for excluding a juror, and found that all can be adequately addressed and enable a deaf juror to perform their tasks effectively. In reaching this conclusion, he drew on several judgments from US courts which had determined that a deaf individual was able to serve on a jury. The four issues concern the accuracy of transliteration of spoken English into sign languages; the presence of an interpreter leading to a slowing down of proceedings; the ability of deaf people to assess the credibility of witnesses; and the presence of an interpreter in the jury room inhibiting the jury's discussion of the case (Lee 1989: 91–113). He concluded that 'the practical experience of service by deaf jurors without fail indicates that no rational basis exists for their exclusion' (Lee 1989: 113). Research by Spencer and colleagues (2017: 332) carried out in Australia also found that 'deaf people have the ability to understand complex legal discourse in a courtroom setting using sign language interpretation and, therefore, are able to discharge the functions of a juror' and that 'residual procedural and logistical issues' and 'reservations from some legal stakeholders' can be addressed (see also Napier et al. 2019). They also argued that, in order to allow deaf persons to participate effectively in juries, it is important to 'dispel . . . perceptions about deaf people' and 'the role of [sign language] interpreters and the process of sign language interpretation would have to be addressed through clear and evidence-based education' directed at stakeholders, such as judges, lawyers, court staff and hearing members of a jury (Spencer et al. 2017: 334–45).

Other concerns regarding the participation of jurors with sensory impairments relate to the accuracy of sign language and interpretation, the belief that involving such jurors will have an adverse impact on the length and cost of a trial (Lam 1997: 49), and that their involvement can prejudice the accused's right to a fair trial (see Boyle 2011). Providing accurate sign language interpretation, or text typed by a transcriber, is vital to ensure that jurors with hearing impairments can follow and contribute to proceedings (Budworth, Ryan and Bartels 2017: 35). This can be facilitated by only using interpreters who are qualified in legal translation, and who have taken an oath to perform their duties honestly and effectively and to not act outside their authority, for example, by attempting to influence the juror or jury in their work, or to reveal confidential information (Budworth, Ryan and Bartels 2017: 40; citing *United States v Dempsey* 1987: 1090). This would also be the case for transcribers or personal assistants (Dickhute 1998: 876). Such oaths could also help to resolve the concerns associated with an interpreter or transcriber being present during jury deliberations. Importantly, Australian research has found that 'deaf people can sufficiently comprehend the content of courtroom discourse when accessing the information through an interpreter' (Napier and McEwin 2015: 27). To ensure a manageable workload, it is be necessary to employ two translators; this can also contribute to ensuring that interpretation is accurate, as there will be a second individual who can both hear what is being said and follow the interpretation.

Employing sign language interpreters or readers, and using technological aids, such as hearing assistive technology (e.g. loop systems or real-time computer-aided transcription services), will sometimes result in extra costs. However, some research indicates that the additional costs are limited and 'no cause for concern' (Budworth, Ryan and Bartels 2017: 35; citing New South Wales Law Reform Commission 2006: 6). Moreover, these costs can be reduced if multiple courts or public authorities pool resources to purchase mobile technological devices which can be used in different settings. In addition, the costs of providing such assistance can result in the availability of a broader and more representative set of jurors (see e.g. Benson 2018: 439 and 464; Boyle 2011: 1–3; Budworth, Ryan and Bartels 2017: 36). Time delays can be avoided by providing simultaneous interpretation and real time captioning of testimony by a transcriber.

Lastly, the right to a fair trial is imperative, and should never be sacrificed for the right of an individual with a disability to participate in a jury (Law Reform Commission (Ireland) 2013: 58). Article 10 of the *Universal Declaration of Human Rights* (UDHR) addresses this right and provides that:

> Everyone is entitled in full equality to a fair and public hearing by an independent and impartial tribunal, in the determination of his rights and obligations and of any criminal charge against him.

These elements of a fair trial are also reflected in other human rights treaties, such as Article 14 of the *International Covenant on Civil and Political Rights* (ICCPR) and Article 6 of the *European Convention on Human Rights* (ECHR).

Nevertheless, the composition of juries is not addressed explicitly in such definitions. There is little evidence to suggest that allowing a person with a sensory impairment to be a juror would compromise the fairness of the trial. Moreover, it can be argued that juries should be made up of a representative cross-section of society (see *Taylor v Louisiana* 1975: 528), and should therefore include people with sensory impairments to a representative degree. As early as 1980, one author argued that the right to a fair trial 'is arguably threatened more by the exclusion of deaf persons from the jury selection process than by the potential effects of a juror's deafness during a trial' (Manson 1980: 968). Therefore, if appropriate arrangements are made for jurors with sensory impairments to participate, they should, in principle, be able to carry out their task just as effectively as other jurors, and this may even contribute to the fairness of any trial, as it would ensure juries are more representative of society at large. Consequently, individuals should not be excused from the jury, save for instances where appropriate arrangements cannot be made, or where the circumstances of a particular case warrant their removal (Spencer et al. 2017: 346).

While the literature reviewed in this chapter largely argues that persons with sensory impairments are capable of being jurors, this view is not universal. McConnell (1984: 209), writing in the US almost four decades ago, argued that 'the perceptually handicapped juror cannot bring the same independence of reflection and judgment to his [or her] task as the juror who can see and hear'. He argued that research had shown that individuals can best retain information if they are able to access it through both spoken word and visually, and that blind or deaf jurors are at a 'demonstrable disadvantage' in terms of their ability to retain information as a result (McConnell 1984: 212). However, McConnell did not clarify whether this research involved people with sensory impairments, and is therefore equally applicable to them. He also argued that a blind juror is unable to understand visual evidence, even when this is described to them. McConnell (1984: 214) concluded that '[i]f the parties to a lawsuit can be forced to accept perceptually handicapped jurors then their constitutional right to trial by jury has been fundamentally altered'. This five-page paper, which is now almost 40 years old, was the only publication identified in the literature review which argued that persons with sensory impairments were not able to carry out the tasks of a juror in general, and is out of line with the overwhelming majority of both older and more recent publications on this issue.

Removing Barriers to Jury Participation Experienced by People With Sensory Disabilities

This sub-section briefly considers how barriers to jury participation experienced by persons with sensory disabilities can be removed. In many cases, this will involve the provision of reasonable accommodation(s) (Martínez-Pujalte 2018: 344–49), which should be tailored to the needs of the individual and the specific case they are called to assess. It is important that the obligation to provide reasonable accommodation(s), and non-discrimination law more generally, is extended to the activities of a jury. The provision of sign language interpreters and transcribers for jurors with a hearing impairment, as well as technological aids, and a reader for a juror who is blind, are forms of reasonable accommodation which have already been mentioned. Other forms of accommodation could include the provision of information in accessible formats, including orally, Braille, large print, digital format and videos/film clips with subtitles; reserving seats with the best line of sight to the witness stand for jurors with visual or hearing impairments; providing additional lighting so that jurors who use lip reading can see other trial participants clearly; scheduling breaks as needed; and allowing service animals to accompany jurors with disabilities. Numerous other actions can also facilitate the participation of jurors with visual or hearing impairments, including appropriate training for court staff; ensuring that prospective jurors are not automatically excluded because of an impairment; and having a clear policy that reasonable accommodations will be provided for qualified jurors who request them.

Lastly, where jurors are randomly selected from lists such as those mentioned earlier, it is important to also include other lists which may have a broader scope, such as lists of holders of identity cards or lists of individuals who have a national insurance or taxpayers' number or code (Bleyer, McCarty and Wood 1995a: 252–54, 1995b: 275; Boyle 2011: 29–34).

International and European Law on Jury Participation and Persons With Sensory Disabilities

This section analyses the implications of international law (in particular the CRPD) and European Union law (*Employment Equality Directive 2000/78/ EC*) for jury participation by persons with sensory disabilities.

The CRPD

The Right to Physical Access and Information in the Courtroom

International law recognised the rights to access information and physical spaces prior to the adoption of the CRPD. The ICCPR, for example, provides that every 'citizen shall have the right and the opportunity' to have 'access, on general terms of equality, to public service' and the right to 'seek, receive and impart information' (Articles 4, 19, 25(c) and 26). Similar rights can be sourced in other United Nations conventions, such as the *International Convention on the Elimination of all forms of Racial Discrimination* (ICERD), which guarantees to everyone equality before the law, including in the enjoyment of the right to access any place or service intended for use by the general public (Article 5(f)).

However, in practice, these rights provided limited protection to persons with disabilities, as they lacked the disability specific perspectives which are now found in the CRPD. The CRPD recognises that persons with disabilities have the right to meaningful contact with and equal participation in the wider community as persons without disabilities (Stein and Lord 2008: 175–76). This notion of participatory justice represents a tipping point in how law and society responds to ability equality (Harpur and Stein 2022b). The participatory dynamic animates the CRPD in general (Harpur and Stein 2022a: 75), including in the context of courtroom-related activities. Rights to informational and physical access to courtrooms can be sourced from the CRPD in Article 9 (on accessibility) and Article 21 (on freedom of expression and opinion, and access to information), and can be viewed as disability specific affirmations of pre-existing human rights (Committee on the Rights of Persons with Disabilities 2014: para. 4).

In combination, Articles 9 and 21 of the CRPD create a right to physical and informational access to courtrooms. Article 9(1) requires State Parties to identify and eliminate obstacles to access to the physical environment and to information in 'all aspects of life'. This right to accessibility is a collective right. *General Comment 2* (CRPD Committee 2014: para. 25) contrasts the group focus of the right to accessibility with the individual right to reasonable accommodation. As a consequence, the duty to provide accessibility is an ex-ante duty, with States Parties having the duty to provide accessibility before receiving an individual request to enter or use a place or service. States Parties therefore need to set accessibility standards. The CRPD's Article 21(a) expands upon the right to access information found in its Article 9, requiring that State Parties enshrine the right to receive and impart information, including where the information is intended for the general public. This includes accepting and facilitating the use of sign languages, Braille, augmentative and alternative communication, and all other accessible means, modes and formats of communication that persons with disabilities choose in official interactions (Article 21(b)). This creates rights to access and accessible information provided by both public and private actors and in both public and private spaces (see e.g. the requirement that State Parties ensure private bank communications are accessible; Committee on the Rights of Persons with Disabilities 2013: para. 10.2(a)). The CRPD relies on a broad concept of 'communication', which is defined in Article 2 to include 'languages, display of text, Braille, tactile communication, large print, accessible multimedia . . . written, audio, plain-language, human-reader and augmentative and alternative modes, means and formats of communication' (see Varney 2018: 587).

In the context of court proceedings, the CRPD Committee (2015: para. 32) has identified that State Parties should ensure deaf persons are provided with sign language interpretation in all judicial procedures. Accordingly, Articles 9 and 21 create a right for persons with disabilities to receive and impart information in courtrooms; by extension, this includes jury members.

The Equal Right to Participate in Juries

The principles of human dignity, equality and non-discrimination are at the core of international human rights law. Equality and non-discrimination are the only human rights mentioned in the *United Nations Charter* (Preamble para. 2 and Articles 55–56), while human dignity, equality and non-discrimination are referred to in the UDHR (Preamble para. 1), the ICCPR (Articles 4 and 26) and the *International Covenant on Economic, Social and Cultural Rights* (ICESCR) (Preamble and Articles 2 and 13). Despite the importance of the equality principle, United Nations treaty bodies have not produced consistent commentaries on the principle (Vandenhole 2005: 33 and 289), and this is clearly apparent in the case of persons with disabilities prior to the adoption of the CRPD. The CRPD has reinforced the understanding that persons with disabilities have the right to equality and provides incidental rights to ensure this right can be exercised. The right to equality grants persons with disabilities a substantive right to participate on juries.

Although the organisation of jury systems, including how individuals are appointed to a jury, differs across State Parties to the CRPD, the right to equality is common. The equality principle in the CRPD found in Article 5 is of general application and permeates the entire Convention. As observed by the CRPD Committee in *General Comment No 6* (2018: para. 7), equality and non-discrimination are at the heart of the CRPD and evoked consistently throughout its substantive articles with the repeated use of the wording 'on an equal basis with others', which links all substantive rights of the CRPD to its non-discrimination principle in Article 5. For Article 5(1) of the CRPD starts from the position that all persons are equal before and under the law, and that they are entitled, without any discrimination, to the equal protection and equal benefit of the law. This prohibits *de jure* or *de facto* discrimination in any field regulated and protected by public authorities. While the equality guarantee does not create a right to participate in juries, it does create a right to equal treatment when it comes to jury participation. Since the CRPD adopts a substantive equality approach (Fredman 2011: 25), requiring proactive support to realise the equality guarantee (Corsi 2018: 157–60), State Parties must provide persons with disabilities with support to enable them to have equal opportunities to participate on juries.

The Right to Access Justice and the Right to Participate on Juries

Whereas there is a strong right to justice under international human rights law, that right had not translated into a right to participate in juries prior to the CRPD. Rights to an effective remedy and to a fair hearing are enumerated in the international bill of rights, the UDHR (Article 10) and the ICCPR (Article 14(1)), as well as in a range of other United Nations conventions, including the ICERD (Articles 5(a) and 6)), the *Convention on the Elimination of All Forms of Discrimination Against Women* (CEDAW) (Articles 7, 8 and 15), the *Convention against Torture* (CAT) (Articles 13 and 14), the *Convention on the Rights of the Child* (CRC) (Article 12), the *International Convention on the Protection of the Rights of All Migrant Workers* (ICRMW) (Articles 18 and 83) and the *Convention for the Protection of All Persons from Forced Disappearance* (Articles 2, 8, 11 and 17). These provisions all reinforce the connection between effective access to justice and the realisation of human rights; however, they do not expressly provide a right to participate on juries to advance justice.

In contrast to other human rights conventions, the CRPD (Articles 13 and 14) has expanded both the rights to an effective hearing and to a fair hearing (Lawson and Flynn 2013: 10). Article 13 of the CRPD requires States Parties to ensure 'effective access to justice for persons with disabilities on an equal basis with others . . . in order to facilitate their effective role as direct and indirect participants in all phases of legal proceedings', 'including through the provision of procedural and age-appropriate accommodation' (see Flynn 2018: 384–89). A distinction needs to be drawn here between 'procedural and age-appropriate accommodations' and 'reasonable accommodations'. Article 13 does not restrict the State's obligation to provide accommodations by requiring that ccommodations do not amount to a disproportionate or undue burden. Accordingly, the duty upon States Parties to provide both procedural and age-appropriate accommodations is absolute. The extent of this duty must be considered within the context of the justice system. The reach of the system is significant and can result in a person spending the rest of their life in prison, gaining protection from a domestic violence order, obtaining compensation rather than living in poverty or having their right to act as a full citizen protected. Accordingly, if jury participation is held to fall under Article 13, State Parties are under considerable obligations to ensure a full and equal experience.

When adopting Concluding Observations directed at States Parties, the CRPD Committee has interpreted the right to justice to include a right to participate in juries. The Committee, for example, was concerned about the 'absence of measures such as those for the provision of reasonable accommodation that would enable persons with disabilities in assuming positions as judges, members of the jury or other functions in the judiciary' in India (Committee on the Rights of Persons with Disabilities 2019a: 7). Similarly, in its Concluding Observation on the United Kingdom, the CRPD Committee (2017: 6) was concerned about regulations which excluded persons with hearing impairments from participation in jury proceedings, and that the provision of personal assistants/interpreters was not deemed to constitute a procedural accommodation. The CRPD Committee (2017: 6) recommended that the United Kingdom ensure that all persons with disabilities were provided with 'adequate procedural accommodation within the justice system, and enable in particular deaf persons through the use of sign language interpreters, to fully and equally participate as jurors in court proceedings'. Accordingly, the CRPD Committee has concluded that access to justice includes a right to participate in juries with appropriate support.

The Right to Participate in Public and Political Affairs

Prior to the adoption of the CRPD, the right to engage in political and public affairs did not extend to participation in juries. The UDHR recognised a right to representative government and to public service (Article 21). Similarly, the ICCPR created a right to take part in the conduct of public affairs and to public service (Article 25; see also Human Rights Committee 1996: para. 1). This right to participate in public affairs was restated in subsequent conventions (see e.g. CEDAW: Article 7; CRC: Article 12; ICRMW: Article 41; *Indigenous and Tribal Peoples Convention*: Articles 6 and 7). Even though jury participation is related to public affairs, jurisprudence of the Human Rights Committee confirms that the ICCPR's Article 25 does not extend to jury duty (Joseph and Castan 2013: 732; Nowak 2005: 570).

The CRPD has extended the right to participate in public affairs to include the judicial branch of government. Even though the title of Article 29 of the CRPD refers to both public and political rights, the *chapeau* (introductory text of a treaty that broadly defines its principles, objectives and background) only guarantees full and effective participation in the exercise of political rights. The *chapeau* provides that State Parties must guarantee to persons with disabilities political rights through a range of measures. Article 29(b) illustrates that protecting political rights is only possible where persons with disabilities have their right to participate in public affairs protected. Article 29(b) requires States '[t]o promote actively an environment in which persons with disabilities can effectively and fully participate in the conduct of public affairs, without discrimination and on an equal basis with others, and encourage their participation in public affairs'. Grobelaar Du Plessis and Njau (2018: 861) explain that Article 29(b) 'broadens the significance of participation of persons with disabilities in decision-making beyond the scope of political rights'. Reflecting this reasoning, the CRPD Committee (2019b: 10) has held that the right to participate in public affairs includes a right to participate in all branches of government, including the political, legislative and judicial branches. When the participation provided for in the *chapeau* is realised in the judicial branch, persons with disabilities should be able to effectively and fully participate on juries.

The Right to Work as a Juror

Whereas jury participation in common law jurisdictions is associated with citizenship, in some civil law jurisdictions legally qualified individuals are employed as jurors. In such situations, the right to work and employment are relevant. The right to work and employment has been recognised in the international bill of rights (UDHR: Article 23(1); ICESCR: Article 6; ICCPR: Article 8(3)(a)), a range of other UN human rights conventions (ICERD: Article 5(e)(i); CEDAW: Article 11(1)(a); CRC: Article 32), as well as in regional instruments, including the *European Social Charter (Revised)* of 1996 (Article 1; see also *African Charter on Human and Peoples' Rights*: Article 15; *Additional Protocol to the American Convention on Human Rights in the Area of Economic, Social and Cultural Rights*: Article 6). The International Labour Organization conventions are also relevant, with the *Vocational Rehabilitation and Employment (Disabled Persons) Convention* being most pertinent to workers with disabilities.

The CRPD requires proactive efforts to realise the right to access (Article 9(2)(h)), and universal design (see Harpur 2013: 540–41). Universal design is defined in the CRPD to include the 'design of products, environments, programmes and services to be usable by all people, to the greatest extent possible, without the need for adaptation or specialized design' (Article 2). Where universal design does not meet the needs of all individuals with a disability, the CRPD requires that individualised reasonable accommodations are made (Harpur 2017: chapter 2). The duty to make reasonable accommodations and adjustments is a key aspect of the CRPD (Lord and Brown 2011: 273), and is an important aspect of the right to work (CRPD: Article 27(1)(i)). The understanding of what is reasonable is situational and differs between rights protected under the Convention. For example in *Devers v Kindilan Society* (2010: 261), Justices Ryan, Mansfield and McKerracher of the Full Court of the Federal Court of Australia found that the notion of 'access' to employment in Australian disability anti-discrimination law only arises in relation to access to the benefits associated with employment and not to employment per se. Thus, the Full Court found that whereas disabled persons have an entitlement to access education, the duty in the employment space requires less from employers when compared to educators.

There is also more expected from public sector employers than from private sector employers. This is illustrated by the fact that while the CRPD requires State Parties to 'employ' persons with disabilities in the public sector, they are only required to 'promote' employment in the private sector (Article 27(1)(g)–(h)). This means that where juror membership is a form of employment, State Parties have a duty to create universally accessible courtrooms and to make reasonable accommodations to enable jurors to exercise their right to work.

Individual Communications Concerning the Right to Jury Duty

The CRPD Committee has issued communications in *Beasley* and *Lockrey* against Australia. Gemma Beasley and Michael Lockrey were both Australian citizens who were selected, eligible and excited by the opportunity to serve as jurors. When both Beasley and Lockrey respectively contacted the Office of the Sheriff of New South Wales who had issued the jury summons and informed it of their sensory impairments that required accommodation, the fact they were deaf caused each to be excluded from exercising their right to jury participation. The CRPD Committee found that Australia had breached Articles 5, 9, 13, 21 and 29 of the CRPD in preventing Beasley and Lockrey from participating as jurors due to their deafness.

The CRPD Committee concluded that Australia had not taken 'the necessary steps to ensure reasonable accommodations were provided' and so had violated its Article 5 obligations under the CRPD (*Beasley v Australia* 2016: 15; *Lockrey v Australia* 2016: 15). It determined that 'communication' guaranteed in Article 2 of the CRPD included languages, and thus extended to alternative modes of communication. This meant Australia was required to provide access to sign language interpretation and steno-captioning to enable communication on juries (*Beasley v Australia* 2016: 16). The Committee also found providing sign language interpretation or steno-captioning would not constitute a disproportionate or undue burden (*Beasley v Australia* 2016: 15; *Lockrey v Australia* 2016: 15). Similarly, when addressing Article 21, the Committee held that steno-captioning came within the definition of 'communication' in Article 2 of the Convention and the failure to provide these modes of communication constituted a breach of Article 21 (*Beasley v Australia* 2016: 16; *Lockrey v Australia* 2016: 16).

In both *Beasley* and *Lockrey*, the CRPD Committee noted that the performance of jury duty is associated with active citizenship, and thus constitutes an important aspect of civic life within the meaning of the CRPD's Article 9(1) (*Beasley v Australia* 2016: 15–16; *Lockrey v Australia* 2016: 16). The Committee determined that Australia's refusal to provide Beasley with Auslan (sign-language) interpretation and Lockrey with steno-captioning violated their respective rights to access the jury. Article 9 is even more significant in jurisdictions where jurors are employed, as it expressly references workplaces at Article 9(1)(a). In contrast, participation on a jury in some (common law) jurisdictions is associated with citizenship, which is not expressly referenced in this article of the CRPD.

The CRPD Committee also found that Australia had breached Articles 13 and 29 in both Communications. The Committee observed that juries form a part of the Australian legal system and therefore State Parties have obligations under Article 13 (*Beasley v Australia* 2016: 16–17; *Lockrey v Australia* 2016: 17). The Committee also noted that jury service relates to citizenship, and that State Parties are subject to duties under Article 29 regarding participation in juries (*Beasley v Australia* 2016: 16–17; *Lockrey v Australia* 2016: 17).

States' duties are not limited to the provision of means of communication to jurors with sensory impairments. The refusal by the Office of the New South Wales Sheriff to provide basic accommodations was also addressed. The Committee on the Rights of Persons with Disabilities (2019c: paras. 25–26) has subsequently commented on the access of persons with disabilities to juries in its second *Concluding Observations on Australia*. When addressing Article 13 of the CRPD, the Committee (2019c: para. 25(a)) explained it was concerned that in Australia 'only some states and territories have passed legislation to support the equal participation of persons with disabilities in the jury system'. The Committee (2019c: para. 26(a)) recommended that Australia 'develop legislation in all states on the equal participation of persons with disabilities in the jury system'. The language of the Committee in this 2019 *Concluding Observation* was broad and did not limit Australia's obligation to providing appropriate means of communications. Providing 'equal participation' will require a profound shift in how Australia approaches jurors with a disability. It will require consideration of all the measures which limit equal access and participation on juries. Equal participation is a high bar.

European Union Law

The 27 Member States of the European Union have transferred specific powers and competences to the European Union. Those powers and competences are set out in two treaties: the *Treaty on the European Union* (*TEU*), and the *Treaty on the Functioning of the European Union* (TFEU). The European Union is obliged to act in accordance with a set of fundamental (or human) rights, as set out in the *Charter of Fundamental Rights of the European Union* (EU Charter), and its Member States are also bound by the Charter when implementing EU law. The EU is a party to the CRPD and is bound by the Convention to the extent of its competences (Waddington 2011). In addition to the treaties and EU Charter, which amount to primary law, the EU has adopted a wide range of secondary legislation which is binding on the Member States, and which must be transposed into national law. The Court of Justice of the European Union (CJEU) interprets EU law. Most interpretation by the CJEU takes place through preliminary references made by national courts, asking how EU law should be interpreted in specific cases. National courts have an obligation to apply EU law in line with the interpretation given by the CJEU.

The EU has some competence to adopt legislation in the field of criminal law (see *European Union Instruments in the Field of Criminal Law and Related Texts* 2019); however, jury membership is not addressed in this body of law. The EU also has the competence to adopt legislation to prohibit discrimination on several grounds, including disability, under Article 19 of the TFEU. In 2000 the EU adopted the *Employment Equality Directive 2000/78/EC*, which prohibits *inter alia* disability discrimination in the fields of employment and vocational training. In addition to prohibiting direct and indirect discrimination, harassment and an instruction to discriminate, the Directive requires that Member States establish a duty to provide a reasonable accommodation to a person with a disability. All Member States have transposed this Directive, meaning that they have national law which prohibits disability discrimination in the field of employment.

Although EU law does not, on the face of things, address the participation by persons with disabilities in juries, the CJEU has been asked to interpret EU law in a case when this was at issue (*TC and UB v Komisia za zashtita ot diskriminatsia and VA* 2021; see Waddington 2022). The case originated in Bulgaria and concerned the legality of excluding an individual (VA) who was blind from working as a juror under the *Employment Equality Directive.* In Bulgaria professional jurors sit and deliberate alongside professional judges. VA had been admitted as a juror but, at the discretion of judge UB, was not permitted to serve as a juror; VA's request to be reassigned to another judge was not acted on by judge TC. Following VA's complaint to the Bulgarian Commission for the Protection against Discrimination, the two judges were found to have discriminated against VA and ordered to pay fines. They unsuccessfully appealed against this decision and, ultimately, Bulgaria's Supreme Administrative Court made a preliminary reference to the CJEU seeking clarification on how to interpret the Directive in the context of this case.

The CJEU quickly found that 'activities of a juror constitute paid, professional activity' in the context of Bulgaria, meaning that the case fell within the material scope of the *Employment Equality Directive*, and that VA had a disability within the meaning of the Directive (*TC, UB v VA* 2021: paras. 37 and 39). It also found that the failure to allow her to work as a juror constituted a difference in treatment directly based on disability (*TC, UB v VA* 2021: para. 42). The case therefore turned on whether this exclusion could be justified on the basis of a genuine and determining occupation requirement, meaning the objective pursued was legitimate, and the requirement was proportionate (*TC, UB v VA* 2021: para. 43), as well as necessary.

The Court found that the objective pursued, namely, 'ensuring full compliance with the principles of criminal procedure, including those of immediacy and direct assessment of evidence', was capable of constituting a legitimate aim and the complete exclusion of a blind juror was an appropriate means for achieving that aim (*TC, UB v VA* 2021: paras. 53 and 55). It also concluded that vision could be a genuine and determining occupation requirement for the work of a juror in certain cases involving 'examination and assessment of visual evidence . . . in so far as such examination, and assessment of that evidence cannot be made by means of, *inter alia*, medico-technical equipment' (*TC, UB v VA* 2021: para. 52).

In determining whether the total exclusion of VA from working as a juror was necessary to achieve the pursued objective, the Court recalled the obligation in the Directive on employers to make reasonable accommodations for persons with a disability to enable them 'to have access to, participate in, or advance in employment, unless such measures would impose a disproportionate burden on the employer' (*TC, UB v VA* 2021: para 54). This obligation is established in Article 5 of the *Employment Equality Directive*, and should be understood in light of the CRPD and Article 26 of the European Union's Charter (*TC, UB v VA* 2021: paras. 57–60). The CJEU also noted that VA had not been subject to 'an evaluation of her individual ability to perform her duties and . . . [there had been no] investigation of the possibility of rectifying any difficulties that may arise' (*TC, UB v VA* 2021: para. 56). The Court concluded that, subject to a determination by the referring court, the total exclusion of VA from working as a juror had gone beyond what was necessary to achieve the legitimate aim. In reaching this conclusion, the CJEU took into account the fact that VA, following the introduction of an electronic allocation of jurors, had successfully worked as a juror (*TC, UB v VA* 2021: para. 63). As a result, it held that the *Employment Equality Directive* (Articles 2(2)(a) [prohibition of direct discrimination] and 4(1) [genuine and determining occupational requirement exception]), read in light of Articles 21 and 26 of the EU Charter and the CRPD, 'must be interpreted' as precluding 'that a blind person be totally deprived of any possibility of performing the duties of a juror in criminal proceedings' (*TC, UB v VA* 2021: para. 64).

The judgment makes it clear that a complete exclusion of a blind person from working as a juror is not permissible under the Directive, but that exclusion is possible for certain cases which 'involve examination and assessment of visual evidence' (*TC, UB v VA* 2021: para. 52). In determining whether a blind juror can carry out her work in such cases, an individual evaluation must take place. Moreover, reasonable accommodations should be provided, and the individual's ability should be assessed in light of the provision of those accommodations. With regard to the latter the CJEU refers to 'medico-technical equipment' which could enable a blind person to examine and assess evidence (*TC, UB v VA* 2021: para. 52), while also noting the concept of reasonable accommodations should be 'understood broadly'. In its ruling, the Court explicitly referred to Article 5(3) of the CRPD, which also establishes a duty to reasonable accommodation, as well as Article 27 of the CRPD, which covers work and employment. The duty to provide an accommodation is removed if doing so would result in a disproportionate burden.

In terms of wider implications of the judgment, two issues arise. Firstly, this case fell within the scope of EU law because being a juror is a form of employment in Bulgaria. This is certainly not always the case and, in common law countries at least, jury membership is a civic duty, and citizens are randomly selected to serve on a jury. Consequently, any discrimination against such jurors would fall outside the scope of the Directive. This is because of the limited scope of the *Employment Equality Directive*, and EU law more generally. Advocate General Saugmandsgaard Øe (2021: para.57), who issued an advisory Opinion to the Court before it ruled in the case, noted that 21 of the 27 EU Member States involve jurors to some degree in the justice system, and 15 Member States adopt an approach similar to that found in Bulgaria, whereby jurors sit alongside judges. However, it is not clear whether Bulgaria is the only Member State which provides for the employment of jurors, and, as noted, the judgment in VA is only directly relevant in those states in which jurors have that status.

Secondly, this case concerned an individual who was blind. Quite naturally, the Court did not consider the situation of individuals with other impairments. However, Advocate General Saugmandsgaard Øe (2021: para. 66) noted in his Opinion that 'it is in principle necessary for . . . jurors be (sic) able to hear the oral argument'. Moreover, he alluded to the fact that, in the context of common law systems, the prohibition of a '13th person' during jury deliberations may constitute a barrier to the provision of reasonable accommodations to persons with disabilities (Saugmandsgaard Øe 2021: para. 90).

Conclusion

Historically, persons with disabilities have been excluded from society. This has extended to jury participation. The CRPD has transformed how society approaches persons with disabilities. Under the Convention, persons with sensory disabilities have a right to participate on juries and States Parties have a positive duty to ensure they can exercise this right. The CRPD promotes full participation in society of persons with disabilities, which includes physical and informational access to public spaces such as courtrooms. Moreover, participation in the legal process as jurors is supported through the right to equal treatment. Even though the CRPD does not expressly reference a right to jury participation, such a right is covered by Article 13, on 'Access to justice'. Participation in public and political life can also provide the basis for a right to participate in juries. In some civil law jurisdictions, jury participation is a form of employment; the right to work and employment supports the inclusion of persons with disabilities in juries. This is particularly significant in the EU, where disability discrimination is prohibited in the employment context. International jurisprudence illustrates how the right to jury participation operates.

The participatory dynamic adopted in the CRPD must enliven law reform efforts. Reflecting this approach, the VLRC (2020: 9–11) has embraced the new participatory dynamic in responding to its terms of reference and the 43 questions posed in its Consultation Paper. Persons with sensory disabilities have previously been unable to access supports or interpreters during the trial or in the jury room or ensure that information is communicated in formats that they can consume. The CRPD requires that laws are reformed so that persons with sensory disabilities can benefit from accommodations. In addition to providing supports for persons with sensory disabilities, the CRPD requires courtroom processes to be altered to become more inclusive. This can require trial adjustments and requires that discriminatory bias does not influence the operation of peremptory challenges. Eliminating bias from peremptory challenges cannot be addressed by practitioner guidelines or warnings from the judge alone. Procedures must be built into the peremptory challenges process to interrogate where bias may emerge; discriminatory practices should be regarded as unethical conduct and sanctioned accordingly. Including a blind or deaf juror can be perceived as increasing the cost to litigants, and the state should reimburse any related accommodation expenses.

Australian legislators have a history of reversing laws which excluded vulnerable groups from society. It was not until 1964 that women were able to serve on juries and Indigenous people were only included as jurors in the 1960s, when they were added to electoral rolls (Taylor 2017); yet they still experience considerable discrimination at the hands of white juries (Anthony and Longman 2016). While it is always hard to predict how a law reform commission report will be received, it is hard to imagine how Victoria, one of four jurisdictions in Australia with a human rights charter (*Charter of Human Rights and Responsibilities Act 2006* (Vic)), could continue to deny so profoundly the human rights of persons with sensory disabilities. We anticipate the final VLRC report, which was completed in July 2022 but to date has not been tabled in the Victorian Parliament and therefore made public, will provide transformational recommendations. We hope it will act as a tipping point for law makers and the profession to act, so that participation on juries becomes a right for all, and not just a right for those who happen not to have a sensory disability.

References

Cases

Beasley v Australia (2016) *Committee on the Rights of Persons with Disabilities, 'Views Adopted by the Committee Under Article 5 of the Optional Protocol, Concerning Communication No. 11/2013'*, UN Doc CRPD/C/15/11/2013. Available https://tbinternet.ohchr.org/_layouts/15/treatybodyexternal/Download.aspx?symbolno=CRPD%2FC%2F15%2FD%2F11%2F2013&Lang=en (accessed 31 December 2022).

Devers v Kindilan Society (2010) 116 ALD 23.

Fox v Percy (2003) 214 CLR 118.

Lockrey v Australia (2016) *Committee on the Rights of Persons with Disabilities, 'Views Adopted by the Committee Under Article 5 of the Optional Protocol, Concerning Communication No. 13/2013'*, UN Doc CRPD/C/15/D/13/2013. Available https://tbinternet.ohchr.org/_layouts/15/TreatyBodyExternal/Download.aspx?symbolno=CRPD/C/15/D/13/2013&Lang=en (accessed 31 December 2022).

Taylor v Louisiana (1975) 419 US 522.
TC and UB v Komisia za zashtita ot diskriminatsia and VA (2021) (C-824/19) ECLI:EU:C:2021:862 (*TC, UB v VA)*. Available https://eur-lex.europa.eu/legal-content/EN/TXT/?uri=CELEX:62019CJ0824 (accessed 31 December 2022).
United States v Dempsey (1987) 830 F 2d 1084 (10th Cir).

Legislation and International Instruments

Additional Protocol to the American Convention on Human Rights in the Area of Economic, Social and Cultural Rights (1988) Opened for signature 17 November, ILM 28 (entered into force 16 November 1999).
African Charter on Human and Peoples' Rights (1981) Opened for signature 27 June, 1520 UNTS 217 (entered into force 21 October 1986).
Americans with Disabilities Act of 1990, 42 USC.
Charter of Fundamental Rights of the European Union (2000) Proclaimed 7 December, OJ 2016/C 202/02 (entered into force 1 December 2009).
Charter of Human Rights and Responsibilities Act 2006 (Vic).
Charter of the United Nations (1945) Opened for signature 26 June, 1 UNTS XVI (entered into force 24 October 1945).
Consolidated Version of the Treaty on European Union (2007) Opened for signature 13 December, OJ 2012/C 326/13 (entered into force 1 December 2009).
Consolidated Version of the Treaty on the Functioning of the European Union (2007) Opened for signature 13 December, OJ 2012/C 326/47 (entered into force 1 December 2009).
Convention Against Torture and Other Cruel, Inhuman or Degrading Treatment or Punishment (CAT) (1984) Opened for signature 10 December, 1465 UNTS 85 (entered into force 26 June 1987).
Convention on the Elimination of All Forms of Discrimination Against Women (CEDAW) (1979) Opened for signature 18 December, 1249 UNTS 13 (entered into force 3 September 1981).
Convention on the Rights of Persons with Disabilities (CRPD) (2007) Opened for signature 30 March, 2515 UNTS 3 (entered into force 3 May 2008).
Convention on the Rights of the Child (CRC) (1989) Opened for signature 20 November, 1577 UNTS 3 (entered into force 2 September 1990).
Council Directive 2000/78/EC of 27 November 2000 Establishing a General Framework for Equal Treatment in Employment and Occupation (Employment Equality Directive) (2000) OJ L 303/16.
European Convention for the Protection of Human Rights and Fundamental Freedoms, As Amended by Protocols Nos. 11 and 14 (ECHR) (1950) Opened for signature 4 November, ETS 5 (entered into force 3 September 1953).
European Social Charter (Revised) (1996) Opened for signature 3 May, ETS 163 (entered into force 1 July 1999).
European Union Instruments in the Field of Criminal Law and Related Texts (2019) Council of the European Union. Available www.consilium.europa.eu/media/41918/eu-instruments-in-the-field-of-criminal-law-and-related-texts_december-2019.pdf (accessed 31 December 2022).
Indigenous and Tribal Peoples Convention (No 169) (1989) Opened for signature 27 June, 1650 UNTS 383 (entered into force 5 September 1991).

International Convention for the Protection of All Persons from Enforced Disappearance (2007) Opened for signature 6 February, 2716 UNTS 3 (entered into force 23 December 2010).

International Convention on the Elimination of All Forms of Racial Discrimination (ICERD) (1965) Opened for signature 21 December, 660 UNTS 195 (entered into force 4 January 1969).

International Convention on the Protection of the Rights of All Migrant Workers and Members of Their Families (ICRMW) (1990) Opened for signature 18 December, 2220 UNTS 3 (entered into force 1 July 2003).

International Covenant on Civil and Political Rights (ICCPR) (1966) Opened for signature 16 December, 999 UNTS 171 (entered into force 23 March 1976).

International Covenant on Economic, Social and Cultural Rights (ICESCR) (1966) Opened for signature 16 December, 993 UNTS 3 (entered into force 3 January 1976).

Universal Declaration of Human Rights (1948) *GA Res 217A(III)*, 3rd sess, 183rd plen mtg, UN Doc A/810.

Vocational Rehabilitation and Employment (Disabled Persons) Convention (No. 159) (1983) Opened for signature 20 June, 2121 UNTS 235 (entered into force 20 June 1985).

Books, Journal Articles and Other Texts

Anthony, T. and Longman, C. (2016) 'Blinded by the White: A Comparative Analysis of Jury Challenges on Racial Grounds', *International Journal for Crime, Justice and Social Democracy*, 6(3): 25–46.

Benson, J. (2018) 'Stricken: The Need for Positive Statutory Law to Prevent Discriminatory Peremptory Strikes of Disabled Jurors', *Cornell Law Review*, 103(2): 437–64.

Bleyer, K., McCarty, K.S. and Wood, E. (1995a) 'Access to Jury Service for Persons with Disabilities', *Mental and Physical Disability Law Reporter*, 19(2): 249–54.

Bleyer, K., McCarty, K.S. and Wood, E. (1995b) 'Jury Service for People with Disabilities', *Judicature*, 78(6): 273–75.

Boyle, C. (2011) 'A Consideration of the Eligibility of Blind or Deaf People for Jury Service in Ireland', *Hibernian Law Journal*, 10: 1–40.

Budworth, B., Ryan, T. and Bartels, L. (2017) 'Reigniting the Lamp: The Case for Including People Who Are Blind or Deaf as Jurors', *University of Western Australia Law Review*, 42(2): 29–55.

Committee on the Rights of Persons with Disabilities (2013) *Communication No. 1/2010: Views Adopted by the Committee*, 9th sess, 15–19 April 2013, UN Doc CRPD/C/9/D/1/2010. Available https://documents-dds-ny.un.org/doc/UNDOC/GEN/G13/446/93/PDF/G1344693.pdf (accessed 31 December 2022).

Committee on the Rights of Persons with Disabilities (2014) *General Comment No. 2 – Article 9: Accessibility*, 11th sess, UN Doc CRPD/C/GC/2. Available https://tbinternet.ohchr.org/_layouts/15/TreatyBodyExternal/Download.aspx?symbolno=CRPD/C/GC/2 (accessed 31 December 2022).

Committee on the Rights of Persons with Disabilities (2015) *Concluding Observations on the Initial Report of Croatia*, 13th sess, UN Doc CRPD/C/HRV/CO/1. Available https://documents-dds-ny.un.org/doc/UNDOC/GEN/G15/098/80/PDF/G1509880.pdf (accessed 31 December 2022).

Committee on the Rights of Persons with Disabilities (2017) *Concluding Observations on the Initial Report of the United Kingdom of Great Britain and Northern Ireland*, 18th sess, UN Doc CRPD/C/GBR/CO/1. Available https://tbinternet.ohchr.org/_layouts/15/treatybodyexternal/Download.aspx?symbolno=CRPD%2FC%2FGBR%2FCO%2F1 (accessed 31 December 2022).

Committee on the Rights of Persons with Disabilities (2018) *General Comment No. 6 – Article 5: Equality and Non-discrimination*, 19th sess, UN Doc CRPD/C/GC/6. Available https://tbinternet.ohchr.org/_layouts/15/treatybodyexternal/Download.aspx?symbolno=CRPD/C/GC/6 (accessed 31 December 2022).

Committee on the Rights of Persons with Disabilities (2019a) *Concluding Observations on the Initial Report of India*, 22nd sess, UN Doc CRPD/C/IND/CO/1. Available https://tbinternet.ohchr.org/_layouts/15/treatybodyexternal/Download.aspx?symbolno=CRPD%2FC%2FIND%2FCO%2F1 (accessed 31 December 2022).

Committee on the Rights of Persons with Disabilities (2019b) *Concluding Observations on the Initial Report of Vanuatu*, 21st sess, UN Doc CRPD/Vut/CO/1. Available https://tbinternet.ohchr.org/_layouts/15/treatybodyexternal/Download.aspx?symbolno=CRPD%2FC%2FVUT%2FCO%2F1 (accessed 31 December 2022).

Committee on the Rights of Persons with Disabilities (2019c) *Concluding Observations on the Combined Second and Third Periodic Reports of Australia*, 22nd sess, UN Doc CRPD/C/AUS/CO/2–3. Available https://tbinternet.ohchr.org/_layouts/15/treatybodyexternal/Download.aspx?symbolno=CRPD%2FC%2FAUS%2FCO%2F2-3 (accessed 31 December 2022).

Corsi, J.L. (2018) 'Article 5: Equality and Non- Discrimination', in I. Bantekas, M.A. Stein and D. Anastasiou (eds) *The UN Convention on the Rights of Persons with Disabilities: A Commentary*, New York: Oxford University Press, 140–70.

Crehan, M.J. (1997) 'Seating the Blind Juror', *Judicature*, 81(3): 104–10.

Crehan, M.J. (1998) 'The Disability-based Peremptory Challenge: Does It Validate Discrimination Against Blind Prospective Jurors', *Northern Kentucky Law Review*, 25(3): 531–52.

Dickhute, N.L. (1998) 'Jury Duty for the Blind in the Time of Reasonable Accommodations: The ADA's Interface With a Litigant's Right to a Fair Trial', *Creighton Law Review*, 32(3): 849–81.

Flynn, E. (2018) 'Article 13: Access to Justice', in I. Bantekas, M.A. Stein and D. Anastasiou (eds) *The UN Convention on the Rights of Persons with Disabilities: A Commentary*, New York: Oxford University Press, 383–401.

Fredman, S. (2011) *Discrimination Law*, 2nd edn, Oxford: Oxford University Press.

Grobelaar Du Plessis, I. and Njau, J. (2018) 'Article 29: Participation in Political and Public Life', in I. Bantekas, M.A. Stein and D. Anastasiou (eds) *The UN Convention on the Rights of Persons with Disabilities: A Commentary*, New York: Oxford University Press, 834–62.

Harpur, P. (2013) 'From Universal Exclusion to Universal Equality: Regulating Ableism in a Digital Age', *Northern Kentucky Law Review*, 40(3): 529–65.

Harpur, P. (2017) *Discrimination, Copyright and Equality: Law Opening the E-Book for the Print Disabled*, Cambridge: Cambridge University Press.

Harpur, P. and Stein, M.A. (2022a) 'The CRPD as a Global Tipping Point for the Participation of Persons with Disabilities', in W.R. Thompson (ed) *Oxford Research Encyclopedia of Politics*, Oxford: Oxford University Press. Available https://oxfordre.com/politics/display/10.1093/acrefore/9780190228637.001.0001/acrefore-9780190228637-e-245 (accessed 31 December 2022).

Harpur, P. and Stein, M.A. (2022b) 'The UN Convention on the Rights of Persons with Disabilities and the Global South', *Yale Journal of International Law*, 47(1): 75–117.

Human Rights Committee (1996) *General Comment No 25: The Right to Participate in Public Affairs, Voting Rights and the Right of Equal Access to Public Service (Article 25)*, 57th sess, 1510th plen mtg, UN Doc CCPR/C/21/Rev.1/Add.7. Available https://tbinternet.ohchr.org/_layouts/15/treatybodyexternal/Download.aspx?symbolno=CCPR%2FC%2F21%2FRev.1%2FAdd.7 (accessed 31 December 2022).

Joseph, S. and Castan, M. (2013) *The International Covenant on Civil and Political Rights: Cases, Materials and Commentary*, 3rd edn, Oxford: Oxford University Press.

Kaiser, D.N. (1984) 'Juries, Blindness, and the Juror Function', *Chicago-Kent Law Review*, 60(2): 191–207.

Lam, S. (1997) 'The Thirteenth Juror: A Deaf Person's Right to Serve as a Juror and Have an Interpreter Present', *John F. Kennedy University Law Review*, 8: 47–70.

Law Reform Commission (Ireland) (2013) *Jury Service*, Report No. 107–2013. Available www.lawreform.ie/_fileupload/Reports/r107.pdf (accessed 31 December 2022).

Lawson, A. and Flynn, E. (2013) 'Disability and Access to Justice in the European Union: Implications of the UN Convention on the Rights of Persons with Disabilities', *European Yearbook of Disability Law*, 4: 7–44.

Lee, R. (1989) 'Equal Protection and a Deaf Person's Right to Serve as a Juror', *New York University Review of Law and Social Change*, 17(1): 81–117.

Lord, J.E. and Brown, R. (2011) 'The Role of Reasonable Accommodation in Securing Substantive Equality for Persons with Disabilities: The UN Convention on the Rights of Persons with Disabilities', in M.H. Rioux, L.A. Basser and M. Jones (eds) *Critical Perspectives on Human Rights and Disability Law*, Leiden: Martinus-Nijhoff Publishers, 273–307.

Lord, J.E. and Stein, M.A. (2020) 'The Committee on the Rights of Persons with Disabilities', in P. Alston and F. Mégret (eds) *The United Nations and Human Rights: A Critical Appraisal*, 2nd edn, Oxford: Oxford University Press, 547–78.

Majid, A.A. (2007) 'Disability Per Se is Not Bar to Jury Service', *Journal of Legal Technology Risk Management*, 1(1): 8–21.

Manson, H.C. (1980) 'Jury Selection: The Courts, The Constitution, and the Deaf', *Pacific Law Journal*, 11(4): 967–92.

Martínez-Pujalte, A-L. (2018) 'La Participación de las Personas con Discapacidad en la Institución del Jurado. A Propósito de la Ley Orgánica 1/207, de 13 Diciembre', *Revista de Derecho Político*, 103: 331–53.

McConnell, J.G. (1984) 'Blind Justice or Just Blindness', *Chicago-Kent Law Review*, 60(2): 209–14.

McEwin, A. (2015) 'Shut Out of the Jury Room: Deaf People and Jury Service in NSW', *Human Rights Defender*, 24(1): 25–26.

Napier, J. and McEwin, A. (2015) 'Do Deaf People Have the Right to Serve as Jurors in Australia', *Alternative Law Journal*, 40(1): 23–27.

Napier, J., Spencer, D., Hale, S., San Roque, M., Shearim, G. and Russell, D. (2019) 'Changing the International Justice Landscape: Perspectives on Deaf Citizenship and Jury Service', *Sign Language Studies*, 19(2): 240–66.

New South Wales Law Reform Commission (2006) *Blind or Deaf Jurors*, Report No. 114. Available www.lawreform.justice.nsw.gov.au/Documents/Publications/Reports/Report-114.pdf (accessed 31 December 2022).

Nowak, M. (2005) *UN Covenant on Civil and Political Rights: CCPR Commentary*, 2nd rev edn, Kehl: NP Engel.

Saugmandsgaard Øe, H. (2021) *Opinion of Advocate General Saugmandsgaard Øe, Case C-824/19 TC, UB v Komisia za zashtita ot diskriminatsia, VA*, ECLI:EU:C:2021:324. Available https://eur-lex.europa.eu/legal-content/GA/TXT/?uri=CELEX:62019CC0824 (accessed 31 December 2022).

Spencer, D., San Roque, M., Napier, J. and Hale, S. (2017) 'Justice is Blind as Long as it Isn't Deaf: Excluding Deaf People From Jury Duty – An Australian Human Rights Breach', *Australian Journal of Human Rights*, 23(3): 332–50.

Stein, M.A. and Lord, J.E. (2008) 'Jacobus tenBroek, Participatory Justice, and the UN Convention on the Rights of Persons with Disabilities', *Texas Journal on Civil Liberties & Civil Rights*, 13(2): 167–85.

Taylor, T. (2017) *Indigenous Constitutional Recognition: The 1967 Referendum and Today*, Parliament of Australia. Available www.aph.gov.au/About_Parliament/Senate/Powers_practice_n_procedures/pops/Papers_on_Parliament_68/Indigenous_Constitutional_Recognition_The_1967_Referendum_and_Today (accessed 31 December 2022).

Vandenhole, W. (2005) *Non-Discrimination and Equality in the View of the UN Human Rights Treaty Bodies*, Antwerp: Intersentia.

Varney, E. (2018) 'Article 21: Freedom of Expression and Opinion, and Access to Information', in I. Bantekas, M.A. Stein and D. Anastasiou (eds) *The UN Convention on the Rights of Persons with Disabilities: A Commentary*, New York: Oxford University Press, 582–603.

Victorian Law Reform Commission (2020) *Inclusive Juries – Access for People who are Deaf, Hard of Hearing, Blind or Have Low Vision*, Consultation Paper. Available www.lawreform.vic.gov.au/wp-content/uploads/2022/06/VLRC_Inclusive-Juries-Consultation-Paper-forweb_appendices.pdf (accessed 31 December 2022).

Waddington, L. (2011) 'The European Union and the United Nations Convention on the Rights of Persons with Disabilities: A Story of Exclusive and Shared Competences', *Maastricht Journal of European and Comparative Law*, 18(4): 431–53.

Waddington, L. (2022) 'Case Note on Case C824/19 Komisia za zashtita ot diskriminatsia – No Blanket Exclusion on Blind Person from Being Employed as a Juror', *European Human Rights Cases Updates*, 2: 1–8.

Weis, A. (1997) 'Peremptory Challenges: The Last Barrier to Jury Service for People with Disabilities', *Willamette Law Review*, 33(1): 1–66.

Part IV

Transforming Mental Health Law

12 Challenging the Foundations of Mental Health Law

Using Articles 12 and 14 of the CRPD as a Framework to Deconstruct and Reimagine Mental Health Law

Anna Arstein-Kerslake[1]

Introduction

Throughout history, society has responded to differences in mental health in varying ways. Western society has moved from the highly restrictive and often crude institutionalisation of 'lunatics' to modern psychotherapy, medication, and community treatment orders (Wise 2013). Mental health practices have moved on from Victorian-era commitment in asylums. Most mental health treatment is now focused on facilitating 'wellness' – however, the predominance of involuntary treatment and detention remains a constant in most mental health law. The result is that individuals with a mental health disability continue to be subjected to a greater risk of paternalistic state intervention and denial of autonomy and decision-making rights.

Those who have not experienced involuntary treatment or detention or have not felt its repercussions vicariously through a loved-one or close friend, may not understand its impact. One of the most powerful ways to understand its impact is through first-hand experiences. The following passage is the story of a leading mental health activist, whose experiences led to her involvement in the movement to abolish such treatment.

> I told them that, if they felt I was a voluntary patient, they should understand what their use of power really was. I wanted there to be no question of meaning, no sideways threat or verbal coercion. Such things, though often the essence of oppression, are rarely recognised as such; I wanted utter clarity.
>
> 'You'll have to drag me, if you want me in this place, because I will not go willingly'. It seemed the only stronger way to say what the words 'habeas corpus' had failed to. I was loud, but I made no physical move, no threat . . .
>
> . . . I was grabbed, handled by two men, and dragged back to the seclusion room along some fifty to a hundred feet of corridor from the front of the hospital's locking doors to the adolescent acute unit. There, I told them that they had made their point, and they could let me go.

DOI: 10.4324/9781003350644-16

> They had other ideas. I was thrown onto a bare mattress in the seclusion room and two became five. They had me by my hands and feet, one person to a limb, and one of them was on top of me with his knee on my back, the pressure of his weight constricting my chest.
>
> I could barely breathe. I thought I might suffocate right then and there . . .
>
> . . . Their position was superior and I was overpowered. To them it was just another takedown and restraint. To me, it was something all the darker.
>
> I realised they owned me. Completely. I understood there was nothing I could do to resist them. I felt my very powerlessness as they prepared the shot. Any moment, they would be inserting a needle into my body . . .
>
> . . . It took many years for me to overcome what happened that day and reclaim my voice. It took years for me to be able to speak of that day.
>
> Aubrey Ellen Shomo (2013)

Aubrey's experiences are a sobering reminder of the impact of forced treatment and detention on an individual. They highlight the violence and trauma that people with mental health disability are experiencing – or are at risk of experiencing. Her story is not an isolated incident. Forums have developed around the world where people are speaking out about the harm that they have experienced from mental health systems, including the Center for the Human Rights of Users and Survivors of Psychiatry (CHRUSP), the World Network of Users and Survivors of Psychiatry (WNUSP) and Mad in America: Science, Psychiatry, and Community. This harm is often a result of mental health law that is not sufficiently protecting the right of people with mental health disability to make decisions regarding their own treatment.

This failure of mental health law may be due to the origins of mental health law, which are largely incongruent with the protection of the rights of people with mental health disability. Some of the first known legal instruments that dealt with mental health were in Roman law from around 450 BCE. These instruments were created to protect the family property and wealth of people experiencing mental health difficulties and did not attempt to protect their rights generally (Allan 2002: 24–25). Much of modern mental health legislation has evolved from the emergence of mental health institutions in the later part of the 18th century, particularly in England and France (Pols 2006; Joseph 2015; Mills 2014). The emergence of these institutions necessitated the development of legislation to regulate such 'madhouses'. These laws aimed to ensure that 'sane' individuals were not being detained – however, they provided no protection for individuals with mental health disability, including in instances of clear neglect and ill-treatment (Allan 2002: 26).

Later, mental health legislation evolved to include some protection from neglect and ill-treatment but continued to focus on delineating appropriate uses of coercion and control of patients. Instead of protecting the rights of people with mental health disability, it focused on protecting mental health professionals by legislating for the permissible exercise of coercion and control via detention and forced treatment (because without such legislation, their actions would likely attract penalties under assault, kidnapping and other criminal laws) (Allan 2002: 26–27; Wise 2013). In the 20th century, there was a move towards attempting to protect patients' rights. However, in many cases, such attempts consisted of maintaining much of the existing mental health legislation and adding on some protections for patients' rights – as occurred in England and elsewhere. The result is mental health legislation that continues to authorise mental health professionals' use of coercion and control, while also attempting to protect the rights of people with mental health disability (Fennell 2010). This fundamental tension that exists in mental health law – between the rights of mental health professionals and the rights of people with mental health disability – may be contributing to the relatively weak protection of the rights of people with mental health disability and the need for a human rights instrument, like the United Nations *Convention on the Rights of Persons with Disabilities* (CRPD), to demand a radical transformation of such laws.

The traumatic experiences of people engaging with mental health systems, as described earlier, are evidence of a need for greater rights protection for people with mental health disability. Such experiences were one of the key drivers of the creation of Articles 12 and 14 of the CRPD, which respectively protect the rights to legal capacity and liberty in relation to people with disability (Dhanda 2006). It is important to note that not all people engaging with mental health systems have negative and/or traumatic experiences. However, there are major user/survivor movements across the globe that have highlighted the immense numbers of people who are experiencing profound trauma in mental health systems (Beresford 2012; Tomes 2006). This should be enough to stimulate a transformation of these systems and a better application of human rights law that will allow for the protection of the rights of people with mental health disability, while also creating and maintaining access to high quality mental health support and treatment, where desired.

The drafters of Article 12 and 14 CRPD recognised this need for the transformation of mental health systems. While the text of the articles is a result of compromise and diplomacy – and is, therefore, not exclusively a product of activism – it seems evident that the drafters recognised that two of the core gaps in rights protection for people with mental health disability are in relation to autonomy and liberty. As such, Article 12 was created to protect the Right to Equal Recognition Before the Law – including the right to legal capacity, or the right to make legal decisions, including mental health treatment decisions (McSherry 2012; Dhanda 2006; Arstein-Kerslake 2017; Flynn and Arstein-Kerslake 2014). Article 14 was created to protect the Right to Liberty – including the right to not be deprived of liberty on the basis of mental health disability. These articles were drafted in a collaborative process between activists, civil society groups, and state delegations – as was the entire CRPD. It was the first time that people with mental health disability had such direct involvement in the drafting of a human rights instrument (Dhanda 2006). The result is two ground-breaking articles in a legally binding international human rights instrument that reflect the lived experiences of people with mental health disability (Dhanda 2006; Kayess and French 2008). They challenge the foundations of mental health law and provide a framework for deconstructing and reimagining mental health law. Professor Bernadette McSherry was one of the first scholars to begin exploring what these articles mean for mental health law. She began to ask how our existing mental health systems could incorporate protections for these rights and whether there is a need for a radical re-thinking of mental health law (McSherry 2012, 2014; McSherry and Weller 2010; McSherry and Freckelton 2013; Arstein-Kerslake et al. 2017; Maker et al. 2017). In the following sections, this chapter will provide an overview of the CRPD demands that McSherry identified in her work and will then begin to explore some of the possible solutions.

CRPD Demands for Mental Health Law

The CRPD provides a revolution in the way disability is treated in law (Quinn and Arstein-Kerslake 2012). It is no longer acceptable to hide disability issues away in social policy and welfare debates. The CRPD has made it clear that the rights of persons with disabilities are a justice issue (Kayess and French 2008). They belong in every corner of the law. This can be seen in the comprehensive nature of the rights covered in the CRPD, ranging from the right to health, to the right to cultural materials, to the right to be free from discrimination.

Articles 12 and 14 CRPD are particularly challenging for mental health law. Several of the other articles are also implicated as they relate to the repercussions of mental health laws that deny decision-making and autonomy to people with mental health diagnoses, such as: Article 19, Living Independently and Being Included in the Community; Article 15, Freedom from Torture; Article 17, Personal Integrity; and Article 23, Respect for Home and the Family. However, Articles 12 and 14 have content that challenges mental health law at its core.

Article 12 CRPD

Article 12 guarantees equal recognition before the law of people with disabilities. This right has its roots in the *International Covenant on Civil and Political Rights* (ICCPR) which states, in Article 6, 'Everyone shall have the right to recognition everywhere as a person before the law'. Jurisprudence and scholarly work on this right have been relatively scarce, in comparison with other rights (Arstein-Kerslake 2017). Forty years after the ICCPR, the CRPD sets out the right as follows:

1. States Parties reaffirm that persons with disabilities have the right to recognition everywhere as persons before the law.

2. States Parties shall recognize that persons with disabilities enjoy legal capacity on an equal basis with others in all aspects of life.
3. States Parties shall take appropriate measures to provide access by persons with disabilities to the support they may require in exercising their legal capacity.
4. States Parties shall ensure that all measures that relate to the exercise of legal capacity provide for appropriate and effective safeguards to prevent abuse in accordance with international human rights law. Such safeguards shall ensure that measures relating to the exercise of legal capacity respect the rights, will and preferences of the person, are free of conflict of interest and undue influence, are proportional and tailored to the person's circumstances, apply for the shortest time possible and are subject to regular review by a competent, independent and impartial authority or judicial body. The safeguards shall be proportional to the degree to which such measures affect the person's rights and interests.
5. Subject to the provisions of this article, States Parties shall take all appropriate and effective measures to ensure the equal right of persons with disabilities to own or inherit property, to control their own financial affairs and to have equal access to bank loans, mortgages and other forms of financial credit, and shall ensure that persons with disabilities are not arbitrarily deprived of their property.

This is a more comprehensive description of the right than has ever before been included in an international human rights instrument (Arstein-Kerslake 2014). By guaranteeing people with disabilities the right to legal capacity on an equal basis with others in all areas of life, Article 12 challenges all laws that deny individual decision-making and legal capacity on the basis of disability. This has immediate implications for mental health law. Mental health laws vary by jurisdiction, but generally regulate the process around involuntary treatment, detention, and other issues related to the interaction between individuals with a mental health diagnosis and legal and medical systems. For the most part, they depend upon a diagnosis of disability – a mental health diagnosis – for the application of the law. Where there is a diagnosis, mental health law often empowers mental health professionals to deny the legal capacity of individuals and make decisions on their behalf. Mental health professionals often have good intentions; nonetheless, they are frequently denying the voice and legal capacity rights of the individual. Article 12 CRPD is the first international human rights article that has put this issue sharply into perspective and forces the re-examination of mental health law, its purpose, effectiveness, and compliance with human rights obligations (Arstein-Kerslake and Flynn 2016; Dhanda 2006; McSherry 2014, 2012; McSherry and Weller 2010).

In 2014, the Committee on the Rights of Persons with Disabilities adopted the first General Comment on the Right to Equal Recognition Before the Law (Arstein-Kerslake and Flynn 2016). A General Comment is an authoritative interpretation of international law. The General Comment adopted by the Committee affirms that Article 12 challenges legal capacity denials that occur in mental health legislation – and asserts that legal capacity should not be denied on the basis of decision-making skills. Instead, it demands that our legal systems create mechanisms to ensure that the will and preference of all people is respected on an equal basis. While there has been some resistance to the General Comment, it is generally accepted that, at a minimum, Article 12's demand for the recognition of legal capacity on an equal basis for disabled people requires a re-examination of mental health law and its denial of legal capacity on the basis of mental health disability.

Article 14 CRPD

Article 14 of the CRPD guarantees liberty and security of people with disabilities on an equal basis. It states:

1. States Parties shall ensure that persons with disabilities, on an equal basis with others:
   - (a) Enjoy the right to liberty and security of person;
   - (b) Are not deprived of their liberty unlawfully or arbitrarily, and that any deprivation of liberty is in conformity with the law, and that the existence of a disability shall in no case justify a deprivation of liberty.
2. States Parties shall ensure that if persons with disabilities are deprived of their liberty through any process, they are, on an equal basis with others, entitled to guarantees in accordance with international human rights law and shall be treated in compliance with the objectives and principles of this Convention, including by provision of reasonable accommodation.

Laws that permit involuntary detention on the basis of mental health disability are contradictory to the text of this Article. Those who are interested in maintaining the status quo of mental health law may argue that this text could be interpreted to allow deprivations of liberty on the basis of mental health disability, as long as there is appropriate process, and the deprivation does not occur arbitrarily or unlawfully. (See further discussion of arbitrary detention by Dawson and Matthews in Chapter 8 of this volume.) However, there are several flaws with such an argument. The most pronounced is that such an interpretation would essentially render Article 14 meaningless. The drafters had a clear intention to challenge mental health law that permits differential treatment on the basis of disability. This is outlined in the Committee on the Rights of Persons with Disabilities' Guidelines on Article 14 and it is also reflected in the 'United Nations Basic Principles and Guidelines on the right of anyone deprived of their liberty to bring proceedings before a court' developed by the Human Rights Council's Working Group on Arbitrary Detention (2015), which states:

> Courts, while reviewing the arbitrariness and lawfulness of the deprivation of liberty of persons with disabilities, shall comply with the State's

obligation to prohibit involuntary committal or internment on the grounds of the existence of an impairment or perceived impairment, particularly on the basis of psychosocial or intellectual disability or perceived psychosocial or intellectual disability, as well as with their obligation to design and implement de-institutionalization strategies based on the human rights model of disability. The review must include the possibility of appeal.

This is an indication that the wider human rights community is in concurrence (see also Special Rapporteur on torture and other cruel, inhuman or degrading treatment or punishment 2013). For disability – including intellectual and psychosocial disability – is no longer a justification for the denial of rights, including the deprivation of liberty and the denial of legal capacity. Most mental health law specifically permits the deprivation of liberty for people diagnosed with a mental health disability – often in the form of detention in a psychiatric/mental health ward or other closed environment that is professed to be for the purposes of treatment. Paragraph 1(b) of Article 14 CRPD, in particular, explicitly states that 'disability shall in no case justify a deprivation of liberty'. This phrase, immediately following the text prohibiting unlawful or arbitrary deprivations of liberty, suggests that the existence of disability cannot be used as a justification to legitimise a deprivation of liberty that would otherwise be unlawful or arbitrary. In other words, a deprivation of liberty that would amount to an unlawful or arbitrary deprivation of liberty for non-disabled people must also be considered unlawful or arbitrary for disabled people – including people with mental health disability. This is radical, because it is precisely the existence of disability that has historically been deemed sufficient to legitimise a deprivation of liberty via mental health law that permits involuntary commitment to a mental health treatment facility or other setting. This type of approach to legal capacity denial has been identified as a 'status-based' denial, because it is predicated on the individual having the 'status' of disabled person (Dhanda 2006; McSherry 2012). Such deprivations were – and in many cases, still are – considered to be lawful and not arbitrary under most domestic law. Article 14's implication that deprivations of liberty on the basis of disability may be considered arbitrary and/or unlawful challenges this fundamental element of mental health law – and, arguably, makes mental health law as we know it a violation of human rights law.

Towards Compliance: Disability-Neutral Mental Health Law

The implementation of Articles 12 and 14 of the CRPD is underway in many countries. However, many challenges are raised in this implementation process. As discussed, one of the greatest challenges for the implementation of Articles 12 and 14 is that they require that legal capacity and liberty not be denied on the basis of disability. Therefore, where the law denies legal capacity or liberty, it will have to be on a basis other than disability. This is already done in many areas of the law. For example, the criminal law denies legal agency in certain areas to individuals who have been convicted of a crime. Once an individual is convicted of a crime, the court can limit the individual's legal agency in a variety of ways. One way is by sentencing them to a period of incarceration, where their legal agency is severely limited, and they cannot engage in legal relationships or transactions in the same way as those who are not incarcerated. It must be noted here that incarceration is being used as an example of where the law currently denies legal capacity on a basis other than disability – however, the use of this example is not meant to condone carceral solutions to social problems. Incarceration is exorbitantly expensive; frequently ineffective in any type of reform or rehabilitation goals; and often perpetuates racist, sexist, and gendered social structures (Davis et al. 2022; Sánchez-Eppler 1993).

Another example of legal capacity denial on a basis other than disability is bankruptcy. After bankruptcy, in most jurisdictions, an individual's legal agency is restricted because they are not free to engage in the same financial transactions as others. Similarly, the demand of Articles 12 and 14 is that when the law denies an individual the freedom to be recognised as a legal person, make legal decisions, or take legal actions, then it must be done on an equal basis for disabled and non-disabled people (Arstein-Kerslake and Flynn 2016). However, many would argue that decision-making denial in the context of mental health (in other words, coercion) should never be allowed, regardless of disability status (Minkowitz 2006; Dhanda 2006; Arstein-Kerslake 2017). This argument is a powerful one, particularly because it is difficult to imagine a disability-neutral form of legal capacity denial in the context of mental health treatment.

It is important to note that the Articles require that disability-neutral denials are non-discriminatory in both purpose and effect – in other words, they must be both disability neutral on their face, as well as disability neutral in their application and impact (Arstein-Kerslake and Flynn 2016). It is also important to note that the examples of criminal law and bankruptcy used earlier are merely being used here to demonstrate that legal capacity denial can occur in an ostensibly disability-neutral manner. However, the criminal justice system is often prejudicial and profoundly disadvantageous towards disabled people (Kanter 2010; Dowse, Baldry and Snoyman 2009).

As mentioned earlier, mental health law is predicated on legitimising the removal of legal capacity and liberty from individuals diagnosed with a mental health disability. Although the history of mental health law is quite fraught, and there continues to be resistance to the implementation of Articles 12 and 14 among the mental health profession, many mental health professionals and scholars now have the goal of creating modern mental health law with the aim of minimising harm and facilitating treatment and support for people with mental health disability (Zinkler 2022; Moro et al. 2022). (It is critical to note here that there is also a strong argument that there continues to be rather more nefarious motivations behind modern mental health law – such as maintaining the staggeringly large mental health industry that includes a large pharmaceutical industry, as well as the ever-growing mental health hospital industry and professional industry) (see Srivastava and Sumant 2021; Mills 2014; Clark 2014). The challenge that Articles 12 and 14 bring to the fore is to create mental health law that meets the goals of minimising harm and facilitating treatment and support for people with mental health disability *without* removing their legal capacity or liberty on the basis of their mental health disability.

Creating Compliance

To create Article 12 and 14 compliant mental health law, then, legal capacity and liberty must be denied in a disability-neutral manner. One way to meet this requirement is to deny legal capacity and liberty on the basis of an individual's 'dangerous' conduct (Hewitt 2008; McSherry 2012; Flynn and Arstein-Kerslake 2017). However, the determination that conduct is 'dangerous' is highly subjective and has already been an area of critique in mental health law (Large et al. 2008a, 2008b; Otto 1994). One of the main critiques is that the conduct of those diagnosed with a mental health disability is often deemed to be 'dangerous' when it would not be so characterised for people who are not diagnosed with a mental health disability. For these reasons, the solution does not lie in creating disability-neutral mental health law on the surface – if that law, in practice, may have the same oppressive effect as existing law.

Another option is to only deny legal capacity and liberty when an individual has relinquished such legal capacity and liberty explicitly, through advanced directives or other means (McSherry and Weller 2010; Sellars et al. 2017). This creates an Articles 12 and 14 compliant solution for many instances where an individual would prefer others to make legal decisions on their behalf. It may not be a comprehensive solution, however, because it is not available, for example, in emergency cases where there is a risk of severe harm and an individual does not have an advanced directive and is not communicating any willingness to relinquish decision-making power to another individual.

However, there are other solutions that do not necessitate the denial of legal capacity or the imposition of forced treatment even where advance planning has not been possible or emergency situations raise the risk of harm. There is a well-developed – and growing – body of research into such solutions, with Bernadette McSherry's work at the forefront of this body of research (Gooding et al. 2018; McSherry and Maker 2021). They include changes to mental health laws to prioritise alternatives to denial of legal capacity or liberty, such as the use of de-escalation techniques and environmental changes to prevent or overcome crisis situations. They also include peer-led initiatives and family-based support – as well as acceptance of dignity of risk. Such research has made it possible to begin to assert that we can feasibly implement Articles 12 and 14 – we can move to a mental health system that only denies legal capacity and liberty when an individual has voluntarily relinquished such legal capacity and liberty.

These solutions are not only preferable because they are compliant with Articles 12 and 14, but because implementing such solutions will usher in a new era of mental health law that respects the decision-making of people with mental health disability on an equal basis with others. Such law would foster acceptance of all forms of decision-making – it would not pathologise neuro-diversity – as existing mental health law often does (Lollini 2018; Rowland 2015). It would celebrate our neurodiverse world that includes many different forms of cognition and decision-making. It would also require mental health professionals to focus on understanding and supporting people with mental health disability, as opposed to 'curing' them or corralling them into some form of humanity that is determined to be 'normal'.

There is always a faction of naysayers who assert that these solutions cannot work in crises and emergency situations. Perhaps they are right; or, perhaps it is worth the effort to work across disciplines, let ourselves be led by people with mental health disability, and seek to develop innovative new ways to protect the right to legal capacity and liberty of people with mental health disability *even* in crises or emergency situations – which is, after all, when such solutions are needed the most. Such endeavour will likely, at least, lead to a world where we are working together to listen to the voice of people with mental health disability and seeking to maximise their rights protection.

There is not room in this chapter to fully explore all the possible solutions and challenges to the demands of Articles 12 and 14 (Gooding et al. 2018; McSherry and Maker 2021; Wilson 2022). However, there is space to highlight the most important lesson that Articles 12 and 14 bring to mental health law: there is an imperative – both a human rights imperative and a moral imperative – to ensure that disabled people enjoy legal capacity on an equal basis with others and are free from deprivations of liberty on an equal basis with others. This imperative provides an opportunity to re-examine mental health law and ask whether it can be reconstructed to not only respect the legal capacity and liberty of disabled people on an equal basis with others, but also whether it can be transformed into a tool to facilitate the realisation of all human rights of people with mental health disability.

Transforming Mental Health Law

The transformation that Articles 12 and 14 are asking for must be distinguished from previous mental health law reform efforts. Many of these efforts have resulted in rights language being included in mental health legislation. However, they have not changed the core function of mental health law as a means to facilitate the removal of legal capacity and liberty from people with mental health disability (McSherry and Maker 2021). The transformation required for mental health law to comply with Articles 12 and 14 may require the dismantling of mental health law – as it is currently known – and the construction of a new legal structure. The new structure would need to be free of the corporate interests in the mental health industry. It would also need to acknowledge and seek to break away from the oppressive and violent history of mental health law. Primarily, it would need to have, at its core, the purpose of protecting the rights of people with mental health disability on an equal basis with others – ensuring that legal capacity is never denied on the basis of disability. Perhaps it should not be the role of mental health law to deny legal capacity at all. Perhaps the role of mental health law should be the protection of the legal capacity and liberty of people with mental health disability. This type of role could transform mental health law from a weapon often used against disabled people, into a tool – as mentioned earlier – for the realisation of the human rights of people with mental health disability.

This discussion of dismantling existing mental health law is not approached lightly or naively. (See also discussion of the difficulties and opportunities of transforming mental health law under the CRPD by Bartlett in Chapter 4 of this volume.) There is a massive mental health infrastructure that currently exists. An important portion of that structure is providing significant benefit to people with mental health disability. There is evidence to indicate that the portion providing the greatest benefit is the portion that is not denying the legal capacity of people with mental health disability (Gooding et al. 2018; McSherry and Maker 2021). Instead, it is the portion that meets the need of people with mental health disability – and meets people with mental health disability where they are at. Some individuals are ready to use psychotropic medication and they benefit greatly from it. Others have profoundly adverse effects when using psychotropic medications and would prefer a life without them. Some are happy to engage regularly with mental health professionals and often feel safer in a setting with mental health professionals close by. Others do not feel safe with mental health professionals and have a strong preference for developing their own, often community-based, supports (Daya, Hamilton and Roper 2020; Daya et al. 2020). What Articles 12 and 14 provide is a framework for developing these positive aspects and transforming our mental health law to establish and maintain systems where the decisions of people with mental health disability are respected and enforced.

Transformation of mental health law cannot be accomplished overnight – it is a huge task, and there are risks involved in such an endeavour. However, in many ways, the tides have already turned towards a new understanding of mental health law. This change is occurring quite naturally with the momentum building from activists with lived-experience of mental health disability and human rights advocates and scholars around the world (Gooding et al. 2018; Minkowitz 2006, 2014; Dhanda 2006, 2012; Flynn et al. 2018; McSherry 2014, 2012; Maker et al. 2017; McSherry and Weller 2010; McSherry and Freckelton 2013; McSherry and Maker 2021; see also Cameron in Foreword, Wilson et al. in Chapter 1, Katterl and Friel in Chapter 14, Jayakody and Perera in Chapter 15 of this volume). Bernadette McSherry is one of the leaders of this shift, and her work has significantly contributed to this momentum for change.

Mental health professionals are also critical agents of change, and there are growing networks of professionals seeking to eliminate forced treatment, legal capacity denials, and deprivation of liberty in mental health systems (Daya, Hamilton and Roper 2020; Daya et al. 2020). In these ways, the transformation that Articles 12 and 14 demand does not need to be viewed as radical disruption or violent revolution. It can be viewed as an inevitable evolution that has already begun and will serve to improve not only our mental health systems, but also our society. There will be fewer individuals traumatised by forced treatment and detention, and there will be mental health systems that operate to serve the needs of people with mental health disability, as opposed to protecting the choices of mental health professionals.

Conclusion: The Future of Mental Health Law

Based on the developments discussed in this chapter, it is reasonable to question whether mental health law is headed for deconstruction and ultimately abolition. What is clear is that there is an ever-present need to protect the rights of people with mental health disabilities on an equal basis with others. Human rights trends are moving towards the elimination of mental health law that protects mental health practitioners by outlining when and how they can override or ignore the wishes and decisions of individuals with mental health diagnoses. Instead, it is calling for a legal system to protect those wishes and decisions.

Note

1 For a discussion of these issues in the context of Australian legislation, see the following article in *Precedent*, the Australian Lawyers Alliance's bi-monthly journal. Arstein-Kerslake, A. (2015) 'Challenging the Foundations of Mental Health Law', *Precedent*, 128: 32–36.

References

Allan, A. (2002) 'The Past, Present and Future of Mental Health Law: A Therapeutic Jurisprudence Analysis', *Law in Context: A Socio-Legal Journal*, 20(2): 24–53.

Arstein-Kerslake, A. (2014) 'A Call to Action: The Realization of Equal Recognition Under the Law for People with Disabilities in the EU', *European Yearbook of Disability Law*, 5: 75–102.

Arstein-Kerslake, A. (2017) *Restoring Voice to People with Cognitive Disabilities*, Cambridge: Cambridge University Press.

Arstein-Kerslake, A. and Flynn, E. (2016) 'The General Comment on Article 12 of the Convention on the Rights of Persons with Disabilities: A Roadmap for Equality Before the Law', *The International Journal of Human Rights*, 20(4): 471–90.

Arstein-Kerslake, A., Gooding, P., Andrews, L. and McSherry, B. (2017) 'Human Rights and Unfitness to Plead: The Demands of the Convention on the Rights of Persons with Disabilities', *Human Rights Law Review*, 17(3): 399–419.

Beresford, P. (2012) 'Psychiatric System Survivors: An Emerging Movement', in N. Watson, A. Roulstone and C. Thomas (eds) *Routledge Handbook of Disability Studies*, Abingdon: Routledge, 151–64.

Clark, J. (2014) 'Medicalization of Global Health 2: The Medicalization of Global Mental Health', *Global Health Action*, 7(1): 24000.

Davis, A.Y., Dent, G., Meiners, E.R. and Richie, B.E. (2022) *Abolition. Feminism. Now*, Chicago: Haymarket Books.

Daya, I., Hamilton, B. and Roper, C. (2020) 'Authentic Engagement: A Conceptual Model for Welcoming Diverse and Challenging Consumer and Survivor Views in Mental Health Research, Policy, and Practice', *International Journal of Mental Health Nursing*, 29(2): 299–311.

Daya, I., Maylea, C., Raven, M., Hamilton, B. and Jureidini, J. (2020) 'Defensive Rhetoric in Psychiatry: An Obstacle to Health and Human rights', *The Lancet Psychiatry*, 7(3): 231.

Dhanda, A. (2006) 'Legal Capacity in the Disability Rights Convention: Stranglehold of the Past or Lodestar for the Future?' *Syracuse Journal of International Law and Commerce*, 34(2): 429–62.

Dhanda, A. (2012) 'Universal Legal Capacity as a Universal Human Right', in M. Dudley, D. Silove and F. Gale (eds) *Mental Health and Human Rights: Vision, Praxis, and Courage*, Oxford: Oxford University Press, 177–88.

Dowse, L., Baldry, E. and Snoyman, P. (2009) 'Disabling Criminology: Conceptualising the Intersections of Critical Disability Studies and Critical Criminology for People with Mental Health and Cognitive Disabilities in the Criminal Justice System', *Australian Journal of Human Rights*, 15(1): 29–46.

Fennell, P. (2010) 'Institutionalising the Community: The Codification of Clinical Authority and the Limits of Rights-Based Approaches', in B. McSherry and P. Weller (eds) *Rethinking Rights-Based Mental Health Laws*, Oxford: Hart Publishing, 13–49.

Flynn, E. and Arstein-Kerslake, A. (2014) 'Legislating Personhood: Realising the Right to Support in Exercising Legal Capacity', *International Journal of Law in Context*, 10(1): 81–104.

Flynn, E. and Arstein-Kerslake, A. (2017) 'State Intervention in the Lives of People With Disabilities: The Case for a Disability-neutral Framework', *International Journal of Law in Context*, 13(1): 39–57.

Flynn, E., Arstein-Kerslake, A., de Bhailís, C. and Serra, M.L. (eds) (2018) *Global Perspectives on Legal Capacity Reform: Our Voices, Our Stories*, London: Routledge.

Gooding, P., McSherry, B., Roper, C. and Grey, F. (2018) *Alternatives to Coercion in Mental Health Settings: A Literature Review*, Melbourne Social Equity Institute. Available https://socialequity.unimelb.edu.au/__data/assets/pdf_file/0012/2898525/Alternatives-to-Coercion-Literature-Review-Melbourne-Social-Equity-Institute.pdf (accessed 20 December 2022).

Hewitt, J.L. (2008) 'Dangerousness and Mental Health Policy', *Journal of Psychiatric and Mental Health Nursing*, 15(3): 186–94.

Joseph, A.J. (2015) 'The Necessity of an Attention to Eurocentrism and Colonial Technologies: An Addition to Critical Mental Health Literature', *Disability & Society*, 30(7): 1021–41.

Kanter, A.S. (2010) 'The Law: What's Disability Studies Got to Do With It or an Introduction to Disability Legal Studies', *Columbia Human Rights Law Review*, 42(2): 403–80.

Kayess, R. and French, P. (2008) 'Out of Darkness Into Light – Introducing the Convention on the Rights of Persons with Disabilities', *Human Rights Law Review*, 8(1): 1–34.

Large, M.M., Nielssen, O., Ryan, C.J. and Hayes, R. (2008a) 'Mental Health Laws That Require Dangerousness for Involuntary Admission May Delay the Initial

Treatment of Schizophrenia', *Social Psychiatry and Psychiatric Epidemiology*, 43(3): 251–56.

Large, M.M., Ryan, C.J., Nielssen, O.B. and Hayes, R.A. (2008b) 'The Danger of Dangerousness: Why We Must Remove the Dangerousness Criterion From our Mental Health Acts', *Journal of Medical Ethics*, 34(12): 877–81.

Lollini, A. (2018) 'Brain Equality: Legal Implications of Neurodiversity in a Comparative Perspective', *New York University Journal of International Law and Politics*, 51(1): 69–134.

Maker, Y., McSherry, B., Paterson, J.M. and Arstein-Kerslake, A. (2017) 'Legal Issues: Supporting People with Decision-making Impairments: Choice, Control and Consumer Transactions', *Journal of Law and Medicine*, 24(4): 756–62.

McSherry, B. (2012) 'Legal Capacity Under the Convention on the Rights of Persons with Disabilities', *Journal of Law and Medicine*, 20(1): 22–27.

McSherry, B. (2014) 'Mental Health Laws: Where to from Here', *Monash University Law Review*, 40(1): 175–97.

McSherry, B. and Freckelton, I. (eds) (2013) *Coercive Care: Rights, Law and Policy*, Abingdon: Routledge.

McSherry, B. and Maker, Y. (eds) (2021) *Restrictive Practices in Health Care and Disability Settings: Legal, Policy and Practical Responses*, Abingdon: Routledge.

McSherry, B. and Weller, P. (eds) (2010) *Rethinking Rights-Based Mental Health Laws*, Oxford: Hart Publishing.

Mills, C. (2014) *Decolonizing Global Mental Health: The Psychiatrization of the Majority World*, London: Routledge.

Minkowitz, T. (2006) 'The United Nations Convention on the Rights of Persons with Disabilities and the Right to Be Free from Nonconsensual Psychiatric Interventions', *Syracuse Journal of International Law and Commerce*, 34(2): 405–28.

Minkowitz, T. (2014) 'Rethinking Criminal Responsibility From a Critical Disability Perspective: The Abolition of Insanity/Incapacity Acquittals and Unfitness to Plead, and Beyond', *Griffith Law Review*, 23(3): 434–66.

Moro, M.F., Pathare, S., Zinkler, M., Osei, A., Puras, D., Paccial, R.C. and Carta, M.G. (2022) 'The WHO QualityRights Initiative: Building Partnerships Among Psychiatrists, People with Lived Experience and Other Key Stakeholders to Improve the Quality of Mental Healthcare', *The British Journal of Psychiatry*, 220(2): 49–51.

Otto, R.K. (1994) 'On the Ability of Mental Health Professionals to Predict Dangerousness: A Commentary on Interpretations of the Dangerousness Literature', *Law and Psychology Review*, 18: 43–68.

Pols, H. 2006, 'The Development of Psychiatry in Indonesia: From Colonial to Modern Times', *International Review of Psychiatry*, 18(4): 363–70.

Quinn, G. and Arstein-Kerslake, A. (2012) 'Restoring the "Human" in "Human Rights": Personhood and Doctrinal Innovation in the UN Disability Convention', in C. Gearty and C. Douzinas (eds) *The Cambridge Companion to Human Rights Law*, Cambridge: Cambridge University Press, 36–55.

Rowland, M. (2015) 'Angry and Mad: A Critical Examination of Identity Politics, Neurodiversity, and the Mad Pride Movement', *Journal of Ethics in Medicine*, 9: 1–3.

Sánchez-Eppler, K. (1993) *Touching Liberty: Abolition, Feminism, and the Politics of the Body*, Berkeley: University of California Press.

Sellars, M., Fullam, R., O'Leary, C., Mountjoy, R., Mawren, D., Weller, P., Newton, R., Brophy, L., McEwan, T. and Silvester, W. (2017) 'Australian Psychiatrists'

Support for Psychiatric Advance Directives: Responses to a Hypothetical Vignette', *Psychiatry, Psychology and Law*, 24(1): 61–73.
Shomo, A.E. (2013) 'Remembering A Restraint', in *Mad in America: Science, Psychiatry, and Community*, 26 June. Available www.madinamerica.com/2013/06/remembering-a-restraint/ (accessed 20 December 2022).
Special Rapporteur on Torture and Other Cruel, Inhuman, or Degrading Treatment or Punishment (2013) *Report of the Special Rapporteur on Torture and Other Cruel, Inhuman or Degrading Treatment or Punishment*, Juan E. Méndez, Human Rights Council, UN Doc A/HRC/22/53. Available www.ohchr.org/sites/default/files/Documents/HRBodies/HRCouncil/RegularSession/Session22/A.HRC.22.53_English.pdf (accessed 20 December 2022).
Srivastava, A. and Sumant, O. (2021) *Mental Health Market Size, Share, Key Analysis, Forecast – 2030*, Allied Market Research. Available www.alliedmarketresearch.com/mental-health-market-A11770 (accessed 20 December 2022).
Tomes, N. (2006) 'The Patient as a Policy Factor: A Historical Case Study of the Consumer/Survivor Movement in Mental Health', *Health Affairs*, 25(3): 720–29.
Wilson, K. (2022) 'The CRPD and Mental Health Law: The Conflict About Abolition, the Practical Dilemmas of Implementation and the Untapped Potential', in F. Felder, L. Davy and R. Kayess (eds) *Disability Law and Human Rights: Theory and Policy*, Cham: Palgrave Macmillan, 171–97.
Wise, S. (2013) *Inconvenient People: Lunacy, Liberty and the Mad-Doctors in Victorian England*, London: Vintage Books.
Working Group on Arbitrary Detention (2015) *United Nations Basic Principles and Guidelines on the Right of Anyone Deprived of their Liberty to Bring Proceedings Before a Court*, Human Rights Council, UN Doc A/HRC/30/37. Available https://ap.ohchr.org/documents/dpage_e.aspx?si=A/HRC/30/37 (accessed 20 December 2022).
Zinkler, M. (2022) 'Non-coercive Techniques for the Management of Crises in Mental Health Settings in Germany – A Narrative Review', *International Review of Psychiatry*, forthcoming. Available www.tandfonline.com/doi/abs/10.1080/09540261.2022.2087493 (accessed 20 December 2022).

13 The Digital Turn in Mental Health and Disability Law

Actuarial Traditions and AI Futures of Risk Assessment From a Human Rights Perspective

Piers Gooding and Yvette Maker

Introduction

In 2019, senior members of the Trump administration, including the then President Donald Trump and Vice President Mike Pence, were briefed on a proposal called, 'SAFEHOME – Stopping Aberrant Fatal Events by Helping Overcome Mental Extremes' (Wan 2019). SAFEHOME involved experimentation to explore whether 'technology including phones and smartwatches can be used to detect when mentally ill people are about to turn violent' (Wan 2019). The programme would sit within a proposed new research arm of the US government called the 'Health Advanced Research Projects Agency', to be modelled after the Defence Advanced Research Projects Agency (DARPA).

SAFEHOME was not adopted during Donald Trump's term in office. Yet, the proposal highlights the proximity of ideas about algorithmic risk management with policies concerning mental health, 'preventive policing' and emerging technologies of biometric monitoring and surveillance. SAFEHOME builds on experiments in preventive policing in recent years, particularly in the US, which involve flows of mental health-related data from disparate public and private systems. In 2018, for example, the Florida state legislature authorised the collection and digitisation of certain types of student mental health data and its distribution through a state-wide police database (Travis 2019). Authorities reportedly intended to correlate the data with social media monitoring activity, with the purported aim of preventing gun violence (Travis 2019). Also in 2018, municipal police in Canada collated non-criminal information about individuals who had self-harmed or attempted suicide (Office of the Privacy Commissioner of Canada 2017). The information was then circulated to US border authorities, who used it to deny several Canadians entry into the US (Office of the Privacy Commissioner Canada 2017). These examples, too, highlight the growing potential for risk management in mental health policy and in policing more generally to be linked to the automated and data-driven technologies that power the contemporary information economy.

Our mentor and colleague Bernadette McSherry has explored such links, drawing on her longstanding work on predictive analytics in assessment tools

DOI: 10.4324/9781003350644-17

that are used both to define and diagnose mental health conditions and in efforts to predict future violence or recidivism among individuals deemed to pose a risk (see e.g. McSherry 2014, 2017; McSherry and Freckelton 2013; McSherry and Keyzer 2011). McSherry's more recent works on the technological frontiers of these developments have examined efforts to detect and treat mental health conditions using social media data and other health-related datasets (McSherry 2018) and the use of algorithms in forensic psychiatry to predict risk of harm (McSherry 2020). McSherry's work so far has been unique in applying a human rights lens to these technological developments in forensic mental health. In this chapter we seek to extend on that work and, in doing so, contribute to the growing, global conversation on the implications of data-driven, automated and AI-enabled technology in the mental health and disability contexts (see e.g. Gooding and Kariotis 2021; Gooding and Resnick 2020; Human Rights Council 2021; Marks 2019, 2020; Paterson and Maker 2021; Valentine, D'Alfonso and Lederman 2022), as well as in criminal law and health and social care more generally (see e.g. Eubanks 2018). Our aim is to extend the discussion to the range of techniques that use – or claim to use – automated or AI-enabled technology to assess mental health-related risk. Due to the 'black box' and proprietary nature of much of this technology, it is not always clear what processes are in use, but they range from the automation of statistical or actuarial processes to more sophisticated technologies that use machine learning, neural networks or natural language processing to make predictions, recommendations or decisions (OECD 2019). These techniques and devices share both similarities to, and differences from, earlier risk assessment techniques that utilised actuarial methods and algorithms to produce estimates of individuals' likelihood of reoffending or other forms of 'riskiness'.

We draw on McSherry's work to review technological developments in forensic mental health risk assessment and consider critiques of these developments. This includes concerns raised about the use of automated and AI-enabled technology in risk assessment that build on concerns about traditional forms of risk assessment, as well as critiques that draw on human rights principles and laws. We then connect this work with recent discussion about the contribution and limitations of a human rights-based approach, particularly compared to an approach that foregrounds ethics, to critically assessing the social and other human consequences of AI and automated decision-making. Arguments in favour of such an approach are growing in volume, largely on the basis that human rights provide widely accepted normative standards against which to assess these consequences and mechanisms for overseeing their use, which more conventional analyses based on principles of 'ethical' AI arguably do not. Other scholars and commentators seek alternative political, legal and ethical approaches that aim to move beyond the binary confines of ethics and human rights (see e.g. Benthall and Goldenfein 2020; McQuillan 2022), though we contain our focus for the purposes of this chapter to ethics and human rights as proposed governance or analytical frameworks.

We conclude that the use of automation and AI-enabled technology in risk assessment in forensic mental health contexts raises substantially the same issues that already exist in longer standing critiques of traditional risk assessments. These principally relate to bias, confounding variables and issues of transparency. However, we also consider that the extent or nature of some of these issues is significantly different in several senses. This includes differences associated with the speed and scale of decisions that are possible (such as automated risk assessment of arrested individuals awaiting trial based on massive, population-level datasets) the opacity of AI and other automated approaches that add to existing problems with transparency in risk assessment, and the major legal implications in areas such as privacy and discrimination that are raised by the monitoring and surveillance capabilities of new biometric technologies that may be used in risk assessment. We argue that efforts toward accountability in the use of these risk assessment technologies must address the needs and rights of people with disability, including mental health-related or psychosocial disability, in order to respond to growing calls for societal use of automation, AI and other data-driven technologies in such a way that protects and promotes the human rights of these groups on an equal basis with others (Whittaker et al. 2019; Human Rights Council 2021).

Actuarial Risk Assessment in Mental Health and the Digital Turn

The use of predictive analytics in forensic mental health settings is not new. By 1990, according to Robert Castel (1991), risk management had become a core professional responsibility of all those involved with psychiatry. Various techniques were designed to identify and measure levels, signs and indicators of 'risk' or 'dangerousness'. These techniques built on a longer tradition in the criminal law context. As far back as the 1920s, statisticians in Europe and North America were taking steps to formalise the assessment of parolees' likelihood of recidivism (Mathiesen and Rutherford 2006: 95).

Early risk assessment techniques in forensic mental health and other criminal justice settings involved actuarial methods based on regression, and then evolved to relying on algorithmic risk assessment that provides a probabilistic estimate of the likelihood of reoffending (Stevenson and Doleac 2019; McSherry 2020). Slobogin (2012: 198) has explained that the latter involve 'actuarial prediction devices that rely on empirical discovery of factors associated with recidivism, which are then weighted and combined according to an algorithm that produces recidivism probability estimates'. Such predictive work has served several purposes, including informing bail or parole decisions and determining whether a person should be subject to 'preventive justice', such as post-release monitoring or post-sentence detention and supervision (McSherry 2020). Proponents offered such approaches as a way for courts and mental health professionals to improve on 'unstructured' decision-making. Unstructured decision-making in risk assessment, which essentially refers to discretionary judgments by authorised individuals, is broadly considered to be 'notoriously bad, biased, and reflexive, and often relies on stereotypes and generalizations that ignore the goals of the system' (Slobogin 2021: ix). The aim of standardised risk assessment has been to replace such an approach with one that is efficient, predictable, accurate and consistent, and hence to aspire to 'objectivity' and 'certainty in decisions about preventive justice' (McSherry 2020: 30). It has also been suggested that some newer systems, such as those that use biometric monitoring techniques to make a human 'machine-readable', can circumvent the need for subjective patient reporting or clinical observation (see e.g. Resnick and Appelbaum 2019). This latter view carries controversial value judgments about the relative merit of 'overcoming' the subjective viewpoints of an individual and their mental health practitioners, in favour of 'objective' biometric data about that person, such as voice activity, bodily motion and heart and respiratory rates (Resnick and Appelbaum 2019; cf. McQuillan 2018). We will discuss such biometric or 'passive monitoring' shortly.

The first two decades of the 21st century have seen risk assessment for the purpose of managing individuals rise in prominence in mental health service provision in many countries (Holmes 2013; Slemon, Jenkins and Bungay 2017) and throughout society (Lupton 2013). Today, psychiatric services in many parts of the world are centrally concerned with pre-emptive interventions to prevent some future harm (Mossman 2009; Holmes 2013; Szmukler and Rose 2013; Slemon, Jenkins and Bungay 2017). In the US, for example, Christopher Slobogin (2021: vii) notes that almost every state has 'authorized the use of algorithms that purport to determine the recidivism risk posed by people who have been charged or convicted of crime'.

While it may not be new for government agencies, health providers and private companies to collect and hold large volumes of information about people, or to attempt to make individuals more 'calculable' (Miller and Rose 1995), the quantity and detail of the data which they are now able to collect – and the rapid speed with which it flows through complex communication ecosystems – is unprecedented. In other words, the preoccupation with risk among mental health practitioners has expanded alongside the acceleration of digital approaches to health care, making it unsurprising that steps have been taken to digitise predictive analytics in risk assessment and management (McSherry 2020).

Contemporary data-based approaches to risk assessment can deal in ever-expanding datasets, increasingly complex algorithms and exponential increases in computational power. These deterministic systems range from those that employ relatively simple binary logic, through to those that utilise 'deep learning' or machine learning which make probabilistic predictions based on complex algorithms and massive datasets (Zalnieriute, Bennett Moses and Williams 2019: 432). Some approaches just automate actuarial and statistical processes of the past. Others seek to identify new patterns or correlations in data and formulate rules on that basis. Experiments currently underway include the application of natural language processing and machine learning to forensic eHealth records (Le et al. 2018) and the use of machine learning on patient registries using a range of sociodemographic, judicial and psychiatric variables to determine whether 'early intervention' should occur (Trinhammer et al. 2022).

As noted, experiments are underway to use automated software to classify human behaviours using remote technologies to monitor or surveil individuals. One iteration, 'passive monitoring', refers to generation of data about individuals that does not require them to actively respond (Resnick and Appelbaum 2019), as compared to 'active monitoring' where a respondent might provide mood self-reports. In one Austrian study, ten patients in a psychiatric hospital were given a mobile phone with an application (or app) that was 'based on smartphone behavior and activity monitoring' over a 12-month period (Grünerbl et al. 2015). The app generated data, used with the consent of patients, that was 'usable [by clinicians] as an "objective" measurement that help[ed] detect state changes to guarantee the availability of in-time treatment' (Grünerbl et al. 2015: 142). The researchers compared evaluations of patient mood using sensors that generated information concerning phone-use, voice and bodily movement, to evaluations using standard scales (such as the Hamilton Depression Scale). The results indicated a 'state change detection precision and recall of over 97%' (Grünerbl et al. 2015: 142), suggesting close to perfect accuracy.

In the context of the US, Kimberly Resnick and Paul Appelbaum (2019: 457) have explored the implications of being able to set 'objective parameters that correlate with mental health status and create an opportunity to use Big Data and machine learning to refine diagnosis and predict behavior'. They consider how these approaches could be applied to the forensic mental health and criminal law context. Examples include:

- accused persons who are found not guilty by reason of mental impairment being subject to continuous monitoring and real-time analysis of body data that generate 'electronic biomarkers' of relapse in ways that 'bypass the limitations of approaches that rely on self-report and clinical interview of insanity acquittees';
- defendants who have been diverted by the legal system into specialty mental health courts being subjected to passive monitoring arrangements, which again, monitor for relapse; and
- 'offenders with mental illnesses [more generally being] given the option of passive monitoring or entering or remaining in confinement' (Resnick and Appelbaum 2019: 461–63).

These possibilities highlight a complicating dimension to the discussion of forensic mental health risk assessment today; namely, that recent technological developments create the possibility of ongoing, passive monitoring and surveillance of persons through remote technologies and through real-time, automated, algorithmic analysis of the data generated. In such circumstances, the assessment of some future harm is no longer conducted at a single point in time, such as during a pre-trial or post-conviction assessment by a psychologist or psychiatrist. Instead, remote risk assessment can occur on a continuous basis. This could be posited as a logical (and individualised) progression from current electronic monitoring of convicted persons and forensic mental health patients through the use of radio-frequency or GPS data (see Miller 2015; Bartels and Martinovic 2017).

Notably, continuous, remote monitoring or 'passive monitoring' operates in ways that go beyond assessment, having the potential to generate more than merely clinical data (notwithstanding that what counts as 'clinical data' may be contested). For example, Resnick and Appelbaum (2019: 463) point out that the generation of a body of data through compulsory monitoring would be almost 'irresistible to law enforcement and prosecutors', at least in the US, given that such data 'is likely to be considered nontestimonial by the courts and thus will likely fall outside the bounds of psychotherapist – patient privilege, even if it is being gathered for clinical purposes'. These possibilities start to break down the distinction between risk assessment (taking steps to evaluate the likelihood of future offending) and risk management (taking steps to reduce risk). For a related discussion, see Chapter 10 by Christopher Slobogin in this volume.

The use of passive monitoring in contemporary risk assessment, therefore, raises the much larger issue of biometric monitoring and surveillance, where 'biometric monitoring' refers to the tracking of individuals' characteristics related to changes in human traits and body parameters, such as bodily motion, location, voice activity, and heart and respiratory rates. There is a growing body of law reform and research activity on the legal, ethical, political and social dimensions of biometric monitoring and surveillance (see Kak 2021), including criticism of the epistemological aspiration to 'overcome' the subjective account of the individual or care professional in favour of purportedly objective technical measures (McQuillan 2018). For the purpose of this chapter, what is important is that both forms of risk assessment, whether single-point-in-time assessment or 'remote, continuous assessment' (and management) using biometric monitoring and surveillance, rely on statistical methods and probabilistic reasoning in predicting some future harm. These methods and forms of reasoning regarding risk assessment have been the subject of criticism from multiple angles, even as others have pointed to benefits, such as greater accuracy and the reduction of bias, that may be made possible by such methods.

Critique of Risk Assessment in Mental Health Settings: Old and New

McSherry notes at least three criticisms of forensic mental health risk assessments that are especially pertinent to the more recent developments in data-driven and AI-enabled technologies. First, she draws critical attention to the specific variables used in risk assessment, and the variable-based approach itself (McSherry 2013). Risk assessment tools typically focus on 'the main risk variables or factors associated with the risk of reoffending', with some exclusively assessing historical or '"static" risk factors that cannot change over time and that cannot be changed through treatment and intervention' (McSherry 2013: 45). Static factors may include the age of first offending and the offender's prior criminal history. Consequently, many assessments do not consider 'current clinical variables (such as response to treatment or motivation), protective factors (such as stable employment) or variables that reduce the risk of reoffending (such as physical illness or frailty)' (McSherry 2013: 45). AI-enabled approaches could – in theory – better accommodate some of the dynamic factors that exist in a person's life, for example by generating and analysing data on a multitude of contemporaneous factors in a person's life. As we will discuss further later, such approaches would seemingly require the disclosure of large volumes of private data about an individual, and the manner in which dynamic variables are weighted may be obscure and difficult to review or contest.

A second major criticism of forensic mental health risk assessment that McSherry identifies is the application of group data to individuals and the resulting likelihood of bias – a problem that would appear to be amplified by automated approaches based on ever larger, population-level datasets. Risk categorisation involves classifying an individual in relation to a group, such as 'high risk', 'medium risk' or 'low risk'. Yet assessors 'cannot say where, in this group, a given person lies and, therefore, cannot identify the precise risk an individual poses' (McSherry 2020: 30). In criminal law trials, this nuance may be missed by judges unless they receive expert witness guidance on how to interpret the results. Bias is also likely where risk assessment tools are developed based on one population and then used to assess risk in individuals of a different population. An example is a risk assessment tool developed using data from non-Indigenous offenders that is applied to Indigenous offenders. According to Kelly Hannah-Moffat (2013: 278), judges and other legal decision-makers may also mistake correlation and causation when actuarial risk tools are used in sentencing:

> Instead of understanding that an individual with a high risk score shares characteristics with an aggregate group of high-risk offenders, practitioners are likely to perceive the individual *as* a high-risk offender.

Hannah-Moffat (2013) highlights a risk that courts and practitioners will struggle with the meaning of probabilistic scoring and overlook the substandard evidence of risk assessment tools.

Bias is a concern consistently raised in the digital context. Lorna McGregor (2023) has argued that automating risk assessment is unlikely to resolve the highly contested nature of risk prediction, particularly 'in the absence of agreement on the factors that can be used to predict risk, and the exclusion of data points that may serve as a proxy for bias or discrimination'. It is now well-accepted that datasets that fuel automated systems, including those that utilise AI, can themselves incorporate or perpetuate bias in one or more respects. Datasets are created by humans, and choices made by humans about what data to collect in the first place, what data to include in training datasets, and how that data is organised or tagged can result in individual and systemic biases (conscious or unconscious), which become built into such systems. The link between actuarial prediction and automated tools is important here: automation in many cases relies on the same kinds of statistical analysis, so embeds concerns about the bias that McSherry and others allude to in earlier actuarial methods. As McSherry (2020) has indicated, dataset choice affects mathematical analysis whether by actuaries or computers.

A well-known example of such bias emerging in the criminal law context is COMPAS (Correctional Offender Management Profiling for Alternative Sanctions), an automated decision-making tool used by judges in some US jurisdictions to inform sentencing decisions based on an assessment of an individual's risk of recidivism (Angwin et al. 2016). COMPAS was shown to produce a higher rate of 'false positive' results for black defendants than for white defendants; in other words, it was more likely to incorrectly predict that black people assessed by the system would re-offend when compared to results for white people (Angwin et al. 2016; cf. Flores and Bechtel 2016). The tool did not explicitly use race as a variable for predicting the risk of reoffending, but race correlated with variables that are themselves correlated with risk classification, such as poverty, joblessness and social marginalisation, producing biased results (Angwin et al. 2016). It is inevitable that similar forms of bias will emerge in experiments with algorithmic risk assessment and prediction in forensic mental health settings.

A third critique of actuarial risk assessment that McSherry (among others) has raised is specific to the use of AI and other automated systems; namely, that such systems tend to obfuscate, or at least lack transparency, in one or more senses (see Pasquale 2016). Such opacity may exist on several levels, including in the use of pretentious language, with technology vendors exaggerating or cultivating a mystique around technological capabilities (see Paterson 2022). Obfuscation also appears in the internal operation of AI-enabled systems, with some systems remaining inscrutable or hard to explain as to how conclusions are reached. There are several potential sources of this opacity, including the sheer scale of data being used and the high number of variables being used in AI and machine learning systems which entails 'a degree of unavoidable complexity' (Burrell 2016: 5); and intentional secrecy in service to proprietary interests, with private companies imposing confidentiality clauses and intellectual property protections over data and algorithms (see Slobogin 2021: 109–10). Questioning the outcomes produced by these tools – even on fundamental matters such as which of an individual's characteristics were taken into account in the tool's calculation of that person's level of risk, and how variables were weighted – is made more difficult by the lack of transparency in the development and use of some partially or fully automated risk assessment tools. Another source of obfuscation may be a lack of explainability in the sense of the translation of technical concepts and decision outputs into intelligible, comprehensible formats suitable for evaluation by auditors, regulators, researchers and users and, related to this, limited technical literacy on the part of users/subjects/affected persons (Burrell 2016).

On this point about transparency, McSherry has suggested that '[t]he results generated and the methodology underlying risk assessment tools must be interpretable in order for appropriate judicial decisions to be made' (McSherry 2020: 36–37). Slobogin (2021: 111) more forcefully argues that '[e]ven if it turns out that advanced machine-learning [risk assessment instruments] are demonstrably more accurate than simpler versions (which is unlikely), they should be banned from criminal proceedings, at least when they are "inscrutable"'. Slobogin cites a fundamental compromise to fairness when litigants, policymakers and decision-makers are not provided with accurate and clear information about how the software works. Others have concluded that the use of predictive algorithms cannot be legitimised in sentencing decisions but have 'left open the door for legitimate use in treatment decisions' (van Eijk 2020: 119), a point to which we will return later in this chapter.

Concerns about transparency and avoiding 'black box' decision-making also tie into a persistent criticism of the way statistical methods and probabilistic reasoning have been used to give risk assessment the veneer of objectivity and certainty. A framing of algorithmic risk assessment as a 'technical' approach – whether using AI or not – conveys a view of a neutral, administrative and objective process for improving public safety (Rose 1998). A secondary effect of this projected certainty is that the stronger the public confidence in the accuracy of such assessments, misplaced though this may be, the more likely that 'moral outrage' will be attributed to public authorities who bear an implied culpability when certain types of tragedy occur, such as a person completing suicide or harming others during a mental health crisis (Szmukler and Rose 2013) – and the greater the social acceptability of and even public demand for intrusions on individuals deemed 'risky'. Digital forms of monitoring and assessment may amplify this misleading projection of facticity, and further pave the way for expanded preventive detention powers. As the SAFE-HOME example suggests, these intrusions are likely to disproportionately affect those with mental health conditions and psychosocial disabilities.

Such an 'allure of certainty' raises the possibility that automated risk assessment and management will be unreflectively normalised in preventive justice or psychiatric schemes, repeating harms of earlier opaque and misguided risk assessment approaches. Along these lines, Nikolas Rose (1998: 190–91) has offered the following critique of 'risk thinking' more broadly and the associated technologies and discourses of risk:

> Given that clinicians are not experts in the methodology and statistics 'black boxed' within risk-assessment scales, the populations upon

> which they are standardized, the generalization from one population to another, the moral and social judgments involved in decisions as to what does or does not count as dangerous behavior in the populations on which the scales were developed, the 'false positive rates', the effects of changes since the time the scales were constructed, the implications of national and cultural variation, what are the implications of their uncritical clinical acceptance of the 'objectivity' of such scales? . . . [T]he facticity conferred by scales and numbers, in which the decisions, calculations, techniques, and assumptions of the methods disappear into the apparent objectivity of the single number, not only serves to increase the appearance of accuracy. It also serves to decrease contestability and to imply specious pre-vision.

This critique was made in 1998 in terms that could well apply to concerns about the use of automated and AI-enabled risk assessment technologies in mental health settings a quarter of a century later. Yet, today, adding to this already perplexing array of factors for which to account, are ever-new forms of software, proprietary barriers to algorithmic methods and datasets, cheaper and more sophisticated monitoring and surveillance technologies and an increasingly interconnected communication ecosystem.

A final relevant point is that some mental health practitioners have raised ethical concerns about the pressure they face from courts to provide risk assessments for purposes such as continued supervision or detention after a sentence is complete (see e.g. Sullivan, Mullen and Pathé 2005). As McSherry outlines, this risk assessment role can leave clinicians feeling pressed to serve as 'agents of supervision, social control and monitoring' rather than as 'independent clinicians' (McSherry 2014: 787; see also Sullivan, Mullen and Pathé 2005; Gunn 2000). In the digital context, a related concern is the potential for automation to generate cheap, if limited, software and monitoring devices that will be attractive to system administrators who are drawn to a substitute for more expensive, expert and empathetic professionals (Pasquale 2020).

Indeed, with regards to the role of mental health experts, McSherry (2020) has observed that perhaps the most prominent strategy to constrain an unreflective reliance on algorithmic risk assessment, though one that remains contentious, is 'structured professional judgment'. Structured professional judgment combines statistical or actuarial risk prediction with clinical methods; in other words, clinicians use risk prediction tools alongside their professional judgment to make decisions or recommendations about a person's 'risk'. It was proposed to improve upon the *unstructured* decision-making by judges, parole authorities and mental health professionals described earlier, while mitigating the mechanistic, inflexible and opaque qualities of 'purely' algorithmic assessment. This proposition has been broadly convincing to both courts and in the forensic mental health field, and structured professional judgment 'has become an accepted forensic method to help identify those who are at low, moderate or high risk of harming others' (McSherry 2020: 23).

For McSherry (2020: 38), structured professional judgment seems to offer 'the "least worst" option' currently available, even as it remains contentious and raises 'serious ethical and human rights issues because of the consequences for the individuals concerned'. McSherry's work highlights the potential role of a human rights lens in identifying better than 'least worst' options for reform and change, to which we now turn.

Human Rights: False Hope or a Targeted Mechanism of Accountability?

McSherry's work applies a human rights lens to the issues raised by digital technological developments in the mental health context. Although there is a growing body of work concerning automation and human rights more broadly (Access Now 2018; Amnesty International and Access Now 2018; McGregor, Murray and Ng 2019), little if any has provided an explicit focus on automation in the mental health context generally (for a notable exception, see Cosgrove et al. 2020), or the forensic mental health context in particular.

Researchers concerned with the consequences for humans and human society of AI and automated decision-making have tended *in general* to focus on 'ethical' approaches to such technologies, drawing on, for instance, bioethics or virtue ethics approaches (Fjeld et al. 2020), and ethical framing has been extended to the mental health context (e.g. Luxton 2015; Capon et al. 2016; Lederman et al. 2020; Martinez-Martin 2020; Martinez-Martin et al. 2020). Ethical principles for assessing, designing and utilising AI have also been proposed by industry, governments, international and intergovernmental organisations and professional associations as an appropriate means to guide the design, development and deployment of AI (see e.g. Berendt 2019; Jobin, Ienca and Vayena 2019; Fjeld et al. 2020). The proliferation of these non-binding codes, guidelines and recommendations for ethical AI has been attributed at least partly to industry resistance to stronger regulation of the design, development and use of AI and automated decision-making (United Nations General Assembly 2019). Such ethics statements typically identify a set of principles that should guide the development and use of AI to benefit humans, or at a minimum to avoid harm. While there is considerable variation in their content, they commonly include principles of transparency, fairness, non-maleficence, responsibility, privacy and trust, as well as concepts associated with social justice and human rights, such as equity, justice and access. The criticisms of forensic mental health risk assessment discussed in the preceding section map onto several of these principles, including issues of bias, transparency, privacy and trust, as well as justice related to the use of these tools in determining a person's 'riskiness'.

Ethical principles for AI provide some framework for assessing and responding to the issues raised by automated and AI-enabled risk assessments in the context of mental health. Yet assessing AI and automated decision-making on the basis of ethical principles has been criticised for several reasons. The most relevant for present purposes is that statements of ethical AI principles tend to be articulated in overly broad terms without reference to normative underpinnings (Algorithm Watch 2019). In consequence, they are open to multiple interpretations (Pizzi, Romanoff and Engelhardt 2020) – including interpretations that may require a much lower standard than that established in human rights instruments (Smuha 2021) – and also to manipulation (Rességuier and Rodrigues 2020). This means 'there are serious problems of conceptual incoherence, conflicts among norms are rarely acknowledged, meaningful input is rarely sought from stakeholders and accountability mechanisms are absent' (United Nations General Assembly 2019: para 40; see also Yeung, Howes and Pogrebna 2020: 76–106).

A second criticism is that, while ethics-based statements often mention elements of accountability such as 'transparency' and 'responsibility', they do not tend to identify or prescribe mechanisms for enforcement of standards or consequences for breach (Fukuda-Parr and Gibson 2021: 42). This relates to broader criticisms of the origin of many statements of ethical AI principles in self-regulation efforts by the tech industry, which include allegations of 'ethics-washing' whereby Big Tech has avoided or delayed the imposition of binding forms of regulation while giving the appearance of being socially responsible (Wagner 2018; Hagendorff 2020).

Human rights principles, such as equality and non-discrimination, are sometimes mentioned in statements of ethical principles, or human rights is mentioned in general as one of a series of ethical principles for assessing the harms and benefits of AI (Fjeld et al. 2020; Fukuda-Parr and Gibbons 2021: 37). However, there has only recently been attention on the potential of a human rights approach to become the over-arching framework (rather than a subset of ethics) to address the limitations of ethics-based analyses and provide 'a sound normative framework to steer AI-systems towards the good' (Smuha 2021).

The main purported advantages of the human rights perspective are that it provides a set of internationally agreed-upon values and that those values are, at least to an extent, enforceable via laws, principles and standards whose interpretation and application is supported by existing enforcement mechanisms and a wealth of jurisprudence, research and other guidance (Latonero 2018; Berthet 2019; Aizenberg and van den Hoven 2020; Yeung, Howes and Pogrebna 2020; Smuha 2021). Fukuda-Parr and Gibbons (2021: 34–35) highlight several features of a human rights approach that set it apart from other statements of AI ethics, including its focus on structural issues and power imbalances; its imposition of obligations on States and other parties to ensure the realisation of rights (not to simply refrain from breaching them); and its underpinning by guiding principles including universality, equality and non-discrimination, participation, and accountability and remedy. These authors have also noted the growing attention on the human rights implications of technology from 'the UN human rights machinery', with special rapporteurs and other mandates 'call[ing] for studies and debates to develop norms, principles and standards' (Fukuda-Parr and Gibbons 2021: 34).

Criticisms have been levelled at human rights approaches to the assessment, design and deployment of AI and automated decision-making. Some of these engage long-standing critiques of human rights law, including that it is not enforceable in the conventional sense – the extent to which it is implemented and enforced varies greatly and depends in many states on international commitments (demonstrated via ratification of international instruments) being implemented in domestic law (see Yeung, Howes and Pogrebna 2020).

Two other criticisms are specific to human rights approaches to automated and AI-enabled technologies. The first is that existing recommendations for human rights-compliant AI tend not to appreciate or account for the technical complexities involved (Floridi 2010); the second is that attempts to articulate human rights requirements provide limited practical guidance for their implementation because they are stated at similar levels of generality to statements of AI ethics (Smuha 2021). Other critiques take aim at the foundations of human rights, including concerns that core tenets of humanism and liberalism in the era of Big Data not only fail to prevent the expansion of inequality and widespread social harm but potentially entrench it and work to guarantee the supremacy of private firms over individuals (see e.g. Benthall and Goldenfein 2020; McQuillan 2021).

Deeply engaging with these broad critiques is beyond the scope of this chapter. For our purposes, it is notable that there have been some recent efforts to develop practical human rights guidance in the context of AI and automated decision-making. These efforts have at least begun addressing concerns about the ambiguous practical applicability of human rights. For example, the UN Special Rapporteur for the Rights of Persons with Disabilities, Gerard Quinn, published a 2022 thematic study on artificial intelligence and its impact on persons with disabilities (Human Rights Council 2021). Quinn observed that 'there has been little detailed assessment of the direct benefits and potential harms of artificial intelligence for the world's approximately 1 billion persons with disabilities' (Human Rights Council 2021: 6). He concluded that 'a fundamental reset of the debate [about artificial intelligence] is needed, based on more evidence and greater consideration of the rights and obligations contained in the Convention on the Rights of Persons with Disabilities and other human rights instruments' (Human Rights Council 2021: 17).

McSherry's leading steps to apply human rights to contemporary developments in forensic mental health risk assessment point to several of the advantages, and limitations, of a human rights approach to the issues discussed earlier. Of primary concern for McSherry has been the human right to liberty, which she asserts is clearly violated by risk assessment tools that are used to justify and facilitate indefinite and preventive detention (McSherry 2013, 2020). McSherry (2017: 69) has argued that 'human rights may be able to provide a framework for change despite the intractable nature of risk as a criterion for detention of those with mental impairment' and has discussed this approach specifically in relation to predictive algorithms for preventive detention (see also McSherry 2020).

Key to any such change is enforceability of human rights protections, which is variable at domestic levels throughout the world. McSherry (2020: 30) notes the tendency for community protection arguments that support the use of preventive detention to trump rights arguments in countries such as Australia and New Zealand, which have 'relatively weak rights protection', even where preventive detention regimes have been declared to constitute human rights violations by the Human Rights Council. In contrast, limits have been placed on preventive detention schemes in states with stronger human rights protections, including challenges to such a scheme in Germany which resulted in the Federal Constitutional Court declaring preventive detention orders unconstitutional on the basis that they violated the right to liberty (McSherry 2020: 34–36). McSherry acknowledges that these protections are not absolute, despite preventive detention constituting a 'clear' violation of the right to liberty, which touches on criticisms of human rights law lacking enforceability in many places. We would nevertheless agree with McSherry's (2020: 36) assertion that '[j]urisprudence having an influence rather than being binding is still better than having no influence at all'.

To date, McSherry's work has not specifically engaged with the way that automated and AI-enabled risk assessment tools might be utilised to *promote* and *protect* the rights of accused and convicted persons. Raso and colleagues (2018: 20), for example, suggest that certain risk assessment tools, including those that use machine learning, could actually strengthen people's right to liberty where their use results in 'low-risk' individuals benefitting from greater pre-trial release and shorter sentences, with the wider community also benefitting from a lower crime rate. A US policy simulation study of pre-trial detention practices using New York data, for example, concluded that 42% more arrestees would be released as 'low risk' if a risk assessment instrument using machine learning replaced cash bail (Kleinberg et al. 2017). Slobogin (2021: fn 166) points to numerous other studies indicating that jurisdictions using risk assessment instruments can release a greater number of people without raising crime rates. He concludes that overall, when properly regulated, with peer review and vetting, training for judges, lawyers and correctional officials, and a willingness to abandon the measures if hypothesised benefits fall short, risk assessment tools can be a crucial means of safely and humanely dismantling the massive jail and prison complex in the US (Slobogin 2021: 158–63). This is arguably an optimistic picture, and one that appears to take specific aim at the anomalously high rates of US incarceration. Further, Slobogin adds the caveat that if after all those steps of rigorous peer review and auditing were taken, and the scheme was found not to have achieved its aims, that it probably ought to be abandoned (Slobogin 2021: 163). Regardless, such a pragmatic approach does not negate the rights concerns that these technologies raise to those affected, particularly those deemed 'high risk' and others whose subjection to risk assessment results in longer detention or more intensive monitoring.

Potential Avenues for Research on Rights and Algorithmic Risk Assessment

If one adopts the human rights framework, there is clear scope to extend McSherry's focus on the right to liberty to other human rights issues raised by automated and AI-enabled risk assessments, including the rights articulated in the International Covenant on Civil and Political Rights (ICCPR) and Convention on the Rights of Persons with Disabilities (CRPD). This could include rights concerning equality before the law and non-discrimination, health, protection from arbitrary arrest and detention, rights to a fair hearing and the presumption of innocence, and (perhaps particularly in the light of increased technological capacity for remote monitoring and surveillance) rights to protection from interference with privacy and family life.

Gerard Quinn, in his aforementioned report, argued that equality and non-discrimination must be the primary considerations when assessing the rights implications of AI for disabled people (Human Rights Council 2021). The possibility of bias in the training data for risk assessment tools clearly raises concerns about the violation of this right, although arguments that some digital tools may reduce racial and other disparities in bail and sentencing raise the possibility that some technologies may actually enhance the protection of this right (Raso et al. 2018: 20).

The possibility of individuals being erroneously classified as 'high-risk', and subsequently detained on that basis, or the use of risk assessment technology where the basis on which individuals have been assessed as high risk and detained is not transparent or open to appeal, raise questions about such individuals' enjoyment of the right to be free from arbitrary arrest and detention (ICCPR: Article 9). The combination of proprietary interests, inherent complexity and inscrutability of automated systems makes it especially difficult to challenge algorithmic determinations in court settings and also raises concerns in relation to the rights to a fair hearing and to be presumed innocent until found guilty (ICCPR: Article 14; CRPD: Article 14). Automated risk assessment systems rely on the generation, storage and analysis of large and even vast amounts of personal data, raising significant privacy concerns, which are acute in the context of 'passive monitoring' and surveillance. Such matters may constitute violations of the freedom from arbitrary or unlawful interference with privacy, family, home and correspondence articulated in the ICCPR (Article 17) and the CRPD (Article 22). In this sense, it is possible that measures to promote 'fairness' or human rights compliance in one respect will have contrary consequences in another – such as measures to improve the quality of personal data used to train automated systems, which may result in less biased systems but may have deleterious consequences for individuals' privacy.

The right to the highest attainable quality of physical and mental health on an equal basis with others may also be undermined by data-driven evaluation of individuals, including through monitoring and surveillance (CRPD:

Article 25). Dainius Pūras, then UN Special Rapporteur on the Right to the Highest Attainable Physical and Mental Health, has warned (albeit briefly) of the negative impact on the right to health of expanding surveillance technologies that 'categorize an individual for commercial, political or additional surveillance purposes' (Human Rights Council 2020: para 75). An example might be involuntary 'monitoring conditions' on people detained in forensic psychiatric settings in the form of electronic ankle bracelets, which proceed against the submissions of medical practitioners, and in a manner that hinders the rehabilitation and treatment of the individuals concerned (see e.g. Miller 2015). Others have argued that the very designation of people as 'high risk' through predictive algorithmic approaches to sentencing could violate rights-based protection of human dignity given that it impacts 'the degree to which a person is free to form his or her own intentions and is able to act in accordance with them without interference' (Ward 2011: 106).

Further work is clearly required to move from this kind of general discussion of human rights implications to detailed consideration in the mental health context and in relation to specific technologies such as forensic risk assessments. Fruitful exploration may include close analysis of the applicability of existing mechanisms for the realisation and enforcement of each of the above human rights to specific applications of AI and automation, and consideration of the implementation of AI-specific human rights measures proposed by bodies such as the European Commission's AI High-Level Expert Group, the UN Special Rapporteur on the Rights of Persons with Disabilities and the Australian Human Rights Commission, such as human rights impact assessments, auditability requirements, ex-ante oversight, stakeholder consultation and procedures for redress (High-Level Expert Group on Artificial Intelligence 2019; Human Rights Council 2021; Australian Human Rights Commission 2021).

Cross-disciplinary and inter-disciplinary work, which brings together mental health, legal and computer science scholars, including those working from a lived experience of both mental health conditions and detention or supervision in forensic mental health systems, may be necessary to investigate the utility and implementation of these and other measures in relation to forensic mental health risk assessment.

There has been some commentary from people with lived experience of mental health conditions or psychosocial disabilities, among which prominent concerns include: promoting a 'right to explanation' concerning algorithmic decision-making for individuals (both the right of an individual to understand how a decision about them using algorithmic technology was made, but also to query the values that go into a particular algorithmic decision system) (Carr 2020); the risk of discrimination or harm where sensitive personal information is leaked, stolen, sold or scraped from social media and other 'public' fora (Consumers of Mental Health Western Australia 2018); and concerns about the deployment of data-driven technologies in coercive psychiatric interventions and in policing (Harris 2019; Carr 2020). However, such commentaries are scarce, and there seems to be a general marginalisation of lived experience perspectives from research concerning algorithmic and data-driven approaches to mental health (Gooding and Kariotis 2021).

As a final point, the aim or even mandate to elevate the subjective standpoint of disabled persons, which is incorporated throughout the CRPD, also appears to run counter to some of the theoretical aims behind automated prediction tools, offering important avenues for future work. Jackie Leach Scully and Georgia Van Toorn (2021) have argued that broader 'datafication' of the human body will delineate increasingly rigid boundaries between normality and disability. This impulse to quantify and distinguish embodied difference, they argue, 'diverts attention from the realities of disabled lives, at a time when disability scholars and activists are arguing for more rather than less attention to the lived experience of disability' (Scully and Van Toorn 2021).

One expression of this attention to the lived experience of disability in the forensic mental health context, is the call for 'collaborative risk assessment and management' in forensic mental health settings. Sarah Markham (2020: 5) suggests that collaborative risk assessment and management requires 'a more fluid and responsive culture with increased emphasis on relational safety and epistemic regard for patient self-insight and testimony'. Although collaborative risk assessment is outside the scope of this chapter, it seems another potentially generative line of enquiry in broader discussions about risk assessment today, given such an approach appears to be antithetical to the aim of using passive monitoring and Big Data analytics to 'overcome the limitations' of the subjective accounts of patients/service users and clinicians (see also Markham 2021).

Another possibility, given the ambivalent impact of the automated and AI-enabled approaches to risk assessment discussed in this chapter, is that it may be more productive to get past the binary idea that either computers can improve on the fallibility of human decisions, or that humans can improve on the fallibility of computer decisions. Instead, it may be more helpful to acknowledge that what lies beneath these debates are longstanding and intractable tensions in law of rules and equality on the one hand, and discretion and individuality on the other (Goldenfein 2019). Structured professional judgment may well have to remain the 'least worst option' for mediating these tensions (McSherry 2020: 38), which next invites questions of (1) what makes a good professional judgment or decision; and (2) what role automated and AI-enabled approaches might play in making them. Human rights clearly have something to offer in this respect.

As a final point, the broader critique of a human rights approach to automation and AI warrants continued attention. Taken seriously, such critiques could help to either refine rights-based efforts, where critical viewpoints are addressed within a human rights framework, or divert those who find the criticisms convincing to seek strategies beyond what human rights would seem to offer.

Conclusion

The digital, data-informed evaluation of persons is advancing. The world is at the beginning of a long project of critiquing and regulating AI and other algorithmic technologies and understanding the role they play in attempts to make individuals more 'calculable'. Risk assessment in the forensic mental health context is one such area in which the legal and regulatory landscape is likely to change considerably in coming years – particularly in light of efforts to integrate biometric monitoring and surveillance capabilities of increasingly ubiquitous sensor technologies. The Trump administration's serious consideration of the 'SAFEHOME' proposal seems likely to be a portent of future efforts along these lines. Further study of these developments and their profound implications for people's human rights could contribute to efforts to guide the design, use, regulation and broad governance of AI and automation in this field more generally. Bernadette McSherry's leading scholarship provides a rich corpus from which to build this work.

References

Access Now (2018) *Human Rights in the Age of Artificial Intelligence.* Available www.accessnow.org/cms/assets/uploads/2018/11/AI-and-Human-Rights.pdf (accessed 15 December 2022).

Aizenberg, E. and van den Hoven, J. (2020) 'Designing for Human Rights in AI', *Big Data & Society*, *7*(2): 1–14.

Algorithm Watch (2019) *No Red Lines: Industry Defuses Ethics Guidelines for Artificial Intelligence.* Available https://algorithmwatch.org/en/industry-defuses-ethics-guidelines-for-artificial-intelligence/ (accessed 15 December 2022).

Amnesty International and Access Now (2018) *The Toronto Declaration: Protecting the Right to Equality and Non-discrimination in Machine Learning Systems.* Available www.torontodeclaration.org/declaration-text/english/ (accessed 15 December 2022).

Angwin, J., Larson, J., Mattu, S. and Kirchner, L. (2016) 'Machine Bias', *ProPublica*, 23 May. Available www.propublica.org/article/machine-bias-risk-assessments-in-criminal-sentencing?token=TiqCeZIj4uLbXl91e3wM2PnmnWbCVOvS (accessed 15 December 2022).

Australian Human Rights Commission (2021) *Human Rights and Technology – Final Report.* Available https://tech.humanrights.gov.au/sites/default/files/2021-05/AHRC_RightsTech_2021_Final_Report.pdf (accessed 15 December 20220).

Bartels, L. and Martinovic, M. (2017) 'Electronic Monitoring: The Experience in Australia', *European Journal of Probation*, 9(1): 80–102.

Benthall, S. and Goldenfein, J. (2020) 'Data Science and the Decline of Liberal Law and Ethics', *Social Science Research Network*. Available https://doi.org/10.2139/ssrn.3632577 (accessed 15 December 2022).

Berendt, B. (2019) 'AI for the Common Good?! Pitfalls, Challenges, and Ethics Pen-testing', *Paladyn: Journal of Behavioral Robotics*, 10(1): 44–65.

Berthet, A. (2019) *Why Do Emerging AI Guidelines Emphasize 'Ethics' over Human Rights?* OpenGlobalRights. Available www.openglobalrights.org/why-do-emerging-ai-guidelines-emphasize-ethics-over-human-rights/ (accessed 15 December 2022).

Burrell, J. (2016) 'How the Machine "Thinks": Understanding Opacity in Machine Learning Algorithms', *Big Data & Society*, 3(1): 1–12.

Capon, H., Hall, W., Fry, C. and Carter, A. (2016) 'Realising the Technological Promise of Smartphones in Addiction Research and Treatment: An Ethical Review', *International Journal of Drug Policy*, 36: 47–57.

Carr, S. (2020) '"AI Gone Mental": Engagement and Ethics in Data-driven Technology for Mental Health', *Journal of Mental Health*, 29(2): 125–30.

Castel, R. (1991) 'From Dangerousness to Risk', in G. Burchell, C. Gordon and P. Miller (eds) *The Foucault Effect: Studies in Governmentality*, Chicago: University of Chicago Press, 281–98.

Consumers of Mental Health Western Australia (2018) *9 Days Left to Make an Informed Decision about My Health Record*, 6 November. Available https://comhwa.org.au/blog/9-days-left-to-make-an-informed-decision-about-my-health-record (accessed 15 December 2022).

Cosgrove, L., Karter, J., Mcginley, M. and Morrill, Z. (2020) 'Digital Phenotyping and Digital Psychotropic Drugs: Mental Health Surveillance Tools That Threaten Human Rights', *Health and Human Rights Journal*, 22(2): 33–40.

Eubanks, V. (2018) *Automating Inequality: How High-Tech Tools Profile, Police, and Punish the Poor*, New York: St Martin's Press.

Fjeld, J., Achten, N., Hilligoss, H., Nagy, A. and Srikumar, M. (2020) 'Principled Artificial Intelligence: Mapping Consensus in Ethical and Rights-Based Approaches to Principles for AI', *Social Science Research Network*. Available https://doi.org/10.2139/ssrn.3518482 (accessed 15 December 2022).

Flores, A.W. and Bechtel, K. (2016) 'False Positives, False Negatives, and False Analyses: A Rejoinder to "Machine Bias: There's Software Used Across the Country to Predict Future Criminals. And It's Biased Against Blacks"', *Federal Probation*, 80(2): 38–46.

Floridi, L. (2010) 'Information Ethics', in L. Floridi (ed) *The Cambridge Handbook of Information and Computer Ethics*, Cambridge: Cambridge University Press; Cambridge Core, 77–98.

Fukuda-Parr, S. and Gibbons, E. (2021) 'Emerging Consensus on "Ethical AI": Human Rights Critique of Stakeholder Guidelines', *Global Policy*, 12(S6): 32–44.

Goldenfein, J. (2019) 'Algorithmic Transparency and Decision-Making Accountability: Thoughts for Buying Machine Learning Algorithms', in S. Bluemmel (ed) *Closer to the Machine: Technical, Social, and Legal Aspects of AI*, Melbourne: Office of the Victorian Information Commissioner, 41–60.

Gooding, P. and Kariotis, T. (2021) 'Ethics and Law in Research on Algorithmic and Data-Driven Technology in Mental Health Care: Scoping Review', *JMIR Mental Health*, 8(6): e24668.

Gooding, P. and Resnick, K. (2020) 'Psychiatry and Law in the Digital Age: Untangling the Hype, Risk and Promise', *International Journal of Law and Psychiatry*, 70: 101553.

Grünerbl, A., Muaremi, A., Osmani, V., Bahle, G., Öhler, S., Tröster, G., Mayora, O., Haring, C. and Lukowicz, P. (2015) 'Smartphone-Based Recognition of States and State Changes in Bipolar Disorder Patients', *IEEE Journal of Biomedical and Health Informatics*, 19(1): 140–48.

Gunn, J. (2000) 'Future Directions for Treatment in Forensic Psychiatry', *The British Journal of Psychiatry*, 176(4): 332–38.

Hagendorff, T. (2020) 'The Ethics of AI Ethics: An Evaluation of Guidelines', *Minds and Machines*, 30(1): 99–120.

Hannah-Moffat, K. (2013) 'Actuarial Sentencing: An "Unsettled" Proposition', *Justice Quarterly*, 30(2): 270–96.

Harris, L. (2019) 'The Rise of the Digital Asylum', *Mad In America*, 15 September. Available www.madinamerica.com/2019/09/the-rise-of-the-digital-asylum/ (accessed 15 December 2022).

High-Level Expert Group on Artificial Intelligence (2019) *Ethics Guidelines for Trustworthy AI*, European Commission. Available https://digital-strategy.ec.europa.eu/en/library/ethics-guidelines-trustworthy-ai (accessed 15 December 2022).

Holmes, A. (2013) 'Is Risk Assessment the New Clinical Model in Public Mental Health?' *Australasian Psychiatry: Bulletin of Royal Australian and New Zealand College of Psychiatrists*, 21(6): 541–44.

Human Rights Council (2020) *Report of the Special Rapporteur on the Right of Everyone to the Enjoyment of the Highest Attainable Standard of Physical and Mental Health*, UN Doc A/HRC/44/48. Available www.ohchr.org/en/documents/thematic-reports/ahrc4448-right-everyone-enjoyment-highest-attainable-standard-physical (accessed 15 December 2022).

Human Rights Council (2021) *Report of the Special Rapporteur on the Rights of Persons with Disabilities*, UN Doc A/HRC/49/52. Available www.ohchr.org/en/documents/thematic-reports/ahrc4952-artificial-intelligence-and-rights-persons-disabilities-report (accessed 15 December 2022).

Jobin, A., Ienca, M. and Vayena, E. (2019) 'The Global Landscape of AI Ethics Guidelines', *Nature Machine Intelligence*, 1(9): 389–99.

Kak, A. (2021) *Regulating Biometrics: Global Approaches and Urgent Questions*, AI Now Institute. Available https://ainowinstitute.org/regulatingbiometrics.pdf (accessed 15 December 2022).

Kleinberg, J., Lakkaraju, H., Leskovec, J., Ludwig, J. and Mullainathan, S. (2017) *Human Decisions and Machine Predictions*, NBER Working Paper Series No. 23180. Available www.cs.cornell.edu/home/kleinber/w23180.pdf (accessed 15 December 2022).

Latonero, M. (2018) *Governing Artificial Intelligence: Upholding Human Rights & Dignity*, Data & Society. Available https://datasociety.net/library/governing-artificial-intelligence/ (accessed 15 December 2022).

Le, D.V., Montgomery, J., Kirkby, K.C. and Scanlan, J. (2018) 'Risk Prediction Using Natural Language Processing of Electronic Mental Health Records in an Inpatient Forensic Psychiatry Setting', *Journal of Biomedical Informatics*, 86: 49–58.

Lederman, R., D'Alfonso, S., Rice, S., Coghlan, S., Wadley, G. and Alvarez-Jimenez, M. (2020) *Ethical Issues in Online Mental Health Interventions*, ECIS 2020 Research Papers. Available https://aisel.aisnet.org/ecis2020_rp/66/ (accessed 15 December 2022).

Lupton, D. (2013) *Risk*, 2nd edn, Abingdon: Routledge.

Luxton, D.D. (2015) *Artificial Intelligence in Behavioral and Mental Health Care*, London: Academic Press.

McGregor, L. (2023) *Detention and Its Alternatives under International Law*, Oxford: Oxford University Press.

Markham, S. (2020) 'Collaborative Risk Assessment in Secure and Forensic Mental Health Settings in the UK', *General Psychiatry*, 33(5): e100291.

Markham, S. (2021) 'The Omnipresence of Risk and Associated Harms in Secure and Forensic Mental Health Services in England and Wales', *Social Theory & Health*. Available https://link.springer.com/article/10.1057/s41285-021-00167-z (accessed 15 December 2022).

Marks, M. (2019) *Artificial Intelligence Based Suicide Prediction*, Social Science Research Network. Available https://papers.ssrn.com/abstract=3324874 (accessed 15 December 2022).

Marks, M. (2020) 'Algorithmic Disability Discrimination', in A. Silvers, C. Shachar, I.G. Cohen and M.A. Stein (eds) *Disability, Health, Law, and Bioethics*, Cambridge: Cambridge University Press, 242–54.

Martinez-Martin, N. (2020) 'Chapter Three – Trusting the Bot: Addressing the Ethical Challenges of Consumer Digital Mental Health Therapy', in I. Bárd and E. Hildt (eds) *Developments in Neuroethics and Bioethics: Ethical Dimensions of Commercial and DIY Neurotechnologies*, Cambridge, MA: Academic Press, 69–91.

Martinez-Martin, N., Dasgupta, I., Carter, A., Chandler, J. A., Kellmeyer, P., Kreitmair, K., Weiss, A. and Cabrera, L.Y. (2020) 'Ethics of Digital Mental Health During COVID-19: Crisis and Opportunities', *JMIR Mental Health*, 7(12): e23776.

Mathiesen, T. and Rutherford, A. (2006) *Prison on Trial*, 3rd edn, Winchester: Waterside Press.

McGregor, L., Murray, D. and Ng, V. (2019) 'International Human Rights Law as a Framework for Algorithmic Accountability', *International & Comparative Law Quarterly*, 68(2): 309–43.

McQuillan, D. (2018) 'Mental Health and Artificial Intelligence: Losing Your Voice', *openDemocracy*. Available www.opendemocracy.net/en/digitaliberties/mental-health-and-artificial-intelligence-losing-your-voice-poem/ (accessed 15 December 2022).

McQuillan, D. (2021) 'Post-Humanism, Mutual Aid', in P. Verdegem (ed) *AI for Everyone? Critical Perspectives*, London: University of Westminster Press, 67–83.

McQuillan, D. (2022) *Resisting AI: An Anti-fascist Approach to Artificial Intelligence*, Bristol: Bristol University Press.

McSherry, B. (2013) *Managing Fear: The Law and Ethics of Preventive Detention and Risk Assessment*, New York: Routledge.

McSherry, B. (2014) 'Throwing Away the Key: The Ethics of Risk Assessment for Preventive Detention Schemes', *Psychiatry, Psychology and Law*, 21(5): 779–90.

McSherry, B. (2017) 'Preventive Justice, Risk of Harm and Mental Health Laws', in T. Tulich, S. Bronitt and S. Murray (eds) *Regulating Preventive Justice*, New York: Routledge, 61–74.

McSherry, B. (2018) 'Computational Modelling, Social Media and Health-Related Datasets: Consent and Privacy Issues', *Journal of Law and Medicine*, 25(4): 894–98.

McSherry, B. (2020) 'Risk Assessment, Predictive Algorithms and Preventive Justice', in J. Pratt and J. Anderson (eds) *Criminal Justice, Risk and the Revolt against Uncertainty*, Cham: Springer International Publishing, 17–42.

McSherry, B. and Freckelton, I. (eds) (2013) *Coercive Care: Rights, Law and Policy*, Abingdon: Routledge.

McSherry, B. and Keyzer, P. (eds) (2011) *Dangerous People: Policy, Prediction, and Practice*, New York: Routledge.

Miller, P. and Rose, N. (1995) 'Production, Identity, and Democracy', *Theory and Society*, 24(3): 427–67.

Miller, S. (2015) 'The Use of Monitoring Conditions (GPS Tracking Devices)Re CMX [2014] QMHC 4', *Psychiatry, Psychology and Law*, 22(3): 321–26.

Mossman, D. (2009) 'The Imperfection of Protection Through Detection and Intervention', *Journal of Legal Medicine*, 30(1): 109–40.

Office of the Privacy Commissioner of Canada (2017) *Disclosure of Information about Complainant's Attempted Suicide to US Customs and Border Protection Not*

Authorized Under the Privacy Act. Available www.priv.gc.ca/en/opc-actions-and-decisions/investigations/investigations-into-federal-institutions/2016–17/pa_20170419_rcmp/ (accessed 15 December 2022).
Organisation for Economic Co-operation and Development (OECD) (2019) *Artificial Intelligence in Society*, Paris: OECD Publishing.
Pasquale, F. (2016) *The Black Box Society: The Secret Algorithms That Control Money and Information*, Cambridge, MA: Harvard University Press.
Pasquale, F. (2020) *New Laws of Robotics: Defending Human Expertise in the Age of AI*, Cambridge, MA: Belknap Press of Harvard University Press.
Paterson, J.M. (2022) 'Misleading AI: Regulatory Strategies for Algorithmic Transparency in Technologies Augmenting Consumer Decision-Making', *Loyola Consumer Law Review*, 34(SI): 558–81.
Paterson, J.M. and Maker, Y. (2021) *AI in the Home: Artificial Intelligence and Consumer Protection*, Social Science Research Network. Available https://papers.ssrn.com/sol3/papers.cfm?abstract_id=3973179 (accessed 15 December 2022).
Pizzi, M., Romanoff, M. and Engelhardt, T. (2020) 'AI for Humanitarian Action: Human Rights and Ethics', *International Review of the Red Cross*, 102(913): 145–80.
Raso, F., Hilligoss, H., Krishnamurthy, V., Bavitz, C. and Levin, K. (2018) *Artificial Intelligence & Human Rights: Opportunities & Risks*, Berkman Klein Center for Internet & Society Research Publication. Available https://dash.harvard.edu/handle/1/38021439 (accessed 15 December 2022).
Resnick, K.S. and Appelbaum, P.S. (2019) 'Passive Monitoring of Mental Health Status in the Criminal Forensic Population', *The Journal of the American Academy of Psychiatry and the Law*, 47(4): 457–66.
Rességuier, A. and Rodrigues, R. (2020) 'AI Ethics Should Not Remain Toothless! A Call to Bring Back the Teeth of Ethics', *Big Data & Society*, 7(2): 1–5.
Rose, N. (1998) 'Governing Risky Individuals: The Role of Psychiatry in New Regimes of Control', *Psychiatry, Psychology and Law*, 5(2): 177–95.
Scully, J.L. and Van Toorn, G. (2021) *Datafying Disability: Ethical Issues in Automated Decision Making and Related Technologies – AABHL 2021*, 19 November. Available www.aabhlconference.com/3563 (accessed 15 December 2022).
Slemon, A., Jenkins, E. and Bungay, V. (2017) 'Safety in Psychiatric Inpatient Care: The Impact of Risk Management Culture on Mental Health Nursing Practice', *Nursing Inquiry*, 24(4): e12199.
Slobogin, C. (2012) 'Risk Assessment', in J. Petersilia and K.R. Reitz (eds) *The Oxford Handbook of Sentencing and Corrections*, New York: Oxford University Press, 196–214.
Slobogin, C. (2021) *Just Algorithms: Using Science to Reduce Incarceration and Inform a Jurisprudence of Risk*, Cambridge: Cambridge University Press.
Smuha, N.A. (2021) 'Beyond a Human Rights-Based Approach to AI Governance: Promise, Pitfalls, Plea', *Philosophy & Technology*, 34(1): 91–104.
Stevenson, M.T. and Doleac, J.L. (2019) *Algorithmic Risk Assessment in the Hands of Humans*, Social Science Research Network. Available https://papers.ssrn.com/sol3/papers.cfm?abstract_id=3489440 (accessed 15 December 2022).
Sullivan, D.H., Mullen, P.E. and Pathé, M.T. (2005) 'Legislation in Victoria on Sexual Offenders: Issues for Health Professionals', *The Medical Journal of Australia*, 183(6): 318–20.
Szmukler, G. and Rose, N. (2013) 'Risk Assessment in Mental Health Care: Values and Costs', *Behavioral Sciences & the Law*, 31(1): 125–40.

Travis, S. (2019) 'Florida Wants to Amass Reams of Data on Students' Lives', *Sun-Sentinel.Com*, 9 July. Available www.sun-sentinel.com/local/broward/parkland/florida-school-shooting/fl-ne-school-shooting-database-deadline-20190709-i4oc-smqeivdmrhpauhyaplg52u-story.html (accessed 15 December 2022).

Trinhammer, M.L., Merrild, A.C.H., Lotz, J.F. and Makransky, G. (2022) 'Predicting Crime During or After Psychiatric Care: Evaluating Machine Learning for Risk Assessment Using the Danish Patient Registries', *Journal of Psychiatric Research*, 152: 194–200.

United Nations General Assembly (2019) *Report of the Special Rapporteur on Extreme Poverty and Human Rights 11 October*, UN Doc A/74/493. Available www.ohchr.org/en/documents/thematic-reports/a74493-digital-welfare-states-and-human-rights-report-special-rapporteur (accessed 15 December 2022).

Valentine, L., D'Alfonso, S. and Lederman, R. (2022) 'Recommender Systems for Mental Health Apps: Advantages and Ethical Challenges', *AI & SOCIETY*. Available https://pubmed.ncbi.nlm.nih.gov/35068708/ (accessed 15 December 2022).

van Eijk, G. (2020) 'Algorithmic Reasoning: The Production of Subjectivity Through Data', in R. Peeters and M. Schuilenburg (eds) *The Algorithmic Society*, Abingdon: Routledge, 119–34.

Wagner, B. (2018) 'Ethics as An Escape from Regulation. From "Ethics-Washing" To Ethics-Shopping?' in E. Bayamlioğu, I. Baraliuc, L. Janssens and M. Hildebrandt (eds) *Ethics as An Escape from Regulation: From "Ethics-Washing" To Ethics-Shopping?* Amsterdam: Amsterdam University Press, 84–89.

Wan, W. (2019) 'White House Weighs Controversial Plan on Mental Illness and Mass Shootings', *Washington Post*, 9 September. Available www.washingtonpost.com/health/white-house-considers-controversial-plan-on-mental-illness-and-mass-shooting/2019/09/09/eb58b6f6-ce72-11e9–87fa-8501a456c003_story.html (accessed 15 December 2022).

Ward, T. (2011) 'Human Rights and Dignity in Offender Rehabilitation', *Journal of Forensic Psychology Practice*, 11(2–3): 103–23.

Whittaker, M., Alper, M., Bennett, C.L., Hendren, S., Kaziunas, L., Mills, M., Morris, M.R., Rankin, J., Rogers, E., Salas, M. and West, S.M. (2019) *Disability, Bias, and AI*, AI Now. Available https://ainowinstitute.org/disabilitybiasai-2019.pdf (accessed 15 December 2022).

Yeung, K., Howes, A. and Pogrebna, G. (2020) 'AI Governance by Human Rights Centred-Design, Deliberation and Oversight: An End to Ethics Washing', in M.D. Dubber, F. Pasquale and S. Das (eds) *The Oxford Handbook of Ethics of AI*, New York: Oxford University Press, 76–106.

Zalnieriute, M., Bennett Moses, L. and Williams, G. (2019) 'The Rule of Law and Automation of Government Decision-Making', *Modern Law Review*, 82(3): 425–55.

14 Regulating Rights

Developing a Human Rights and Mental Health Regulatory Framework

Simon Katterl and Sharon Friel

Introduction

In Australia, all states and territories permit the use of compulsory mental health treatment, including restrictive practices such as seclusion and restraint (for an overview see McSherry 2021). The use of compulsory mental health treatment and restrictive practices in many countries has been criticised for being contrary to international human rights law (Maylea and Hirsch 2017; McSherry and Maker 2021), being counter-therapeutic and placing consumers in vulnerable positions where further abuse may occur (Victorian Equal Opportunity and Human Rights Commission 2019). When introducing such laws, governments argue safeguards and regulatory oversight bodies protect against this (see e.g. Victoria 2014: 477). In 2011, Bernadette McSherry and Susan Klauber (2011) pointed out the need in Australia for independent mental health commissions that can investigate complaints. Over a decade later, the needs remain not only in Australia, but in many countries with legislation enabling compulsory treatment, for effective regulatory oversight of clinical mental health settings. This chapter seeks to extend on McSherry and Klauber's (2011) early calls for specialisation by providing principles for effective regulatory oversight that embed human rights within clinical mental health settings. The key question being asked in this research is: how can specialist mental health regulators with complaints-based and systemic functions best protect human rights in clinical mental health services?

Victoria, a state of Australia, provides an example of where such public policy questions arise. With a population of 6.5 million people, 1% of whom identify as Aboriginal or Torres Strait Islander, Victoria's demographics are shifting towards greater religious and cultural diversity (Australian Bureau of Statistics 2022). Victoria's mental health system is also undergoing change following the Royal Commission into Victoria's Mental Health System (Royal Commission), on which Professor Bernadette McSherry served as a commissioner. In 2014, the Victorian government introduced new mental health laws that saw the state as a 'leader' in mental health reform (Cannold 2014). While allowing for compulsory mental health treatment, these laws included safeguards to protect consumers' rights. These comprised access to independent

DOI: 10.4324/9781003350644-18

non-legal advocacy (Weller et al. 2019), advance statements to express one's treatment preferences when placed on a compulsory treatment order (*Mental Health Act 2014* (Vic): sections 19–22), principles to guide decision-making (*Mental Health Act 2014* (Vic): section 11(1)) and specific obligations regarding informed consent (*Mental Health Act 2014* (Vic): sections 68–71).

Accompanying these safeguards were regulatory oversight bodies. These included the Mental Health Tribunal and the Office of the Chief Psychiatrist which both had roles to administer and secure compliance with the *Mental Health Act 2014* (Vic). Of particular interest was the introduction of Australia's first specialist mental health complaints regulator, the Mental Health Complaints Commissioner (MHCC). The MHCC was established in part in response to calls from sector leaders like Professor McSherry for an independent and specialist complaints agency (McSherry and Klauber 2011). The Victorian Parliament granted broad investigative and compliance powers as part of a broader agenda to reduce the use and duration of compulsory treatment and better protect consumer rights (Victoria 2014: 471).

The *Mental Health Act 2014* (Vic) and the Victorian mental health system failed to live up to expectations. The Victorian government and mental health providers did not embed mental health and human rights laws into the governance and operation of the mental health system (Katterl and Maylea 2021). The leadership of people with lived experience working within the mental health system was limited or resisted (Edan et al. 2021). Due to these and other factors, such as under-funding of mental health services (Victorian Auditor-General's Office 2019a), breaches of the *Mental Health Act 2014* (Vic) were common. For example, safeguards such as advance statements were routinely ignored (Maylea et al. 2018), while the decision-making principles had minimal impact on practice (Royal Commission into Victoria's Mental Health System 2021: Volume 4, 32–33). Rights were breached by clinicians with such regularity as to be rendered 'illusory' (Maylea et al. 2021). In 2021 the Royal Commission handed down its five-volume final report which found that the mental health system regularly breached human rights (Royal Commission into Victoria's Mental Health System 2021: Summary and Recommendations 4). (For further discussion of the Royal Commission and its findings see also Donnelly in Chapter 2 and Weller in Chapter 3 of this volume.)

The Royal Commission's 74 recommendations (65 detailed recommendations in the final report, plus nine recommendations in the interim report) were fully accepted by the Victorian Government. It recommended a new Mental Health and Wellbeing Act and a new regulatory oversight regime (Royal Commission into Victoria's Mental Health System 2021: Summary and Recommendations, 42 and 44: Department of Health 2022). The MHCC is due to be dissolved and a new Mental Health and Wellbeing Commission (MHWC) established in its place. The MHWC will regulate compliance with new mental health laws through similar complaints, investigative and compliance powers, in addition to broader powers to conduct public inquiries at its own behest (Royal Commission into Victoria's Mental Health System 2021: Volume 4, 59).

However, it is unclear whether introducing a new regulator will ensure greater compliance with mental health laws and human rights than has occurred under the 2014 Act. While some research has examined the efficacy of tribunals that authorise treatment orders (Carney, Tait and Beaupert 2008; Maylea and Ryan 2017; Boyle and Walsh 2021), with the exception of McSherry and Klauber's (2011) work, there has been less examination of complaints and systems-wide regulators who can inquire into broad parts of the system. In Victoria, several sector advocates and experts have criticised the MHCC for its performance, in particular its failure to pursue compliance with the *Mental Health Act 2014* (Vic) (Katterl 2021a; Ore 2022; Ore and Davey 2022). A full assessment of the MHCC is difficult, however, given Victoria is the only Australian jurisdiction with a specialist mental health regulator. Calls for greater national guidance on mental health complaints (Productivity Commission 2020: 1118) illustrate that it is unclear what good regulatory practice *is* within clinical mental health settings.

The subsequent sections of this chapter outline its method, which primarily constitutes a rapid review of the literature on regulatory practice and approaches to power within health, mental health and regulatory settings. From this literature, the chapter puts forward a new framework to inform and assess regulatory practice within clinical mental health settings: the Human Rights and Mental Health Regulatory Framework (HRMHRF). The final substantive section of this chapter uses the MHCC as an opportunity to apply the HRMHRF to examine how it had performed as a specialist mental health regulator.

Developing a Human Rights and Mental Health Regulatory Framework

The HRMHRF was developed with two principal functions in mind. First, it aims to inform the design and operation of new regulatory bodies intersecting with the complex legal and ethical terrain in mental health. Second, it assists regulators, governments and civil society to evaluate the performance of a mental health regulator. The development of a principles-based framework was based on a core research question: how can specialist mental health regulators with complaints-based and systemic functions best protect human rights in clinical mental health services? From that question, the following sub-questions were developed:

- What are the key concepts that underpin responsive and risk-based regulation?
- How do theories of power in policy and health policy impact on regulation of clinical mental health services?

A rapid review of the academic and 'grey' literature (e.g. policy documents, NGO reports and reports from civil society) informed the development of a framework of principles with which to assess regulation of clinical mental health services. This chapter follows a similar methodology set out by England's Care Quality Commission (CQC) for a review that examined effective regulatory methods across all health care (Marsden et al. 2020). Rather than reflecting a systematic approach, this rapid review adopts *a priori* key theoretical perspectives and then iteratively examines the literature, whereby key research and its references become a platform for identifying other relevant research that responds to the research questions. This methodology has been termed the 'berrypicking' model (Bates 1989).

Responsive and risk-based regulation theoretical perspectives were chosen given their prominence, standing and application in health contexts. The seminal text *Responsive Regulation: Transcending the Deregulation Debate* has, at April 2022, been cited on Google Scholar 5,862 times and has informed health care regulation (Healy and Dugdale 2009; Smith-Merry et al. 2017). Similarly, risk-based regulatory approaches have been well researched (Black 2005, 2010) and used as a common framework to regulate health services in resource-constrained environments (Spittal, Bismark and Studdert 2019; Therapeutic Goods Administration 2021). Finally, theories of power in health care and systems, mental health care and systems, as well as broader public policy are all included, owing to their prominence in mental health research and the Royal Commission's final report (Royal Commission into Victoria's Mental Health System 2021: Volume 3, 19–23).

In searching for literature for this analysis, the review used Google Scholar and Google with a combination of terms relating to regulation[1] and mental health.[2] This rapid review took a flexible approach to its research, examining both peer-reviewed and 'grey' literature, given the latter is often the only time mental health regulation is discussed. The literature review process gathered a broad number of publications, then reduced these to 87 publications based on relevance. Seventy were peer-reviewed, while 17 were from grey literature. Within this chapter the term 'human rights' is used broadly to encompass international human rights law that generates obligations on State signatories, domestic human rights law such as the *Charter of Human Rights and Responsibilities Act* 2006 (Vic) and domestic mental health laws that contain rights said to embed human rights principles, such as the *Mental Health Act 2014* (Vic). The obligations on mental health regulators are more directly related to enforcement of domestic human rights and mental health law, but they may promote and are influenced by international human rights obligations on states.

Key Concepts Underpinning Responsive and Risk-Based Approaches to Regulation

The rapid review of the literature indicated there were six key concepts underpinning responsive regulation and four central elements of risk-based approaches. These are set out in turn.

Responsive Regulation

Responsive regulation advocates for a flexible approach to regulating entities, with the strategic and considered use of enforcement and the involvement of third parties (Ayres and Braithwaite 1992). A common regulatory approach for diverse industries (see e.g. Freiberg 2017: 443–44), including in health care (for early advocacy by Professor McSherry, see Macleod and McSherry 2006; Healy and Dugdale 2009), responsive regulation centres on six key concepts:

- contingency – regulators should use a mixture of regulatory methods and tools to meet the circumstances of each stakeholder that is regulated;
- enforcement hierarchy – there should be a 'regulatory conversation' with the regulated stakeholder that starts with the least regulatory intervention possible, escalating up to more severe interventions and sanctions where lower-level interventions prove ineffective or unhelpful;
- flexibility – regulators should be flexible and respond to the circumstances of each regulated entity, rather than apply a uniform approach;
- tripartism – third parties should be involved in the regulatory process;
- parsimony – the judicious use of sanctions and limited regulatory resources for greatest impact; and
- empowerment of parties – ensuring that those being regulated and those impacted by the regulatory problem are enabled to partake in developing a regulatory strategy to fix the problem (Braithwaite, Healy and Dwan 2005: 36).

This review will provide more context on four concepts, avoiding duplication or overlap between some concepts. These are contingency and flexibility (treated together in this chapter), an enforcement hierarchy and tripartism.

CONTINGENCY AND FLEXIBILITY

Contingency and flexibility – using a diversity of methods while responding to each regulated entity's circumstances – may also be considered 'responsiveness' (Ayres and Braithwaite 1992; Macleod and McSherry 2006; Braithwaite 2011). In health care, no single regulatory method is likely to achieve desired outcomes (Berrill and Healy 2009), therefore regulators are encouraged to use a mix of rewards and sanctions (Braithwaite, Makkai and Braithwaite 2007). This should furthermore be done in a way that sends consistent messages (Berrill and Healy 2009: 9). However, this mix should be enacted in a way that communicates clear regulatory methods to organisations (Healy and Dugdale 2009: 9).

Responsiveness requires an understanding of each regulated organisation (Braithwaite, Makkai and Braithwaite 2007; Parker and Nielsen 2017). 'Motivational postures' research provides a framework for this understanding (Braithwaite et al. 1994; Braithwaite 2003). This research refers to the 'sets of beliefs and attitudes that sum up how actors feel about and wish to position themselves in relation to another actor' (Braithwaite, Makkai and Braithwaite 2007: 290). Responsive regulators using motivational postures seek to understand an organisation's beliefs about the regulator or law and seek to shape those beliefs as well as apply tailored regulatory interventions (Braithwaite 2016). Understanding motivational postures has been crucial to several regulatory spaces (Braithwaite et al. 1994; Braithwaite 2003; Smith-Merry et al. 2017), with calls for this to be applied to better regulation of clinical mental health services (Katterl 2021b).

ENFORCEMENT HIERARCHY

Responsive regulation requires judicious enforcement. Good regulators have a clear 'account of how and why to combine deterrent and cooperative regulatory enforcement strategies' (Nielsen and Parker 2009: 377). The 'enforcement pyramid' or 'pyramid of sanctions' is a well-established framework for guiding such strategies (Ayres and Braithwaite 1992). The pyramid – which has a large base at the bottom that narrows to a point at the top – signifies a range of regulatory tools and interventions that can be used with more interventionist, restrictive or sanction-oriented tools at the top of the pyramid. The pyramid assumes voluntary compliance at the bottom, where a regulator uses less interventionist tools such as education and capacity building, but signifies that where those tools don't prove effective in motivating compliance, the regulator should move up the pyramid (Ayres and Braithwaite 1992; Braithwaite 2011; Parker and Nielsen 2017).

The pyramid has informed several regulatory environments (Braithwaite, Makkai and Braithwaite 2007; Braithwaite, Murphy and Reinhart 2007; Healy and Dugdale 2009; Young 2015). Many contemporary regulators are empowered with broad functions to achieve their aims, including education, complaints and investigatory powers (see a suite of functions provided to the regulator – the Victorian Equal Opportunity and Human Rights Commission – under the *Equal Opportunity Act 2010* (Vic): parts 8 and 10). Use of these powers is crucial, with regulatory interventions by the CQC in England resulting in sector improvements (Smithson et al. 2018). The Victorian Ombudsman has illustrated how transparency, persuasion and 'shaming' can result in improvements, even in the absence of compliance powers (Victorian Ombudsman 2021). Such examples highlight the importance of regulators maintaining a commitment to enforcement (Freiberg 2017: 447).

TRIPARTISM

Being responsive to organisations carries risks of regulators becoming captured by those organisations (Ayres and Braithwaite 1991; Carpenter and Moss 2013). Tripartism aims to address this and refers to the inclusion of third parties in the regulatory process to hold the regulator accountable (Ayres and Braithwaite 1991). This can be achieved through public disclosure of regulatory activities, including external third parties in regulatory dealings with industry, as well as allowing third parties to unilaterally take a cause of action against an industry actor without the regulator. Such approaches open up the 'smoke-filled rooms' where regulatory decisions are made to necessary public scrutiny (Ayres and Braithwaite 1992: 57–58). Such approaches reflect a devolution of power from regulators to third parties (Gray and van Rooij 2021). Components of tripartism are found in health regulation (Bouwman et al. 2016), mental health regulation (Weingart et al. 2005; Bouwman et al. 2016; de Kam et al. 2020; Wiig et al. 2020) and in calls for strengthening human rights oversight processes (Minty 2019; Marsh 2021).

Involvement of third parties often invites inclusion of lived experience expertise (Victorian Mental Illness Awareness Council 2020a; Katterl 2021a). People working from a lived experience perspective can improve monitoring (Stevens 2015: 19; Caruana 2018: 35–38) and engagement activities (Caruana 2018: 37). Importantly, people who are using health services may act as a third party regulator by directing their own care and enforcing their rights, in turn shaping the quality of service delivery (Healy 2017; Quick 2017: 164–65). Where effective (Healy and Walton 2016; O'Donovan and Madden 2018; Katterl 2021a), complaints processes provide another tripartite method (Bouwman et al. 2016). (For discussion of the meaning and importance of lived experience see also Jayakody and Perera in Chapter 15 of this volume.)

Risk-Based Regulation

Risk-based regulation refers to an approach where regulators' decision-making processes and resource-allocation decisions are shaped by an assessment of what risks regulated entities pose to the regulator's objectives (Baldwin and Black 2016). Such an approach enables regulators to guide limited resources to the issues or risks that matter most to the regulator and stakeholders (Black 2005: 156). Four central elements of risk-based regulatory approaches are: (1) clarifying the regulatory objectives; (2) identifying risks to those objectives; (3) setting standards; and (4) assigning resources for monitoring and enforcement.

CLARIFY THE REGULATORY OBJECTIVES

A risk-based regulator must figure out the risks 'to what' that needs to be controlled (Black and Baldwin 2010: 184). These objectives serve as the 'north star' for the regulator conducting its day-to-day operations (Windholz 2017: 145) and may be reflected in policy or legislative objectives or functions (see e.g. the *Mental Health Act 2014* (Vic): section 228; *National Disability Insurance Scheme Act 2013* (Cth): section 181E(1)(a)). For many health care regulators, objectives might be to ensure patient safety (Healy and Dugdale 2009) or prevent improper conduct by practitioners (Spittal, Bismark and Studdert 2019). In mental health, it may be protection of human rights, with regulators often having multiple or evolving objectives (see Carney et al. 2017; Katterl 2021a: 152).

IDENTIFY RISKS TO THOSE OBJECTIVES

A regulator must document the historical, current and emerging risks to its objectives (Beaussier et al. 2016; Freiberg 2017: 458). Examples of this are the 'Risk Regulation Regime', which argues that regulators must understand risk and responses to risk within each agency and policy area's context (Hood, Rothstein and Baldwin 2001: 28). This approach recognises that there are both normative and technical elements about what constitutes a risk and what matters to regulators (Baldwin and Black 2016). Once the regulator confirms possible risks it must assess the regulatory space for those risks and determine its tolerance for particular risks, as not all can be eliminated (Freiberg 2017: 459).

While risk is featured in mental health law, McSherry (2013) and others (Sawyer 2017) have focused on how the law functions – for justifiable and unjustifiable reasons – to regulate the behaviour and treatment of *consumers*, rather than *mental health providers*. For example, all Australian jurisdictions contain expressed or implied tests that ask those authorising compulsory treatment to assess whether the person is at risk of harm to themselves or another person (see *Mental Health Act 2015* (ACT): sections 58, 66 and 101; *Mental Health Act 2007* (NSW): sections 12, 14 and 68; *Mental Health and Related Services Act 1998* (NT): section 14; *Mental Health Act 2016* (Qld): sections 3 and 12; *Mental Health Act 2009* (SA): section 21; *Mental Health Act 2013* (Tas): sections 6 and 40; *Mental Health Act 2014* (Vic): section 5; *Mental Health Act 2014* (WA): section 25). Unfortunately, the policy within these jurisdictions often lacks a sufficient focus on the risk that care poses to a person's rights (Katterl and Maylea 2021), such as during the early points of detention where the risk of torture or ill-treatment is greatest (Carver and Handley 2017: 8).

SET STANDARDS

Risk-based regulators must set standards that distinguish desired states from less desired states (Hood, Rothstein and Baldwin 2001: 23). Regulators may publish these standards so that regulated entities and other stakeholders are able to assess risk. In health care, England's CQC publishes a series of standards for quality and safe health care (see also in Victoria: Commissioner for Children and Young People 2019). The CQC assesses providers on the aforementioned five rating domains on a four-point scale (inadequate, requires improvement, good, outstanding). These assessments are done via in-depth inspections (Smithson et al. 2018; CQC 2021). In mental health there are standards developed by the Victorian Office of the Chief Psychiatrist that outline how services can provide safe and quality care in line with their legal obligations (Department of Health and Human Services 2020), though their legal effect is uncertain (Victorian Auditor-General's Office 2019b: 67).

ASSIGN RESOURCES FOR MONITORING AND ENFORCEMENT

Those activities which pose the greatest risk to the regulator's objectives should attract greater resources (Freiberg 2017: 461). This provides monitoring and enforcement, as well as the allocation of resources, with a clear and transparent rationale (Hampton 2005: 27). In Australia, data from the Australian Health Practitioner Regulation Agency (AHPRA) has been used to develop algorithms that can assist regulators to identify clinicians that are at a high risk of complaints (Spittal, Bismark and Studdert 2019; Jago et al. 2021), responding to concerns that health governance has been too reactionary to risks (Duckett, Cuddihy and Newnham 2016; Spittal, Bismark and Studdert 2019). The CQC again provides examples of how resources may be allocated, with its use of 'special measures' to deal with escalating risk to quality and safety (Gedling Eye Reporter 2022; for public examples see Meredith 2022). Services that are rated inadequate can be placed on 'special measures' which attracts increased support and oversight from the CQC. However, if a service does not make necessary improvements within a defined period, the CQC will take measures to de-register them. Both risk and responsive regulatory theories provide this focus on enforcement. However, a central concept implicit behind questions of enforcement is power.

Theories of Power in Health Policy, Mental Health and Regulation and the Regulation of Clinical Mental Health Service

Power inequalities between individuals and groups have been long acknowledged in politics (Machiavelli 2014), health governance, mental health policy (Bennetts, Cross and Bloomer 2011; Juntanamalaga et al. 2019; Edan et al. 2021) and regulatory policy (Gray and van Rooij 2021). It has many definitions: power can mean coercive power *over* another person, but can also mean *collaborative* power (power with) and a sense of *empowerment* (power to or power within) (Dahl 1957).

Theories of Power in Health Governance and Policy

Power is regularly implicated in health governance and policy and in particular the inequities in access and outcomes for consumers (Walt 1994; Sriram et al. 2018). The Health Equity Power Framework (HEPF) (Friel et al. 2021) analyses power in three distinct ways:

- types – the structural, institutional, economic, physical, discursive, moral, expert and network types of power;
- forms – the visible, hidden and invisible forms of power; and
- spaces – the closed, invited and claimed spaces of power.

When power manifests in these ways, different framings of and approaches to health problems and solutions may be privileged by those who enjoy greater power. As a result of this, health inequities can emerge, not just as a consequence of health service delivery but from diverse policy areas (e.g. international trade, social protection, planning and infrastructure).

Theories of Power in Mental Health Policy and Systems

Power is heavily implicated in mental health policy, but also in service delivery and systems. For example, power is noted in the relationships between clinicians and consumers (Weller et al. 2019; Boyle 2022; Victoria Legal Aid 2020; Maylea et al. 2021) and between consumer workers and fellow clinical staff (Edan et al. 2021). These power imbalances are reflected more broadly in the design and operation of the mental health system (Royal Commission into Victoria's Mental Health System 2021: Volume 3, 18), including the use of laws that permit compulsory mental health treatment (Roper 2019).

Several strategies attempt to address these power imbalances. These include greater opportunities for leadership for consumer lived experience workers within mental health systems (Happell and Roper 2006; Scholz, Gordon and Happell 2017), giving greater prominence to human rights obligations within the system (Katterl and Maylea 2021), and moving from top-down forms of system management towards more collaborative approaches (Roper, Grey and Cadogan 2018; McSherry 2023). The latter is commonly called 'co-design' (McKercher 2020) or 'co-production' (Roper, Grey and Cadogan 2018), prioritising a focus on power-sharing and inclusion at all stages of decision-making in projects, services or systems that impact mental health consumers.

Theories of Power in Regulation

Power is also relevant to regulatory theory and practice in general. The reduction of domination – the arbitrary power of a party or group over another – is a normative goal of responsive regulation (Braithwaite 2013; Burford, Braithwaite and Braithwaite 2019: 2–3). The appropriate distribution and use of power is also central to responsive regulation, with the approach navigating a third way beyond traditional 'command and control' and laissez-faire approaches to regulation (Ayres and Braithwaite 1992).

Power also impacts *how* the regulatory process works or fails. For example, power imbalances and strict hierarchies can undermine citizens' interactions with regulators (Gray and van Rooij 2021), including during health complaints processes (O'Donovan and Madden 2018). This highlights the need for regulators to actively redress power imbalances between parties (Creutzfeldt 2016: 444). In the absence of such corrective actions, regulators may suffer from regulatory capture (see e.g. Grabosky and Braithwaite 1986). Together, these accounts of risk and responsive regulations, with an awareness of power-dynamics as they relate to mental health, law and regulation, may provide principles for improved regulatory practice of clinical mental health services.

The Human Rights and Mental Health Regulatory Framework

Guidance has been called for to assist regulators to deal with complaints after their performance has been questioned (Productivity Commission 2020: 1118). This framework takes a broad approach, acknowledging that some regulators have broader systemic powers than purely a complaints function. Therefore, any framework or guidance should encapsulate how regulators should judiciously exercise *all* these powers and functions.

This chapter puts forward the HRMHRF as a framework for effective regulatory practice in clinical mental health settings. The HRMHRF draws on the previously described peer-reviewed and grey literature that focus on responsive and risk-based regulation, as well as theories of power. From this literature key concepts and findings are transformed into principles that can protect and promote human rights in mental health settings. Such principles are built on the understanding that clinical mental health settings are characterised by human rights breaches (Maylea et al. 2021) and significant power imbalances (Weller et al. 2019; Victoria Legal Aid 2020), which may be remedied in part through effective regulatory oversight (Katterl 2021a). The HRMHRF identifies seven key principles for effective practice, and they are elaborated next (see Figure 14.1).

Indicators to each of these principles are set out in Table 14.1.

Application of the Framework

The HRMHRF may inform the design and evaluation of current or new regulatory strategies. Victoria's reforming mental health system provides a prime opportunity to do so. In the following sections the chapter introduces the legislative powers and policy landscape surrounding the MHCC and the key sources of information to conduct a public assessment of their performance. Following this, the chapter assesses the MHCC against the seven principles identified in the HRMHRF.[3]

Figure 14.1 Human Rights and Mental Health Regulatory Framework

Table 14.1 Human Rights and Mental Health Regulatory Framework

Principle	*Explanation/indicators*
Clear objectives	Establishment and articulation of clear regulatory objectives for promoting and protecting human rights. Indicators include: • Statutory objectives that clearly state a focus on protecting and promoting human rights • Public evidence of how the regulatory process has a rational connection to promoting and protecting human rights • Communications strategies and activities that indicate statutory objectives of promoting and protecting human rights
Be responsive	Respond to mental health service's circumstances and level of motivation to respect and comply with human rights. Indicators include: • An understanding of the characteristics, capacities and motivations of each mental health service • Use of a diverse set of regulatory methods to achieve the regulatory goal of rights protection and promotion • A framework for promoting good practice, supporting capacity building and deterring wilful non-compliance
Regulate risk	Allocate resources and regulatory interventions to actors or system components that pose a significant risk to human rights. Indicators include: • A framework for identifying where risks to human rights are greatest • Tools to monitor those risks through existing complaints and other regulatory processes • A strategy to apportion resources to system components and specific mental health services that pose greatest risk to mental health consumers' human rights
Effective standards	Set a mix of prescriptive and outcome-focused standards to measure compliance with human rights. Indicators include: • Published practice guidelines or frameworks that articulate standards • The use of outcomes-focused or principle-based standards and prescriptive standards based on the flexibility and certainty needed • Standards that indicate how the regulator makes decisions regarding its use of powers
Judicious enforcement	Ensure the deliberate, transparent and robust use of enforcement measures. Indicators include: • Evidence of deliberate and considered use of education and capability-focused regulatory strategies • Evidence that the regulator monitors implementation or the effectiveness of recommendations or education and capability-development regulatory strategies • Evidence of the use of more coercive regulatory measures, such as investigations, enforceable undertakings and compliance notices, where less interventionist regulatory strategies have proved ineffective

(*Continued*)

Table 14.1 (Continued)

Principle	*Explanation/indicators*
Tripartism	Engage third parties in the regulatory process, including people with lived experience. Indicators include: • Publishing of routine regulatory and complaints information that enables monitoring by civil society organisations • Recruitment of civil society organisations, including lived experience organisations, to assist with investigations and provide resolutions advice • Routine coordination with other regulatory organisations to achieve statutory objectives
Balance power	Take positive steps to identify, name and address power imbalances between complainants, mental health services and the regulator as part of the regulatory process and as an outcome of the regulatory process. Indicators include: • A framework for how the regulator understands, identifies and responds to the different types, forms and spaces where power operates in the regulatory process • Measures of change at the systems level, regulatory process and the service-provision level changes in power relations • Evidence that the regulator has people in leadership roles with lived experience

Victoria's Principal Mental Health Regulator

Established after the Victorian government recognised concerns from the community about the state's more generalist health care regulator (Victorian Government 2008; McSherry and Klauber 2011), the MHCC commenced operations in July 2014 at the same time as the then new *Mental Health Act 2014* (Vic). The MHCC has a broad range of functions that focus on education, complaints management and assisting quality improvement in the system (see Table 14.2). The Royal Commission recommended that a new Mental Health and Wellbeing Commission (MHWC) incorporate similar powers to those of the MHCC and have a focused systems monitoring function. Table 14.2 sets out the current functions of the MHCC.

To inform the development of the MHWC, the MHCC is assessed based on publicly available data, including:

- complaints data and analysis in annual reports and obtained via freedom of information;
- independent stakeholder feedback surveys obtained via freedom of information;
- policy documents such as the 'Driven by Lived Experience Framework and Strategy' (LE Strategy);
- submissions to the Royal Commission into Victoria's Mental Health System;
- web content, including complaints stories, information on the complaints process and tools developed such as the internal complaints self-assessment tool;

Table 14.2 Functions of the Mental Health Complaints Commissioner established in the *Mental Health Act 2014* (Vic)

Education (section 228(g))	To provide information, education and advice to mental health service providers about their responsibilities in managing complaints made by consumers
Accept and investigate complaints (section 228(a))	To accept, assess, manage and investigate complaints relating to mental health services providers
Formal (conciliation) and informal (mediation) resolution (section 228(b))	To endeavour to resolve complaints in a timely manner using formal and informal dispute resolution as appropriate, including conciliation
Make recommendations (section 228(j))	To identify, analyse and review quality, safety and other issues arising out of complaints and to provide information and make recommendations for improving the provision of mental health services
Accept undertakings (section 243(4)(e))	Accept an undertaking given by a mental health service provider to take remedial action in relation to the complaint
Issue compliance notices (section 260(1))	May serve a compliance notice on a mental health service provider who has not complied with an undertaking or acted or engaged in a practice in contravention of the *Mental Health Act 2014* (Vic) or the regulations

- communications content, such as social media posts;
- external commentary and feedback on the MHCC and other regulatory agencies;
- external data on the prevalence and nature of human rights issues within Victoria's mental health system.

It is important to note that there has been no independent evaluation of the MHCC and much of this data is presented *by* the MHCC. Therefore, it may not reflect more critical lived experience views and risks bias in favour of the MHCC's performance.

Principle 1: Clear Objective (Human Rights Protection)

Indicators

- statutory objectives that clearly state a focus on protecting and promoting human rights;
- public evidence of how the regulatory process has a rational connection to promoting and protecting human rights;
- communications strategies and activities that indicate statutory objectives of promoting and protecting human rights.

The MHCC does not include clear objectives to protect and promote human rights. Part of the challenges for the MHCC is that despite its core message of safeguarding rights (MHCC 2022a) these functions or objectives are not reflected in section 228 of the *Mental Health Act 2014* (Vic). This contrasts with other Australian regulators, such as the National Disability Insurance Scheme Quality and Safeguards Commission, who have explicit rights and compliance functions (*National Disability Insurance Scheme Act 2013* (Cth), section 181E(1)(a)). This absence leaves the MHCC on less firm legislative terrain to forcefully pursue protection and the promotion of human rights.

Perhaps connected to a lack of objectives, the MHCC has not articulated a clear framework that coordinates its regulatory activities towards human rights protection. This absence results in an inconsistent connection between human rights and its regulatory practice (counter-example see Commissioner for Children and Young People 2019). For example, the 'Complaints stories' on the MHCC's website do positively foreground human rights protection and the MHCC's response in diverse areas such as compulsory treatment, restrictive interventions and inclusive forms of service delivery (MHCC 2021a). By contrast, there is little evidence that the MHCC's 'It's OK to complain' campaign and online self-assessment tool is connected to its regulatory functions and human rights protection. Rather than reflect a commitment to human rights protection, the campaign and self-assessment tool (which is voluntary and anonymous) appears to devolve governance and handling of complaints to services, with a lack of oversight of how they implement the initiative as an explicit design feature of the MHCC's processes (see further under Principle 3).

Principle 2: Be Responsive

Indicators

- an understanding of the characteristics, capacities and motivations of each mental health service;
- use of a diverse set of regulatory methods to achieve the regulatory goal of rights protection and promotion;
- a framework for promoting good practice, supporting capacity building and deterring wilful non-compliance.

The MHCC is not a responsive regulator. Examination of 'Complaints stories' does not demonstrate an understanding that services present diverse characteristics, capacities and motivations (e.g. motivational postures). Complaints stories appear to indicate a homogenous set of mental health services and an assumption that individual complaints must be handled separate to system or service trends (MHCC 2021b). While the complaints stories provide an example of how the MHCC broadly approaches complaints on different topics, they do not reveal how it tailors its response to different actors. This suggests that complaints may be dealt with in isolation from the systemic features of the mental health service. For example, there may be multiple complaints of the same kind that have generated the same or similar recommendations from the MHCC, warranting an escalated response if those recommendations have not been implemented. Information obtained via freedom of information revealed that South West Healthcare had routinely failed to provide evidence to the MHCC of its failure to report outcomes on internal complaints in breach of the *Mental Health Act 2014* (Vic), with little visible enforcement from the regulator (MHCC 2021b: 27–28). In the absence of the MHCC publishing the recommendations it makes to mental health services, it is difficult to ascertain whether any such strategy exists (Katterl 2021a).

Complaints data reveal that there is a significant disparity between services in Victoria. For example, information obtained under the freedom of information request noted previously illustrated that between 2019 and 2020 some services had zero or single digit complaints per 1,000 consumers, whereas other services had up to 27 complaints per 1,000 consumers. Despite this disparity, there is minimal evidence that the MHCC has used its regulatory powers to respond to services that perform worse and have repeated complaints. The limited public data available on the MHCC's regulatory actions makes it challenging to assess, creating a mixed picture. Pointing to some measure of responsiveness, it appears that the MHCC chose to participate in a national news story that highlighted potentially poor practice at a Victorian clinical mental health service, Mercy Health (Choahan 2021). Mercy Health has the highest rates of complaints over a sustained period, both directly to the service and independently to the MHCC.[4] This may indicate that the MHCC chose to escalate its responses publicly because previous regulatory activities were insufficient to promote change. However, such conclusions remain speculative as the MHCC does not release the recommendations it makes to mental health services.

Principle 3: Regulate Risk

Indicators

- a framework for identifying where risks to human rights are greatest;
- tools to monitor those risks through existing complaints and other regulatory processes;
- a strategy to apportion resources to system components and specific mental health services that pose greatest risk to mental health consumers' human rights.

The MHCC presents limited commitment to a risk-based approach. The MHCC states that it takes a risk-based approach (Coulson Barr 2020: 25) and it may be stated that some processes around seclusion and restraint reflect resources being directed to complaints that present a high risk to human rights (MHCC 2022b). However, it has not articulated a clear regulatory strategy. Therefore, it is unclear if it allocates resources based on risks to human rights. This is concerning given some aspects or periods of detention pose a greater risk to human rights (Carver and Handley 2017: 8), and that some services (Victorian Mental Illness Awareness Council 2020b; see MHCC 2021b) and clinicians perform more poorly when it relates to quality of care or ethical practice (Spittal, Bismark and Studdert 2019).

Several examples indicate that the MHCC does not adopt a risk-based approach. The component of the service that may interface with the greatest risk – the oral complaints process where consumers often call from a place of detention – has been criticised for failing to resolve consumers' concerns (Maylea 2020: 10; Katterl 2021a: 154). The 'It's Ok to complain' campaign (MHCC 2022c), which encourages consumers to complain directly to their service rather than the MHCC, represents another failure of risk-based regulation. While devolution of regulation is entirely appropriate in risk-based regulatory approaches (Haines 2017: 181), the MHCC has minimal measures to ensure that mental health services' internal complaints processes are effective. The tools developed by the MHCC for services to improve their internal complaints are voluntary and anonymous, meaning the MHCC has no visibility or indication if its efforts have been effective. This occurs despite the MHCC also writing to services to state that their existing complaints processes and reporting are in breach of the *Mental Health Act 2014* (Vic) (MHCC 2021c: 27–28). This runs contrary to a risk-based approach and may in fact place consumers at greater risk of human rights breaches by encouraging them to pursue fruitless internal complaints processes.

Principle 4: Effective Standards

Indicators

- published practice guidelines or frameworks that articulate standards;
- the use of outcomes-focused or principle-based standards and prescriptive standards based on the flexibility and certainty needed;
- standards that indicate how the regulator makes decisions regarding its use of powers.

The MHCC presents a positive but incomplete picture regarding the use of effective standards. Complaints stories indicate how mental health principles are intended to apply to a range of regulatory settings. All stories at a general level indicate how the MHCC can utilise its powers, including stories that indicate where an enforceable undertaking was accepted (MHCC 2021c). Together these may serve as proxies for standards that outline outcomes or prescriptive-based standards, as well as how the MHCC signals using its powers.

However, this falls short of the principle required here. This content may be better characterised as examples of how standards are *applied*, rather than standards *themselves*. Moreover, these stories do not explain the underlying rationale for how the MHCC makes decisions about when and how to use its regulatory powers. Complaints stories would be more useful as an extension or example of standards than as standards themselves.

Principle 5: Judicious Enforcement

Indicators

- evidence of deliberate and considered use of education and capability-focused regulatory strategies;
- evidence that the regulator monitors implementation or the effectiveness of recommendations or education and capability-development regulatory strategies;
- evidence of the use of more coercive regulatory measures, such as investigations, enforceable undertakings and compliance notices, where less interventionist regulatory strategies have proved ineffective.

The MHCC lacks a clear strategy or commitment to enforcement. In eight years of operation there has been in excess of 12,000 complaints made to the office, with no compliance notices used by the MHCC (Ore and Davey 2022). Enforceable undertakings, whereby the MHCC accepts undertakings by a service to comply with the *Mental Health Act 2014* (Vic), are also low. In its 2020–21 annual report (MHCC 2021a), there were no enforceable undertakings compared to four in the year 2019–20 (MHCC 2020a), two in the year 2018–19 (MHCC 2019) and one in the year 2017–18 (MHCC 2018).

This under-enforcement was reflected in experiences of complainants via independent survey results of the MHCC. For example, 54% of respondents (consumers and carers) disagreed that their complaint resulted in positive changes for themselves (ORIMA Research 2020: 13). However, 65% did note that they believed it had a positive impact on the service and others' experience of it. When discussing concerns around the MHCC's effectiveness, some stated 'nothing changed', 'I tried to get help, but no one cares' and that the MHCC was just a 'sounding board'. Several were under the belief that the MHCC did not have sufficient powers, stating that they needed more powers and asking, what is the point of an investigative body if it has no authority? (ORIMA Research 2020: 14). This is concerning given the MHCC does in fact have significant coercive powers that have remained unused, begging the question why mental health consumers were under this misapprehension.

These reflections come at the same time as the Royal Commission's final report found that the community and consumers had lost trust in Victorian regulators due to under-enforcement (Royal Commission into Victoria's Mental Health System 2021: Volume 4, 266). While the MHCC states that it does monitor implementation of its recommendations, as this principle requires, it does not appear to have an enforcement strategy. For example, data obtained via freedom of information revealed that the South West Healthcare mental health service recorded no outcomes to the MHCC in the 2018–2020 period in breach of the *Mental Health Act 2014* (Vic), with no corresponding recorded MHCC enforcement measure (MHCC 2021b: 27–28). This failure to enforce despite evidence of non-compliance renders voluntary and less coercive regulatory interventions ineffective (Ayres and Braithwaite 1992; Kagan, Gunningham and Thornton 2011; Parker and Nielsen 2017).

Principle 6: Tripartism

Indicators

- publishing of routine regulatory and complaints information that enables monitoring by civil society organisations;
- recruitment of civil society organisations, including lived experience organisations, to assist with investigations and provide resolutions advice;
- routine coordination with other regulatory organisations to achieve statutory objectives.

The MHCC presents a complex picture regarding tripartism. The LE Strategy and consumer, carer and clinical members of its Advisory Council point to elements of tripartism. The LE Strategy states that lived experience is engaged in the MHCC's strategy and quality activities, its education and engagement activities, leadership as well as its complaints and investigations activities (MHCC 2020b: 13–14). However, on the latter complaints and investigations activities, there is no evidence that third parties such as consumer or carer peak bodies are involved in the regulatory process. Information from some members of the Advisory Council – a body set up with consumer, carer and clinician representatives to advise the MHCC – indicates positive experiences (MHCC 2021d: 31). However, like the LE Strategy, there is little evidence that Advisory Council members (who are not MHCC staff) are involved in the regulatory process. Therefore, it is unclear whether this involvement is truly tripartite in nature or placative.

Tripartism is heavily hampered by the MHCC's poor data disclosure practices and limited leadership in coordinating safeguard and oversight bodies.

The MHCC has until May 2022, resisted releasing service-level data that enables comparisons amongst mental health services (Katterl 2021a). While the MHCC now does report this data, they have redacted some of the most crucial data – the recommendations it has made to services to improve their quality (MHCC 2022d). This is despite the practice being advocated for (Katterl 2021a) and common with other oversight agencies (see e.g. Victorian Ombudsman 2020).

Principle 7: Balance Power

Indicators

- a framework for how the regulator understands, identifies and responds to the different types, forms and spaces where power operates in the regulatory process;
- measures of change at the systems level, regulatory process and the service-provision level changes in power relations;
- evidence that the regulator has people in leadership roles with lived experience.

The MHCC's articulation of, and commitment to, addressing power imbalances presents another incomplete picture. Within Victoria's mental health system there are significant power imbalances between mental health providers, including clinicians and consumers who access the system. This power imbalance found in the relations between consumers and clinicians (Victoria Legal Aid 2020: 16–20) is codified in the laws that permit compulsory treatment (Roper 2019) and is expressed in frequent examples of disempowerment (Maylea et al. 2018) and breaches of the law by services (Maylea et al. 2021).

There are indications that the MHCC understands this. Importantly, the agency has leadership from people with lived experience, including one of the current assistant commissioners (MHCC 2022e). Moreover, the regulator's LE Strategy highlights that it is built on a principle of addressing power imbalances between consumers and mental health services (MHCC 2020b: 10). However, while it notes power, the LE Strategy and other public documents do not identify different types, forms and spaces where power can operate in the MHCC's regulatory process. They also fail to articulate *how* they would ameliorate or measure changes in those power imbalances. Critically, the LE Strategy does not make a commitment to the central mechanism by which power imbalances may be addressed: enforcement of consumer rights. Indeed, consumers who have used the MHCC have described it as a 'toothless tiger' and question the agency's sincerity in protecting their rights (Victoria Legal Aid 2020: 17; Royal Commission into Victoria's Mental Health System 2021: Volume 4, 263).

It is also unclear what mechanisms the MHCC has put in place to guard against regulatory capture. Given the strength of contact, the small number of providers and the significant power the mental health sector holds, the risks of regulatory capture of the agency are significant, with these elements being signalled by Grabosky and Braithwaite (1986) as risk factors for regulatory capture. While advisory mechanisms put in place by the MHCC could guard against this (MHCC 2016), these do not have decision-making capacity and there is no evidence that they are routinely privy to the operational regulatory decisions where capture may develop (Ayres and Braithwaite 1991: 441).

Conclusion

As mental health systems reform and come to grips with the human rights implications of their practices, two reform paths will need to develop concurrently. On the one hand, mental health laws will need to continue to progressively align with international human rights laws that indicate an abolition of compulsory mental health treatment (Committee on the Rights of Persons with Disabilities 2014; Maylea and Hirsch 2017) and positive duties on the State to provide quality support, housing and voluntary care (McSherry and Wilson 2015). On the other, mental health laws will need to show greater effect on *actual practice* from practitioners and the *lived experience* of those using services. It is this latter path that this chapter contributes to.

This chapter aims to fill a gap in the literature at the nexus of regulation, mental health and human rights. Good mental health regulation should reduce rather than increase experiences of domination (Braithwaite 2013). The HRMHRF provides a starting point for designing and evaluating mental health regulators who oversee clinical mental health environments, particularly those that regulate clinical mental health services. Centring responsive and risk-based approaches to regulation, as well as multi-layered approaches to power, the HRMHRF focuses on seven key principles for effective regulatory practice:

- clear objectives (human rights protection);
- regulation of risk to those objectives;
- being responsive;
- effective standards;
- judicious enforcement;
- tripartism;
- balance power.

The chapter uses the discontinuation of the MHCC in Victoria as an opportunity to examine it against the HRMHRF. It highlights positive signs in standard-setting and some inclusion of lived experience voices to balance power. However, these positive signs are hampered by a lack of statutory objectives that align the MHCC towards human rights protection. Under those absent objectives, the MHCC has lacked clear regulatory goals, impeding the ability to assess risk and respond to differently performing mental health services. Central to this has been a lack of enforcement of laws and rights accompanied by closed rather than tripartite approaches to regulatory practice. Power imbalances between mental health services and consumers appear largely undisrupted by the MHCC's practice.

Post-Royal Commission, Victoria will create the new MHWC. Based on the Royal Commission's final report, the legal architecture of this regulator will be similar to the MHCC, with some minor enhancements. Except for the first principle, the HRMHRF framework focuses less on the legal design of mental health regulators, and more on their culture and practices. It is only with improvements to the latter that better mental health services can be achieved and human rights can move from words to deeds.

Notes

1 Including 'risk-based regulation', 'responsive regulation', 'health care', 'healthcare', 'tripartism'.

2 Including 'Mental Health Act 2014', 'Charter of Human Rights and Responsibilities Act 2006', 'Mental Health Complaints Commissioner', 'Mental Health and Wellbeing Commission', 'Chief Psychiatrist', 'Care Quality Commission', 'Care Quality Commission' AND 'mental health', 'power imbalances', 'consumer leadership'.

3 Thank you to Treasure Jennings, the Mental Health Complaints Commissioner, for providing feedback on an early version of this chapter. The authors encouraged the commissioner to publish a response on points of disagreement that were maintained.

4 This excludes Forensicare complaints recorded by the MHCC (2021c), as mental health consumers in Forensicare – a forensic mental health service – are detained for much longer periods under the *Crimes (Mental Impairment and Unfitness to be Tried) Act 1997* (Vic), meaning the likelihood of making a complaint dramatically increases with the length of detention.

References

Australian Bureau of Statistics (2022) *Snapshot of Victoria: High Level Summary Data for Victoria in 2021*. Available www.abs.gov.au/articles/snapshot-vic-2021 (accessed 28 December 2022).

Ayres, I. and Braithwaite, J. (1991) 'Tripartism: Regulatory Capture and Empowerment', *Law & Social Inquiry*, 16(3): 435–96.

Ayres, I. and Braithwaite, J. (1992) *Responsive Regulation: Transcending the Deregulation Debate*, New York: Oxford University Press.

Baldwin, R. and Black, J. (2016) 'Driving Priorities in Risk-Based Regulation: What's the Problem?' *Journal of Law and Society*, 43(4): 565–95.

Bates, M.J. (1989) 'The Design of Browsing and Berrypicking Techniques for the Online Search Interface', *Online Review*, 13(5): 407–24.

Beaussier, A-L., Demeritt, D., Griffiths, A. and Rothstein, H. (2016) 'Accounting for Failure: Risk-based Regulation and the Problems of Ensuring Healthcare Quality in the NHS', *Health, Risk & Society*, 18(3–4): 205–24.

Bennetts, W., Cross, W. and Bloomer, M. (2011) 'Understanding Consumer Participation in Mental Health: Issues of Power and Shange', *International Journal of Mental Health Nursing*, 20(3): 155–64.

Berrill, J. and Healy, J. (2009) 'Hospital Licensure, Certification and Accreditation', in J. Healy and P. Dugdale (eds) *Patient Safety First: Responsive Regulation in Healthcare*, Crows Nest: Allen & Unwin, 273–98.

Black, J. (2005) 'The Development of Risk-based Regulation in Financial Services: Just "Modelleing Through"?' in J. Black, M. Lodge and M. Thatcher (eds) *Regulatory Innovation: A Comparative Analysis*, Cheltenham: Edward Elgar Publishing, 156–80.

Black, J. (2010) 'The Role of Risk in Regulatory Processes', in R. Baldwin, M. Cave and M. Lodge (eds) *The Oxford Handbook of Regulation*, Oxford: Oxford University Press, 302–48.

Black, J. and Baldwin, R. (2010) 'Really Responsive Risk-based Regulation', *Law & Policy*, 32(2): 181–213.

Bouwman, R., Bomhoff, M., Robben, P. and Friele, R. (2016) 'Patients' Perspectives on the Role of Their Complaints in the Regulatory Process', *Health Expectations*, 19(2): 483–96.

Boyle, M. (2022) 'Power in the Power Threat Meaning Framework', *Journal of Constructivist Psychology*, 35(1): 27–40.

Boyle, S. and Walsh, T. (2021) 'Procedural Fairness in Mental Health Review Tribunals: The Views of Patient Advocates', *Psychiatry, Psychology and Law*, 28(2): 163–84.

Braithwaite, J. (2011) 'The Essence of Responsive Regulation', *University of British Columbia Law Review*, 44(3): 475–520.

Braithwaite, J. (2013) 'Relational Republican Regulation', *Regulation & Governance*, 7(1): 124–44.

Braithwaite, J. (2016) *Restorative Justice and Responsive Regulation: The Question of Evidence*, RegNet Research Paper, 2016/51. Available https://regnet.anu.edu.au/sites/default/files/uploads/2016-10/SSRN_2016_updated_Braithwaite%20J.pdf (accessed 28 December 2022).

Braithwaite, J., Healy, J. and Dwan, K. (2005) *The Governance of Health Safety and Quality*. Available https://regnet.anu.edu.au/research/publications/3626/governance-health-safety-and-quality (accessed 28 December 2022).

Braithwaite, J., Makkai, T. and Braithwaite, V.A. (2007) *Regulating Aged Care: Ritualism and the New Pyramid*, Cheltenham: Edward Elgar Publishing.

Braithwaite, V. (2003) 'Dancing with Tax Authorities: Motivational Postures and Non-compliant Actions', in V. Braithwaite (ed) *Taxing Democracy: Understanding Tax Avoidance and Evasion*, Aldershot: Ashgate Publishing, 15–39.

Braithwaite, V., Braithwaite, J., Gibson, D. and Makkai, T. (1994) 'Regulatory Styles, Motivational Postures and Nursing Home Compliance', *Law & Policy*, 16(4): 363–94.

Braithwaite, V., Murphy, K. and Reinhart, M. (2007) 'Taxation Threat, Motivational Postures, and Responsive Regulation', *Law & Policy*, 29(1): 137–58.

Burford, G., Braithwaite, J. and Braithwaite, V. (2019) 'Introduction: Restorative and Responsive Human Services', in G. Burford, J. Braithwaite and V. Braithwaite, *Restorative and Responsive Human Services*, New York: Routledge, 1–19.

Cannold, L. (2014) 'Victoria a True Leader in Mental Health Reform', *ABC News*, 27 February. Available www.abc.net.au/news/2014-02-28/cannold-victoria-a-true-leader-in-mental-health-reform/5289940 (accessed 28 December 2022).

Care Quality Commission (2021) *Ratings*. Available www.cqc.org.uk/what-we-do/how-we-do-our-job/ratings (accessed 28 December 2022).

Carney, T., Tait, D. and Beaupert, F. (2008) 'Pushing the Boundaries: Realising Rights Through Mental Health Tribunal Processes?' *Sydney Law Review*, 30(2): 329–56.

Carney, T., Walton, M., Chiarella, M. and Kelly, P. (2017) 'Health Complaints and Practitioner Regulation: Justice, Protection or Prevention?' *Griffith Law Review*, 26(1): 65–88.

Carpenter, D. and Moss, D.A. (2013) *Preventing Regulatory Capture: Special Interest Influence and How to Limit It*, New York: Cambridge University Press.

Caruana, S. (2018) *Enhancing Best Practice Inspection Methodologies for Oversight Bodies with an Optional Protocol to the Convention Against Torture Focus*, Winston Churchill Memorial Trust of Australia. Available www.churchilltrust.com.au/project/to-enhance-best-practice-inspection-methodologies-for-oversight-bodies-with-an-optional-protocol-to-the-convention-against-torture-focus/ (accessed 28 December 2022).

Carver, R. and Handley, L. (eds) (2017) *Does Torture Prevention Work?* Liverpool: Liverpool University Press.

Choahan, N. (2021) 'Phoebe Thought She Would Be Safe at the Hospital. But the Staff Forced Her to Meet with Her Husband', *ABC News*, 2 October. Available www.abc.net.au/news/2021-10-03/melbourne-hospital-misdiagnosed-family-violence-victim/100277596 (accessed 28 December 2022).

Commissioner for Children and Young People (2019) *Regulatory Approach*. Available https://ccyp.vic.gov.au/assets/resources/Regulatory-Approach/CCYP-Regulatory-approach-Final.pdf (accessed 28 December 2022).

Committee on the Rights of Persons with Disabilities (2014) *General Comment No. 1 – Article 12: Equal Recognition Before the Law*, 11th sess, UN Doc CRPD/C/GC/1.

Coulson Barr, L. (2020) *Witness Statement of Dr Lynne Coulson Barr OAM to the Royal Commission into Victoria's Mental Health System*, 4 June. Available http://rcvmhs.archive.royalcommission.vic.gov.au/Coulson_Barr_Lynne.pdf (accessed 28 December 2022).

Creutzfeldt, N. (2016) 'What Do We Expect from an Ombudsman? Narratives of Everyday Engagement with the Informal Justice System in Germany and the UK', *International Journal of Law in Context*, 12(4): 437–52.

Dahl, R.A. (1957) 'The Concept of Power', *Behavioral Science*, 2(3): 201–15.

de Kam, D., Kok, J., Grit, K., Leistikow, I., Vlemminx, M. and Bal, R. (2020) 'How Incident Reporting Systems Can Stimulate Social and Participative Learning: A Mixed-methods Study', *Health Policy*, 124(8): 834–41.

Department of Health (2022) *Mental Health Reform*, Victoria State Government. Available www.health.vic.gov.au/mental-health/mental-health-wellbeing-reform (accessed 28 December 2022).

Department of Health and Human Services (2020) *Chief Psychiatrist Guidelines*, Victoria State Government. Available www2.health.vic.gov.au/about/key-staff/chief-psychiatrist/chief-psychiatrist-guidelines (accessed 28 December 2022).

Duckett, S., Cuddihy, M. and Newnham, H. (2016) *Targeting Zero: Supporting the Victorian Hospital System to Eliminate Avoidable Harm and Strengthen Quality of Care – Report of the Review of Hospital Safety and Quality Assurance in Victoria*, Department of Health and Human Services (Vic). Available www.health.vic.gov.au/sites/default/files/migrated/files/collections/research-and-reports/h/hospital-safety-and-quality-assurance-in-victoria.pdf (accessed 28 December 2022).

Edan, V., Sellick, K., Ainsworth, S., Alvarez-Varquez, S., Johnson, B., Smale, K., Randall, R. and Roper, C. (2021) 'Employed But Not Included: The Case of

Consumer-workers in Mental Health Care Services', *The International Journal of Human Resource Management*, 32(15): 3272–301.

Freiberg, A. (2017) *Regulation in Australia*, Leichhardt: Federation Press.

Friel, S., Townsend, B., Fisher, M., Harris, P., Freeman, T. and Baum, F. (2021) 'Power and the People's Health', *Social Science & Medicine*, 282: 114173.

Gedling Eye Reporter (2022) 'Mental Health Hospital in Arnold Rated "Inadequate" and Remains in Special Measures Following CQC Inspection', *Gedling Eye*, 15 March. Available www.gedlingeye.co.uk/news/mental-health-hospital-in-arnold-rated-inadequate-and-remains-in-special-measures-following-cqc-inspection/ (accessed 28 December 2022).

Grabosky, P. and Braithwaite, J. (1986) *Of Manners Gentle: Enforcement Strategies of Australian Business Regulatory Agencies*, Melbourne: Oxford University Press.

Gray, G. and van Rooij, B. (2021) 'Regulatory Disempowerment: How Enabling and Controlling Forms of Power Obstruct Citizen-based Regulation', *Regulation & Governance*, 15(3): 800–21.

Haines, F. (2017) 'Regulation and Risk', in P. Drahos (ed) *Regulatory Theory: Foundations and Applications*, Acton: Australian National University Press, 181–96.

Hampton, P. (2005) *Reducing Administrative Burdens: Effective Inspection and Enforcement*, HM Treasury. Available www.regulation.org.uk/library/2005_hampton_report.pdf (accessed 28 December 2022).

Happell, B. and Roper, C. (2006) 'The Myth of Representation: The Case for Consumer Leadership', *Australian e-Journal for the Advancement of Mental Health*, 5(3): 177–84.

Healy, J. (2017) 'Patients as Regulatory Actors in Their Own Health Care', in P. Drahos (ed) *Regulatory Theory: Foundations and Applications*, Acton: Australian National University Press, 591–610.

Healy, J. and Dugdale, P. (2009) *Patient Safety First: Responsive Regulation in Health Care*, Crows Nest: Allen & Unwin.

Healy, J. and Walton, M. (2016) 'Health Ombudsmen in Polycentric Regulatory Fields: England, New Zealand, and Australia', *Australian Journal of Public Administration*, 75(4): 492–505.

Hood, C., Rothstein, H. and Baldwin, R. (2001) *The Government of Risk: Understanding Risk Regulation Regimes*, Oxford: Oxford University Press.

Jago, R., van der Gaag, A., Stathis, K., Petej, I., Lertvittayakumjorn, P., Krishnamurthy, Y., Gao, Y., Caceres Silva, J., Webster, M., Gallagher, A. and Austin, Z. (2021) 'Use of Artificial Intelligence in Regulatory Decision-making', *Journal of Nursing Regulation*, 12(3): 11–19.

Juntanamalaga, P., Scholz, B., Roper, C. and Happell, B. (2019) '"They Can't Empower Us": The Role of Allies in the Consumer Movement', *International Journal of Mental Health Nursing*, 28(4): 857–66.

Kagan, R.A., Gunningham, N. and Thornton, D. (2011) 'Fear, Duty, and Regulatory Compliance: Lessons from Three Research Projects', in C. Parker and V. Lehmann Nielsen (eds) *Explaining Compliance: Business Responses to Regulation*, Northampton: Edward Elgar Publishing, 37–58.

Katterl, S. (2021a) 'Regulatory Oversight, Mental Health and Human Rights', *Alternative Law Journal*, 46(2): 149–56.

Katterl, S. (2021b) 'The Importance of Motivational Postures to Mental Health Regulators: Lessons for Victoria's Mental Health System in Reducing the Use of Force', *Australasian Psychiatry*, 29(6): 683–86.

Katterl, S. and Maylea, C. (2021) 'Keeping Human Rights in Mind: Embedding the Victorian Charter of Human Rights into the Public Mental Health System', *Australian Journal of Human Rights*, 27(1): 58–77.
Machiavelli, N. (2014) *The Prince and Other Writings*, San Diego: Canterbury Classics.
Macleod, A. and McSherry, B.M. (2006) 'Regulating to Ensure Patient Safety in Hospitals: Towards a Comprehensive Framework', *Journal of Law and Medicine*, 14(2): 228–43.
Marsden, J., Bazzard, D., Breeze, K., De'Ath, A. and Thwaites, A. (2020) *Rapid Literature Review on Effective Regulation: Implications for the Care Quality Commission*. Available www.cqc.org.uk/sites/default/files/20200128%20Effective%20Regulation%20Literature%20Review%20Final%20report.pdf (accessed 28 December 2022).
Marsh, D. (2021) 'Disability Versus Work Health and Safety: A Safe Workplace and the Right to an "Ordinary Life": Commentary on "Regulating Disability Services: The Case of Australia's National Disability Insurance Scheme Quality and Safeguarding System" (Hough 2021)', *Research and Practice in Intellectual and Developmental Disabilities*, 8(2): 111–18.
Maylea, C. (2020) *Witness Statement of Dr Christopher Maylea to the Royal Commission into Victoria's Mental Health System*, 31 March. Available http://rcvmhs.archive.royalcommission.vic.gov.au/Maylea_Chris.pdf (accessed 28 December 2022).
Maylea, C. and Hirsch, A. (2017) 'The Right to Refuse: The Victorian Mental Health Act 2014 and the Convention on the Rights of Persons with Disabilities', *Alternative Law Journal*, 42(2): 149–55.
Maylea, C., Jorgensen, A., Matta, S., Ogilvie, K. and Wallin, P. (2018) 'Consumers' Experiences of Mental Health Advance Statements', *Laws*, 7(2): 22.
Maylea, C., Katterl, S., Johnson, B., Alvarez-Vasquez, S., Hill, N. and Weller, P. (2021) 'Consumers' Experiences of Rights-based Mental Health Laws: Lessons from Victoria, Australia', *International Journal of Law and Psychiatry*, 78: 101737.
Maylea, C. and Ryan, C.J. (2017) 'Decision-making Capacity and the Victorian Mental Health Tribunal', *International Journal of Mental Health and Capacity Law*, 23: 87–108.
McKercher, K.A. (2020) *Beyond Sticky Notes: Co-design for Real: Mindsets, Methods, and Movements*, Sydney: Beyond Sticky Notes.
McSherry, B. (2013) *Managing Fear: The Law and Ethics of Preventive Detention and Risk Assessment*, New York: Routledge.
McSherry, B. (2021) 'Australian Mental Health Laws and Human Rights', in P. Gerber and M. Castan (eds) *Critical Perspectives on Human Rights Law in Australia*, Sydney: Thomson Reuters, 409–32.
McSherry, B. (2023) 'Interdisciplinary Collaboration in the Mental Health Sector: The Role of the Law', in M. Donnelly and B. Kelly (eds) *Routledge Handbook of Mental Health Law*, Abingdon: Routledge.
McSherry, B. and Klauber, S. (2011) 'Who Do I Turn To? Resolving Complaints By Mental Health Consumers and Carers', *Journal of Law and Medicine*, 18(4): 669–76.
McSherry, B. and Maker, Y. (eds) (2021) *Restrictive Practices in Health Care and Disability Settings: Legal, Policy and Practical Responses*, Abingdon: Routledge.
McSherry, B. and Wilson, K. (2015) 'The Concept of Capacity in Australian Mental Health Law Reform: Going in the Wrong Direction?' *International Journal of Law and Psychiatry*, 40: 60–69.

Mental Health Complaints Commissioner (MHCC) (2016) *Our Advisory Council Commences Operation*. Available www-azure.mhcc.vic.gov.au:443/news-and-events/news/our-advisory-council-commences-operation (accessed 28 December 2022).

Mental Health Complaints Commissioner (MHCC) (2018) *Annual Report 2017–2018*. Available www.mhcc.vic.gov.au/annual-reports (accessed 28 December 2022).

Mental Health Complaints Commissioner (MHCC) (2019) *Annual Report 2018–2019*. Available www.mhcc.vic.gov.au/annual-reports (accessed 28 December 2022).

Mental Health Complaints Commissioner (MHCC) (2020a) *Annual Report 2019–2020*. Available www.mhcc.vic.gov.au/annual-reports (accessed 28 December 2022).

Mental Health Complaints Commissioner (MHCC) (2020b) *Our Driven by Lived Experience Framework and Strategy*. Available www.mhcc.vic.gov.au/driven-lived-experience-framework-and-strategy (accessed 28 December 2022).

Mental Health Complaints Commissioner (MHCC) (2021a) *Complaint Stories*. Available www.mhcc.vic.gov.au/common-public-mental-health-complaint-themes-and-stories (accessed 28 December 2022).

Mental Health Complaints Commissioner (MHCC) (2021b) *Individual Service Provider Complaint Report: South West Healthcare*. Available www.simonkatterlconsulting.com/writing/information-obtained-via-freedom-of-information (accessed 28 December 2022).

Mental Health Complaints Commissioner (MHCC) (2021c) *Michelle – Restrictive Interventions and Public Mental Health Services*. Available www.mhcc.vic.gov.au/michelle-restrictive-interventions-public-mental-health-services (accessed 28 December 2022).

Mental Health Complaints Commissioner (MHCC) (2021d) *Annual Report 2020–2021*. Available www.mhcc.vic.gov.au/annual-reports (accessed 28 December 2022).

Mental Health Complaints Commissioner (MHCC) (2022a) *Mental Health Complaints Commissioner (MHCC)*. Available www.mhcc.vic.gov.au (accessed 28 December 2022).

Mental Health Complaints Commissioner (MHCC) (2022b) *MHCC Introduces More Oversight for Seclusion and Restraint*. Available www.mhcc.vic.gov.au/mhcc-introduces-more-oversight-seclusion-and-restraint (accessed 28 December 2022).

Mental Health Complaints Commissioner (MHCC) (2022c) *It's OK to Complain!* Available www.mhcc.vic.gov.au/its-ok-complain (accessed 28 December 2022).

Mental Health Complaints Commissioner (MHCC) (2022d) *Individual Service Reports*. Available www.mhcc.vic.gov.au/individual-service-reports (accessed 28 December 2022).

Mental Health Complaints Commissioner (MHCC) (2022e) *The Mental Health Complaint Commissioner (MHCC) Leadership Group*. Available www.mhcc.vic.gov.au/commissioner (accessed 28 December 2022).

Meredith, S. (2022) 'Nottinghamshire Mental Health Hospital to Remain in Special Measures', *Medscape*, 15 March. Available www.medscape.com/viewarticle/970285 (accessed 28 December 2022).

Minty, R. (2019) 'Involving Civil Society in Preventing Ill Treatment in Detention: Maximising OPCAT's Opportunity for Australia', *Australian Journal of Human Rights*, 25(1): 91–112.

Nielsen, V.L. and Parker, C. (2009) 'Testing Responsive Regulation in Regulatory Enforcement', *Regulation & Governance*, 3(4): 376–99.

O'Donovan, O. and Madden, D. (2018) 'Why Do Medical Professional Regulators Dismiss Most Complaints from Members of the Public? Regulatory Illiteracy, Epistemic Injustice, and Symbolic Power', *Journal of Bioethical Inquiry*, 15(3): 469–78.

Ore, A. (2022) '"You Don't Have a Choice": Victoria's Mental Health Regulator Criticised Over Complaints Handling', *The Guardian*, 28 May. Available www.theguardian.com/society/2022/may/29/you-dont-have-a-choice-victorias-mental-health-regulator-criticised-over-complaints-handling (accessed 28 December 2022).

Ore, A. and Davey, M. (2022) 'No Action Taken Against Victorian Mental Health Services Despite More Than 12,000 Complaints', *The Guardian*, 25 May. Available www.theguardian.com/society/2022/may/26/no-action-taken-against-victorian-mental-health-services-despite-more-than-12000-complaints (accessed 28 December 2022).

ORIMA Research (2020) *Mental Health Complaints Commissioner: 2020 Stakeholder Feedback Surveys.* Available https://static1.squarespace.com/static/6004b9776f0b7e66aaa48c0a/t/62de68254082dc1fe6f3714c/1658742835486/Orima+report+2020+re+feedback+surveys.pdf (accessed 28 December 2022).

Parker, C. and Nielsen, V.L. (2017) 'Compliance: 14 Questions', in P. Drahos (ed) *Regulatory Theory: Foundations and Applications*, Acton: Australian National University Press, 217–32.

Productivity Commission (2020) *Mental Health: Inquiry Report.* Available www.pc.gov.au/inquiries/completed/mental-health/report.

Quick, O. (2017) *Regulating Patient Safety: The End of Professional Dominance?* Cambridge: Cambridge University Press.

Roper, C. (2019) 'Ethical Peril, Violence, and "Dirty Hands": Ethical Consequences of Mental Health Laws', *Journal of Ethics in Mental Health*, 10: 1–17.

Roper, C., Grey, F. and Cadogan, E. (2018) *Co-production: Putting Principles into Practice in Mental Health Contexts.* Available https://healthsciences.unimelb.edu.au/__data/assets/pdf_file/0007/3392215/Coproduction_putting-principles-into-practice.pdf (accessed 28 December 2022).

Royal Commission into Victoria's Mental Health System (2021) *Final Report.* Available https://finalreport.rcvmhs.vic.gov.au/download-report (accessed 28 December 2022).

Sawyer, A.M. (2017) 'Negotiating the Interface Between Risk Management and Human Rights-based Care', in S. Stanford, E. Sharland, N. Rovinelli Heller and J. Warner (eds) *Beyond the Risk Paradigm in Mental Health Policy and Practice*, Basingstoke: Palgrave, 103–20.

Scholz, B., Gordon, S. and Happell, B. (2017) 'Consumers in Mental Health Service Leadership: A Systematic Review', *International Journal of Mental Health Nursing*, 26(1): 20–31.

Smith-Merry, J., Walton, M., Healy, J. and Hobbs, C. (2017) 'Responses By Hospital Complaints Managers to Recommendations for Systemic Reforms By Health Complaints Commissions', *Australian Health Review*, 41(5): 527–32.

Smithson, R., Richardson, E., Roberts, J., Walshe, K., Wenzel, L., Robertson, R., Boyd, A., Allen, T. and Proudlove, N. (2018) *Impact of the Care Quality Commission on Provider Performance: Room for Improvement?* King's Fund. Available www.kingsfund.org.uk/sites/default/files/2018-09/cqc-provider-performance-report-september2018.pdf (accessed 28 December 2022).

Spittal, M.J., Bismark, M.M. and Studdert, D.M. (2019) 'Identification of Practitioners at High Risk of Complaints to Health Profession Regulators', *BMC Health Services Research*, 19(1): 1–11.

Sriram, V., Topp, S.M., Schaaf, M., Mishra, A., Flores, W., Rajasulochana, S.R. and Scott, K. (2018) '10 Best Resources on Power in Health Policy and Systems in Low- and Middle-income Countries', *Health Policy and Planning*, 33(4): 611–21.

Stevens, J. (2015) *Institutional Culture in Detention: A Framework for Preventive Monitoring*, Penal Reform International and the Association for the Prevention of Torture. Available https://cdn.penalreform.org/wp-content/uploads/2016/01/culture-in-detention-2nd-ed-v6.pdf (accessed 28 December 2022).

Therapeutic Goods Administration (2021) *The TGA's Risk Management Approach*. Available www.tga.gov.au/tgas-risk-management-approach (accessed 28 December 2022).

Victoria (2014) *Parliamentary Debates*, Legislative Assembly, 20 February (Mary Wooldridge, Minister for Mental Health).

Victoria Legal Aid (2020) *Your Story, Your Say: Consumers' Priority Issues and Solutions for the Royal Commission into Victoria's Mental Health System*. Available www.legalaid.vic.gov.au/sites/default/files/vla/vla-your-story-your-say-report.pdf (accessed 28 December 2022).

Victorian Auditor-General's Office (2019a) *Access to Mental Health Services: Independent Assurance Report to Parliament*, March. Available www.audit.vic.gov.au/sites/default/files/2019-03/20190321-Mental-Health-Access.pdf (accessed 28 December 2022).

Victorian Auditor-General's Office (2019b) *Child and Youth Mental Health: Independent Assurance Report to Parliament*, June. Available www.audit.vic.gov.au/sites/default/files/2019-06/050619-Youth-Mental-Health_0.pdf (accessed 28 December 2022).

Victorian Equal Opportunity and Human Rights Commission (2019) *Submission to the Royal Commission into Victoria's Mental Health System*. Available www.humanrights.vic.gov.au/static/c9fa1059faa0e6006e5e521348070ac5/Submission-Royal_commission-Mental_health_system-Jul_2019.pdf (accessed 28 December 2022).

Victorian Government (2008) *Review of the Mental Health Act 1986: Consultation Paper – December 2008*, Melbourne: Mental Health and Drugs Division.

Victorian Mental Illness Awareness Council (2020a) *Response to Royal Commission: Issues Affecting Consumers Labelled With 'Serious and Persistent Mental Illness'*. Available www.vmiac.org.au/wp-content/uploads/Response-to-Royal-Commission-request-.pdf (accessed 28 December 2022).

Victorian Mental Illness Awareness Council (2020b) *Seclusion Report #2: Consumer Friendly Information on Seclusion in Victorian Mental Health Services*. Available www.vmiac.org.au/wp-content/uploads/Seclusion-Report-2-2020-1.pdf (accessed 28 December 2022).

Victorian Ombudsman (2020) *Investigation into the Detention and Treatment of Public Housing Residents Arising From a COVID-19 'Hard Lockdown' in July 2020*. Available www.ombudsman.vic.gov.au/our-impact/investigation-reports/investigation-into-the-detention-and-treatment-of-public-housing-residents-arising-from-a-covid-19-hard-lockdown-in-july-2020/ (accessed 28 December 2022).

Victorian Ombudsman (2021) *Public Housing Residents Still Waiting for an Apology, Ombudsman Says*. Available www.ombudsman.vic.gov.au/our-impact/news/public-housing-residents-still-waiting-for-an-apology-ombudsman-says (accessed 28 December 2022).

Walt, G. (1994) *Health Policy: An Introduction to Process and Power*, London: Zed Press.

Weingart, S.N., Pagovich, O., Sands, D.Z., Li, J.M., Aronson, M.D., Davis, R.B., Bates, D.W. and Phillips, R.S. (2005) 'What Can Hospitalized Patients Tell Us About Adverse Events? Learning From Patient-reported Incidents', *Journal of General Internal Medicine*, 20(9): 830–36.

Weller, P., Alvarez-Vasquez, S., Dale, M., Hill, N., Johnson, B., Martin, J., Maylea, C. and Thomas, S. (2019) 'The Need for Independent Advocacy for People Subject to Mental Health Community Treatment Orders', *International Journal of Law and Psychiatry*, 66: 101452.

Wiig, S., Rutz, S., Boyd, A., Churruca, K., Kleefstra, S., Haraldseid-Driftland, C., Braithwaite, J., O'Hara, J. and van de Bovenkamp, H. (2020) 'What Methods are Used to Promote Patient and Family Involvement in Healthcare Regulation? A Multiple Case Study Across Four Countries', *BMC Health Services Research*, 20(1): 1–15.

Windholz, E. (2017) *Governing Through Regulation: Public Policy, Regulation and the Law*, New York: Routledge.

Young, M.B. (2015) *From Commitment to Culture: The 2015 Review of the Charter of Human Rights and Responsibilities Act 2006*. Available https://files.justice.vic.gov.au/2021-06/summary_report_charter_review.pdf (accessed 28 December2022).

15 Standing Up Against the Weight of History

The Importance of Lived Experience in the Mental Health Context

Erandathie Jayakody and Malitha Perera

Introduction

In Australia, the contemporary mental health system is driven by a centuries-old 'deficit narrative' that has created a bias towards a bio-medical, individualistic approach to understanding and responding to people experiencing mental ill-health. As a result, and despite new models of care, multiple inquiries and various attempts to deliver better supports for people with mental ill-health in Australia, many people affected by mental ill-health, trauma and emotional distress remain marginalised and continue to experience poor outcomes.

In this chapter, we will articulate how this persistent 'deficit' narrative positions people living with mental ill-health as 'other' – incapable, unreliable and even dangerous, requiring individual medical intervention and paternalistic laws to deliver on a promise of safety to the individual and community. We will then explore how this narrative remains embedded within aspects of the mental health system today, particularly in (a) mental health law, (b) the treatment of people with lived experience working in the system (as peer workers, advisors and consultants) and (c) the disregard of the social determinants of mental ill-health. For the purposes of this chapter, the 'mental health system' refers to the clinical and community sector that offers mental health services. Although this chapter examines the broader historical mistreatment of people experiencing mental ill-health across the world, we emphasise developments in our own national context in Australia, with reference to major federal and state governmental reports from the past half century. This includes the recent final report of the Royal Commission into Victoria's Mental Health System (2021) (Victorian Royal Commission), on which Professor Bernadette McSherry was a commissioner.

At the conclusion of this chapter, we briefly explore several strategies and points for further consideration in moving beyond the deficit narrative. First, to bring change, we argue for awareness of the ongoing influence of the conceptual history of mental ill-health, including the need to be clear about the values and social norms embedded within contemporary understandings of mental health. Second, we contend that the concept of 'allyship', that is mental health professionals reflecting on their role in upholding a system built on

DOI: 10.4324/9781003350644-19

flawed foundations and working in partnership with people with lived experience as equals (as discussed later), has transformative potential. Finally, we argue that prioritisation and integration of lived experience perspectives in all aspects of the mental health system, including leadership, is the most effective way to challenge the flawed foundations of mental health policy and practice today.

We write from our experiences working in the mental health sector. The lead author (Jayakody) writes from a lived experience perspective with qualifications in law. The second author (Perera) writes from his experience as an occupational therapist with a public health background. We have each worked in the mental health sector for more than ten years in a variety of settings. We are interested in understanding and challenging the social norms that underpin the mental health system. Bernadette McSherry has insisted throughout her scholarship that law – and particularly mental health legislation – should be viewed in its social and policy context. We would like to extend this approach to include the history that shapes contemporary social and political conditions and link it with McSherry's continued emphasis on the inclusion of lived experience perspectives in research. (For discussion of the history of mental health law see also Arstein-Kerslake in Chapter 12 of this volume.)

Flawed Foundations

According to Davidson, Rakfeldt and Strauss (2010: 30), 'few subjects in medicine are so intimately connected with the history and philosophy of the human mind as insanity. There are still fewer, where there are so many errors to rectify, and so many prejudices to remove'.

The evolution of our understanding of mental ill-health is complex. We will briefly look at two conceptualisations of mental ill-health in Western culture throughout history: a supernatural paradigm and a medical paradigm. We will then examine how the stigma and discrimination experienced by people living with mental ill-health today is driven by these paradigms.

The largely pre-modern, supernatural framing conceptualised mental ill-health as a manifestation of something beyond our comprehension and is attributed to something beyond scientific understanding and the laws of nature. This conceptualisation was discussed in a 1993 report by the Australian Human Rights Commission (AHRC), titled *Report of the National Inquiry into the Human Rights of People with Mental Illness* (better known as the 'Burdekin Report' after its lead commissioner, Brian Burdekin). According to the Burdekin Report:

> Literature available from the Middle Ages in Europe indicates that with the spread of Christianity natural causes were lost sight of and madness was seen as a manifestation of possession by the devil or other evil spirits, heresy, or some other form of immorality.
>
> (AHRC 1993: 38)

Foerschner (2010: 1) summarises the conceptual evolution of mental ill-health in ancient civilisations, and notes that:

> In all of these ancient civilizations, mental illness was attributed to some supernatural force, generally a displeased deity. Most ill health, particularly mental ill health, was thought to be afflicted upon an individual or group of peoples as punishment for their trespasses.

As is well covered, the supernatural understanding of 'madness' gave way in the modern era to the 'medicalised paradigm'. By the 'medicalised paradigm', we mean the framing of mental ill-health as a predominantly biological condition – a 'chemical imbalance' requiring alteration, in which medical intervention is prioritised. This conceptual model takes an individualised approach without regard to the broader context of an individual, including social determinants such as housing, employment and relationships. According to Davidson, Rakfeldt and Strauss (2010: 24), in their examination of Philippe Pinel[1] the 18th and 19th century reformer, Pinel 'was establishing mental ill health to be ill health that belonged, like other illness, under the purview of medicine'.[2] He was also 'arguing that recovery was possible' (Davidson, Rakfeldt and Strauss 2010: 24). Pinel's framing of mental ill-health as a medical condition helped establish psychiatry as a discipline within medicine, and this has been firmly cemented in the second half of the 20th century with the rise of the pharmaceutical industry.

The medical framing meant providing interventions to fix or correct the individual condition, with the aim of restoring them to what is deemed medically normal and acceptable. As the 21st century began, Peter Beresford, a British academic with lived experience, stated in an editorial in the *Journal of Mental Health* that 'it is difficult to think of any other area of medicine, let alone thought or practice more broadly, where prevailing understandings have remained so long glued to their nineteenth century origins' (Beresford 2002: 581). The first two decades of this current century have seen increasing recognition of the broad determinants of mental health such as social, economic and physical factors (World Health Organization 2014). However, this 'social model' understanding of mental ill-health arguably remains overshadowed by the centuries old, established medical paradigm.

Both these framings have created a deficit narrative, positioning people experiencing mental ill-health as either lacking something biologically (medical paradigm) or deviating from what is considered natural (supernatural paradigm). In the supernatural framing, where people were perceived to have sinned or otherwise displeased deities, individuals in many Western countries were required to confess and repent, creating immense shame and stigma. Families often hid relatives to avoid stigmatisation by association, while others were ostracised and shunned to the fringes of society and abandoned to fend for themselves. In extreme cases, where mental ill-health was perceived as witchcraft, they may have been subjected to torture to extract a 'confession' and murdered. Through the 15th to 17th centuries, more than 100,000 presumed 'witches' were burned at the stake in Europe (Farreras 2022). The narrative that a person had sinned also made it possible for society to disregard their experiences and views, and in cases where people experiencing mental ill-health were seen as being under demonic influence, they were regarded as particularly violent and unpredictable. This attitude persists into the contemporary era. As Beresford (2002: 581) notes:

> The increasing association of mental health service users with 'dangerousness' and the constant coupling of cruel and murderous activities with 'mental ill health', as though 'bad' is tantamount to mad, is a defining feature of early twenty-first century discussion.

Conceptualising mental-ill-health as a medical condition requiring intervention to correct biological causes such as a 'chemical imbalance' in the brain, framed the individual as having a fundamental impairment. The individual is seen as 'lacking', 'weak' and 'incapable' and needing to be 'cured', 'fixed' or 'taken care of' until they are restored to what is deemed normal or acceptable by medical authorities and society at large. This narrative attributes all explanation and blame to the individual themselves and ignores external factors and determinants that may be contributing to their mental health. People experiencing mental ill-health have been positioned as 'other' to and less than others, devaluing their human experience and fostering prejudice, stigma and discrimination.

As Mary O'Hagan, an international lived experience advocate, former Mental Health Commissioner in New Zealand, and current Executive Director Lived Experience at the Victorian Department of Health, has stated:

> People often say [discrimination] starts with fear, ignorance, misunderstanding, pity or malice. But these are just some of the clothes discrimination wears. Take off all the clothes and we are left with one thing; the devaluing of madness and the entwined assumptions that mad people are full of nonsense and incompetence.
>
> (New Zealand Ministry of Health 2003: 4)

The deficit narrative that underpinned the mental health system of the 19th century still pervades today's mental health systems, including in mental health law. Despite the social changes and greater recognition of human rights and dignity of people living with mental ill-health, they continue to be marginalised and denied the opportunities to lead meaningful, autonomous lives. The deficit narrative perceiving people living with mental ill-health as other – 'weak', 'incapable' and 'violent' – enables the mental health system to continue overlooking their needs and perspectives, creating a power imbalance that privileges the perspectives of professionals.

When the medical model was emerging in the 18th and 19th centuries, there were no groups with sufficient power and authority to challenge this deficit narrative. Doctors and the medical model were at the right place at the right time in history, and the medical model prevailed. Clinicians were put in charge of the asylums and have continued to have authority in the provision of care for people living with mental ill-health throughout the modern era. Credibility and authority remain with medical professionals, and the people living with the decisions they make are often shut out of making them. This dominance of the medical model also fails to consider the collective experiences of people living with mental ill-health, helping to create a view of social determinants of mental health as being beyond the scope of the mental health system. This has created a mental health system that is inherently biased towards a medicalised and individual approach, where the perspectives of people experiencing mental ill-health are marginalised. This marginalisation within service provision also extends outside those spaces, creating a bias against people experiencing mental ill-health being involved in critical areas such as funding, research and governance arrangements.

The mental health system needs to be fundamentally re-oriented to meet the needs of and empower people living with mental ill-health to take their place as full citizens in society. To do this, long-standing biases against people experiencing mental ill-health need to be recognised and actively challenged. There needs to be meaningful recognition of the perspectives and knowledge of people living with mental ill-health, and the growth of the lived experience workforce is an indication that this change is underway.

Whose Lived Experience Is It Anyway?

Recognising the value of lived experience of people living with mental ill-health is radical. It challenges entrenched frameworks, ideas and biases that have prevailed for centuries, and requires a fundamental re-orientation of the mental health system. As Davidson, Rakfeldt and Strauss (2010: 2) note:

> these movements [including the lived experience workforce] indeed [are] a response to centuries of violence and bloodshed in which people with mental ill-health were stoned, burned at the stake, locked in cages, chained to posts and walls, confined to squalid and inhumane living conditions, insulin-shocked, hydro-shocked, electro-shocked and lobotomized.

The idea of 'lived experience' is currently experiencing a historical moment in mental health discourse and beyond. At the tabling of the final report of the Victorian Royal Commission, psychiatrist Patrick McGorry referred to the lived experience of clinicians.[3] Similarly, Australian political commentator Stan Grant in his 2022 'China Tonight' television programme referred to his own lived experience of living in China, while Pete Buttigieg, candidate for the US presidency in the 2020 Democratic presidential primary, referred to the importance of lived experience in the public policy agenda for people with disabilities (Abrams 2019).

So, whose lived experience matters? Don't we all have a lived experience? Commenting on the concept of lived experience in social policy research McIntosh and Wright (2019: 1) state:

> In our own research, we have found the idea of lived experience both intuitive and useful, but have become increasingly perplexed by its potential to seem vacuous or contradictory – what is any experience if it is not lived? . . . Emergent use of 'lived experience' in the social policy literature tends to pick it up as a free-floating notion, untethered from the theoretical and methodological contexts in which it originated, has been deployed and critiqued.

In 'Exploring the Conceptual History of Lived Experience', Rebecca Duke (2022: 11) notes that the notion of lived experience, at least in part, offers a counterpoint to positivism and 'the strictures of the scientific method with its emphasis on "objective" and unbiased observation and analysis'. Lived experience challenges the notion that 'knowledge, understanding and the conceptualisation of experience can only come about via positive affirmation of theories through strict scientific method' (Duke 2022: 11). Lived experience offers a counterpoint through the interpretation and analysis of knowledge gained by the direct experience of a condition.

In the mental health sector, 'lived experience' carries a specific meaning. It is used to recognise a voice and perspective (the 'consumer' perspective) that has been consistently overlooked and refers to the direct experience of people with lived/living experience of mental ill-health and or recovery. This diverse group is increasingly regarded as 'experts by experience'. Sometimes 'people with lived experience' can also refer to the experience of families, friends and carers that support someone experiencing mental ill-health. For the purposes of this chapter, we will be referring to lived/living experience of mental ill-health and or recovery (the consumer perspective) only.

Lived experience workers are those in designated lived experience positions and are required to primarily draw on their lived experience to inform their work. They must have the ability to use their personal experience to support others or to improve and change practices, policies and systems. When using lived experience at a system level, one must be able to 'contextualise their experience in the wider political, social and economic context' (Byrne et al. 2019: 10). This application of knowledge is sometimes referred to as 'lived experience expertise'. Lived experience expertise is increasingly and often informed by a body of knowledge known as Mad Studies. According to Beresford (2020: 1337):

> Mad studies are a field of scholarship, theory, and activism about the lived experiences, history, cultures, and politics about people who may identify as mad, mentally ill, psychiatric survivors, consumers, service users, patients, neurodiverse, and disabled.

Many clinicians have their own direct experience of lived/living experience of mental ill-health and recovery. They are invariably informed by that experience in addition to the expertise they hold in relation to their professional capacity and discipline. This is indeed valuable, but it is different to occupying a designated lived experience position where one draws on their lived experience as the primary source of knowledge to inform their work. Similarly, many lived experience workers have a background in other disciplines, but that expertise is secondary to their lived experience in the context of their work.

For example, the lead author (Jayakody) has a professional background in law, but primarily works from a lived experience perspective. As a person living with an enduring mental health condition, I have an intimate understanding of how mental ill-health pervades every aspect of one's life: distress, stigma, confusion and grief are all part of the experience. This is combined with the experience of finding peer support, navigating mental health services and treatments. A turning point in my journey was accidentally coming across a peer support network. There is a connection, a shared language and safety that peers offer. It helped me make sense of the distress as well as the experience of seeking support, and the stigma and discrimination experienced along the way. The peer support groups provided a much-needed sense of community and gave me hope that there are many creative ways of making this journey. These are the experiences I draw upon to inform my work. My knowledge is not scientific. Over the years I have learnt to translate these experiences into a broader policy context. For example, I am able to translate the helplessness experienced when seeking treatment and the lack of support for navigating treatments, to inform how power dynamics work at a systems level. (See also discussion of hopelessness in Cameron in the Foreword to this volume.) I am able to draw on the experience of differing responses from others when introducing myself as a lawyer or a lived experience worker, to articulate how stigma and power dynamics play out at a societal level. It is the art of bringing critical theory and a social justice lens to the personal experience. The personal becomes the political. My knowledge and skills as a lawyer enable me to complement and elevate my lived experience perspective; however, knowledge and skill as a lawyer are not my primary source of knowledge.

Increasingly, as noted earlier, in our work the phrase 'lived experience' is being used by clinicians to describe their professional experiences. This adoption of the term has been criticised, as this terminology was meant to elevate the marginalised voices of consumers, and its co-option by clinicians is sometimes referred to as the 'colonisation of Lived Experience'. Caution must be exercised with this type of critique, particularly in colonised nations such as Australia where there is a violent history of subjugation of Aboriginal and Torres Strait Islander people associated with the word 'colonisation'. The effect of colonisation is still being felt by Aboriginal and Torres Strait Islander people, and in our view 'colonisation' is inappropriate as an analogy or metaphor in this context, as the co-optation of emancipatory language like 'lived experience' is not comparable to colonisation of country and its ongoing impacts on Aboriginal and Torres Strait Islander people. Nevertheless, we do see it as inappropriate for clinicians to refer to their professional experience as a 'lived experience' perspective.

As evident through this short discussion, the term 'lived experience' in the mental health context is dynamic and can be contested, requiring a nuanced approach. Care must be taken not to create an oppositional 'us' and 'them' binary. It is important to remember that the locus of the discussion on lived experience is the attempt to recognise and elevate a perspective that has been consistently overlooked. In attempting to recognise this perspective and address power imbalances, (see also Katterl and Friel in Chapter 14 of this volume) care must be taken (a) not to deny the lived/living experience of mental ill-health and recovery experienced by clinicians, and (b) not dilute the lived experience perspective of persons with mental ill-health. The lived experience workforce, in requiring a person to primarily work from a lived experience perspective, ensures that that perspective remains prominent and offers a counterpoint to the established, dominant way of thinking.

The Evidence of Bias

'Structural and systemic bias' refers here to biases in the way structures, practices and policies are developed and maintained to deliver a particular outcome. The underinvestment in the mental health system by successive governments reflects the established bias against people experiencing mental ill-health, and their needs continue to be overlooked and marginalised. This view was supported by the Victorian Royal Commission noted previously, which described an 'overlooked and de-prioritised mental health system' in Victoria (Royal Commission into Victoria's Mental Health System 2021: Volume 1, 9). Underinvestment in Australia is consistent with reports from other OECD (2014) countries, in which spending on mental health services has reportedly grown in recent years but is not consistent with the level of need.

Continuous underinvestment has meant not only poor outcomes for people living with mental ill-health but enormous economic cost to society, according to the Productivity Commission (2020) inquiry into the economic impacts of mental ill-health.[4] There have been many reports that quantify the economic cost of mental ill-health, and in 2018–19 the Australian economic cost of mental ill-health and suicide was estimated to be up to AUD$70 billion (Productivity Commission 2020). These economic costs do little to convey the emotional and human cost to an individual and families and the ultimate toll it takes on society. The Productivity Commission (2020: 9) stated that 'not all of this cost is avoidable, but there is considerable scope for Australia to do better'. In commenting on Victoria's low monetary investment in mental health, Kevin Bell AM KC, former Justice of the Supreme Court of Victoria, noted:

> In human rights terms, this is a matter of obligation, not policy. Victoria is not like a developing nation where lack of resources is an explanation for under-investment in health.
>
> (Royal Commission into Victoria's Mental Health System 2021: Summary and Recommendations, 17)

Allan Fels, inaugural chair of Australia's National Mental Health Commission[5] and a commissioner of Victoria's Royal Commission alongside Bernadette McSherry, similarly stated:

> Mental health is still a fairly low priority for governments. From time to time, politicians talk about taking a big initiative, and momentarily, mental health is at the top of the policy pile. Then other matters intervene, and it falls back down. I've seen this happen time and again. Mental health is the poor cousin of health and social welfare and doesn't get priority when budgets are drawn up.
>
> (Fels 2019: 17)

What drives this underinvestment? Why does mental health remain a low priority for governments despite the enormous economic cost? As Bell clearly articulated, this is a matter of human rights and of obligation, yet Australia has continued to deprioritise mental health. Again, the historical precedent of shunning people experiencing mental ill-health to the fringes of society now continues in the form of underinvestment.

However, although increased investment is important, it does not necessarily translate to good outcomes if it does not adequately address the biases discussed previously, including the power imbalance in professional-consumer encounters, and with attention to the broader determinants of mental health. Change is in the wind, at least in Victoria. This longstanding tendency to underinvest in mental health is being addressed through a new Victorian mental health levy and a dedicated revenue mechanism for funding mental health services, as recommended by the Victorian Royal Commission. Guaranteeing investment through a special levy is one way of addressing this structural bias in mental health funding. However, systemic issues of power imbalance and bias need to be addressed if people living with mental ill-health are to truly benefit from this change. (See also Donnelly in Chapter 2 of this volume.)

The Royal Commission into Victoria's Mental Health System (2021) also recommended that the Victorian Government establish a Mental Health and Wellbeing Cabinet Subcommittee chaired by the Victorian Premier (who is the head of the Victorian state government) to monitor outcomes to inform planning and policy decisions. The Victorian Royal Commission's intention was to keep mental health a priority by keeping it close to the locus of power and control in government. It remains to be seen if this policy structure will remain with successive governments, and history has demonstrated that attempts to prioritise mental health through reporting structures have not been sustained. For example, when the National Mental Health Commission was initially established, it reported directly to the Prime Minister of Australia (the head of the Australian federal government) and federal Cabinet, signalling the prioritisation of mental health. However, this Commission was moved to the Australian Department of Health after a few years and distanced from the centre of power (Fels 2019: 25).

The biases inherent in the practices and policies of the mental health system are best demonstrated through how the lived experience workforce is perceived. For the lead author (Jayakody), it has been all too common to hear disparaging comments about the workforce in over a decade of work. Examples include comments such as: 'this is a very complex role. It is not suitable for someone with a lived experience'; 'people with a lived experience should be given part-time jobs not full-time jobs'; 'peer workers have high turnover rates'; and 'peer workers become unwell'. The implication is clear, that lived experience workers are 'incapable' and 'unpredictable'. These and other such statements were and continue to be made in the presence of lived experience workers. In contrast, if such statements are made regarding race or gender, there is increasing recognition of the prejudice and fallacy of such statements. For example, statements such as 'you can't do this job because you are a woman' or 'this job is not suited to you because you are a migrant' are understood as prejudicial and unacceptable. Both authors are first generation migrants from Sri Lanka, and this is evident in our skin colour, yet these authors have rarely encountered outright racial prejudicial statements in a work setting. The racial prejudice is subtle. However, when the lead author (Jayakody) has clearly identified they have a lived experience and present as a lived experience worker, disparaging statements are made constantly. There have also been instances where the lead author has been told that they are not suited for full time work (because of their lived experience) and denied learning and development opportunities (because of their role as a lived experience worker). The statements about lived experience workers come from the assumption that people with lived experience are unreliable and incompetent because of their mental health challenges. These are the same views as those visible throughout history about people experiencing mental ill-health.

These statements rarely get challenged in today's mental health system. If such statements are challenged, it is invariably by lived experience workers themselves. The fact that such statements are deemed insignificant and not typically called out demonstrates the pervasiveness of the stigma and suggests that it often remains 'hidden' in plain sight. It is demonstrative of the entrenched power imbalances of a mental health system that continues to devalue lived experience perspectives. (See also Katterl and Friel in Chapter 14 of this volume.)

Without recognition of the prejudice, there is an inherent tendency to continue narratives that perpetuate stigma. The conversation is framed around the person's ill-health or deficit rather than the system failure. Examples of systemic problems include the lack of peer supervision, inadequate learning and development opportunities and working in isolation (that is, being the only lived experience worker in the team). Research suggests there is high burnout of lived experience workers (Byrne et al. 2019), which is often interpreted by the sector as the incapability of lived experience workers to cope. There is little regard for inadequate training and hostile working environments that indicate a lack of value in lived experience expertise. Instead, the narrative is simply that that *lived experience workers can't cope.*

This contrasts with the way other workers are described in the mental health system. For example, in 2019 Professor Gordon Parker AO, Scientia Professor of Psychiatry at the University of New South Wales and former Executive Director of the Black Dog Institute, spoke about the shortfalls of the New South Wales public mental health system and noted that junior psychiatrists are leaving the sector:

> I see so many young psychiatrists enter the public sector with a genuine commitment and wish to help those with serious psychiatric problems but who become profoundly disillusioned.
>
> (Aubusson 2019)

The narrative here is not about the capability of the individual; instead, it is about the failure of the system and environmental factors. Likewise, one news report in the *Sydney Morning Herald* reported the situation by noting that 'the "psychiatric breakdown of the public system" is driving away overburdened psychiatrists' (Aubusson 2019). Words like 'disillusioned' and 'overburdened' are used to describe psychiatrists leaving the system, while terms such as 'can't cope' and 'job is too complex' are often used to describe lived experience workers who leave the mental health system.

In a speech titled, 'This is Water', US novelist David Foster Wallace warns of the danger of pervasive phenomena that remain unacknowledged, sometimes described as the 'default setting'. Wallace (2005: 4) begins the speech with a parable to demonstrate his point:

> There are these two young fish swimming along, and they happen to meet an older fish swimming the other way, who nods at them and says, 'Morning, boys. How's the water?' And the two young fish swim on for a bit, and then eventually one of them looks over at the other and goes, 'What the hell is water?'

The inability to recognise and call out false statements in the mental health system is reflective of a default setting that disregards and marginalises the experiences of people experiencing mental ill-health. This has resulted in practices and policies that are biased in favour of the medical framing of mental ill-health as a deficit in the individual.

The default setting of marginalising the lived experience-perspective was evident in the way the Victorian Government established the organisation, Mental Health Reform Victoria. Mental Health Reform Victoria was established in 2020 in response to the interim report recommendations of the Victorian Royal Commission. The Victorian Government appointed a chief executive officer and a 'Senior Advisor, Clinical' upon the establishment of Mental Health Reform Victoria. However, there was no lived experience appointee at the time of this organisational establishment. Lived Experience Advisors were employed only *after* Mental Health Reform Victoria was set up, and they were not employed at an executive level. This setting up of Mental Health Reform Victoria with the absence of a lived experience appointee was ironic, as it was in the same interim report in which the Victorian Royal Commission was unequivocal on the value of lived experience. Two of the ten recommendations in the interim report were about recognising and promoting the lived experience perspective (Royal Commission into Victoria's Mental Health System 2019).

It is interesting to note that in the final report of the Victorian Royal Commission, the commissioners were more explicit in their recommendations; for example, they recommended a requirement to have 'Lived Experience Commissioners' at the new Mental Health Commission and 'Lived Experience Members' in the regional boards (Royal Commission into Victoria's Mental Health System 2021). The Commission evidently saw enforcement of obligations on the mental health system concerning lived experience leadership as one crucial way to combat structural bias. Without an obligation, the mental health system so easily reverts backs to its 'default setting': the centuries old habit of dismissing and marginalising the experiences of people living with mental ill-health.

A Narrow View: Expanding the Frame From the Individual to Society

Bias in favour of the medical framing has also meant that the responsibility for addressing the broad determinants of mental ill-health and distress is placed outside the scope of the mental health system. Often there is little intersection between the mental health system and other systems that address social determinants. Some mental health practitioners view their role as alleviating the distress of an individual through individual treatment and therapy – addressing broader determinates is not considered within their remit. This is a narrow view that is the result of the medical and individualistic approach. Rather, a mental health system which takes into consideration broad determinants and addresses them is required.

Australia's *Mental Health and Suicide Prevention Plan – Final Report*, produced by a House of Representatives Select Committee on Mental Health

Suicide Prevention (2021: 280), concluded that 'evidence to the inquiry suggests clinical interventions, in the absence of broader measures to address social determinants of health, cannot resolve growing mental health concerns in Australia'. It also described the mental health system as operating in 'a palliative' manner (House of Representatives Select Committee on Mental Health Suicide Prevention 2021: 281). This approach, once again, reflects the strong bias towards a medicalised model where mental ill-health is constructed primarily as a biological deficit of the individual for which outcomes relate to reduction in symptoms and distress. Positive outcomes are more than the reduction of symptoms – it is about enabling people to live an autonomous, meaningful life with or without symptoms and distress. This cannot be achieved without explicitly addressing the broader determinants. It is well established that mental ill-health is interlinked with factors such as housing, education, finances and community connections (World Health Organization 2014). The mental health system must address this at the macro level. This includes creating services, roles and incentives to address broad determinants as a core function of the mental health system alongside mental health responses such as treatment and wellbeing supports.

The lead author's (Jayakody) experience of being a tribunal member at the Mental Health Tribunal in Victoria provides an insight into the dynamics of the mental health system. People who are subject to compulsory treatment often say what they want is to 'get on with my life', 'I want to get a job' and 'I want to spend time with friends'. The response from the treating team invariably is that the person is not ready or has not progressed far enough in their recovery journey to begin addressing these needs. The focus of the supports is on addressing the deficits of the person rather than addressing the other contributing factors. There are also many instances of people on compulsory treatment orders being discharged from hospital into temporary accommodation such as motels. This is a prime example of a mental health system operating in a palliative manner. In this example, housing is a critical factor in achieving a good outcome and must be part of the mental health service response. Unfortunately, services are not centred on addressing such determinants.

Another example is the second author's (Perera) experience of working with a young person who was experiencing mental ill-health. The young person had accessed two different mental health services over the past year. Although the services sought to address the young person's distress through medical and psychological interventions, what was also helpful was a referral to a financial counselling service that assisted with longstanding financial difficulties. This addressed an underlying contributor to their distress.

An effective mental health system should be required to address such broader determinants. Provision of, or referral to, legal, housing or financial services may meet these needs. For these services to be considered a critical element, the system needs to be built on a different foundation that not only conceptualises mental ill-health as intrinsically linked to social and economic determinants, but also addresses these determinants by providing holistic support that enables full and effective participation in society.

The Productivity Commission (2020) observed that housing, employment services and services that help the person integrate into the community can be as or more important than health care in supporting a person's recovery. Out of the five priority reforms identified by the Productivity Commission, only one related to improving people's experience with mental health care. The other four acknowledged the broader determinants as they related to prevention, experiences beyond the health system, workplaces (called out in addition to the other services beyond the health system), and incentives and accountability for improved outcomes. The Productivity Commission (2020: Volume 1, 7) described barriers that lead to poor outcomes as:

> [A] narrow view of people seeking treatment and support – mental health services are often based on an incomplete picture of what people are seeking, failing to look beyond the symptoms being presented to work out what help an individual needs to recover and remain well in the longer term, and how to deliver that help most effectively.

Reflecting on the evolution of mental ill-health and the resulting power dynamics, these findings are unsurprising, despite well-established evidence of the relationship between broad social determinants and mental ill-health.

Bias in the Law

Contemporary mental health law is likewise driven by the historical prejudices noted previously. (See also Arstein-Kerslake in Chapter 12 of this volume.) The law is rooted in a deficit narrative that suggests a person with mental ill-health is incapable and dangerous.

Mental health law gives medical professionals power to detain and restrain people experiencing mental ill-health, thus restricting their liberty and undermining their autonomy in a manner that would be illegal in other circumstances. This is justified on the basis of treatment and a promise of safety for the individual and the community. The law is driven by a deficit and medicalised narrative that drives a 'we know best' approach. The root of paternalism is based on 'parens patriae'. As Gooding (2014: 7) articulates:

> The 'parens patriae' power, translating literally as parent of the country, justifies detaining and/or treating a person compulsorily in his or her best interests on the basis of the person not being able to look after his or her own interests.

In contemporary times, 'parens patriae' is typically identified with family law whereby the state acts as the parent of any child or individual needing protection. The assumption behind this paternalistic approach is that people experiencing mental ill-health are, in similar fashion to a child, incapable of making informed decisions about their own life. This then gives authority for the medical professionals to step into the role of 'parent' – to make decisions for people experiencing mental ill-health, and to restrict individual liberty and undermine autonomy, thus disregarding the views of the individual. The role of procedural safeguard mechanisms, like the Mental Health Tribunal in Victoria, is to confirm or reject the role of the medical professionals in their role as the 'parent'.

With increased recognition of human rights, mental health law has been somewhat reoriented to promote the person's autonomy and self-determination, but the entrenched power imbalances against those interests remain. Under Victoria's new *Mental Health and Wellbeing Act 2022* (which will come into effect in September 2023), recommended by the aforementioned Victorian Royal Commission, there is no obligation on the Mental Health Tribunal to provide a 'Statement of Reasons' for its decisions. A 'Statement of Reasons', as the name suggests, is a formal note that articulates why the tribunal made a particular decision. The burden of seeking such a statement is on the individual. In 2020–21, only 238 Statements of Reasons were requested in comparison to the 8,212 Treatment Orders made during that period (Mental Health Tribunal 2021). An agency that exercises power by restricting individual liberty must be held accountable. Instead of creating an obligation on the Mental Health Tribunal, it is framed as a right of the individual. This, in our view, is deeply unjust. Statements of Reasons for decisions will be resource intensive; however, they will create transparency and accountability. Notably, there are other adjudicative bodies in Victoria where there is also no obligation to provide a written Statement of Reasons. For example, the Magistrates Court where the majority of criminal cases are heard, or certain matters before the Victorian Civil and Administrative Tribunal, such as those cases on the Residential Tenancies List and the Guardianship List. However, unlike residential tenancies, mental health legislation involves a significant loss of liberty as it permits people to be detained in hospital and treated with psychiatric drugs without their consent, and unlike the criminal law this occurs where they have not been found guilty of any crime. The lack of a Statement of Reasons for the Guardianship List, however, is objectionable for the same reasons as it is in the mental health context. Further, persons subject to treatment orders may not understand why they are being detained and a Statement of Reasons could help them reflect on their recovery journey and understand what occurred at a later date. Published Statements of Reasons will also create (non-binding) legal precedents and will add to mental health law jurisprudence.

As noted earlier, the prejudicial belief that people experiencing mental ill-health are violent and dangerous also underpins mental health law. The compulsory treatment criteria under the *Mental Health and Wellbeing Act 2022* (Vic) includes the requirement that involuntary intervention is required to prevent a serious deterioration in the person's mental health or physical health, or serious harm to the person or to another person (section 143).[6] The premise here is that detention will keep the individual and the community safe, and the continuation of the narrative that people experiencing mental ill-health are violent justifies their detention for the good of others.

The promise of safety is very much driven by the public discourse reflecting the prejudicial values of our society. Safety of people experiencing mental ill-health, workers and the community are often deemed paramount, even if this involves trauma to persons with mental ill-health. For example, when the Victorian Government announced its intention to work towards ending restraint and seclusion within a decade, (see also Chesterman in Chapter 5 and Freckelton in Chapter 6 of this volume) the immediate response from the Victorian branch of the Australian Medical Association (AMA) was to ridicule and dismiss the idea:

> The plan is right up there with pink elephants flying.
>
> How are we meant to manage these people if we can't use medical and chemical restraint?
>
> The safety of healthcare workers needs to be paramount when changing laws dealing with unpredictable and sometimes psychotic patients, but that has not been done in this case.
>
> (Illanbey 2022)

This response emphasises the paramount importance of the safety of health care workers, and there is no mention of the safety of the person with mental ill-health. The AMA branch also uses dehumanising language referring to 'these people' rather than recognising that persons are in distress and are in need of compassionate care. We contrast the AMA's response with the response by Forensicare (2022):[7]

> We do not agree with recent commentary that reducing or eliminating restrictive practices will increase risks to the community and health care workers. However, we recognise the elimination of restrictive interventions is a challenge and will require substantial investment and change across our mental health and wellbeing systems.

This latter response is not driven by a narrative of paternalism or prejudice but underpinned by a belief that people experiencing mental ill-health deserve and can be provided with care in a compassionate and humane way. They also acknowledge that the change can be challenging and requires substantial investment to reduce the systemic issues which are related to use of restrictive practices.

When the approach to ensure safety for all is driven by the paternalistic narrative, the default position is to respond through restriction of liberty, as one seemingly would towards a child. Instead, if the mental health system is driven by a different narrative wherein this is a person in distress needing support, the instinctive and default response would be to ask how services can provide compassionate and humane care that will alleviate distress and ensure the safety of all. Such an approach would reduce the need for the high rates of compulsory treatment in Victoria.

The change can only be driven by different social norms and a different narrative. As the Royal Commission into Victoria's Mental Health System (2019: Summary, 5) stated in its Interim Report:

> As Victorians, we all bear some responsibility for the system's failings. Inclusive, tolerant, and supportive communities play a vital role in nurturing good mental health and wellbeing, yet it is evident that stigma and discrimination persist.

Moving Forward With Allyship

There needs to be a renewed awareness of the ongoing influence of the conceptual history of mental ill-health in contemporary times. As individuals and as a collective, we must begin to question the fundamental values that drive the discourse on mental health and how people living with mental ill-health are perceived. It is only with this kind of examination that we can begin to change the discourse on mental health and challenge the flawed foundation of the mental health system. This could include, for example, challenging the statements that are made about lived experience workers, questioning the public discourse on the association of mental ill-health and violence, and examining the broader social determinants of ill-health rather than exclusively responding to the deficit of the individual. These types of actions have been pursued in decades of sustained activism by people with lived experience. However, given the historical context noted previously and entrenched power imbalances, true transformation can only be achieved through allyship.

Allyship requires individuals to question their own role in upholding a system built upon such flawed foundations. Allyship does not mean 'helping' people with lived experience – individuals cannot be 'guided by an altruistic urge to save or fix people' (Nixon 2019: 5). People who maintain authority through sustained bias and marginalisation must be open to being challenged and sitting with this discomfort, rather than be defensive and becoming ashamed of that power. This can be confronting, and it requires humility. Margaret Grigg, CEO of Forensicare, recently talked about this discomfort (at a workshop for the Consumers Leading in Governance Program on 17 May 2022 in Melbourne, Victoria). She said, 'it is very difficult to sit and be told that what I was taught as best practice actually harmed people'.

Allyship is about services and policymakers working in partnership with people with lived experience to reflect, challenge and dismantle the existing foundations to ensure the mental health system works from a different starting point. It is about recognising people with lived experience as a valued and equal partner. This requires more than expanding the lived experience workforce – it is about integrating lived experience expertise at leadership levels such as in governance, regulation and funding decisions. Conscious effort is required to prioritise lived experience expertise in the way the system operates. Prioritisation of lived experience does not mean creating a new hierarchy or merely flipping the existing power imbalances in the mental health system, but is about making a conscious and consistent effort to integrate lived experience expertise in the system. Without this prioritisation, history has shown that lived experience expertise will continue to be marginalised.

Conclusion

The science fiction writer Ursula Le Guin once said that 'all privileged lives are based on injustice' (Freedman 2008: 127). In the mental health context, the system is biased against lived experience perspectives and it privileges the medicalised and individualised interpretation of mental ill-health with little regard to social determinants. Legal frameworks are paternalistic and reinforce societal fears based on several fallacies about distress and mental ill-health. Mainstream public discourse continues the centuries-old narrative that people experiencing mental ill-health are illogical, incompetent and dangerous. What would it take us to reorientate ourselves? Do we have the courage?

Notes

1 Philippe Pinel (1745–1826) was a French physician who is sometimes regarded as the father of psychiatry. Pinel was remarkably ahead of his time as he did not view mental ill-health as a bestial or demonic condition. His approach was influenced by the experience of losing a close friend to mental ill-health.
2 It is worth noting that Pinel's thinking was that recovery from mental ill-health was brought about primarily by psychological, rather than physical, means.
3 The final report of the Royal Commission into Victoria's Mental Health System was tabled in a special sitting of the Victorian Parliament on 2 March 2021.
4 The Productivity Commission is the Australian Government's independent research and advisory body on a range of economic, social and environmental issues affecting the welfare of Australians.
5 Australia's National Mental Health Commission is a federal government agency that gives independent policy advice and evidence to the Australian Government on ways to improve Australia's mental health and suicide prevention system.
6 Note that the Victorian Government announced in 2022 an independent inquiry to review the compulsory treatment criteria with the view to reducing rates of compulsory treatment orders. The panel is chaired by Justice Shame Marshall AM, and the lead author (Jayakody) is a member of the inquiry panel. The independent report is expected to be tabled at the end of 2023.
7 Forensicare (Victorian Institute of Forensic Mental Health) is the state-wide specialist provider of forensic mental health services in Victoria. Forensicare is the only agency in Victoria that provides clinical forensic mental health services which span all components of the mental health and criminal justice sectors – giving Forensicare a unique perspective on mental health and public safety issues.

References

Legislation

Mental Health and Wellbeing Act 2022 (Vic).

Books, Journal Articles and Other Texts

Abrams, A. (2019) 'Presidential Candidate Pete Buttigieg Announces His Policy Agenda for People with Disabilities', *TIME*, 2 November. Available https://time.com/5716620/pete-buttigieg-disability-policy-agenda/ (accessed 21 December 2022).

Aubusson, K. (2019) 'Overburdened Psychiatrists Abandon "Broken" Public System', *Sydney Morning Herald*, 29 May. Available www.smh.com.au/healthcare/overburdened-psychiatrists-abandon-broken-public-system-20190528-p51s3j.html (accessed 21 December 2022).

Australian Human Rights Commission (1993) *Report of the National Inquiry Concerning the Human Rights of People with Mental Illness*. Available https://humanrights.gov.au/our-work/publications/report-national-inquiry-human-rights-people-mental-illness (accessed 21 December 2022).

Beresford, P. (2002) 'Thinking About "Mental Health": Towards a Social Model', *Journal of Mental Health*, 11(6): 581–84.

Beresford, P. (2020) ' "Mad", Mad Studies and Advancing Inclusive Resistance', *Disability & Society*, 35(8): 1337–42.

Byrne, L., Wang, Y., Roennfeldt, H., Chapman, M. and Darwin, L. (2019) *Queensland Framework for the Development of the Mental Health Lived Experience Workforce*, Queensland Mental Health Commission. Available www.qmhc.qld.gov.au/documents/qmhclivedexperienceworkforceframeworkwebpdf (accessed 21 December 2022).

Davidson, L., Rakfeldt, J. and Strauss, J. (2010) *The Roots of the Recovery Movement in Psychiatry: Lessons Learned*, Chichester: John Wiley & Sons.

Duke, R. (2022) 'Exploring the Conceptual History of Lived Experience' (forthcoming manuscript).

Farreras, I.G. (2022) 'History of Mental Illness', in R. Biswas-Diener and E. Diener (eds) *Noba Textbook Series: Psychology*, Champaign: DEF Publishers. Available http://noba.to/65w3s7ex (accessed 21 December 2022).

Fels, A. (2019) *Tough Customer: Chasing a Better Deal for Battlers*, Melbourne: Melbourne University Publishing.

Foerschner, A.M. (2010) 'The History of Mental Illness: From "Skull Drills" to "Happy Pills" ', *Inquiries Journal*, 2(9): 1–4.

Forensicare (2022) *Forensicare Position Statement: Eliminating Restrictive Interventions in Mental Health Services*. Available www.forensicare.vic.gov.au/position-statement-eliminating-restrictive-interventions-in-mental-health-services/ (accessed 21 December 2022).

Freedman, C.H. (ed) (2008) *Conversations with Ursula K. Le Guin*, Jackson: University Press of Mississippi.

Gooding, P.M. (2014) 'Change and Continuity in Mental Health Law: The Long Road to the United Nations Convention on the Rights of Persons with Disabilities', *Web Journal of Current Legal Issues*, 20(3): 1–24.

House of Representatives Select Committee on Mental Health Suicide Prevention (2021) *Mental Health and Suicide Prevention Plan – Final Report*. Available www.aph.gov.au/Parliamentary_Business/Committees/House/Former_Committees/Mental_Health_and_Suicide_Prevention/MHSP/Report (accessed 21 December 2022).

Illanbey, S. (2022) 'Doctors Warn Andrews Government's Mental Health Reforms Flawed and Put Lives at Risk', *The Age*, 13 July. Available www.theage.com.au/

national/victoria/doctors-warn-andrews-government-s-mental-health-reforms-flawed-and-put-lives-at-risk-20220708-p5b039.html (accessed 21 December 2022).

McIntosh, I. and Wright, S. (2019) 'Exploring What the Notion of "Lived Experience" Offers for Social Policy Analysis', *Journal of Social Policy*, 48(3): 449–67.

Mental Health Tribunal (Victoria) (2021) *Mental Health Tribunal 2020–21 Annual Report*. Available www.mht.vic.gov.au/annual-reports (accessed 21 December 2022).

Ministry of Health (New Zealand) (2003) *Like Minds, Like Mine: National Plan 2003–2005 – Project to Counter Stigma and Discrimination Associated with Mental Illness*. Available www.likeminds.org.nz/assets/National-Plans/1plan2003-05.pdf (accessed 21 December 2022).

Nixon, S.A. (2019) 'The Coin Model of Privilege and Critical Allyship: Implications for Health', *BMC Public Health*, 19(1): 1–13.

Organisation for Economic Co-operation and Development (OECD) (2014) *Making Mental Health Count: The Social and Economic Costs of Neglecting Mental Health Care*. Available www.oecd.org/health/making-mental-health-count-9789264208445-en.htm (accessed 21 December 2022).

Productivity Commission (2020) *Inquiry Report – Mental Health*. Available www.pc.gov.au/inquiries/completed/mental-health/report (accessed 21 December 2022).

Royal Commission into Victoria's Mental Health System (2019) *Interim Report*. Available http://rcvmhs.archive.royalcommission.vic.gov.au/interim-report.html (accessed 21 December 2022).

Royal Commission into Victoria's Mental Health System (2021) *Final Report*. Available https://finalreport.rcvmhs.vic.gov.au/ (accessed 21 December 2022).

Wallace, D.F. (2005) 'This is Water', *Kenyon Alumni Magazine*, 5 November. Available http://bulletin-archive.kenyon.edu/x4280.html (accessed 21 December 2022).

World Health Organization (2014) *Social Determinants of Mental Health*. Available https://apps.who.int/iris/bitstream/handle/10665/112828/9789241506809_eng.pdf (accessed 21 December 2022).

Afterword

Bernadette McSherry

When the editors told me of their plans to put together a collection of essays drawing on my academic work over the past three decades, I was both delighted and a little daunted. What themes would emerge? What publications would spark debate? It has been fascinating to read all the contributions to this volume from colleagues and friends and to know that scholarship on issues in mental health, disability and criminal law is in such good hands.

I am honoured by the dedication shown by my former doctoral students, Piers Gooding, Jamie Walvisch and Kay Wilson and former postdoctoral research fellow, Yvette Maker, in bringing this collection together. They are all not only fine researchers but wonderful people who I'm sure will inspire many more students, scholars and advocates in the future. My thanks to them, to Andrew Simon-Butler and Sandra Pyke for their research assistance and indexing, to Duncan Cameron for his generous Foreword, to all those involved at Routledge and of course to all the contributors.

This thought-provoking collection has prompted me to reflect on the legislative, policy and practical changes that have occurred over the course of my career. When I began tutoring in law, the internet and mobile phones were still being developed and the height of technology was using overhead projectors to beam text written on transparent sheets onto lecture room walls. The world is now a very different place, but the issues that were being discussed at conferences in the early '90s are mostly echoed in this edited collection.

In 1994, I reported on the XXth International Congress on Law and Mental Health for the *Journal of Law and Medicine* (McSherry 1994a). The plenary session was devoted to the allocation of resources and priority setting in treatment and care of individuals with diagnoses of mental illness. A common refrain throughout the conference was the need for resources to support positive reforms across mental health and criminal justice settings. That refrain led to my positing that:

> The problems associated with the mental health system due to declining morale and conditions of work cannot be solved by the formalistic

DOI: 10.4324/9781003350644-20

> rigidity of the law. Fundamentally it is a question of resources and the organisation of social priorities and education.
>
> (McSherry 1994b: 207)

There remains a substantive divide between what the law may require and what happens in day-to-day practice in mental health, disability and criminal justice settings. For example, as Kathleen Jones (1980: 11) has pointed out, the 'world of the psychiatric ward is a long way from the world of the courts'. Several chapters in this volume eruditely explore this point and provide suggestions for how best to ensure the gap between law and practice is narrowed.

At the International Congress in 1994, syndrome evidence and expert evidence was a hot topic. 'False memory syndrome' and 'battered women syndrome' may have had their day, but there was also a Congress session on predicting 'dangerousness' for the purpose of detaining those found not criminally responsible on the grounds of 'insanity'. That latter topic was also central to a conference held in Vancouver that I reported on the following year (McSherry 1995). As several chapters explore, risk assessment and preventive detention are still very much a concern in many settings. Indeed, the issue of how to identify the risk of future harm through the use of professional judgment and AI-assisted technology has expanded from focusing on those found not criminally responsible, to post-sentence preventive detention regimes, as well as into civil schemes for compulsory treatment.

While teaching and research in criminal law and justice was well established when I began my career, scholarship in mental health and disability laws was less developed, at least in Australasia. The United Nations *Convention on the Rights of Person with Disabilities* had provided a significant framework for questioning why we have laws that enable compulsory detention and treatment of people with disabilities and many of the chapters use this framework for (re)-assessing the scope of state interference in this regard.

Perhaps the most welcome change over the past decade at least is the growing importance placed on lived experience perspectives in research, policy and practice and it is gratifying to see such perspectives expressed throughout this collection. The development of disability studies led to the reframing of disability within academia away from a focus on 'impaired' individuals toward a concept of disability that explored social and cultural processes (Mallett and Runswick-Cole 2014: chapter 1). This shift in focus reflected the refrain 'nothing about us, without us' which became central to disability activism in the 1990s.

The Royal Commission into Victoria's Mental Health System, of which I was one of four commissioners, was keen to ensure 'a central role for people with lived experience of mental illness or psychological distress and families, carers and supporters in the ongoing design and development of the system, and in the delivery of services' (Royal Commission into Victoria's Mental

Health System 2021: Volume 3, 3) and made several recommendations in this regard. While these recommendations are in the process of being implemented, there is much to be learnt from disability activism in ensuring the full and effective participation of people with lived experience from diverse cultural backgrounds in shaping mental health, aged care and criminal justice settings.

Too often, systems are skewed in favour of the privileged and powerful, but it was heartening through the Royal Commission process to learn of healing practices in social and emotional wellbeing services in Aboriginal communities and the range of other community-based activities promoting good health and wellbeing. Those instances of people doing it for themselves I believe supports a spirit of optimism that positive reforms can be 'turbocharged', as my former colleague Duncan Cameron has termed it in his Foreword. As the poet Percy Bysshe Shelley wrote in his Ode to the West Wind (1820):

> *If Winter comes, can Spring be far behind?*

References

Jones, K. (1980) 'The Limitations of the Legal Approach to Mental Health', *International Journal of Law and Psychiatry*, 3(1): 1–15.

Mallett, R. and Runswick-Cole, K. (2014) *Approaching Disability: Critical Issues and Perspectives*, Oxford: Routledge.

McSherry, B. (1994a) 'The XXth International Congress on Law and Mental Health', *Journal of Law and Medicine*, 2: 91–92.

McSherry, B. (1994b) 'Human Rights and Mental Illness: The Legal Framework', *Journal of Law and Medicine*, 1: 205–7.

McSherry, B. (1995) 'Report on Mental Disorder and Criminal Justice Conference', *Journal of Law and Medicine*, 3: 102–4.

Royal Commission into Victoria's Mental Health System (2021) *Final Report*. Available https://finalreport.rcvmhs.vic.gov.au (accessed 22 December 2022).

Index

active monitoring 248
advocacy 62–3
Age Concern New Zealand 119; elder abuse and 114, 120–1, 132; Elder Abuse Response service 120–1, 123, 132; explanation of statistics of 121–3
aged care: closed environments in 114–15, 131
aged care, Australia: chemical restraint in 80, 81, 95–6; Commonwealth powers related to substitute decision-makers 83; decisions on 'personal' matters 82–3; physical restraint in 80; Quality of Care Principles 79–81, 83; restrictive practices in 77, 79–81, 84–5; restrictive practices substitute decision-makers 81–3
aged care cases, New Zealand: *Director of Proceedings v Oceania Care Co Ltd* 118, 119; insights from 119; *Opinion 17HDC00352 2020* 118–19; rarity of 120
Aged Care Commissioner (New Zealand) 116, 120, 130, 132
aged care, New Zealand: cases (*see* aged care cases, New Zealand); *Convention on the Rights of Persons with Disabilities* and 125–6; Health and Disability Commissioner rights breaches reported 117; institutional abuse data 121; lessons from Australia 126–30; staffing issues in 120
Aged Care Quality and Safety Commission (Australia): notifiable incidents 129
algorithmic risk management 244
algorithms: risk algorithms 195; risk assessment and 245, 247
allyship 314–15
arbitrary detention: core principles of (*see* core principles of arbitrary detention); elderly people in secure rest home care, New Zealand (*see* detention of elderly people in secure rest home care, New Zealand); mental health field 140; 'necessary implication' test 146; 'principle of legality' and 145–6; procedures and 151; purposive approach 145; rights-driven approach 145
aural evidence: ability to assess 206
automated decision-making 245, 251, 254, 256
automated or AI-enabled technology 8, 245, 249; 'allure of certainty' and 251–2; bias and 246, 258; cost benefit 253; dynamic factors and 250; ethical principles for assessing 254–5; freedom from unlawful interference with privacy, family, home and correspondence and 258; human rights and 254–7; potential avenues for research 258–60; preventive detention and 252, 256; promotion and protection of rights by 257; right to be free from arbitrary arrest and detention and 258; right to fair hearing and presumed innocence and 258; right to highest attainable quality of physical and mental health and 258–9; right to human dignity and 259; structured professional judgment and 253–4, 260; transparency 251–2

bias: evidence of in mental health systems 305–9; forensic mental health risk assessment and 250–1; mental health law 311–14; risk assessment instruments and 196; use of automated or AI-enabled technology and 246, 258
biometric monitoring 244, 246, 247, 249, 261
blameworthy conduct 197
blind jurors 205–6, 209

Care Quality Commission (England) 270, 274–5
causal matrix: complexity of 178
causal relationship assessment 162; Australian approach 163–5; describing strength of the 'causal relationship' (*see* describing strength of the 'causal relationship'); English approach 165–6; 'psycho-legal challenge' in assessing (*see* 'psycho-legal challenge' in assessing the causal relationship); role of legal practitioners and the court in addressing causation (*see* role of legal practitioners and the court in addressing causation); similarities and differences between Australian and English approaches 166; using 'possibility explanations' to explain causal relationship (*see* 'possibility explanations' and the causal relationship)
causation: 'but for' test 168, 169; direct causation and moral culpability 171; direct and indirect causation and mitigation 171; moral evaluative nature of legal determination regarding 169
chemical restraint: accountability mechanisms for use of 106; adverse reactions to 92, 107; categories of medications in 90–1; common forms and consequences of 90–2; debates on excessive use of 88; definition 90; definitional issues in 98–100, 105; dual purpose conundrum 92–3; individual management plans and 106; National Disability Insurance Scheme providers and 99–100; presence of security guards in administration of 97; Royal Commission into Violence, Abuse, Neglect and Exploitation of People with Disabilities analysis 101–5; threat of as management tool 92; toward future reforms 104–7; use in emergency department setting 94–5; use of force in 92; use in in-patient mental health wards 96–7; use in pre-hospital setting 93–4; use in residential aged care setting 95–6; Victorian Royal Commission recommendations 100–1, 105; views on use of 91
Chief Officer for Mental Health and Wellbeing (Victoria) 24, 34
Chief Ombudsman, New Zealand 132; role of 123–5
closed environments 235; aged care 114–15, 131
Committee on the Rights of Persons with Disabilities 6, 11, 13, 141; Concluding Observations 12, 216; jurors with sensory disabilities and 215–16; jury exclusion and 203; right to participate in public affairs and 214; strands of law reform 13–14; substitute decision-making regimes and 14
Community Treatment Order regime, New Zealand 149
compulsory community treatment 16, 19
compulsory mental health treatment: compulsion and 41; incorrect application of laws 41; unlawful 42; use of restrictive practices 41–2
compulsory monitoring 249
consent model of restrictive practices 74; philosophical problem with 78; substitute decision-makers and 79, 83
Convention on the Rights of Persons with Disabilities: aged care, New Zealand and 125–6; appropriate remedies and 55; changing practice and 55; demands for mental health law 232–5; judicial oversight 55–60; mental health and human rights and 38–42; problem of social change 65–6;

professionals and 55, 60–3; provision of real alternatives 63–5; reasonable accommodation and adjustments and 214; right to health and 39; right to physical access and information in the courtroom and 201–11; social change and 65–6; universal design and 214
convicted offenders: experience of mental health problems by 162
core principles of arbitrary detention: effective access to court or tribunal 140; grounds of detention not arbitrary 139; legal authority must exist 139; prevention against wrongful detention by third parties 140; procedural protections to govern all forms of detention 139–40; regular assessment 140
Correctional Offender Management Profiling for Alternative Sanctions 251
court processes: persons with disabilities and 57–8
Court of Protection (UK) 56–8, 61, 63
courtrooms: right to physical access and information in 210–11, 215
courts: behaviour of 55–60
COVID-19, New Zealand 115, 120–2, 124
criminal offending *see* offending behaviour

dangerousness: as legal criterion 189; sentencing criteria and 189
Daubert criteria 192
deaf jurors 205–7, 209
decarceration, United States of America 189
deficit narrative 298, 301
deprivation of liberty 138, 145, 231, 235, 237, 240; existence of a disability and 140
deprivation of liberty in the name of prevention: as least-drastic means of achieving prevention aim 191; confinement proportional to risk 191–2; provision of rehabilitative services 191
Deprivation of Liberty Standards 14, 59, 154; external impetus law reform and 15; funding 65
describing strength of the 'causal relationship' 175–6; spectrum of causal relationships (*see* spectrum of causal relationships)
detention of elderly people in secure rest home care, New Zealand: adequate review of detention at time it occurs 152–4; adequacy of legal authority invoked 141; areas of doubt in scope of authority to detain 141; common law justification of necessity 142–4; core principles of right not to be arbitrarily detained 139–41; decisions of courts in analogous cases 149–50; differentiating between legal capacity and mental capacity 141; example of interpretive dilemma 146–8; procedural arbitrariness 151–2; requirements of human rights laws 137–8; scope of authority for detention provided by an Adult Guardian Protection Scheme 144–6
dignity and autonomy principle 45
disability neutral mental health law 235–7; creating compliance 237–8
disability sector, Australia: authorisation model of restrictive practice in 75; consent model of restrictive practice in 75

egalitarian injustice 195–6
elder abuse: definition 114, 121
emergency departments: Statement on the Use of Restrictive Practices in Emergency Departments 95; use of chemical restraint in 94–5
enduring power of attorney 144, 153
ethics-washing 255
European Convention on Human Rights: mental health law reform and 14

fairness 186; egalitarian injustice and 195–6; procedural injustice and 198–9; retributive injustice and 196–7
forensic mental health risk assessment: bias and 250–1; lived experience and 259–60; transparency 251–2; use of Big Data and machine learning in 248; variables used in 250

Grigson, James: expert testimony of 192–3

Health and Disability Commissioner (New Zealand) 115–16, 132; rights breaches reported 117
Health Equity Power Framework: methods of analysis of power 276
hearing assistive technology 207–8, 209
human rights: automated or AI-enabled technology risk assessment and 254–7; compulsory mental health treatment powers and 40–2; mental health and the *Convention on the Rights of Persons with Disabilities* 38–42; of persons with disabilities 6; preventive detention and 257
Human Rights and Mental Health Regulatory Framework (Victoria) 269, 288; application of the framework 277–9; development of 269–70
Human Rights Council Working Group on Arbitrary Detention 234–5
Human Rights Review Tribunal (New Zealand) 116–17

impetus for mental health law reform: domestic impetus 15–17; external impetus 13–15
independent mental health advocacy: opt out model 24, 34, 42
indirect relationships in offending behaviour: intellectual disability 171; major depression 171; Post Traumatic Stress Disorder 171
individual management plans 106
informed consent: mental capacity and 40; right to health and mental health and 39–40; Victoria 47, 49
'insanity' defence 162, 163, 167, 178, 182–3
interpreters: qualified in legal translation 207; sign language interpreters 209
involuntary monitoring 259

Jackson reasonable relationship requirement 191–2
juries: equal right to participate in 211–12; exclusion of persons with disabilities 203; right to participate on 213; role in criminal justice system 203
jurisprudence of risk 8, 186, 189; 'fairness' (*see* fairness); 'fit' 190–2; 'validity' (*see* validity)
juror: right to work as 214–15
jurors with sensory disabilities: accuracy of sign language and interpretation concerns 207; Australia 215–16; blind jurors 205–6; Committee on the Rights of Persons with Disabilities Communications 215–16; deaf jurors 205–7; disability discrimination legislation and 205; equal right to participate 211–12; false assumptions regarding ability of 205–9; impact on cost and length of trial concerns 207–8; peremptory strikes of 205; removing barriers to participation 209; right to fair trial concerns 207, 208; right to physical access and information in the courtroom 201–11; technological aids for 209
jury duty: right to *see* right to jury duty
jury participation: legal barriers to 204–5

least restrictive principle 45
legal capacity 13, 40, 47–8; denial of 235, 236, 237, 240; explicit relinquishment of 237
legal culpability: distinguished from moral culpability 167
legal process: persons with disabilities and 59–60
legal representation: persons with disabilities and 57
liberty: deprivation of (*see* deprivation of liberty); explicit relinquishment of 237
Liberty Protection Safeguards 154
lived experience: of clinicians 302, 303; colonisation of 304–5; of disability in the forensic mental health context 259–60; lived experience expertise 303; marginalisation of perspective in mental health system 309; recognition of value of 302; specific meaning of 303
Lived Experience Commissioners (Victoria) 309

mass incarceration 187–8
mental capacity: informed consent and 40; voluntary mental health treatment and 40–1
Mental Capacity Act 2005 (UK): court reluctance and 64; minimisation of role of courts 58; social change and 65–6
mental capacity test 47–8
mental health: human rights and the *Convention on the Rights of Persons with Disabilities* and 38–42; relationship with moral culpability 167; relationship to offending behaviour 161–2
mental health, disability and criminal law: future of 3–9
Mental Health and Wellbeing Act 2022 (Vic): accountability mechanisms for use of chemical restraint 106; decision-making principles and substantive provisions 46–8; definition of 'recovery' 44; dignity and autonomy principle 45; education campaign and implementation plan 49; health and wellbeing principles of 44–6; impact of 49; Independent Review of 36, 42, 50, 77; informed consent and 47, 49; least restrictive principle 45; mental capacity test 47–8; objectives 42–4; supported decision-making principle 45; treatment refusal and 48
Mental Health and Wellbeing Commission (Victoria) 34, 268, 280, 288; Lived Experience Commissioners 309
Mental Health and Wellbeing Commissioner (Victoria) 24
mental health care and treatment: compulsory (*see* compulsory mental health treatment); human rights approach in 49–50; voluntary (*see* voluntary mental health treatment)
Mental Health Complaints Commission (Victoria) 7, 269, 280–1; Balance Power Principle 287–8; Be Responsive Principle 282–3, 288; Clear Objective (Human Rights Protection) Principle 281–2, 288; complaints data 283; 'Complaints Stories' 282–3; Effective Standards Principle 284–5, 288; 'It's OK to complain' campaign 282, 284; Judicious Enforcement Principle 285–6, 288; Regulate Risk Principle 283–4, 288; Tripartism Principle 286–7, 288
Mental Health Complaints Commissioner (Victoria) 268
mental health expert evidence: content 174; describing the strength of the 'causal relationship' (*see* describing the strength of the 'causal relationship'); limits of 174–5; narrative account of relationship between mental health problems and offending 173–4; 'possibility explanations' to explain the causal relationship 172–5; role of in sentencing hearings 169, 171; similarities and differences in Australian and English approaches to 166; *Verdins* principles and 165
mental health in-patients, Australia: restrictive practices and 76–7
mental health law: abolitionist approach to 12, 14; acceptance of all forms of decision-making by 238; automatic review, Ireland 17; bias in 311–14; *Convention on the Rights of Persons with Disabilities* demands for 232–5; disability neutral mental health law (*see* disability neutral mental health law); fundamental tension in 231; future of 240; human rights considerations and 40–2; incorrect application of 42; 'new medicalism' and 16; origins of 230–1; prevention of crisis situations and 237; risk-focused approach to 16; transforming mental health law 238–40
mental health law reform: *European Convention on Human Rights* and 14; impetus for (*see* impetus for mental health law reform); politics of 19; processes in operation 17–18; process in practice 18–20; Turkey 14–15; United Kingdom 12, 15–17; value of comparative work on 12

Mental Health Reform Victoria 309
mental health-related data use: Canada 244; United States of America 244
mental health-related risk: automated or AI-enabled technology and *see* automated or AI-enabled technology
mental health science: sentencing law and 163
mental health system, Australia: bias in 305–9; 'deficit narrative' (*see* deficit narrative); expanding the frame from individual to society 309–11; false statements in 308–9; marginalisation of lived-experience perspective 309; underinvestment in 305–6
Mental Health Tribunal (Victoria) 268, 310; Statement of Reasons 312
mental ill–health: 'chemical imbalance' framing of 300, 301; conceptual evolution of in ancient civilizations 300; medical paradigm 299, 300; moving forward with allyship 314–15; safety of persons experiencing 313; 'social model' understanding of 300; supernatural paradigm 299; witchcraft and 300–1
mental incapacity: abolition of as legal status in United Kingdom 54–5
MIND 18–19
mitigation: direct and indirect causation and 171; indirect causes and 171; limitation of 172
monitoring: active 248; biometric 244, 246, 247, 249, 261; compulsory 249; involuntary 259; passive 247, 248–9, 260
moral culpability: direct causation and 171; distinguished from legal culpability 167; interaction between background variables and situational factors 170; mental impairment as 'background' to commission of offence 171; relationship with mental health conditions 167; sufficiency of causal connection and 172

National Association for Mental Health (UK) *see* MIND
National Disability Insurance Scheme (Australia) 75–6
National Disability Insurance Scheme Commission 99, 104; Quality and Safeguards Commission 76, 78; use of chemical restraint by providers 99–100
National Framework for Reducing and Eliminating the Use of Restrictive Practices in the Disability Service Sector 74–5, 95, 107
National Mental Health Commission (Australia) 89, 306, 307
'necessity explanations' for human conduct 172; impossibility of 173

Oakden Older Persons Mental Health Service: report 88, 95; review of 126–8
offenders: effects and impacts of mental disorder on 178; sentencing of as individuals 180
offending behaviour: connection to mental impairment 171, 178, 182; 'formulation' and 169–70; indirect relationships in (*see* indirect relationships in offending behaviour); role of mental health problems in 8, 161–2, 173–4

parens patriae power 311–12
passive monitoring 247, 248–9, 260
Percy Report 15–16, 18
persons with disabilities: access to justice 57; court processes and 57–8; employment in public sector 215; human rights of 6; legal process and 59–60; legal representation 57; professional involvement and 61
positive behaviour support plans 104
'possibility explanations' and the causal relationship 173, 182; content 174; distinction between 'necessity explanations' 172–3; form 173–4; limits of 174–5
Post Traumatic Stress Disorder 171
power: entrenched imbalances of 6, 307, 312, 314; theories of (*see* theories of power)
pretrial detainees: violence rate amongst 188
preventive detention: automated or AI-enabled technology and 252, 256; human rights and 257; risk assessment and 319; treatment and 191
procedural injustice 198–9

psychiatric practice: 'pharmacological revolution' in 16
'psycho-legal challenge' in assessing the causal relationship 163, 166–7; moral culpability distinguished from legal culpability 167; relevance of 'indirect' causal factors 169–72; role of moral evaluative considerations 167–9
public sector: employment of persons with disabilities by 215

Quality of Care Principles, Australia 79–81, 83

rapid tranquilisation *see* chemical restraint
reciprocity 19
recovery-oriented practice 44
Regional Health and Wellbeing Boards (Victoria) 24, 34
responsiveness 271–2; tripartism 272–3
responsive regulation 271; contingency and flexibility 271–2; enforcement hierarchy 272–3
restrictive practices, Australia: aged care 77, 79–85; elimination of in Victoria 23, 28, 35, 42, 313; health settings 77–8; mental health patients 76–7; regulatory challenge 78–9; unauthorised use 76; voices of carers 105; voices of persons subject to 105
restrictive practices: authorisation model 74–5; compulsory mental health treatment and 41–2; consent model (*see* consent model of restrictive practices); definition 73–4; as 'health' intervention 79; objective of 89; reform movement 89; Senior Practitioner model 84–5
retributive injustice 196–7
Richardson Review 19–20
right to access justice 212–13
right to be free from arbitrary arrest and detention 258
right to be presumed innocent 258
right to equal recognition before the law 231
right to fair trial 207, 208, 258
right to health 36, 258–9; accessibility 38; availability 37–8; *Convention on the Rights of Persons with Disabilities* and 39; evolution of 36–8; informed consent and 39–40; quality 38; relationship to other human rights 38
right to human dignity 259
right to jury duty: European Union law 216–19; individual communications concerning 215–16
right to liberty 29, 39, 63, 64, 129, 138, 231, 234, 256–8
right to mental health 38, 44; informed consent and 39–40
right to participate on juries 213
right to work 214
risk assessment: approach to expert testimony 192; automation and algorithmic technologies in (*see* automated or AI-enabled technology); continued supervision and 253; data-based approaches to 247–8; definition of 'probability' 190; definition of 'violent' 190; dynamic factors 250; forensic mental health (*see* forensic mental health risk assessment); human judgment and 196; importance of 186–9; law's response to the risk and 191; for managing individuals 247; preventive detention and 319; probability and 190; public confidence in 252; remote 249; risk duration period 190–1; scientific assessment and 193; static factors 250; transparency 246
risk assessment instruments 187; arrest prediction 196; bias and 196; community participation in development and application of 199; fairness and (*see* fairness); fit 190–2; incorporation of 'dynamic' risk factors 199; preventive detention and 256; specific probabilities of reoffending and 193; transparency 198; use only in fully adversarial proceedings 198–9; validation of 191–5; validity and (*see* validity)
risk-based regulation 273; assignment of resources for monitoring and enforcement 275; clarification of regulatory objectives 273–4; identification of risks to objectives 274; standard setting 274–5

risk proportionality 191–2
role of legal practitioners and the court in addressing causation: role of prosecution and defence counsel 179–81; sentencing judge's role 179, 181
Royal Commission into Aged Care Quality and Safety 77, 128–30; restrictive practices and 80, 96; Serious Incident Response Scheme 129
Royal Commission of Inquiry into Abuse in Care (New Zealand) 130–2; adoption of Te Reo 131; closed environments and 131; contexts for 130; societal attitude to older people and 131–2; vulnerable adults and 130
Royal Commission into Victoria's Mental Health System *see* Victorian Royal Commission
Royal Commission into Violence, Abuse, Neglect and Exploitation of People with Disabilities 107; accountability mechanisms for administration of chemical restraint 106; analysis of use of chemical restraint 101–5

safety: promise of 313
seclusion 7, 41–2, 75–7, 88, 94, 97–100, 107, 127, 128, 267, 284
sedation 90–1, 95, 107
sentencing: actuarial and clinical risk assessment and 194; calibrated according to risk 187; dangerousness and 189; determinate sentencing 189; 'just desert' sentencing 188, 189; of offender as individual 180; risk period 191; 'violent felony' 190
sentencing courts: current approaches to assessing the causal relationship (*see* causal relationship assessment); 'psycho-legal challenge' in assessing the causal relationship (*see* 'psycho-legal challenge' in assessing the causal relationship)
sentencing guidelines, United Kingdom: culpability and 165–6
Sentencing Hearings: Expert Reports on Mental Functioning of Offenders 166
sentencing hearings: role of expert mental health evidence in 169
sentencing law: mental health science and 163
Sentencing Offenders with Mental Disorders, Developmental Disorders, or Neurological Impairments: Annex A 165
sentencing process: culpability context of 162; role of offender's mental health problems in 8, 162, 173–4
spectrum of causal relationships 176; necessary but not sufficient 177; necessary and sufficient 178; no causal relationship 176–7; significant material contribution 177
Stopping Aberrant Fatal Events by Helping Overcome Mental Extremes 244, 252, 261
structured professional judgment 253–4, 260
substitute decision-makers: Commonwealth powers related to 83; consent model of restrictive practices and 79, 83; restrictive practices substitute decision-makers 81–3
supported decision-making principle 45
systems: systemic consequences between 62–3; values and pressures of 62

theories of power: health governance and policy 275–6; mental health policy and systems 276; in regulation 276–7
therapeutic jurisprudence scholarship: reduction in use of coercion and 106
treatment refusal, Victoria 48
Turkey: mental health law reform 14–15

United Nations Human Rights Committee 141; notion of 'arbitrariness' and 139

validity 186; calibration and 194; certainty and 193; discriminant validity 194; evaluation of risk assessment instruments 194–5; role of risk assessment instruments 194
Verdins effects 169

Verdins principles 163–4, 172, 179, 180; acceptance of 164; expert mental health evidence and 165; Principle I 164–5
Victorian Civil and Administrative Tribunal 312; decisions on 'personal matters' 82–3
Victorian Collaborative Centre for Mental Health and Wellbeing 27–8, 34
Victorian Royal Commission 6, 7, 11, 20–2, 107, 267; compulsory treatment and 23, 35, 42, 49; elimination of restrictive practices 23, 28, 35, 42, 76, 89, 105; implementation of recommendations of 28; legislative reform proposals 22–4, 35, 42; lessons for law reform from 29; *Mental Health Act 2014* (Vic) and 22, 34–5; *Mental Health and Wellbeing Act 2002* (Vic) and 22–4, 34, 42, 89; opt out model 24, 34, 42; outcomes approach 35; recommendations 34–5, 100–1, 268, 280, 306–7, 309, 312; Report 11–12, 19, 25, 34, 161, 298; right to health and 36; systems approach to reform 17, 24–8; systems levers identified by 27; as template for law reform 12; underpinning evidence 24–5
visual evidence: ability to assess 206
voluntary mental health treatment: mental capacity standard 40–1

Wessely Review 19–20, 29
World Health Organization: Mental Health Atlas 12

For Product Safety Concerns and Information please contact our EU
representative GPSR@taylorandfrancis.com
Taylor & Francis Verlag GmbH, Kaufingerstraße 24, 80331 München, Germany

www.ingramcontent.com/pod-product-compliance
Ingram Content Group UK Ltd.
Pitfield, Milton Keynes, MK11 3LW, UK
UKHW020155200926
475702UK00016B/2714

* 9 7 8 1 0 3 2 3 9 6 3 2 3 *